Ancient Chinese Academy, Confucianism, and Society II

As the second volume of a two-volume set that studies the ancient Chinese academy from a socio-cultural perspective, this title investigates the multifaceted roles and political and cultural significance of the academy.

Inaugurated in the Tang dynasty and eventually abolished in the late Qing dynasty, the academy, as a unique cultural and educational organization in Chinese history, exerted extensive and profound influence on ancient Chinese culture, politics, and social life. This title first discusses the state control of the academy and how it functions in social governance, then examines the sacrificial ritual of the academy and its influence on education, enculturation, Confucian orthodoxy, and intellectual ethos, and finally elaborates on the academy's role in enriching the regional cultures in terms of local cultural undertakings and talent cultivation.

The title will be a useful reference for scholars, students, and general readers interested in the cultural history, intellectual history, and educational history of ancient China and especially the Chinese academy culture.

Xiao Yongming, a renowned Professor of History, is the Dean of Yuelu Academy at Hunan University and the Vice President of the China Research Association of Academies. His main research interests are the history of Song and Ming thoughts and Chinese academy culture. He has been a visiting scholar at several universities, including the University of London, National Taiwan University, Cornell University, and the University of Arizona.

Ancient Chinese Academy, Confucianism, and Society II
Politics and Culture

Xiao Yongming

Translated by Li Li and Zhang Xiangting

LONDON AND NEW YORK

First published in English 2023
by Routledge
4 Park Square, Milton Park, Abingdon, Oxon OX14 4RN

and by Routledge
605 Third Avenue, New York, NY 10158

Routledge is an imprint of the Taylor & Francis Group, an informa business

© 2023 Xiao Yongming

Translated by Li Li and Zhang Xiangting

The right of Xiao Yongming to be identified as author of this work has been asserted in accordance with sections 77 and 78 of the Copyright, Designs and Patents Act 1988.

All rights reserved. No part of this book may be reprinted or reproduced or utilised in any form or by any electronic, mechanical, or other means, now known or hereafter invented, including photocopying and recording, or in any information storage or retrieval system, without permission in writing from the publishers.

Trademark notice: Product or corporate names may be trademarks or registered trademarks, and are used only for identification and explanation without intent to infringe.

English Version by permission of The Commercial Press.

British Library Cataloguing-in-Publication Data
A catalogue record for this book is available from the British Library

Library of Congress Cataloging-in-Publication Data

Names: Xiao, Yongming, 1968– author. | Zhang, Xiangting,
    1979– translator. | Li, Li, 1971 June 19– translator.
Title: Ancient Chinese academy, Confucianism, and Society/
    Yongming Xiao ; translated by Zhang Xiangting and Li Li.
Other titles: Ru xue, shu yuan, she hui. English.
Description: Abingdon, Oxon ; New York, NY : Routledge, 2022. |
    Includes bibliographical references and index. | Contents: v. 1.
    Ancient Chinese academy, Confucianism, rise and growth—v. 2.
    Ancient Chinese academy, Confucianism, and Society
Identifiers: LCCN 2022021163 (print) | LCCN 2022021164 (ebook) |
    ISBN 9781032364056 (v. 1 ; hardback) | ISBN 9781032364896
    (v. 1 ; paperback) | ISBN 9781032364049 (v. 2 ; hardback) | ISBN
    9781032364902 (v. 2 ; paperback) | ISBN 9781032364063 (hardback) |
    ISBN 9781032364889 (paperback) | ISBN 9781003332282
    (v. 1 ; ebook) | ISBN 9781003332305 (v. 2 ; ebook)
Subjects: LCSH: Learned institutions and societies—China—History.
Classification: LCC AS445 .X53 2022 (print) | LCC AS445 (ebook) |
    DDC 068.51—dc23/eng/20220506
LC record available at https://lccn.loc.gov/2022021163
LC ebook record available at https://lccn.loc.gov/2022021164

ISBN: 978-1-032-36404-9 (hbk)
ISBN: 978-1-032-36490-2 (pbk)
ISBN: 978-1-003-33230-5 (ebk)

DOI: 10.4324/9781003332305

Typeset in Times New Roman
by Apex CoVantage, LLC

Contents

1	Academy, Society, and Politics	1
2	Academy Sacrificial Rituals and Their Significance	48
3	Academy and Regional Cultural Undertakings	114
	Appendix 1: Rites and Customs in Academies	174
	Appendix 2: Rites and Conduct in Academies	196
	Bibliography	220
	Index	235

1 Academy, Society, and Politics[1]

Academies play multiple roles and have different functions in society. As a base for the creation and dissemination of Confucianism and a place for Confucian scholars to settle down and establish their lives, academies, through their close integration of Confucianism and scholars, have become an important force for societal and cultural governance and have been playing an important role in the social governance system. As the academy is a cultural and educational institution closely related to ideology, its existence and development are bound to gain concern from the autocratic power. Supreme rulers of past dynasties throughout history often tried to adopt various measures and policies to bring academies under the control of state power. As such, the academies' development usually went hand in hand with their being transformed, integrated and controlled by the state. As a matter of fact, academies were basically tools that were dependent on and in the service of the state power after the mid-Qing dynasty. This view is quite different from that of some scholars, who tend to regard the academy as something intermediate between state power and family interests.

Academy and Social Governance

Manipulation of Confucianism Over Society and Role of Confucian Scholars in Society

Social control (or social manipulation) is an essential requisite for the social order to be established and maintained and for society to be harmonious and stable. According to F.W. Blackmar, an American social psychologist,

> The orderly movement of society can not be brought about by chance or maintained without regulative forces, for individuals often seek their own self-interest but tend to be blind to the social interests of the group. Hence, there is a need for "a central controlling force to maintain order."[2]

American sociologist Dennis H. Wrong also pointed out the inherent necessity of social control in all social interactions.[3] This so-called social control is actually to control people's thoughts and behaviors so that human behaviors and

DOI: 10.4324/9781003332305-1

2 Academy, Society, and Politics

mutual relations can be regulated for a good social order and harmonious social relations. In a society, social customs, ethics, religion, philosophy, and law can all influence social psychology and values and thus can provide people with examples of behavioral norms and control their social activities.[4] Among these social regulations, the role of ethical norms and moral customs cannot be ignored. Renowned American jurist, Edgar Bodenheimer, says,

> Although throughout the history of organized societies, law, as a regulator of interpersonal relations, has played a huge and decisive role in any such society, it is quite impossible to have law as the only social control force, and there are still some other tools that can guide behaviour. These tools are often used to supplement or partially replace legal means to achieve the goals of society. They mainly include power, administration, morality, and custom.[5]

Social life itself is rich and diverse and contains many aspects, and law does play a dominant role in many dimensions of social life, but in some other areas, it works little. In this case, the role of social customs, ethics, morality, and religion will thus be more pronounced. This is especially true in traditional Chinese society.

The ethical-political Confucian doctrine played a very important part in social control in traditional Chinese society. When Confucianism became the mainstream social ideology, Confucian teachings, such as values, moral principles, and codes of conduct, occupied a dominant position in regulating people's social relations. Confucian scholars of all ages had a profound understanding of the importance of Confucianism in social control.

Rites were the core element of traditional Confucianism. Confucians of past dynasties laid much emphasis on the function of rites in governing the country. In the chapter "The Eleventh Year of Duke Yin" in *The Commentary of Zuo* (左传·隐公十一年), it is said, "Rites can govern the state, stabilize the community, create order for the people, and benefit the future generations." The chapter "Explanations of the Classics" in *The Book of Rites* (礼记·经解) states,

> In the governance of a state, the rules of propriety serve the same purpose as the steelyard in determining what is light and what is heavy or as a carpenter's line in determining what is crooked and what is straight" and that "there is no better way to govern a country than through rites.

The chapter "Questions of Duke Ai" in *The Book of Rites* (礼记·哀公问) claims, "Rites are the foundation of governance as well as the essence of governance!" Confucius emphasizes that by revering such principles as benevolence, justice, and morality in Confucianism and by taking the lead and setting an example, one can convince the people to do what is right and achieve social harmony and order, thus achieving the ultimate goal of social control. "If people are guided by morality and educated with propriety, they will not only know what shame is but will also correct their misconduct."[6]

As long as those in authority adhere to propriety, the people will not dare to disrespect them; as long as those in authority adhere to righteousness, the people will not dare to disobey them; as long as those in authority attach importance to faith, the people will not dare to be dishonest.[7]

During the Warring States period, Xun Zi explained from the perspective of phylogenetics that Confucian rites came into existence to achieve the purpose of exercising social control through the formulation of various ethical norms and codes of conduct. In this sense, it can be said that social control is a natural function of Confucian rites. Xun Zi says,

People are born with desires and will try to satisfy their desires. However, if there are no rules for them to follow, they will naturally be in conflict with each other. Conflict inevitably leads to social turmoil. The ancient sages hated turmoil so much that they formulated rites as rules for them to follow, which were used to moderately satisfy their desires.[8]

Therefore, the wise emperors of ancient times established rites to regulate the people so that they would have a distinction between the noble and the lowly, the old and young, the wise and the foolish, the virtuous and the incompetent. By so doing, each of them could undertake his own work and feel good about it. They make a salary proportional to their status and their work, and this is the way to make people live together in groups and be in harmony.[9]

From Xun Zi's point of view, as long as there are "standards of propriety and benevolence" set by these ancient wise emperors for the people, and as long as "these standards are used as guidelines for the governance of the state," "people will live together in harmony, peace, and stability." This is the goal of state governance.

The understanding of the pre-Qin Confucians about the social control function of Confucianism was inherited by later generations of Confucian scholars. For example, Zhu Xi, a great Confucian scholar in the Southern Song dynasty, emphasized that Confucian virtue and etiquette were the basic means of governing the country and the people. In his commentary on the chapter "On Governance of the State" in *The Analects of Confucius* (论语·为政), Zhu Xi says,

Politics is a tool for governing the state, and punishment is the law that assists in the governance of the state. Morality and etiquette, however, are fundamental to the governance of the state and morality is the root of etiquette. These factors are interdependent and always accompany the governance of the state. Neither of the two can be ignored. However, while punishment can keep the people away from crime, only morality and propriety can achieve the purpose of improving the moral fiber of the people and raising their moral standards in a subtle way. That is why it is said that governing the people cannot merely rely on minutiae punishments but should be done by fundamentally raising the moral standards of the people.[10]

4 *Academy, Society, and Politics*

Wang Yangming, a great Confucianist of the Ming dynasty and representative of the School of Xin Xue (a philosophy founded by Wang Yangming, referred to as the Theory of Mind, the Yangming School of Mind, or the School of Mind [see Volume 1, Chapter 5]), also attached great importance to the role of Confucian etiquette in governing the people. He thought that the study, promotion, and practice of Confucian etiquette could moralize people and was beneficial to society and the governance of the people. He says,

> The best way to stabilize the country and govern the people is through rites. The various rituals such as coming-of-age ceremonies, weddings, funerals, sacrificial rites, and so on should be understood by all. However, people have now abandoned these rites. How is it possible for them to pursue the beauty of customs in that case? Furthermore, in some remote places on the frontier, people of different nationalities with different customs live at the borders of different countries. It is difficult to change the customs of people who do not understand our rituals. The government knows no means but to resort to punishment to manage and control them. That is really like using fire to control fire. If the people understand etiquette through education, they would understand morality and will thus be easily governed . . . From then on, students have been deeply inspired and enlightened. They discussed among themselves and learned from each other. Afterward, they started to pay attention to moral studies and established moral standards in their own home. This would then extend to the entire village and gradually expand the influence of rituals. Thus, gradually even remote areas like the frontiers will become great places that are like the hometowns of Confucius and Mencius. This is not something difficult."[11]

Not only Confucian scholars were aware of this, but also the emperor, who held the most power as the ruler of the country, attached considerable importance to the social control function of Confucianism. For example, the Kangxi Emperor of the Qing dynasty, when evaluating the social control function of Zhu Xi's Neo-Confucian thought, said,

> If this is not done, one would not be able to understand the relationship between nature and mankind. If this is not done, one would not be able to govern the country well. If this is not done, one would not be able to implement benevolent and righteous policies in the state. And if this is not done, one would not be able to handle the relationship between one's own country and other countries well.[12]

For this reason, the emperor ordered Li Guangdi and his other subordinates to compile *Complete Collection of Zhu Xi* (朱子全书) and *A Compendium on Neo-Confucian Teachings* (性理精义), etc. and issued them throughout the country. Emperor Yongzheng also stated,

If the ruler does not know how to respect Confucian education, how can he be competent and meet the requirements to become a responsible ruler? How then can he be a moral example and set the standards of morality for his own country and other countries?[13]

Confucianism focuses on the consideration and investigation of social problems, with the effective governance of society and the maintenance and optimization of the social order as the starting point of its ideology. In essence, Confucianism is a set of beliefs characterized by active participation in the world with the purpose of governing the world and the people in a peaceful way. It pursues social harmony, stability, and order, with everything in its right place and coexisting harmoniously. To this end, it has put forward a whole set of doctrines and constructed an increasingly complex ideological and theoretical system, of which there is a lot of content on personal spiritual cultivation and the pursuit of maintaining social stability and harmony. Both of them are ultimately related to their social control functions. According to traditional Confucian thinking of "inner sage and outer king" (which is to have both the virtue of the sage and the ability to govern the world like a king) is a necessity in governing the state. The two are actually united as one. Therefore, it can be said that social control is the most fundamental pursuit of Confucianism.

Confucian scholars had several discussions on the way Confucianism exerted societal control. For example, in the chapter "Questions of Duke Ai" in *The Book of Rites* (礼记·哀公问), Confucius mentions,

> Without rites, it would be impossible to serve the gods of heaven and earth; without rites, it would be impossible to distinguish between the positions of rulers and subjects, superiors and subordinates, the elder and the younger; without rites, it would be impossible to distinguish between men and women, father and son, elder brother and younger brother, and between in-laws and friends.[14]

This actually illustrates the various roles that rites play in society. A similar statement is made in the chapter "Summary of the Rules of Propriety" in *The Book of Rites* (礼记·曲礼上):

> Virtue, benevolence, and righteousness cannot be established without rites. Teaching one to be righteous cannot be achieved without rites; arguments and disputes cannot be resolved without rites, and the distinction between the ruler and his subjects, the father and his son, and the elder brother and his younger brother cannot be made without ritual system.[15]

Liu Feng discussed the use of rites to manage society. He points out in *The Integration of Pre-Qin Dynasty Rites in Society* (先秦礼学思想与社会的整合) that in traditional Chinese society,

6 *Academy, Society, and Politics*

rites were a social norm and the most extensive form of social control. It was closely integrated with the law, power, and administration and manifested themselves as an external form of societal control. In addition, rites were also associated with morality and custom and were more intrinsic forms of social control.[16]

He argues that the social control function of rites can be analyzed at two levels: the internal control over people and the external control over social activities. On the one hand, rites achieve their internal control over people by socializing people and internalizing Confucian values and ethical principles. On the other hand, rites manifest themselves as a kind of control that sustains the integration of society at an external institutional level through political systems and laws.[17] This analysis enables us to have a more specific understanding of the social control function of Confucianism from the perspective of rites. It can be said that Confucianism, as the mainstream ideology, played an important role in regulating social relations, establishing social values, maintaining social order, and promoting social integration in all aspects of traditional Chinese social life. In short, Confucianism was an important force of social control in traditional Chinese society.

Associated with Confucianism are scholars who studied, elucidated, and disseminated Confucianism. In the social structure of ancient China, there existed a special social class of scholars in great numbers. In discussing the characteristics of the scholars in the Warring States period, Liu Zehua pointed out that the core members of these scholars were intellectuals. They had their own personalities and were from various social strata. These scholarly exchanges took place between those of different social classes. In terms of social status, the scholars were extremely mobile. They were candidates to become officials but were also part of the masses.[18] This generalization was also generally applicable to scholars after the Tang and Song dynasties. After the Song dynasty, as a result of the great historical transmutation of the Tang and Song dynasties, hierarchical social relations also underwent dramatic changes. Class and social restrictions that influenced people's social life started to disappear. At that time, the number of scholars, mainly Confucian intellectuals, continued to increase. According to Gu Yanwu's estimation in *On Shengyuan* (生员论) (shengyuan, also called xiucai, refers to the holders of the basic degree who passed the entry-level imperial examination in the Ming and Qing dynasties),[19] the number of shengyuan at the end of the Ming dynasty was about 500,000,[20] while Chen Kengzhi argues that the number was 700,000.[21] Meanwhile, according to Zhang Zhongli's research on the gentry class in the 19th century, the number of shengyuan-like students in any period before the Taiping Heavenly Kingdom era was about 460,000 and, after it, 550,000.[22] The ideal "scholars" that the mentioned statistics describe is not completely the same as the concept of "scholars" mentioned here. However, we can surmise that there was a large number of scholars during that period.

As the producers and disseminators of knowledge, scholars were the proponents and demonstrators of Confucian values, ethical principles, and norms. They were also the bearers and embodiment of the spirit of Confucianism. They enjoyed high prestige in the field of spiritual life and played an important role in many aspects of social life. According to Yu Yingshi, a modern Chinese scholar, in order to consolidate the foundation of its political power and rebuild the social order, the government of the Song dynasty turned to the scholars for help and strived to win their cooperation in governing the country. Scholars thus gained relatively higher political status. They "took the governing of the country as their own responsibility" and actively participated in the handling of state and social affairs. This resulted in a situation in which scholars and the emperor "ruled the world together" in the Song dynasty.[23] The situation of scholars in the Ming dynasty was also reflected in Gu Yanwu's *On Shengyuan* (生员论). Gu mentioned the various works that could be done by scholars in the field of politics, claiming that among the scholars, there were "those who often went in and out of the government offices and interfered with the normal management of the government." There were also those who "relied on their own power to participate in the judgment of cases and other government affairs in their hometowns, and those who "befriended government officials, and even some who served as minor officials themselves." Some even "gathered to stir up trouble when government officials did not act according to their will."[24] Gu was strongly critical of such incidents. Even though the situations he talked about do not represent the behavior of the scholarly class as a whole and are not typical, it is conceivable that the then scholars had considerable power and social influence. In his studies on the gentry class in the 19th century, Zhang Zhongli illustrates his argument with a quotation from *The Book of Governors and Magistrates* (牧令书), a must-read manual for magistrates then:

> Intellectuals are the leading force of the people. The people cannot be familiar with all the rules and laws of the government, and only the intellectuals, with their knowledge and a high level of morality, can establish a closer relationship with the people, gain their trust and support, and thus indirectly exhort and guide the people to ensure the teachings of the government can be implemented effectively. Such intellectuals should be respected and valued. If one happens to come across intellectuals coming to the government for business, one should consult them about whether there are thieves in the townships, by what means the people earn their living, and whether the folk customs and manners are righteous. Through such exchanges, it would be possible to understand the actual situation of the people in more depth.[25]

Another Guangdong governor said in his notice,

> You intellectuals are the leading force among the people and are the role models of the people. Since you are the people with higher status and virtue, you should take the initiative to assist me in leading the people in our hometown and make up for my shortcomings.[26]

We can tell from these materials that scholars played an important role in society at that time. In fact, despite the diversified situations at different times, the

8 *Academy, Society, and Politics*

role and influence of scholars in society cannot be ignored. Fei Xiaotong even pointed out that in traditional Chinese society, the scholar-class possessed "social authority"—that is, society's control over the people by virtue of their grasp of social norms and traditions. This "social authority" is not in conflict with political power but is in parallel, forming a situation of "ruling respectively from the top and the bottom." Hence, "local affairs are ruled by the Confucian scholars, while the imperial power rules the government office." Therefore, "the gentry were the true maintainers of the local social order."[27] Even though scholars tend to have different opinions on this point of view, the importance of the role of scholars in traditional society cannot be overlooked.

An important feature of the scholar class was its close ties with all social classes. From a dynamic perspective, there was no unsurmountable gap between the scholar class and other social classes. In the era of imperial examinations and intensified vertical social mobility, some scholars could, after years of study, pass the examinations at different levels and obtain titles such as gongsheng (tribute students), jiansheng (university students), juren (candidates), and jinshi (graduates), which won them a chance to join the government and become a part of the ruling and management class of society. According to research by some scholars, in the Tang dynasty, half of the prime ministers during the rule of Wu Zetian emerged from the imperial examinations, and the number gradually increased since then. During the Xuanzong reign, 87% of prime ministers emerged from the exams.[28] In the Song dynasty, the qualification of jinshi became a prerequisite to becoming a prime minister. Although ennoblement often happened in the Song dynasty, the number of officers who became an official of the government through the imperial examinations was roughly equal to that of those who became an official of the government through ennoblement.[29] These scholars could participate in the decision-making of public affairs or influence the political decisions of the state.

Some erudite scholars merely focused on professional development, caring less about the bureaucratic system and the imperial exams. They worked outside of the political system, teaching, researching, and writing while keeping a certain distance from the authorities. However, most of them thought of themselves as burdened by Confucian thought and believed that Confucian values and norms were more powerful than the ruler of the state. They regulated political activities through Confucianism and even resisted the law through Confucianism. Some considered themselves the conscience of society, and they made comments on celebrities, pointed out the ills of their time, discussed about governance and politics, and influenced and led public opinion and moral evaluation. In various ways, these scholars affected the politics of the country and became a group that exerted pressure on the social system.

Meanwhile, a greater number of scholars played an important role in their social circles. Even though they retired to various villages and towns and lived among the people, they adhered to the traditional Confucian spirit. Some spent most of their lives teaching children and spreading knowledge and culture for a living, while others retired to the farmlands and towns, becoming makers and implementers of etiquette in civilian society and advocates and practitioners of Confucian rites in their daily life. With their own beliefs and conduct, they influenced their relatives and villagers, became models for Confucian culture and education, and played the role of spiritual leaders and moral role models in local society.[30]

From a static point of view, the scholar class was quite influential as they maintained close contact with other social classes and were inextricably linked with each other. Through their intricate social network of teachers and students, relatives, neighbors, classmates, and friends, their ideological views, values, and codes of conduct could reach government officials, dignitaries, and the general public. They could also influence the country's major policies and folk customs. It can be said that scholars played an irreplaceable role in the process of spreading Confucian ethics, moral principles, and ideals to all social classes. Scholars worked as intermediaries so that Confucian moral principles, norms, and values could penetrate into all social strata, transform into universal codes of conduct for members of different social strata, and play a role in the process of social control. In this sense, the socialization of Confucianism and its social control function could not be achieved without the social role of the scholars.

Role of Academy in Social Manipulation and Interlock of Confucianism, Scholars, and Academy

The role of the academy in the social manipulation (control) system has been discussed by scholars over the ages. For example, in the 11th year of the Yongzheng reign in the Qing dynasty (1733), scholar Cheng Tingzuo writes in *Tablet Inscription of Zhongshan Academy* (钟山书院碑记),

> The prosperity and development of education require the upper-level administrators to advocate and implement relevant policies and the lower-level administrators to respond positively to and support these policies so that those who stay close to them are happy to comply and those who do not can be inspired. This is an important aspect of academy education that can both benefit the governance of the country and influence the customs of the people. Such education can also play an important role . . . This is an important period for the country to develop monumentally. From leaders of prefectures to officials at all levels, these people are all actively guiding and promoting the development of education. The entire region is actively pursuing benevolence, justice, and morality and is assisting the government in governing the people through the establishment of academies. How can such a thing be delayed?[31]

Some scholars even pointed out that "the establishment and development of academies can serve as the foundation for the government to govern the people."[32] According to the Confucian thought that "teaching and learning are of top priority in governing a country and in moralizing the people," it was natural that the academy was a cultural and educational organization regarded as

10 Academy, Society, and Politics

an aid to politics and even "the essence of politics." Some foreign scholars also wrote on the role of the academy in social control. For example, American scholar Robert Hymes, in discussing Southern Song dynasty academies, argues that the academy should only be seen as one institution out of a group of local institutions promoted in the new social and political climate of the Southern Song dynasty. Academies and these local institutions had a common purpose, which was to give an organizational structure to the rural society beyond the central government and its local organizations. They were all rural social institutions at the level between the government and the family and could be seen as a substitute for state-specific organizations in the same or earlier period.[33] In traditional Chinese society, where the autocratic monarchy ruled far and wide and where public social space was extremely cramped, the question of whether the academy could serve as an intermediate level between the government and the family, namely, as an alternative to state-specific organizations is worth further exploration. However, Hymes' argument is enlightening, for it allows us to question the role of the academy in the social control system. We believe that academies were an integral part of the social control system and did play a role in controlling society. As a cultural and educational organization, the social control role of academies mainly manifested itself in the form of cultural control.

From a cultural sociology perspective, society is a system capable of self-regulation and self-organization. The realization of social-cultural control occurs as there are many organizational systems that automatically control cultural information.[34] These include the cultural system, education system, public opinion system, group organization system, and so on. It is evident that academies were closely related to them all. In a traditional society, the ethical and moral principles, norms, and rites of Confucianism were important elements of the social and cultural system. They served to strengthen social order and maintain social stability and were an important force in achieving cultural control in society. Meanwhile, the academy was an important place for the creation, renewal, dissemination, and accumulation of Confucian culture and a base for the development of Confucianism. Education was a means to control people's cultural behavior by instilling certain cultural knowledge and ideology, and it controlled people's cultural behavior through the cultivation of psychological and behavioral laws and the construction of cultural education systems, thus realizing the control of people, while the academy was an important place for Confucianism education activities. Teaching was the basic function of the academy and one of its "three major regulations." Public opinion was an invisible force, which achieved the purpose of cultural control over society by influencing people's cultural behavior. As the main place for the creation, interpretation, and promotion of Confucian values, academies often dominated social opinion and had a significant impact on the cultural psychology of the public. Social groups are self-organized systems in society. In social groups, certain group thoughts dominate the behavior of the group and foster the identity and sense of belonging in members of the group. Academies were places where scholars gathered, studied, and lived. They lived together in academies, received training in Confucian knowledge, and were influenced by Confucian values, forming a closed group. Academies also formed a cultural field so that academicians could develop specific values and ideologies through studying and training in Confucian cultural knowledge. They would then form specific behavioral norms that could help realize cultural control over members of the group. As academicians came from various places and were in various social networks, they were inextricably linked to many different social groups. Their values and behavioral norms would thus radiate to different social groups and spread to different social strata, thus expanding the scope of cultural control.

From what was discussed earlier, we can see that academies played an important role in the social control system. It is worth noting that the ultimate realization of the social control function of the academy depended on the close relations between the academies, Confucianism, and scholars. It is the trinity of the academy, Confucianism, and scholar that resulted in academies' being an important force for social and cultural control.

1. Interlock of Academy and Confucianism

If the academies were the external form, then Confucianism was its internal soul. Since its inception, the academy had been a symbol of Confucianism and was naturally linked to it. The educational activities of academies also centered closely around Confucianism.

A distinctive feature of academy education was that it adhered to the traditional Confucian educational philosophy and took explaining traditional Confucian values, teaching traditional Confucian values, and helping the people as its purpose. Educators of academies over the years were consistent in taking explaining Confucian values and advocating the concept of Confucian morality as the purpose of academies despite coming from different eras and having different identities, statuses, and widely different academic orientations. For example, Neo-Confucian Zhang Shi, a representative of the Huxiang School in the mid–Southern Song dynasty, points out in *Restoration of Yuelu Academy in Tanzhou* (潭州重修岳麓书院记) that the establishment of the academy was not just to provide scholars with a place to live and gather or to hunt for fame and fortune. It was also not only to teach students literary skills. Instead, the noble mission of academies was "to nurture talents to spread Confucian values and help the people."[35] Yuan Fu, another Neo-Confucian scholar in the Southern Song dynasty, also mentions in *Records of Xiangshan Academy* (象山书院记), *Restoration of Bailudong Academy* (重修白鹿洞书院记), and other literary works that the purpose of establishing academies was to revitalize Confucianism and "clarify Confucian values."[36]

Was the establishment of Xiangshan Academy in Guixi and Bailudong Academy (also known as White Deer Grotto Academy) in Lufu for nothing? They were done to clarify Confucian values and to distinguish right from wrong so that the intellectuals would stick to their unremitting pursuit despite current events and that they would be able to contribute to the governance of the country.[37]

Huang Yuanzhi, a scholar in the Qing dynasty during the reign of Kangxi, also mentions in *Tablet Inscription* (碑记), which was written for Guixiang Academy

12 *Academy, Society, and Politics*

of Dali, Yunnan Province, "The academy is to gather well-known scholars to teach righteousness, establish good moral models, and formulate ethical norms to eliminate and reduce the bad influence of those who are selfish or unscrupulous."[38]

In line with the educational purpose of academies to clarify and preach Confucian values, academies paid great attention to the inculcation of Confucian ethical and moral concepts in students. What academies taught was also arranged around the core of the inculcation and dissemination of Confucian ethical and moral concepts. Although the specific content taught by academies differed in different periods, they basically included Confucian ethical and moral concepts and the right way to deal with people and situations in daily life. Zhu Xi points out,

> There are definite guidelines and norms for sages to educate the people. The officials in charge of education have to educate the people so that they can understand the principles of life. There should be kinship between father and son, benevolence between monarchs and ministers, distinction of labor between husband and wife, hierarchy between elders and those who are younger, integrity between friends . . ., and what not. These are definite and unshakable guidelines and norms.[39]

In *Statutes of Bailudong Academy* (白鹿洞书院揭示), Zhu Xi claims that these were the purpose of education. He thought that "in the past, the sages educated people so that the people would understand what was right through understanding rites. This allowed them to enhance their moral cultivation, which would extend to influence those around them."[40] Academies should educate students on the most basic Confucian moral principles and norms. Wang Yangming expresses his views on what was taught in academies in *Renovation of Wansong Academy* (增修万松书院记). He thought that the basic content taught in academies was, in a nutshell, the study of basic moral principles, regarding which, he explains through Neo-Confucianism,

> The heart of man is unpredictable, while the heart of Confucianism is righteous and intricate. Working hard and concentrating is the only way to pursue the principles of the world. We have to remain wholehearted and sincere and should not change while pursuing the principles. We must not change our ideals or goals so that we can reconcile our hearts with that of Confucianism and also adhere to the golden rule. This is what it means to study in order to understand the truth of being human . . . If it is to express emotions, it is to show the difference between joy, anger, sorrow, and happiness. If it is to accomplish things, it must conform to the golden rule and be done in accordance with the more than 3,300 rites mentioned in *Classics* (经) and *Songs* (曲). If it is about the ethics of being human, it is about the kinship between fathers and sons, the benevolence and righteousness between monarchs and ministers, the distinction in the division of labor between husbands and wives, the hierarchy between elders and those younger, and the integrity between friends. These three points are the way of the heaven, the earth, and the people.

The officials in charge of educating people use these as their teaching materials when educating the people in the country. Regardless of the past or the present, these are to be taught.

If the rulers can clarify ethics and morals and if the ordinary people can love each other, families will be harmonious, and so will the country. There will then be peace in the world. Therefore, there is no other knowledge than the clarification of ethics and morality.[41]

In the second year of the Jiajing reign in the Ming dynasty (1523), scholar Zhang Yi says in *Tablet Inscription of Chongzheng Academy* (崇正书院碑记),

The knowledge of the sages is based on the laws of nature and is presented in the hearts of man and in the "three principles" and "five constant virtues" (三纲五常)[42], ethics, daily life, and all things. It is used in state governance and is the Confucian values recorded in the classics. It is what the Confucian masters of the past have discovered and clarified, and it is what was used by academies to teach and study.

From these words, it can be seen that what academies implemented was a curriculum based on Confucian ethics and morality. Ming dynasty scholar Yang Lian summarizes what was taught in academies quite comprehensively in "Notes on Shrine of Confucian Ancestors of Bailudong Academy" (白鹿洞书院宗儒祠记):

Education systems such as academies have a long history. It is the Confucian values and doctrines that need to be explained clearly and discussed. The "three principles" and "five constant virtues" are closely related to our body (existence) while the "four natural human consciences"[43] (四端) and innate goodness are governed by our hearts. The Four Books (四书) and Five Classics (五经) are stepping stones to help us improve our cultivation. The various schools of thought are to provide us with the basis for debate and discussion. A person intently studying Confucianism is just like an archer who always expects to hit the target or a traveler who yearns to return home.[44]

It can be seen from the text that the inculcation and dissemination of Confucian ethics was the central task of the daily teaching conducted in academies.

2. Diffusion of Confucianism by Scholars from Academy to Society

In the later period of traditional Chinese society, the academy became an important place for the cultivation and training of Confucian scholars. From the perspective of the historical development of academies, the increasing prosperity of academies in the Song dynasty did enable a large number of scholars to study and learn in academies. Nevertheless, the academies of the Song dynasty were not yet popularized enough.

14 *Academy, Society, and Politics*

Therefore, there are still many talents who are not taught in academies but in schools. However, in the later dynasties, county schools only set up ancestral temples to worship saints and did not have school dormitories anymore. The school still exists, but the actual function of nurturing and shaping talents was lost. That was why there was a need to establish another place to nurture talents.

As a result, academy education spread all over urban and rural areas of the country, becoming the main channel for the nurturing of talents. "Whether it is a big city or a remote area, there are people with special talents and high morals who stand out."[45]

In the process of nurturing talents, academies' primary goal is to indoctrinate and cultivate Confucian moral values. While striving to make Confucian moral values the common value orientation and spiritual belief that governs the social group composed of scholars, academies required the scholars to apply those values to their behavior. This can be seen from the various xuegui (学规, academy rules) and xueyue (学约, academy agreements) issued by different academies across the ages.

Xuegui (学规) and xueyue (学约) were rules and regulations established based on certain talent cultivation goals. Their purpose is to concretize the guiding ideology of running a school and to integrate the goal of talent nurturing into various regulations. By establishing guidelines and norms, scholars would consciously abide by them. Indoctrinating Confucian ethics and morals into students to strengthen their moral consciousness was characteristic of academies through the years. For example, renowned Neo-Confucian scholar Lü Zuqian set forth 11 articles in *Guiyue* (规约) in the fourth year of Qiandao in the Southern Song dynasty (1168). The first article is on filial piety, respect, loyalty, and integrity. It stipulates that

all those who participate in such gatherings must have a foundation of filial piety, respect, loyalty, and integrity. If someone is not filial to his parents and does not love their brothers, not on good terms with his clan, and inconsistent in his words and action, those within the group should lose no time to admonish and advise them. If they do not listen to the advice, they will be punished. If they do not correct their mistakes after they are punished, all those in the group should be told about it so that everyone can work together to help them correct their mistakes. If they do not repent, they will be disqualified from joining the group.

The articles 2 to 11 are also about specific rules of conduct and the nurturing of character. They include, "Do not speak profanity, do not flatter, do not lie, do not be disorganized, do not look down on those who are not of your kind, do not interact with those who engage in bad deeds, and so on." These rules are very detailed.[46]

Another example is what is stated in Zhu Xi's *Statutes of Bailudong Academy* (白鹿洞书院揭示). It is also about the study of moral principles: "There should be kinship between father and son, benevolence between monarchs and subjects, distinction of labor between husband and wife, hierarchy between elders and those who are younger, and integrity between friends." Talking about the key aspects of self-cultivation, he says, "Speak with courtesy and honesty and do things with integrity and respect. Restrain anger and control desires and correct mistakes while pursuing correctness." About the key aspects of handling matters, he says, "Do the right things and do not seek personal gain. Clarify the truth and do not claim the credit." About interacting with others, he says, "Do not do unto others what you don't want others to do unto you. If you are unsuccessful or encounter setbacks and difficulties, reflect on yourself and seek a reason for everything in yourself."[47] *Statutes of Bailudong Academy* (白鹿洞书院揭示) influenced the historical development of academies greatly, and later many academies followed its teachings.

Rules for Learning by Cheng Duanmeng and Dong Zhu (程董学则), formulated by the Song dynasty scholars Cheng Duanmeng and Dong Zhu, attempts to penetrate the central task of inculcating Confucian ethics and moral values into all aspects of daily life in academies. They include such guidelines as being respectful to the place one is living in, standing upright, being proper in one's speech, being dignified in one's appearance, and being neat in clothing, in an attempt to reflect the adherence to Confucian ethics and moral values in different details of daily life. Although the rules of many other academies may vary in their details due to different time periods or different characteristics, their emphasis on indoctrinating and reinforcing Confucian ethics and moral values is consistent. Among the many academy rules, the requirements of ethics and morality were often given special prominence in order to show their emphasis. For example, in the 24th year of the Kangxi reign of the Qing dynasty (1685), the first article of *Rules and Regulations of Bailudong Academy* (白鹿洞书院学规) stipulated by Tang Laihe is to "concentrate on establishing one's moral character."[48] In the 20th year of Qianlong (1755), Wang Mingcong's *Rules and Regulations of Bailuzhou Academy* (白鹭洲书院学规) also states that "concentrating on building one's moral character is the most important task for a scholar."[49] Many other academies also clearly stated that "to engage in learning, one must build one's moral character"[50] and that "there is nothing more fundamental about the purpose of learning than understanding loyalty and filial piety."[51] It can be seen from these rules that the academies tried to make the scholars identify with and believe in Confucianism through the inculcation and indoctrination of Confucian values. Under the circumstances, these scholars naturally became advocates for Confucian values and had them faithfully practiced. In this sense, academies had successfully gained the cultural control over the group of scholars.

It is worth noting that the purpose of education in academies was not only to enhance the moral values of the academy students but also to broaden the horizons of the entire society. Training and educating academy students just served as a starting point to spread Confucian ethics and values to the whole society, to realize the socialization of Confucianism, and eventually to exert the social control function of Confucianism. This was the conscious pursuit of many academy educators and their expectations for scholars.

16 *Academy, Society, and Politics*

Many scholars dedicated to academy education had a clear understanding of the relationship between Confucian scholars of the academy and the mores of the society as a whole. For example, Wang Ji, a scholar of Xin Xue in the Ming dynasty, writes in *On Restoring Academies* (重修书院记), "Education must start with the scholars." Therefore, it was necessary to "inspire and influence the scholars first before advocating the education of the general public on this basis."[52] Wu Rui of the Qing dynasty writes in *Tablet Inscription of Meihua Academy* (梅花书院碑记), "If scholars can get a good education, the customs and habits of the people will be improved."[53] Hao Yulin from the Qing dynasty says in *Records of Tianzhang Academy* (天章书院记),

> Scholars are the role models for the common people to imitate and learn from. Their essays are the characterization of their behavior. If students write well and behave well, the folk customs of the people will be simple and pure. If so, it can reflect the effect of literati support for the country.[54]

During the Daoguang reign, Gui Chaowan, governor of Luancheng, writes in *On Restoring Longgang Academy Tablet* (国朝重修龙冈书院碑), "The responsibility to educate and influence the people lies with the literati. Only those who are proficient in the classics and can clarify Confucian rites can assume the responsibility of persuading people."[55] Zhang Zhidong, a renowned minister in the late Qing dynasty, also says in *A Proposal on Establishment of Guangya Academy* (创建广雅书院折),

> Cultivating good folk customs starts from cultivating the scholars . . . To correct the customs and habits of the people, we must also first start with treating scholars well and nurturing them. When scholars study well, talents will emerge.[56]

It was based on this recognition of the role scholars played in the process of changing customs and traditions that some scholars took building academies and training talents as tasks of urgency.

> If the way of governing the country lies in the edification of the people, then the beginning of edification is to establish schools . . . Now everywhere education administrators are preaching the instructions of the sages and thus it is in this way that edification is promoted. So the ministers understood this intention, and the establishment of academies has spread throughout the whole country.[57]

They hoped that scholars could be cultivated by the academies and would act as role models in various social activities through their words and deeds. They hoped that these role models would further become a reference group expanding their influence throughout society.

> Living together in the academy, discussing and learning from each other . . . Practice love and friendship in the family, and honesty and harmony in the

village. When one is an official, he should adhere to the integrity of justice and righteousness and the promotion of integrity in court.[58]

When scholars are free, they gather together in specific places in the state to teach and learn. If there are things worthy of learning, they will encourage each other. If mistakes are made, they will admonish each other. If they do not achieve success, they will influence and inspire the people of their hometown with filial piety and loyalty. If they achieve great success, they will repay society with knowledge and essays.[59]

This expectation is stated by Li Fu, a Xin Xue scholar during the reign of Yong-zheng in the Qing dynasty, in *Restoration of Xuancheng Academy* (复修宣成书院记). Li Fu believed that it would be narrow-minded to think that the establishment of academies and the training of scholars was only for the purpose of passing the imperial examinations. The effectiveness of academy education did not end with scholars but was linked to the cause of transforming folk customs.

A newly established academy must select outstanding students and gather them together. They must hire highly educated scholars with high moral fiber as the superintendent to conduct daily inspections and monthly examinations. This might seem to only be targeted at a small number of people, but when the scholars of the academies gather to listen to seminars and discuss, academic success can easily be achieved. After the completion of their studies, these scholars will go to different states and counties where they will become educators to guide young people in their studies. The scope of education is very broad, and the common folk can also be educated. Through this, good folk customs and traditions can thus be easily formed.[60]

Obviously, in the process of the spread of Confucianism, the influence of academies was by no means limited to a small group of scholars and could reach the wider society. Since the scholars were all part of their social network, their way of thought, values, and behaviors would have an impact as they were channeled through different networks to different social classes and groups. During the reign of Qianlong in the Qing dynasty, scholar Zhang Zhenyi, in *Tablet Inscription of Rebuilding Dongshan Academy* (重建东山书院碑记), talks about the process of spreading Confucian ethics and moral values from scholars to the family and the world:

The scholars in the capital all teach and learn from each other, imitating the method of studying at Kaoting Academy. They are respectful and study everything exhaustively to build a firm foundation. They take studying the principles of all things to obtain knowledge as the key and take sincerity and righteousness as the heart of the foundation. If this is done, one would see the elevation of one's cultivation. If so, this would have a good influence on the cultivation of a family. If the cultivation of a family is elevated, then this

18 *Academy, Society, and Politics*

would spread throughout the country and the world. Good customs can then be cultivated, and talents can be nurtured.[61]

Cao Yanyue of the Song dynasty writes in *Reconstruction of Book Pavilion in Bailudong Academy* (白鹿书院重建书阁记) that scholars should take "studying hard to gain knowledge and working hard to practice this knowledge" as a starting point to achieve "filial piety in the family, respect for elders in the village, benevolence for the people in prefectures and counties as an official, and good reputation in court."[62] During the reign of Qianlong in the Qing dynasty, Wang Xuntai, magistrate of Xingye County, says in *Records of Shinan Academy* (石南书院记), "The academies are established to cultivate and educate talents. It should be a fundamental place to cultivate good culture and customs." The scholars had to cultivate themselves to cultivate others and eventually reached a state where all in the world shared the same moral values.

They use their knowledge to influence the people from their hometowns, from townships to various villages and elementary schools in these small village clusters. Fathers talk about love and benevolence, while sons talk about filial piety. The people keep each other in check and encourage each other, gradually influencing each other. Under the influence of a unified moral standard, the customs of the people will eventually grow to be the same. This is the effect of education.[63]

This refers to the expansion and penetration of Confucianism into mainstream ideology and the realization of the social control function of Confucianism. Undoubtedly, this was the result of scholars "using their insights to influence the people in their hometowns." Confucianism spread and penetrated all aspects of society through scholars. Due to the close integration of academies, Confucianism, and scholars, academies were able to play an important role in social control.

Politics and State Policies to Academy

As a cultural and educational organization closely integrated with Confucianism and scholars, academies played an essential role in the social control system. However, in traditional Chinese society, "the entire world is under the jurisdiction of the emperor, and the people living on these lands are his subjects." The existence and development of academies were bound to attract the attention and concern of the supreme rulers. So what was the relationship between academies and the imperial power? Was the academy truly, as some scholars have said, "an organizational expression of the rural society above the level of the family" that was separate from the government, or was it just an intermediate space "between state power and family interests"?[64] In this section, we will try to examine the control of the imperial power over the academy and see how the royal steered its institutional policies to exert influence on the evolution of the academies.

According to Li Caidong and Deng Hongbo, academies were non-governmental organizations at the beginning and were considered private schools.[65] From the historical data that we possess, except for Lizheng Academy and Jixian Academy, most academies in the Tang dynasty were almost entirely privately run. These institutions operated autonomously from the authorities. Some of these were private homes used as gathering points for learning. In terms of the scholars' day-to-day remit, these premises facilitated a range of services and purposes for its users – namely, as a place for disciples to gather and learn, a source of land at their own disposal, the site for the construction of academy buildings, the storage space for the accumulation of books, the venue to recruit or select teachers and students, and so on. Regardless of their functions, the schools carried out the activities independently from the state. Perhaps this rudimentary model of a village school run by the people had not yet attracted the attention of the highest authorities. However, the schools' social influence began to spread over time, alongside the gradual development of an institutional system. The combination of the two trends finally caught the attention of the imperial ruler during the Five Dynasties. The late Tang dynasty was established during the Five Dynasties period, with the current regions of Jiangxi, Fujian, Southern Anhui, and Southern Jiangsu as its core. In just a few decades, its cultural endeavors became quite successful, and it stood out amongst the other dynasties.[66] According to Li Caidong's research, during the reign of Mingzong of the Tang dynasty, the scholar known as Luo Tao of Taihe in Jizhou cited illness and sought to return to his hometown. There, he built Kuangshan Academy at the foot of Mount Kuang with the support of the Mingzong Emperor, who granted him the provision of funds and books to establish the school.[67] According to records, this was the first account in history that a Chinese academy had a direct connection with the imperial power.

It is evident that the emperors of the late Tang dynasty sought to strengthen social control and promote social harmony through their orders to build a Confucian culture. Emperor Mingzong's support and high regard for academies could be seen as a manifestation of the cultural and educational policies of the late Tang dynasty. From Emperor Mingzong's edicts, such as "the customs and habits of the people are improving by the day, so much that they are becoming similar to that of Donglu (the hometown of Confucius and Mencius)" and "it is of great help to the education and influence of folk customs and habits," it can be seen that the highest authority of the state had recognized that the academy had helped change and improve society's customs and traditions. Considering the frequent outbreaks of war during the Five Dynasties, it was rare for the Mingzong Emperor to divide his attention amidst all the political chaos and persist with the cause of edification as well as give praise to Kuangshan Academy. It was understandable that during the Ming dynasty, Zeng Gao once exclaimed that it was a rare thing in the Five Dynasties.[68] From the current data, this was indeed the only recorded example of such an incident happening during that era. The significance of this move was that it promoted the development of academies to a certain extent and set precedence for the imperial rulers to incorporate academies into the social control network.

20 *Academy, Society, and Politics*

During the early Song dynasty, there was further development in academies' number, scale, refinement, and regulations. In line with the expansion, the social influence of academies continued to extend as well. Many scholars "chose deep mountains and woods near open and quiet places to teach." In addition, "in most cases, the academies had dozens or even hundreds of people."[69] Among these academies, the more famous ones included Yuelu, Bailudong, Songyang, and Yingtianfu. Yuan Xie, a Neo-Confucian of the Southern Song dynasty, once praised the achievements of academies in the early Song dynasty for promoting learning and cultivating talents. He says in *Continued Tablet Inscriptions of Four Masters of Mingzhou* (四明教授厅续壁记),

> From the reign of Jianlong to the supremacy of Kangding, there were only schools called academies. They included Bailudong Academy, Yuelu Academy, Songyang Academy, Maoshan Academy, and so on. Some notable figures within these institutions were considered role models for future and succeeding scholars. They included Mr. Qi from Nandu, Mr. Sun from Mount Tai, Mr. Hu from Hailing, Mr. Shi from Tulai, and so on. The outstanding figures of that era gathered together, studying and communicating with each other and improving their sense of self-cultivation. The effects of these are obvious and far-reaching.[70]

There were several major academies at that time, and subsequent scholars held different views about them. However, it is certain that the academies had considerable social influence and attracted the ruler's attention. In *Records of Shigu Academy in Hengzhou* (衡州石鼓书院记), Zhu Xi says,

> In the last dynasty, education was not standardized, and scholars often had no place to conduct specialized studies. They often organized among themselves and selected places with beautiful surroundings to establish academies as a place to live, discuss, and study. Government administrators often praised and honored the establishment of such academies.[71]

From various historical materials, we can see the various situations in which emperors from the early Song dynasty praised academies, granted resources, and even summoned the head of the area. Chapter 3 of this book (see Volume 1) has already had a detailed discussion about this. On the one hand, it shows the support and encouragement given by the state's ruler. On the other, it could be argued that autocracy intervened in the establishment of academies. This reflected the importance that the ruler of the state placed on the newly established organizations that were academies.

If the emperor's granting of resources was considered a form of policy orientation, the initiatives taken by the emperors of the early Song dynasty created exemplary conditions for the development of academies. Indeed, as far as the academy is concerned, the state's ruler's praise was an affirmation of the academy's existing status and influence. This, in turn, further extended the academy's influence and improved its status. However, the academies did not flourish rapidly because of this. On the contrary, academies began to show signs of decline in the middle and late Northern Song dynasty. Many scholars who had taught in the academies and famous Confucian scholars left the establishments after the Qingli Education Reform. The renowned Bailudong Academy was effectively destroyed in the spring of 1054 and consequently reduced to ruins. It was left abandoned in its state until the fifth year of the Chunxi reign during the Southern Song dynasty (1178) when Zhu Xi examined the ruins and started preparations to restore the place. There, he claims that

> the academy was left abandoned in ruins, the sounds of people reading and playing music are but just faint echoes. I suggest that we all pick up our tools and tear the grass apart and search through the ruins of the academy.[72]

Meanwhile, Yuelu Academy was almost abandoned in the fourth year of the Shaosheng reign (1097) and had become a governmental drum casting ground.[73] The academies' decline was mainly caused by the prosperity of government schools. From the Qingli Education Reform that led to education development until the Chongning Reform, the Northern Song dynasty government carried out three rounds of campaigns to promote government schools. Official schools flourished rapidly as a result, and their social status and influence were significantly improved. One of the three campaigns' most important and pivotal measures was to link these government schools to the imperial examinations. It was stipulated that scholars must study in a government school for 300 days before taking the imperial examination. In order to seek advancement, scholars began to enter government schools. Under such circumstances, the development of academies was greatly restricted, and thus, their decline was inevitable.

It is obvious that what is behind the growth of government schools and the decline of academies is the leverage of the state's cultural and educational policies. In fact, because of the strong positive correlation between education and ideology, and even social control, it was difficult to imagine that state rulers who were deeply influenced by Confucianism and who believed that "education and learning are the most important things in building and governing a country and edifying the people" would have allowed private forces to play a leading role in the field of education for so long. One theory is that during the early Song dynasty, the absence or lack of a developed official school system and infrastructure meant that academies were the first obvious and ready means of finding, gathering, and nurturing talented individuals whom the country needed for its development. Setting up an official school system would essentially take time before they could be of service to the state in that respect. Hence, the emperors of that era showed their support for academies and utilized them as a stopgap measure.

In the long run, the rulers still preferred schools within the government system and supported them. These tendencies are natural and obvious. The most illustrative example was the summoning of Yuelu Academy's superintendent, Zhou Shi, by the Zhenzong Emperor of Song in the eighth year of Dazhong Xiangfu (1015).

22 *Academy, Society, and Politics*

In the meeting, Emperor Zhenzong tried to retain Zhou, who was a great teacher with outstanding achievements, and offered him the head position at the Imperial College, hoping that he would accept the appointment. Although Zhou declined the offer and returned to Yuelu Academy, the emperor treated him with the utmost respect and granted him funds, clothes, horses, and documents from the internal government. We can see from this incident that government schools took precedence over their private counterparts in the hearts of rulers. Because of this, they would shift their focus to government schools whenever possible and devote their resources to revitalizing the state institutions. It would thus not be difficult to understand why academies no longer received funds, books, and fields from rulers in the mid to late Northern Song dynasty.

At the same time, the initiative of praising and commending academies was accompanied by the transformation and incorporation of such institutions into government schools by the authorities. This happened to several famous academies in the early Song dynasty. According to Vol. 5 of Hong Mai's *Three Essays of Hong Mai* (容斋三笔), in the fifth year of Taiping Xingguo (980), the head of Bailudong was appointed as the chief official of Baoxin County because he "proposed to government officials to turn over his land as public property" and "Bailudong was gradually abandoned."[74] In a similar gesture, Cao Cheng, a citizen of Yingtianfu, during the second year of Dazhong Xiangfu (1009), built 150 school rooms in the former residence of Qi Tongwen and collected more than 1,500 books. The school flourished, and Cao eventually "wanted to hand over the academy to the government."[75] This was subsequently known as Yingtianfu Academy. The efforts to absorb academies into state governance extended in other ways. For example, in October of the second year of Mingdao (1033), "a lecturer was appointed." In November of the second year of Jingyou (1035), "the academy was treated as a local government operated school, and ten hectares of land were given as the operating expenses of the academy." It could be seen that with the granting of funds and field, the nature of the academy had changed, and the privately owned Yingtianfu Academy was essentially transformed into a government-run school.

Furthermore, there are examples of incentive-led initiatives that successfully converted some of the schools. For instance, in September of the second year of the Jingyou reign (1035), "Wang Zeng submitted a request to put in school officials for Songyang Academy and rewarded them with a hectare of land as a source of income."[76] As for Shigu Academy, "a plaque was awarded during the reign of Jingyou in the Song dynasty, and it was not long until it became a government-run school."[77] The head of Yuelu Academy, Sun Zhou, was appointed as an official by the chief minister of waterways named Huang Zong, in the eighth year of the Tiansheng reign (1030).[78] At the same time, the Three-School system of Tanzhou was established in the late Northern Song dynasty. It was the streamlining and integration of Yuelu Academy, Xiangxi Academy, and Tanzhou State Academy into one body, with the latter being the highest institution of the trio.[79] The Three Schools combination was almost fully integrated into government-run schools. Through this, the imperial court further brought academies under control by including their premises and properties into the government. They also placed officials to manage these institutions and conferred official titles to academies or changed them into prefectural or state schools. As a result, the ownership and nature of many academies changed and became very different from the prefectural or village schools Ma Duanlin mentioned previously.

In the early Southern Song dynasty, the conflict between the Song and Jin dynasties, coupled with internal issues and conflicts with other countries, the imperial court was unable to cope with the military struggles against foreign invasion and rebellion within the country. There was little time to care about the state of academies then. But in fact, some scholars at that time hoped for attention from the court to revitalize academies. During the reign of Shaoxing, Hu Hong, a Neo-Confucian scholar and representative of the Huxiang School, wrote to the prime minister, Qin Hui, with a request to revitalize Yuelu Academy. He hoped to become the head of the academy as well.[80] In the sixth year of the Chunxi reign (1179), Zhu Xi served at the Nankang post and prepared to restore the run-down Bailudong Academy. He also wrote to the then prime minister of the Ministry of Rites in *Petition to Rebuild Bailudong Academy* (申修白鹿书院状), explaining his thoughts on restoring the academy and proposing to install a superintendent for the academy whose "salary would be about the same as the officials from the Ministry of Rites." There was no doubt that Zhu Xi had high hopes that the court would support his plan to restore the academy. In the spring of the eighth year of the Chunxi reign (1181), when Zhu Xi was about to leave Nankang to go to eastern Zhejiang, he reported the process of restoration to Emperor Xiaozong and asked for funds and books. In November of the same year, Zhu Xi was summoned to Yanhe Palace, and he asked once again for funds and books. Zhu Xi's action, as Huang Gan said later, was to "request for the reward of plaques and books printed by the government to show the importance of this matter."[81] That was to show that the court supported the revitalization of the academy, reduced the resistance and difficulties in the process, and provided a guarantee for the normal operation and development of the academy. It could be seen from the actions of Hu Hong and Zhu Xi that Confucian scholars hoped to attract the attention of the court and draw on the power of the court for the smooth development of academies. This, however, also brought academies under the control of the imperial court. It could be seen that to these scholars, academies were not organizations independent of imperial rule. The development of academies and the cultural control uses that they offered were inseparable from the support of the imperial court and had to be combined with it. From this, we can have a clearer understanding of the status of academies in the socio-political landscape then.

In fact, although the gradual officialization of academies in the Song dynasty was repeatedly criticized by later researchers, it was a conscious pursuit of Confucian scholars at that time. For example, in *Academies of States and Prefectures* (州郡书院) and *Three Essays of Hong Mai* (容斋三笔), Hong Mai talks about the parallelism of academies and state schools, saying that "it should not be like this compared to moral sensibilities." The two should be combined as one.[82] Some scholars were even dissatisfied with the fact that academies were not under the

24 *Academy, Society, and Politics*

control of the imperial court and were relatively distant from it. For example, Wu Yong wrote in *Postscript to Tablet Inscription of Zonglian Academy by Emperor* (御书宗濂精舍跋记) that he believed academies should be under the government and was dissatisfied with the private nature of many academies. He claims,

> Since the school of thought of Confucianism has changed and the academic lineage has been severed, scholars have established different schools of thought according to their own preferences and exaggerated what they teach and call knowledge. They build buildings near mountains and boast among themselves. Almost all counties and provinces are dotted with academies and places of learning. The original meaning of "having the ruler giving orders to allow education before education was allowed to proceed" has been completely lost.[83]

These scholars were of the view that academies were only in normal operation when they became government schools or were incorporated into the official management system. From here, we can see the position of scholars on the relationship between academies and the imperial rule at that time.

For the Xiaozong Emperor, supporting the restoration of Bailudong Academy and granting it funds and books was undoubtedly an opportunity to exert imperial influence and strengthen control over the academy. Therefore, Zhu Xi's request for funds and books was granted.

Emperor Xiaozong's granting of funds and books to Bailudong Academy had a positive impact on the development of the academy. Thereafter, the academy entered a period of rapid development. Masters of Neo-Confucianism and their disciples played main roles in establishing academies. However, during this period, lectures given by Neo-Confucian scholars were attacked and denigrated. For example, in June of the 15th year of the Chunxi reign (1188), Lin Li, the minister of war, said about the impeachment of Zhu Xi,

> Zhu Xi has no knowledge but only plagiarizes the statements of Zhang Zai and Cheng Yi and calls them Neo-Confucianism. He claims to be the pioneer of Neo-Confucianism and is arrogant, bringing with him dozens of students wherever he goes. He imitates Confucius and Mencius of the Spring and Autumn and Warring States periods, traveling across the country, hoping to gain attention and employment like Confucius and Mencius.[84]

Later, during the Qingyuan Party ban, Neo-Confucianism was regarded as pseudoscience. Neo-Confucian scholars were deemed "pseudo-apprentices" and "rebels" in the political crackdown. Academy lectures were also affected. The imperial court did not directly target academies, and the Neo-Confucianists were still able to establish academies and carry out lectures and write essays. However, Neo-Confucianism had already become the soul of academies due to the close integration of Neo-Confucian studies and academies. Hence, with Neo-Confucianism banned, many Neo-Confucian scholars were persecuted and even

Academy, Society, and Politics 25

exiled. The development of academies was seriously affected, and academies were silenced temporarily.

After the Jiading political reforms by the Ningzong Emperor, Neo-Confucianism became respected and promoted, and scholars of Neo-Confucianism were given important posts once more. They played important roles in the government, from the imperial court to local governments. They continued to restore and establish academies in previous places, and the establishment of academies became a trend. The number of academies increased rapidly. According to Zou Chonghua in *Treatise on Academies in Sichuan in the Song Dynasty* (宋代四川书院考), there were 18 reliable academies in Sichuan Province in the Song dynasty. Of the 18, the establishment date for 14 was known. Four were established before the reign of Emperor Ningzong, while nine were built during the Ningzong reign. In addition, many academies in the country were restored and expanded.[85] For example, Bailudong Academy was renovated and expanded in the tenth year of the Jiading reign (1217), the 11th and 14th year of the Jiading reign, and the sixth year of the Shaoding reign (1233), respectively.[86] The status of the academy also improved day by day. In the fifth year of the Jiading reign (1212), Liu Yue, a disciple of Zhu Xi and the vice superintendent of the Imperial College, submitted a request to the court to make Zhu Xi's *Annotations to the Analects* (论语集注) and *Annotations to Mencius* (孟子集注)[87] official teaching materials. At the same time, they requested for Zhu Xi's "Regulations of Bailudong Academy" (白鹿洞规) to be promulgated and implemented at Taixue (太学, also known as the Imperial College), which was the highest national college in ancient China. The move expressed the desires of Neo-Confucian scholars to have the emperor praise Neo-Confucianism and pay attention to academies. In the first year of the Chunyou reign (1241) when Emperor Lizong visited Taixue, he advocated Neo-Confucianism and also handwrote a copy of *Statutes of Bailudong Academy* (白鹿洞书院揭示) and gifted it to Taixue. This showed that the emperor not only recognized and affirmed this form of schooling but also agreed with the philosophy of education in "Statutes of Bailudong Academy" (白鹿洞书院揭示). It could be said that the relationship between academies and imperial rule reached an unprecedented degree of harmony during this period. The granting of funds is highly symbolic. During the Southern Song dynasty, the emperor gave more than 30 academies funding. Other than the time Emperor Xiaozong granted Bailudong Academy funds during the reign of Chunxi, the other grants were all given during the reign of Ningzong, Lizong, and Duzong.[88]

It is worth noting that during this period, the imperial court's control over academies also reached a new height. In the latter part of the reign of Lizong, there were attempts to further integrate academies within the system. In discussing this issue, Li Caidong cited a large number of historical materials to show that Emperor Lizong had given official positions to some of the superintendents of academies or appointed some officials to act or serve as the superintendents of academies. Some officials of Rites were appointed to serve concurrently as superintendents of academies.[89] It is evident that the imperial court was involved in the appointment of personnel of several academies. In fact, if the superintendent of the academy

26 *Academy, Society, and Politics*

entered the bureaucracy and became an official, the control of the academy would naturally fall into the hands of the court. Some scholars have studied the increasing control over academies by the imperial court in the Song dynasty and concluded that the officialization of the academies was completed in the Song dynasty.[90]

In the Yuan dynasty, the imperial court tightened its control over academies. As early as the eighth year of the Taizong reign of the Yuan dynasty (1236), the government established the first Mongolian Yuan dynasty academy—Taiji Academy. According to the chapter "Schools" in *Continuation of Comprehensive Examination of Literature* (续文献通考·学校考),

> In the eighth year of the Taizong reign, Yang Weizhong, the provincial governor, followed Prince Kuchun in his crusade against the Song dynasty. They collected the writings of Cheng Hao and Cheng Yi (the Chengs, or the Cheng brothers), as well as others, and sent them back to Yanjing, where they built a hall of worship for Zhou Dunyi, a famous Confucian scholar in the Song dynasty. They also established Taiji Academy and hired famous Confucian scholars Zhao Fu, Wang Cui, and some others to teach at the academy. That was the beginning of the first Yuan dynasty academy.[91]

This was during the period of the war between the Yuan dynasty and the Song dynasty. The establishment of Taiji Academy during the war was done by the government as a political strategy. They wanted to use Confucianism, with the academy as its symbol, to promote the inheritance and succession of culture. This would thus dilute the cultural and psychological aversion of the people caused by their occupation and rule of the nation and enhance the rationality of its regime. After the eradication of the Song dynasty, such political strategies continued to be used. At that time, a large number of scholars who were influenced by ideology to be loyal to the emperor and patriotic to the country suffered from the pain of the fall of their country. They had a backlash against the new government and did not want to pledge loyalty to the Yuan rulers. They were unwilling to enter government organizations to teach or allow their children to study in government-run academies. Many scholars thus chose academies under such circumstances. Some lived in seclusion in the countryside, established academies, and taught there as citizens of the fallen Song empire. This could, on the one hand, provide them with a place to stay or make a living without serving the new empire. On the other hand, it satisfied the scholars' children in need of education outside of government-run academies. Through such intermediaries, academies became entangled with realpolitik.

Fortunately, the rulers of the Yuan dynasty adopted an open attitude toward this issue. They accepted and acknowledged the choices of this group of people and adopted policies that supported the establishment of private academies. In March of the 28th year of the Zhiyuan reign (1291), Emperor Shizu of Yuan promulgated a policy to

> establish elementary schools in each county and hire mature and knowledgeable teachers. Otherwise, an individual can also hire a private teacher, or their

fathers or elder brothers could decide for them. Other places where sages and scholars have lectured and schools organized by families who are happy to contribute to public welfare will be established as academies.[92]

Such a policy was wise as it took advantage of the situation and was aimed at resolving conflicts instead of intensifying them. At the beginning of the Yuan dynasty, the policy was effective in softening the hearts of the people, quelling resistance, gaining the support of the literati, and maintaining the stability of the situation. It could be said that in the political environment of the early Yuan dynasty, this academy policy successfully served political uses.

In addition, because the Song and Yuan dynasties differed greatly in terms of race and culture, the academies, where scholars gathered and knowledge was disseminated, became politically sensitive places. The academies of that time were faced with the questions of in what manner and form academies from the previous dynasty should exist in the new dynasty and how various symbols with specific meanings in academies should be reorganized and accepted by the new regime. The solution would have a great impact on the future development and positioning of academies. The rulers of the Yuan dynasty adopted a flexible and pragmatic attitude to this, and the issue was resolved smoothly. The resolution of Daozhou Lianxi Academy in the 31st year of the Zhiyuan reign (1294) was representative. In the 31st year of the Zhiyuan reign, the Quanzhou, Yongzhou, and Daozhou County Supervision Bureaus stated that the

> Daozhou Lianxi Academy kept the words written by the imperial censor from the late Song dynasty and had a golden seal plaque in its building that had "Chen Kui Ge" written on it. The academy also retained old imperial documents and provincial journals from the Song dynasty.

They believed that "after the fall of the Song dynasty, areas south of the lower reaches of the Yangtze River were subordinate for nearly 20 years." However, in the academies, "those words were written by the emperor of the fallen Song dynasty, and there was the original state seal on it." The book shouldn't be handed down by scholars but should be confiscated and burned. Meanwhile, there were seven statues of Zhou Dunyi and the others in the main hall of the academy. Zhou Dunyi and other "representatives of Confucianism of the fallen Song dynasty should not occupy the place of Confucius." Regarding such incidents, "if not restrained by unified rules and regulations, there might be a promotion of a culture of treachery and hypocrisy, which will confuse the common folk and lead to problems."[93] Hence, academies were required to display statues of Confucius instead, and the imperial documents of the fallen Song dynasty were confiscated. This caused the academy to be involved in realpolitik. However, the political small-mindedness and short-sightedness were also very obvious. Linking the historical act of Emperor Lizong granting books to the fostering of treachery and hypocrisy was overly sensitive. It could easily cause conflicts and pit the government against others. Furthermore, there were many incidents of collecting the

28 *Academy, Society, and Politics*

books and plaques of the previous dynasty. If all were confiscated and burned, it would involve many people and cause alarm. Second, Zhou Dunyi and the others were regarded only as "representative figures of Confucianism in the fallen Song dynasty." Their influence in the succession of Confucianism was not granted importance. The Mongolian Yuan regime honored and venerated Confucianism since its rise to promote cultural orthodoxy. Yet such acts defeated the purpose of the Yuan dynasty, and these were just what some scholars of insight in the Yuan regime were very much concerned about. As a result, the matter was reported and properly handled by the court. The officials concerned were reprimanded, and the books and stele were returned to the academy. Furthermore, the court highly praised Zhou Dunyi, saying that

> Mr. Zhou's doctrine had been inherited from theories from thousands of years ago. It was passed on to Messrs. Cheng Hao and Cheng Yi. He kept the original moral principles and promoted the clarification of the system of benevolence, justice, and rites for most scholars. He has made a great contribution to Confucianism and brought blessings to the people.[94]

The original symbolic system of the academy was maintained and used as a tool by the imperial powers after interpretation.

With the Yuan government's support and encouragement, the Yuan dynasty academies showed a flourishing scene. According to Bai Xinliang, there were 406 academies in the Yuan dynasty; 282 academies were new and 124 were restored.[95] At that time, the academies were spread throughout the country. There was a concentration in the number of academies in areas south of the lower reaches of the Yangtze River, while the academies in the northern region and some remote areas also achieved varying degrees of development. Although the number of academies in the Yuan dynasty was not significant compared to the Southern Song, later Ming, and Qing dynasties, the number was still considered considerable given the relatively short reign of the Yuan dynasty. At that time, scholar Xu Youren talked about the development of academies in the Yuan dynasty:

> After the country was unified in the Yuan dynasty, the education system became especially complete. There are schools in every county, prefecture, and town. Each school has a special position for academic officials. I was worried that insufficient education and guidance would lead to poor folk culture. Academies were specially established where the sages used to live, where high-ranking officials and nobles live, where people of high moral prestige visited, and where people advocated benevolence and personal cultivation live, to promote education. Plaques were also inscribed for schools, and special posts were set up for school officials. Rules and regulations for all schools were also established. The world is so big, and whether in remote villages or places, whether deep in the mountains or barren valleys, there are unknown numbers of newly founded schools.[96]

Zhu Yizun of the Qing dynasty writes in *Hearsay of Old Matters from Under the Sun* (日下旧闻) that

> there was no other dynasty in which the establishment of academies was more prosperous than the Yuan dynasty. Every school had a superintendent who was in charge of management, and wages were provided. This was the same almost throughout the entire country.[97]

It is worth noting that along with the prosperity of academies in the Yuan dynasty was the strengthening of the control over academies by the imperial court. At the beginning of the Mongolian Yuan regime, the rulers appeared to be enlightened and supported academies to ease conflicts and soften the hearts of the people. However, the political strategy changed after political stability was achieved. The rulers tried to incorporate academies, which were directly related to ideology, into the system to enhance social control, making them part of the national education system rather than a private organization outside of the system. Xu Zi points out in *Research on Academies of the Yuan Dynasty* (元代书院研究) that in the late Zhiyuan reign of the Yuan dynasty (1271–1294), the Yuan government revised and changed its permissive and lenient policy toward academies and took measures to strengthen their control of academies from several aspects. On the one hand, the establishment of academies was controlled and managed, and various strict and cumbersome procedures to approve the establishment of an academy were stipulated. On the other hand, the government controlled the leadership and economy of the academies by appointing superintendents and allotting fields to strengthen its control over academies. At the same time, the imperial court and the local governments at all levels directly participated in the establishment of academies, which increased the proportion of government-run academies.[98] Through these measures, the rulers established complete rule over academies from the establishment to the daily management. Academies became, to a large extent, tools to reflect the will of the ruler. While Zhu Yizun writes in *Hearsay of Old Matters from Under the Sun* (日下旧闻) that "there was no other dynasty in which the establishment of academies was more prosperous than in the Yuan dynasty." He also emphasizes that "every school had a superintendent who was in charge of management and wages were provided." These could be said to be the characteristics of government schools in the Yuan dynasty.

The Ming dynasty was an important period for the development of academies. Academies developed greatly in terms of number, types, distribution area, and social influence. However, the destruction and banning of academies occurred frequently in the Ming dynasty, and the relationship became more evident between academies and social reality and politics. The control of state power on academies was also further strengthened.

In the early Ming dynasty, the development of academies declined. In the first year of Hongwu (1368), Emperor Taizu decreed the establishment of two academies in Zhusi and Nishan of Qufu, Shandong Province, and appointed a

30 *Academy, Society, and Politics*

superintendent for each school. However, the main function of the two academies was ancestral worship. This indicated that the emperor had established the academies out of respect for Confucianism and to worship Confucius rather than for the promotion and advocacy for academies. According to research by scholars, from the early Ming to the mid-Ming dynasty, a period spanning nearly 100 years, the development of academies was stagnant. Many of the academies of the Song and Yuan dynasties were incorporated into the local government schools. Many famous academies, such as Bailudong Academy, Yuelu Academy, and Bailuzhou Academy, were in a state of disrepair and did not have any management. Although some local officials at that time rebuilt and restored some schools—for example, Wu Yubi, who built Xiaopi Academy; Hu Juren, who built Nangu Academy, Liwu Academy, and Bifeng Academy; and Lou Liang, who built Yunge Academy— the scale and influence of these academies were insignificant. On the whole, the development of academies was stagnant. It was a sharp contrast to the prosperity of government schools at that time.[99] As early as the winter of the second year of Hongwu (1369), Zhu Yuanzhang ordered all counties, prefectures, and townships to set up schools.

> Teaching positions should be set up in government schools in the counties, prefectures, and townships . . . Teachers and students are provided with six dou of food every month. The administrative department will distribute fish and meat, and the salaries of school officials will vary with different positions.

Those with excellent grades in the county, prefecture, and town schools would also obtain an "excellent student qualification" and would be able to participate in the township examinations to become a candidate for middle and lower-level officials of the local government. The central government schools were well regulated and were given many rewards. The various measures to promote learning and education in the early Ming dynasty led to prosperous government schools. In the chapter "Elections" in *History of the Ming Dynasty* (明史·选举志), it is stated that

> Confucian schools were established throughout the country at different levels of administrative divisions, such as counties, prefectures, and townships . . . The voices of various schools were heard, and different rules and regulations were established. Whether in remote villages or places, whether they were at the end of the world, such an education style was prevalent.[100]

The enthusiasm of supreme rulers about setting up official schools and their total disregard for academies in the early Ming dynasty formed a sharp contrast. The reason for the contrast had something to do with the emperor's understanding of academies. The cultural and educational policies promulgated were determined by the ruler's needs. Emperor Taizu of the Ming strongly promoted education and talent cultivation and popularized education to establish social order after a long period of turmoil and war. There was a need to cultivate talents needed by various bureaucratic institutions. This was linked to governance. To the Taizu Emperor, "To govern a country, one has to first educate, and at the basis of education are schools." Since this task was so important, it should be undertaken by the state whenever possible. The private nature of the academy was thus excluded. If we link the early Ming emperors trying to strengthen ideological control and create a situation in which "many different methods and approaches are summed in one, and many truths are summed in one principle" so that "there would be no more than one person in charge of the family and there would not be different customs and traditions in the country," then the various initiatives of the authoritarian government could be explained.

During the reign of Chenghua, government schools began to fail, and the imperial examinations grew increasingly corrupt. Academies began to be resurrected to meet the needs of talents. The policy concerning academies in the Ming dynasty also started to change. The government began to repair and construct academies. According to Vol. 50 of *Continuation of Comprehensive Examination of Literature* (续文献通考),

> On the 20th year of Chenghua, he ordered Guixi County of Jiangxi to rebuild Xiangshan Academy. In the first year of the reign of Hongzhi, Zhou Muyan of the Ministry of Personnel Affairs was assigned to build Xuedao Academy in Changshu County. In the first year of the Zhengde reign, Shao Bao, deputy envoy of the Department of Justice of Jiangxi Province, was sent to restore Lianxi Academy of Dehua County.[101]

Such acts have a guiding effect. With renowned scholars such as Zhan Ruoshui and Wang Yangming choosing academies as a place to gather disciples and lecture, by the years of Zhengde and Jiajing, academies began to enter their heyday. A large number of famous academies were restored, and a large number of new academies were established in various places. In the chapter "Biographies of Confucian Scholars" of *the Ming Dynasty* (明史·儒林传), it is stated,

> During the reign of Zhengde and Jiajing, Wang Shouren gathered his disciples in the army, and Xu Jie, as the head of a hundred officials, publicly lectured. The government was touched by such a culture. Hence, literati in the countryside and retired people of virtue publicly lectured and created academies that became known to all and were very impactful.

However, the growth of the power of academies and the expansion of their social influence would undoubtedly hinder the implementation of ideological control and political autocracy and hinder the expansion of royal power. In such a situation, the power of the emperor began to suppress and crack down on academies. Four large-scale closures and bans and the destruction of academies happened nationwide in the Ming dynasty in the 16th year of Jiajing (1537), the 17th year of Jiajing, the seventh year of Wanli (1579), and the fifth year of Tianqi (1625).[102] The specific reasons and processes of the four waves of incidents were

32 *Academy, Society, and Politics*

different, but the basic reason was the same. Academies were suppressed and attacked by the autocratic monarchy.

According to the chapter "Schools" in *Continuation of Comprehensive Examination of Literature* (续文献通考·学校考四), in February of the 16th year of the Jiajing reign (1537), imperial historian You Jujing submitted a petition to reprimand famous scholar Zhan Ruoshui, who was then the minister of the Ministry of Justice in Nanjing. You accused Zhan of "advocating and promoting his unorthodox doctrine, widely recruiting students who did not follow the correct path, and setting up an academy without permission."[103] You requested for the academy to be banned for setting the people on the right path. Emperor Shizong "comforted and retained Ruoshui with generous treatment and ordered the relevant departments to disband the academy." In April of the following year, Xu Zan, the minister of the Ministry of Justice, submitted another petition, saying that "allowing the building of more academies and gathering students to evaluate and debate on government affairs interferes with government affairs. Academies should be disbanded immediately." In the end, Emperor Shizong issued an edict to ban and destroy academies. In the 16th and 17th years of Jiajing, academies were banned and destroyed. On the surface, it was nothing but a power struggle among individual officials. However, it was, in fact, a measure of the ruler to strengthen ideological control. Since Emperor Chengzi of the Ming dynasty promulgated *Complete Works of Four Books* (四书大全), *Complete Collection of the Five Classics* (五经大全), and *Complete Collection on Neo-Confucian Teachings* (性理大全), Zhu Xi's school of thought established a unique position in academia and became the guiding ideology of governance. Zhu Xi's school of thought also became part of the core teachings in academies. "The current code of conduct of literati, the content and methods used by academies to educate students are all based on Mr. Zhu Xi's thought and education."[104] However, since the Zhengde and Jiajing era, Wang Yangming and Zhan Ruoshui developed academies and held lectures. Most of what they taught was different from Zhu Xi's school of thought. As a matter of fact, many of the academies at that time had become important bases for the development and dissemination of Yangmingism, which undoubtedly caused an impact on the orthodox ideology that used Zhu Xi's theory as a tool to unify thought and clamp down on public opinion. Therefore, as early as the first year of Jiajing (1522), when the trend of Yangmingism gradually emerged, some petitioned the Shizong Emperor to denounce Yangmingism as a foreign school of thought and requested for it to be "strictly prohibited in order to correct the habits and thoughts of students."[105] In the eighth year of Jiajing (1529), Emperor Shizong denounced Wang Yangming for "unrestrained speech, discrediting Confucianism, gathering disciples, being deceitful, and teaching things that are not right." This resulted in the saying that "scholars practice evil doctrines" at that time. Obviously, the emperor's rebuke defined the teachings in academies then and also foreshadowed the inevitable destruction and bans of academies. The two petitions submitted by You Jujing and Xu Zan in the 16th and 17th years of Jiajing, respectively, detailing why academies should be banned and destroyed, were just the repetition and concretization of the emperor's rebuke.

In fact, in the mid-Ming dynasty, the autocratic power had already penetrated the daily teaching of some academies. For example, in the 39th year of Jiajing (1560), Sun Guangzu, the country magistrate of Qimen, Anhui Province, established a hall to teach culture in Dongshan Academy. He went to the academy every month and

> spoke with the students about the study of cultivating themselves and corrected the way they thought. He also interviewed the heads and deputy heads of each village and gave instructions to them face to face. He repeatedly emphasized and explained the emperor's requirements and guided them with the eight codes of good behavior.[106]

Government officials used academies as a place to talk about the emperor's edicts. This showed that some academies began to serve the autocratic rule and were in the social control network and played a direct role in it. Of course, there were not many such academies. Most academies did not directly serve the autocratic rule but were on the opposite end of it.

In the spring of the seventh year of Wanli (1579), "the edict to ban and destroy all academies" was given. This was the third time the Ming dynasty banned and destroyed academies.[107] At that time, Zhang Juzheng was the chief minister. From the standpoint of maintaining authoritarian rule and controlling ideology, Zhang Juzheng was very disgusted and cynical about the style of gathering students to teach in an academy. He denounced academy lectures as "empty talk." In the second year of being chief minister, he submitted a petition to "disallow the establishment of academies, the gathering of disciples in groups, and the calling on other parties to wander around and talk about nothing." In the seventh year of Wanli (1579), academies were finally banned and destroyed. Provincial academies were all converted into public administrative offices. Zhang Juzheng's move, of course, involved his personal tendencies, his experiences, and power struggle. However, the basic motivation for this act was to suppress the voices of different classes and groups, strengthen control over ideology, and maintain autocratic rule. On these points, Zhang had a conscious and clear understanding. In "A Reply to Tu Pingshi of the South Division on Learning" (答南司成屠平石论为学), Zhang talks about the interference and threat brought about by academy lectures to the stability of autocratic rule:

> There are many of them, and they have joined forces to interfere in government politics. These people will seriously and directly impact the governmental order of the imperial court and disrupt the people's judgment of right and wrong. . . . During the reign of Jiajing to Longqing, the court was deeply affected by this bad behavior, and the bad influences continued. This is something that officials responsible for education should take note of.

Zhang spoke as someone who was in charge of education. His motive for banning and destroying academies was to put an end to "differences" and to avoid "shaking the court and cause chaos." Academies advocated freedom in speech, debate, pluralism, and the inclusion of different viewpoints in lectures. Some scholars even argue that "the differences are the reason for the lectures." Although the lectures discussed academic issues rather than political issues, the autocratic rule thought that the spiritual orientation of such lecturing was incompatible with or even contrary to the goal of a "one culture education." In order to maintain the autocratic rule and create a unified ideology, it was necessary to remove academies that posed as an obstacle and eliminate the freedom of thought that was embodied in academy lectures. From these three incidents of banning and destroying academies, it could be seen that the control of the autocratic rule over academies was further strengthened. The control rose to a new level from the control over the academy's economy and administration in the previous dynasty to control at the spiritual level.

In the fifth year of Tianqi (1625), there was a fourth banning and destruction of academies in the Ming dynasty. The fuse of this incident was the clash between two political factions at that time. At that time, a group of scholars led by Gu Xiancheng and Gao Panlong used Donglin Academy as their base for academic research and dissemination. They also delivered lectures "ridiculing the imperial government and gave judgment on the people." This resulted in a great social impact. Donglin Academy became the center of political activities, and there, public opinion was independent of the imperial court. They were dissatisfied with Wei Zhongxian and other court officials for their dictatorship. This incurred hatred from Wei Zhongxian and the others. The Weis cooked up charges and persecuted the scholars who lectured at Donglin Academy and made a move to ban and destroy Donglin Academy and all academies in the country.

The ban and destruction of academies may seem to be a political struggle between parties with different political attitudes and positions at that time. The ban and destruction of academies was just a means for Wei Zhongxian and the party of eunuchs he led to attack and persecute the sages of Donglin Academy. But essentially, this was still a destruction of the free spirit of the academy by the autocratic rule. The eunuchs, led by Wei Zhongxian, took advantage of the incompetence of Emperor Xizong and caused trouble. They took power and began to play the role of an autocratic ruler. Meanwhile, the scholars of Donglin Academy relied on the tradition of free lectures at the academy. They used the academy as a base to discuss political affairs and criticize corruption in realpolitik. This was an extension of the academy's free spirit. However, the autocratic rule would not allow the academy to do anything that was beyond the control of the rule. Hence, academies suffered serious blows. It was obvious that Wei Zhongxian and the others did not only attack those who studied and lectured at Donglin Academy and used it as a base for political activities but also wanted to attack the academy's spirit of free lectures that they embodied. Such free lecture spirit might threaten the stability of the autocratic rule and was targeted as such. It could be said that the banning of academies at the end of the Ming dynasty was actually a fierce fight between the autocratic rule and the free spirit of the academy. On this, Huang Zongxi, a Ming and Qing philosopher, in reflecting on the relationship between academies and the socio-political environment, says,

When schools become academies and achieve nothing, the imperial court will be glorified by them. If they achieve something, the imperial court will think to regard it as a mistake and be humiliated by it. The ban of pseudo-studies and the destruction of academies was nothing but the victory of the strong power of the imperial court.[108]

The four different times academies were banned and destroyed in the Ming dynasty were the result of the imperial rule's attempt to implement ideological control, stifling the spirit of freedom of learning in academies.

The Qing dynasty was the heyday of the development of the academy. At that time, the number of academies reached an unprecedented number of more than 4,300. There was also considerable progress in the scale, system, and social influence of academies. The policy concerning academies underwent a process of changes in the Qing dynasty. During the Shunzhi reign of the early Qing dynasty, the development of academies was suppressed and not until the reign of Emperor Kangxi, where academies slowly restored and their development encouraged. During the reign of Yongzheng and Qianlong, academies were strongly supported, and the establishment of academies was advocated. Such policy adjustment and change were centered around strengthening social order. It was still, at the core, a means to strengthen the autocratic rule.

In the beginning, the Qing government adopted various measures to strengthen their social control and to consolidate their rule. In the ninth year of Shunzhi (1652), inscription tablets were used to distribute the teachings throughout the nation. There were eight articles inscribed on the tablet, including the following:

Students are not allowed to submit opinions on any issues involving the military and the people. Those who violate the relevant regulations will be punished by expulsion and the cancellation of school status.

Students are not allowed to gather and form alliances, societies, parties, and the like to influence and control the political functions of the government and decide on matters in the township. Any writings by the students are not allowed to be freely published and printed. Those who violate the relevant regulations will be subjected to punishment by the administrator.

These rules and regulations deprived scholars of many freedoms of speech, association, and publication. It indicated the intent of the ruler to place scholars under the strict control of the royal power. The teachings on the inscription tablets were promulgated and issued throughout the country and became the keynote of the Qing dynasty's educational and cultural policies and the rules in many of the academies in the Qing dynasty. For example, Yuelu Academy not only put the tablet on the left of Minglun Hall in the ninth year of Shunzhi but also included the full text in the tablet in the chapter "Rules of the Academy" of *A Sequel to Yuelu Academy Annals* (岳麓书院续志·书院规条) during the reign of Tongzhi.

36 *Academy, Society, and Politics*

A paragraph was also added to the rules, stating that "the imperial court established academies and selected students . . . to nurture virtuous talents to serve the court."[109] The smaller academies in remote areas are no exception. For example, Chenhou Academy, located in Beixiang (now Liao City, Zixing County), Xingning (now Zixing), Hunan, was a private rural academy founded by the township during the reign of Xianfeng. However, in the second year of Tongzhi (1863), the academy still stressed in its rules:

> The records of the academy respectfully record the articles and inscriptions written by the emperor himself on the discipline of scholars, as well as the famous remarks of various sages and academic figures. The most important parts of the texts were selected and printed to help students who come forth to study and learn from each other to understand and master the rules of education.[110]

Until the 31st year of Guangxu (1905), Shishan Academy in Shishan County, Nan'an, Fujian Province, continues to stipulate in *Ten Rules of Shishan Academy* (诗山书院课规十则),

> The teachers and administrators responsible for the supervision and management of the academy must display and hang on the walls of the lecture hall and dormitories inscriptions written by the emperor, articles written to admonish scholars by the previous emperor, the edicts issued by every emperor, Mr. Zhu Xi's rules for Bailudong Academy, and so on. This is done so that students will see them every day and would be able to remind themselves at all times.[111]

This shows the strong and profound influence that these rules had on academies. In the same year the tablet was issued, the Shunzhi Emperor also promulgated a policy to inhibit the development of academies:

> Each academy official will supervise the teaching and learning of the classics by the students and Confucian scholars to ensure that they practice what is taught. Disallow the establishment of academies, the gathering of disciples in groups, and the calling on other parties to wander around and talk about nothing.[112]

The implementation of this policy was mainly based on the fact that the imperial regime was new and the political structure was not yet stabilized. There were resistance activities from time to time, and scholars who suffered the pain of the fall of their country strongly opposed and resisted foreign rule. They lived in isolation as citizens of a fallen nation and ignored the new dynasty. As a gathering place for scholars, academies were easily used by anti-Qing forces as the dynasty changed and became the center of activity for the resistance forces. At the same time, academies and realpolitik were closely connected since the end of the Ming dynasty. Scholars satirized political affairs, judged certain figures, and actively participated in realpolitik, standing in opposition to the ruling authorities. Hence, the Qing rulers could not help but maintain considerable suspicion of academies and were even wary of and hostile against them. The ban disallowing "the establishment of academies and the gathering of disciples in groups" was a targeted preventative measure.

However, the fact was that academies did not just go silent. As early as the early years of Shunzhi, some local officials began to actively repair academies that were damaged in the war. Li Caidong, governor of Jiangxi, Cai Shiying, together with his clan and provincial departments, restored the four major academies of Jiangxi around the tenth year of Shunzhi (1653). These academies were Ehu, Bailu, Bailuzhou, and Youjiao. They also hired teachers to give lectures at these academies. In the 14th year of Shunzhi, government official Yuan Kuoyu requested to restore Shigu Academy of Hengyang, and his request was approved by the court.[113] In the chapter "Academies" in *Comprehensive Examination of Literature of the Qing Dynasty* (清朝文献通考·学校七), Vol. 69, it is recorded,

> Governor Yuan Kuoyu submitted a report to the court, saying that Shigu Academy of Hengyang was dedicated to the famous Han dynasty minister Zhuge Liang, the famous minister of the Tang dynasty Han Yu, and the famous minister of the Song dynasty Zhu Xi. The wise figures of the past generations used to gather their students here and give lectures throughout the Yuan and Ming dynasties. The academy was destroyed due to the war at the end of the Ming dynasty, and the rituals were interrupted from then on. I now ask for permission to take the lead in donating funds to restore the academy as a way to express my respect for the sages of the past and to encourage young students to perform the relevant rituals on time every year. The emperor agreed.[114]

Yuan's restoration of Shigu Academy did not break the ban on the establishment of new academies. However, the approval of the imperial court and the support for the initiative showed that the policies concerning academies had relaxed at that time. This impacted the restoration and establishment of future academies. According to Bai Xinliang, the number of restored and reconstructed academies from the previous dynasty nationwide was 61, and 45 new academies were established during the reign of Shunzhi.[115]

This loosening of academy policy in the early Qing dynasty is somewhat related to the increasing stability of the political situation, the boosting of the ruler's confidence, and the weakening of wariness against the academy. During the reign of Kangxi, as internal conflicts calmed, the attitude toward academies born by the rulers began to change even further. Policies concerning academies began to undergo significant changes. The Kangxi Emperor was an ambitious monarch. He loved the Confucian culture and agreed with the idea of governing the country through moral construction and spiritual refinement. He attached great importance to the role of moral culture and ideological building in administering

38 *Academy, Society, and Politics*

the country and the people. Taiwanese scholar Huang Jinxing pointed out that Emperor Kangxi had attempted to combine governance with Confucianism to fully extend autocratic rule. Before the reign of Kangxi, the long-term political ideal of Confucianism, which was the "unity of governance and religion," was not really implemented institutionally. Governance and religion were undertaken separately by the ruler and scholars. Since the Song dynasty, scholars had often relied on the transmission of the Confucian Way to contend with the regime. To achieve the purpose of combining the transmission of the Confucian Way and governance, Emperor Kangxi dispelled the foothold of the scholars who used the transmission of Confucianism to criticize political authority, extended political power into the cultural field, and actively intervened in the tradition of culture and thought to gain cultural power which had the transmission of Confucianism as its symbol.[116] Academies were bases for innovation and dissemination of Confucianism and an important symbol of the Confucian Way (道统, also translated into "Daotong" or "Confucian orthodoxy" elsewhere in this book). And the dissemination of the Confucian Way was the basis and support for scholars' self-esteem, self-respect, and resistance to imperial rule. The supreme ruler's goal of combining the dissemination of the Confucian Way and governance was reflected in policies concerning academies. Academies were no longer beyond governance or in opposition to the imperial ruler. Instead, academies were brought into the system and were made as a tool for socio-political control by autocratic rule. According to Bai Xinliang, after the Revolt of the Three Feudatories was suppressed in the 20th year of his reign (1681), Emperor Kangxi actively supported the construction of academies in various places and "issued edicts to the provinces to build academies for students." He also gave books to famous academies and gave funds dozens of times to promote the construction of academies throughout the country. Under the lead of Emperor Kangxi, the officials of various places established academies one after another, and the number of academies increased rapidly. In total, there were 537 new academies built throughout the nation, and 248 academies from the previous dynasties were reconstructed during the reign of Kangxi.[117]

Thereafter, although the development of academies was restricted during the early years of the reign of Yongzheng due to concerns of private academies having malicious intentions, the policy changed soon, under the premise of transforming their nature from being privately owned to being government-run, from banning them to strongly supporting their construction. Emperor Yongzheng, in the 11th year of his reign (1733), ordered the governors in the provincial capitals to set up academies and gave each a thousand taels to fund this.[118] Twenty-three academies in 19 provinces received funding from the court and became provincial academies. Furthermore, the establishment of academies and the teaching of scholars were clearly defined as the responsibilities of various officials. These measures resulted in the positive development of academies. At the same time, this clear policy orientation also led to the rapid development of government-run academies throughout the country.

During the Qianlong reign, the policy of promoting and encouraging the development of academies continued. Emperor Qianlong also repeatedly issued edicts to pay attention to the establishment of academies and put forward specific requirements. Under the ardent support and encouragement of the imperial court, the development of academies flourished. The number of academies increased to more than 4,300 academies throughout the country.[119] The status of academies rose as well. American scholar Benjamin A. Elman believed that "the status of academies was the highest in the hierarchy of the education system in the Qing dynasty." At the same time, Qing dynasty academies had an unprecedented geographical distribution, covering 19 provinces and regions across the country. Academies were built in culturally developed areas, such as prefectures, counties, and townships, and even in remote areas, such as Yunnan and Gansu.

Accompanying the development of academies in the Qing dynasty was the combination of academies and state power. The development of academies in the Qing dynasty came at the cost of their autonomy, independence, and the free spirit of teaching. For example, when Donglin Academy was rebuilt during the reign of Kangxi, Xiong Cilyu, a representative figure of Confucianism at that time, wrote *Restoration of Donglin Academy* (重修东林书院记) in the 26th year of Kangxi (1687). He wrote from a Confucian standpoint and reflected on the banning and destruction of academies in the Ming dynasty. He believed that the academies' teachings and principles of Confucianism were something that "the rulers and people would have liked to see and hope for." However, "recently, the lectures have led to dissatisfaction and anger from the emperor and the prime minister," resulting in strict impositions and prohibitions. If the matter were to be pursued, "our group should be obliged to bear corresponding responsibility." The main reason for that was that

> as our group's reputation grows and we participate in more and more activities and communicate more frequently, there are many people who claim to be members of our group. However, they are not, and they have caused negative impacts, and this issue needs to be restricted and regulated.

Hence, after the restoration of Donglin Academy,

> I hope that all aspiring scholars in our group will take silent study as true cultivation and take serious cultivation as the best form of education. Do not regard being good at debating as a talent and do not look down on others because they have different opinions and views.[120]

It is evident that Xiong did not agree with the academies' lectures in the late Ming dynasty. He blamed the destruction and banning of academies on the lectures. This reflects the position of early Qing Confucian scholars but also reflects the desires of the emperor, which was to abandon the tradition of free lectures and have academies be completely subordinate to the power of the state and become a tool controlled by the state and to be used by the state.

Influenced by this, many academies of the early Qing dynasty indeed broke away from the tradition of free lectures. For example, in "Mr. Wu Jinhua's Examination

40   *Academy, Society, and Politics*

on Meeting Rules of Donglin Academy" (吴觐华先生审订东林会约), it is written,

> I hope that there will not be any discussion about whether someone is right or wrong, nor will there be talk of using power to oppress others in this place of lecture. There should not be any anonymous letters to denunciate someone or report someone. Any matter involving the mundane should not enter through this place.
>
> From then on, other than the discussion of the classics and the Way, things that happened in the imperial court and the county, and any discussion or criticism of others should not be engaged in even if one hears about it. If one is asked about it, he should not reply. One should just study diligently and complete his studies and live up to the expectations of his superiors and family. That is the most important thing now.[121]

This talk regarding studies and how the Donglin scholars "were concerned about national, family, and world affairs" during the late Ming dynasty were completely different. Such incidents did not just happen at one academy. For example, "Meeting Rules of Guanzhong Academy" (关中书院会约), written by a Confucian scholar named Li Yong during the reign of Kangxi, stipulates that students "should not discuss the merits of officials or the affairs of the court or anything related to it."[122] In the early Qing dynasty, Huangu Academy of Huizhou also had "Meeting Rules of Huangu Academy" (还古会约), which stipulates that "one should not talk about the successes or failures of the court or gossip about affairs of the ministers."[123] The reason why scholars were required to be so careful with their words and actions was undoubtedly related to the political environment at that time. "Meeting Rules of Donglin Academy" (东林会约), mentioned earlier, states, "If such situations are not firmly forbidden from the beginning, it will lead to jealousy and resentment and cause slander and all sorts of unfavorable things." Not concerning oneself with external matters and focusing on studies was "the most important task of the day." Just as Gu Weiying points out, the loss of the podium for free lectures meant that academies had lost their predominant role in education.[124] Their departure from the tradition of free lectures and their betrayal of the creed of "shouldering the responsibility of the world" just shows their submission and dependence on the autocratic power.

Since the reign of Yongzheng, the government further officialized academies by allocating funds, selecting students, granting exam rights, selecting superintendents, awarding awards, and managing the daily affairs of the academies. The dependence academies had on the state grew greatly as well. Just as some scholars have pointed out, the main purpose of the imperial court's allocation of funds to the academies was to facilitate control so that they would not become a tool for individuals to oppose the government. This was an argument that touched on the essence of the matter.[125] In fact, Emperor Qianlong, in the first year of his reign (1736), positioned academies as the "study of old states" and required the academies to "nurture talents for the use of the court."[126] We can see from here that academies had already been incorporated into the system by then and were subordinate to the state power. The mission of academies also changed from a place for scholars to gather and discuss knowledge and give free lectures to an official institution that cultivated talents for the imperial court. If we say, before the Qing dynasty, the academy had some degree of autonomy and scholars were able to exert social control outside of autocratic power by spreading Confucian values and mores, then after the middle of the Qing dynasty, it completely metamorphosed into an instrument that depended heavily on the state and thus became subservient to the authoritarian power.

Notes

1 Notes of Translators: In the process of translation, the translators have consulted many sources, especially for the endnote section, such as Wikipedia and ChinaKnowledge. de, for which they are pretty grateful. We are also deeply grateful to Sun Lin （孙琳）, Wang Zongqiang（王宗强）and Kong Xiaohan（孔小菡）for their generous and kind help.

2 Sun, Benwen 孙本文. "Shehuixue yuanli" 社会学原理. In *Minguo congshu* Vol. 15 民国丛书第二编第15册 (Shanghai: Shanghai Bookstore Publishing House, 1992), 142–143.

3 Wrong, Dennis H. 丹尼斯·H. 朗. *Quanli lun*权力论 (Beijing: China Social Sciences Press, 2001), 3.

4 See Sima, Yunjie 司马云杰. *Wenhua shehui xue*文化社会学 (Beijing: China Social Sciences Press, 2001), 293. Edgar, Bodenheimer E. 博登海默. *Falixue fazhexue jiqi fangfa*法理学法哲学及其方法 (Beijing: Huaxia Publishing House, 1987), 224.

5 Edgar, Bodenheimer E. 博登海默. *Falixue fazhexue jiqi fangfa*法理学法哲学及其方法 (Beijing: Huaxia Publishing House, 1987), 224.

6 Zhu, Xi 朱熹. "Weizheng" 为政. In *Sishu zhangju jizhu lunyu jizhu* Vol. 1四书章句集注论语集注卷一 (Beijing: Zhonghua Book Company, 1983), 54.

7 Zhu, Xi 朱熹. "Zilu" 子路. In *Sishu zhangju jizhu lunyu jizhu* Vol. 7 四书章句集注论语集注卷七 (Beijing: Zhonghua Book Company, 1983), 142.

8 Wang, Xianqian 王先谦. "Lilun Vol. 19" 礼论第十九. In *Zhu zi jicheng* 诸子集成 (Shanghai: Shanghai Bookstore Publishing House, 1986), 231.

9 Wang, Xianqian 王先谦. "Rongru Vol. 4" 荣辱第四. In *Zhuzi jicheng*诸子集成 (Shanghai: Shanghai Bookstore Publishing House, 1986), 44.

10 Zhu, Xi 朱熹. "Weizheng" 为政. In *Sishu zhangju jizhu lunyu jizhu* Vol. 1 四书章句集注论语集注卷一 (Beijing: Zhonghua Book Company, 1983), 54.

11 Wang, Shouren 王守仁. "Bie lu shi" 别录十. In *Wang yangming* Vol. 18 王阳明卷十八 (Shanghai: Shanghai Chinese Classics Publishing House, 1992), 54.

12 Qing, Gaozong 清高宗. "Yu zuan zhuzi quan shu xu" 御纂朱子全书序. In *Siku quan shu* Vol. 720 四库全书第720册 (Shanghai: Shanghai Chinese Classics Publishing House, 1987), 1.

13 Pang, Zhonglu 庞钟璐. *Wenmiaosi diankao* Vol. 1 文庙祀典考卷一 (Taibei: Taibei Chinese Rites and Music Society, 1977), 12.

14 Ruan, Yuan阮元. "Aigongwen di ershiqi" 哀公问第二十七. In *shisan jing zhushu* 十三经注疏 (Beijing: Zhonghua Book Company, 1980), 1611.

15 Ruan, Yuan 阮元. "Qu li shang di yi" 曲礼上第一. In *shisan jing zhushu*十三经注疏 (Beijing: Zhonghua Book Company, 1980), 1231.

16 Liu, Feng 刘丰. *Xianqin lixue sixiang yu shehui de zhenghe* 先秦礼学思想与社会的整合 (Beijing: People's Publishing House, 2003), 101.

42 *Academy, Society, and Politics*

17 See Liu, Feng 刘丰. *Xianqin lixue sixiang yu shehui de zhenghe* 先秦礼学思想与社会的整合 (Beijing: People's Publishing House, 2003), 100–221.
18 See Liu, Zehua 刘泽华. *Xianqin shi ren yu shehui* 先秦士人与社会 (Tianjin: Tianjin People's Publishing House, 1988), 15–47.
19 Shengyuan, also called Xiucai, referring to those who have passed the entry-level imperial examination in the Ming and Qing dynasties.
20 See Gu, Yanwu 顾炎武. "Shengyuan lun shang" 生员论上. In *Gu tinglin shiwen ji* 顾亭林诗文集 (Beijing: Zhonghua Book Company, 1959), 667.
21 See Chen, Jian 陈铿. "Cong xingshi yinyuan kan ming qing zhiji de difang shishen" 从醒世姻缘看明清之际的地方士绅. In *(Journal of Xiamen University* Vol. 4 (1984).
22 See Zhang, Zhongli 张仲礼. *Zhongguo shenshi guanyu qi zai shijiu shiji zhongguo shehui zhong zuoyong de yanjiu* 中国绅士关于其在十九世纪中国社会中作用的研究, Trans. Li Rongchang (Shanghai: Shanghai Academy of Social Sciences Press, 1991).
23 See Yu, Yingshi 余英时. *Zhuxi de lishi shijie* 朱熹的历史世界 (Beijing: SDX Joint Publishing Company, 2004), 199–230.
24 See Gu, Yanwu 顾炎武. "Shengyuan lun shang" 生员论上. In *Gu tinglin shiwen ji*顾亭林诗文集 (Beijing: Zhonghua Book Company, 1959), 667.
25 See Chen, Jian 陈铿. "Cong xingshi yinyuan kan ming qing zhiji de difang shishen" 从醒世姻缘看明清之际的地方士绅. In *(Xiamen daxue xuebao* Vol. 4 (1984).
26 See Zhang, Zhongli张仲礼. *Zhongguo shenshi guanyu qi zai shijiu shiji zhongguo shehui zhong zuoyong de yanjiu*中国绅士关于其在十九世纪中国社会中作用的研究 (Shanghai: Shanghai Academy of Social Sciences Press, 1991).
27 See Yu, Yingshi 余英时. *Zhuxi de lishi shijie*朱熹的历史世界 (Beijing: SDX Joint Publishing Company, 2004), 199–230.
28 Gu, Yanwu 顾炎武. "Shengyuan lun生员论." In *Gu tinglin shiwen ji*顾亭林诗文集 (Beijing: ZhongHua Book Company, 1994), 667.
29 Wang, Fengsheng 王凤生. "Shenshi" 绅士. In *Zhengshu jicheng* Vol. 9 政书集成第九辑 (ZhengZhou: ZhongZhou Ancient Books Publishing House, 1996), 737.
30 Zhang, Zhongli 张仲礼. *Zhongguo shenshi guanyu qi zai shijiu shiji zhongguo shehui zhong zuoyong de yanjiu*中国绅士关于其在十九世纪中国社会中作用的研究 (Shanghai: Shanghai Academy of Social Sciences Press, 1991), 33.
31 Cheng, Tingzuo 程廷祚. "Zhongshan shuyuan bei ji" 钟山书院碑记. In *Congshu jicheng xubian* Vol. 190 丛书集成续编第190册 (Taibei: Taibei Xinwenfeng Publishing Company, 1998), 760.
32 Qin, Maoshen 秦懋绅. "Guo yihou xiujian jingyi shuyuan ji" 郭邑侯修建敬一书院记. In *Zhonguo fangzhi congshu* Vol. 93 中国方志丛书第93号 (Taibei: Taibei Chengwen Publishing House, 1985), 320.
33 See Han, Mingshi韩明士. "Lujiuyuan shuyuan yu xiangcun shehui wenti" 陆九渊书院与乡村社会问题. In *Songdai sixiangshi lun*宋代思想史论 (Beijing: Social Science Literature Press, 2003), 445–474.
34 See Sima, Yunjie 司马云杰. *Wenhua shehui xue* 文化社会学 (Beijing: China Social Sciences Press, 2001), 358.
35 Zhang, Zhe 张栻. "Tanzhou chongxiu yuelu shuyuan ji" 潭州重修岳麓书院记. In *Si ku quan shu* 四库全书 (Shanghai: Shanghai Chinese Classics Publishing House, 1987), 506.
36 Yuan, Fu 袁甫. "Xiangshan shuyuan ji" 象山书院记. In *Si ku quan shu* Vol. 1175 四库全书第1175册 (Shanghai: Shanghai Chinese Classics Publishing House, 1987), 487.
37 Yuan, Fu 袁甫. "Chong xiu bailu shuyuan ji" 重修白鹿书院记. In *Si ku quan shu* Vol. 1175 四库全书第1175册 (Shanghai: Shanghai Chinese Classics Publishing House, 1987), 490.

38 Huang, Yuanzhi 黄元治. "Guixiang shuyuan bei" 桂香书院碑. In *dali xianzhi gao* Vol. 27 大理县志稿卷二十七., 27.

39 Li, Jingde 黎靖德. *Zhuzi yu lei* Vol. 8 朱子语类卷八 (Beijing: Zhonghua Book Company, 1986), 129.

40 Zhu, Xi 朱熹. "Bailu dong shuyuan jieshi" 白鹿洞书院揭示. In *Zhu zi quan shu* 朱子全书 (Shanghai: Shanghai Chinese Classics Publishing House; Anhui Education Publishing House, 2002), 3587.

41 Wang, Shouren 王守仁. "Zeng xiu wansong shuyuan ji" 增修万松书院记. In *Zhongguo lidai shuyuan zhi* 中国历代书院志 (Nanjing: Jiangsu Education Publishing House, 1995), 217.

42 The "three principles" and "five constant virtues" (三纲五常) generally refer to the ethical and moral standards advocated by the feudal Chinese society. In Confucius' thought, by setting various regulations about rituals and systems, they define an individual's specific position, personal behaviors, and the corresponding duty and power, thereby differentiating among people in a community in terms of age, kinship, and social status. Later, the "five constant virtues" (benevolence, righteousness, propriety, wisdom, and trustworthiness) were considered the moral principles of Confucianism and exerted a great influence on Chinese life and culture.

43 The concept of "four natural human consciences" (四端) was first put forward by Mencius, which refers to the sense of compassion, sense of shame, sense of humility, and sense of justice. In later days, they were regarded as the basis for the "five constant virtues."

44 Zhang, Yi 张绎. "Chongzheng shuyuan bei ji" 崇正书院碑记. In *Jianshui zhouzhi* Vol. 15 建水州志卷十五, 10.

45 Yang, Lian 杨廉. Bailudong shuyuan zongruci ji 白鹿洞书院宗儒祠记. Li Mengyang 李梦阳. "Bailudong shuyuan xinzhi Vol. 6" 白鹿洞书院新志卷六. In *Wenzhi san* Vol. 10 文志三第十. Zhu, Ruixi 朱瑞熙 et al. *Bailudong shuyuan guzhi wu zhong* 白鹿洞书院古志五种, 108–109.

46 See Lü, Zuqian 吕祖谦. "Qiandao sinian jiuyue guiyue" 乾道四年九月规约. In *Lüzuqian quan ji* Vol. 1 吕祖谦全集第1册 (Hangzhou: Zhejiang Chinese Classics Publishing House, 2008), 359–360.

47 Zhu, Xi 朱熹. "Bailudong shuyuan jieshi" 白鹿洞书院揭示. In *Zhuzi quan shu* 朱子全书 (Hefei: Anhui Education Publishing House, 2002), 3586–3587.

48 Tang, Laihe 汤来贺. "Bailudong shuyuan xuegui" 白鹿洞书院学规. In *Zhongguo lidai shuyuan zhi* Vol. 2 中国历代书院志第2册 (Nanjing: Jiangsu Education Publishing House, 1995), 102.

49 Wang, Mingzong 王铭琮. "Bailuzhou shuyuan xuegui" 白鹭洲书院学规. In *Zhongguo lidai shuyuan zhi* Vol. 2 中国历代书院志第2册 (Nanjing: Jiangsu Education Publishing House, 1995), 586.

50 Tao, Shu 陶澍. "Suzhou ziyang zhengyi liang shuyuan gaoshi" 苏州紫阳正谊两书院告示. In *Xuxiu siku quan shu* Vol. 1053 续修四库全书第1053册 (Shanghai: Shanghai Chinese Classics Publishing House, 2002), 601.

51 "Jinhua shuyuan xuegui tiaoyue shier ze" 金华书院学规条约十二则. In *Shehong xianzhi* Vol. 7 射洪县志卷七. 4.

52 Wang, Ji 王畿. "Chongxiu shuyuan ji" 重修书院记. In *Zhongguo Lidai shuyuan zhi* Vol. 2 中国历代书院志第2册 (Nanjing: Jiangsu Education Publishing House, 1995), 160–161.

53 Wu, Rui 吴锐. "Meihua shuyuan bei ji" 梅花书院碑记. In *Zhongguo fangzhi congshu* Vol. 408 中国方志丛书第408号 (Taibei: Taibei Cheng Wen Publishing House, 1985), 1073.

54 Hao, Yulin 郝玉麟. "Tianzhang shuyuan ji" 天章书院记. In *Zhongguo fangzhi congshu* Vol. 110 中国方志丛书第110号 (Taibei: Taibei Cheng Wen Publishing House, 1985), 819.

44 *Academy, Society, and Politics*

55 Gui, Chaowan 桂超万. "Guochao chongxiu longgang shuyuan bei" 国朝重修龙冈书院碑. In *Luancheng xian zhi* Vol. 14 栾城县志卷十四, 30.

56 Zhang, Zhidong 张之洞. "Chuangjian guangya shuyuan zhe" 创建广雅书院折. In *Zhang zhidong quanji* Vol. 22 张之洞全集卷二十二 (Shijiazhuang: People's Publishing House, 1998), 585.

57 Gao, Qi 高琦. "Xinjian shuyuan ji" 新建书院记. In *Funing fu zhi* Vol. 13 福宁府志卷十三, 26.

58 Yuan, Pu 袁甫. "Fanjiang shutang ji" 番江书堂记. In *Siku quan shu* Vol. 1175 四库全书第1175册 (Shanghai: Shanghai Chinese Classics Publishing House, 1987), 495.

59 Huang, Pengnian 黄彭年. "Lianchi shuyuan ji" 莲池书院记. In *Xuxiu siku quan shu* Vol. 1552 续修四库全书第1552册 (Shanghai: Shanghai Chinese Classics Publishing House, 2002), 628.

60 Li, Fu 李绂. "Fuxiu xuancheng shuyuan ji" 复修宣成书院记. In *Xuxiu siku quan shu* Vol. 1421 续修四库全书第1421册 (Shanghai: Shanghai Chinese Classics Publishing House, 2002), 560.

61 Zhang, Zhenyi 张振义. "Chongjian dongshan shuyuan beiji" 重建东山书院碑记. In *Zhongguo fangzhi congshu* Vol. 240 中国方志丛书第240号 (Taibei: Taibei Chengwen Publishing House, 1985), 726.

62 Cao, Yanyue 曹彦约. "Bailu shuyuan chongjian shuge ji" 白鹿书院重建书阁记. In *Siku quan shu* Vol. 1167 四库全书第1167册 (Shanghai: Shanghai Chinese Classics Publishing House, 1987), 190.

63 Wang, Xuntai 王巡泰. "Shinan shuyuan ji" 石南书院记. In *Xuxiu xingye xianzh*i Vol. 9 续修兴业县志卷九, 31–32.

64 Han, Mingshi 韩明士. "Lu jingyuan shuyuan yu xiangxun shehui wenti" 陆九渊、书院与乡村社会问题. In Tian, Hao 田浩. *Songdai xixiang shilun*宋代思想史论, Trans. Yang, lihua 杨立华et al. (Beijing: Social Sciences Literature Press, 2003), 445–475.

65 See Li, Caidong 李才栋. "jianlun wohuo shuyuan de qiyuan" 简论我国书院的起源. In *Yuelu shuyuan yiqianlingyishi zhounian jinian wenji* Vol. 1 岳麓书院一千零一十周年纪念文集第1辑 (Changsha: Hunan University Press, 1986), 207–213. See Deng, Hongbo 邓洪波. *Zhongguo shuyuan shi*中国书院史 (Changsha: Hunan Education Publishing House, 1994), 1–26.

66 See Li, goujun 李国钧. *Zhongguo shuyuan shi* 中国书院史 (Changsha: Hunan Education Publishing House, 1994), 27–28.

67 See Li, Caidong 李才栋. *Jiangxi gudai shuyuan yanjiu*江西古代书院研究 (Nanchang: Jiangxi Education Publishing House, 1993), 31–32.

68 See Li, Caidong 李才栋. *Jiangxi gudai shuyuan yanjiu*江西古代书院研究 (Nanchang: Jiangxi Education Publishing House, 1993), 31–32.

69 Lü, Zuqian 吕祖谦. "Bailudong shuyuan ji" 白鹿洞书院记. In Huang, lingyu 黄灵庚et al. *Lüzuqian quanji* Vol. 1 吕祖谦全集第1册 (Hangzhou: Zhejiang Chinese Classics Publishing House, 2008), 100.

70 Yuan, Xie 袁燮. "Siming jiaoshou ting xu bi ji" 四明教授厅续壁记. In *Siku quan shu* Vol. 1157 四库全书第1157册 (Shanghai: Shanghai Chinese Classics Publishing House, 1987), 121.

71 Zhu, Xi 朱熹. "Hengzhou shigu shuyuan ji" 衡州石鼓书院记. In *Zhuzi quan shu* 朱子全书 (Shanghai: Shanghai Chinese Classics Publishing House; Hefei: Anhui Education Publishing House, 2002), 3783.

72 Zhu, Xi 朱熹. "Xun bailudong guzhi ai qi yousui yi fuxingjian gantan youzuo" 寻白鹿洞故址爱其幽邃议复兴建感叹有作. In *Zhuzi quan shu* 朱子全书 (Shanghai: Shanghai Chinese Classics Publishing House, 2002), 469 (Hefei: Anhui Education Publishing House, 2002), 469.

73 See Yang, Shenchu 杨慎初, Zhu, Hanmin 朱汉民, and Deng, Hongbo 邓洪波. *Yuelu shuyuan shilue* 岳麓书院史略 (Changsha: Yuelu Press, 1986), 20.

Academy, Society, and Politics 45

74 Hong, Mai 洪迈. "Zhoujun shuyuan" 州郡书院. In *Rongzhai suibi·rongzhai sanbi* Vol. 5 容斋随笔·容斋三笔卷五 (Shanghai: Shanghai Chinese Classics Publishing House, 1978), 477.

75 Wang, Yinglin 王应麟. "Songchao sishuyuan" 宋朝四书院. In *Siku quan shu* Vol. 947 四库全书第947册 (Shanghai: Shanghai Chinese Classics Publishing House, 1987), 353.

76 Zhang, Tingyu 张廷玉et al. "Xuexiao kao" 学校考. In *Xu wenxian tongkao* Vol. 50 续文献通考卷五十 (Hangzhou: Zhejiang Chinese Classics Publishing House, 1988), 3241.

77 Quan, Zuwang 全祖望. "Da zhangshichi zhengshi wen si da shuyuan yiezi" 答张石痴征士问四大书院贴子. In *Xuxiu siku quan shu* Vol. 1430 续修四库全书第1430册 (Shanghai: Shanghai Chinese Classics Publishing House, 2002), 228.

78 See Hu, Hong 胡宏. "Yu qinhui zhi shu" 与秦会之书. In *Hugongji* 胡宏集 (Beijing: Zhonghua Book Company, 1987), 105.

79 See Yang, Shenchu 杨慎初, Zhu, Hanmin 朱汉民, and Deng, Hongbo 邓洪波. *Yuelu shuyuan shilue* 岳麓书院史略 (Changsha: Yuelu Press, 1986), 22–23.

80 See Hu, Hong 胡宏. "Yu qinhui shu" 与秦桧之书. In *Huhong ji* 胡宏集 (Beijing: Zhonghua Book Company, 1987), 105.

81 Huang, Chu 黄蜍. "Nankangjun xinxiu bailu shuyuan ji" 南康军新修白鹿书院记. In *Siku quan shu* Vol. 1168 四库全书第1168册 (Shanghai: Shanghai Chinese Classics Publishing House, 1987), 220.

82 See Hong, Mai 洪迈. "Zhoujun shuyuan" 州郡书院. In *Rongzhai sui bi · rongzhai sanbi* Vol. 5 容斋随笔·容斋三笔卷五 (Shanghai: Shanghai Chinese Classics Publishing House, 1978), 477–478.

83 Wu, Yong 吴泳. "Yushu zonglian jingshe baji" 御书宗濂精舍跋记. In *Siqu quan shu* Vol. 1176 四库全书第1176册 (Shanghai: Shanghai Chinese Classics Publishing House, 1987), 373.

84 Li, Xinchuan 李心传. "Yezhengze lun linhuangzhong xi weixue dao zhimu yi fei zhengren" 叶正则论林黄中袭为学道之目以废正人. In *Siqu quan shu* Vol. 60 四库全书第60册 (Shanghai: Shanghai Chinese Classics Publishing House, 1987), 517.

85 See Zou, Chonghua 邹重华. "Songdai sichuan shuyuan kao-jianlun songdai shuyuan yanjiu de ruogan wenti" 宋代四川书院考--兼论宋代书院研究的若干问题. In *Zhongguo shuyuan* Vol. 3中国书院第3辑 (Changsha: Hunan Education Press, 2000), 140–151.

86 See Li, Caidong 李才栋. *Bailudong shuyuan shilue* 白鹿洞书院史略 (Beijing: Education Science Press, 1989), 76–81.

87 Tuo, Tuo 脱脱et al. "Liuyue zhuan" 刘爚传. In *Songshi* Vol. 401 (Beijing: Zhonghua Book Company, 1985), 12171.

88 See Li, Caidong 李才栋. *Bailudong shuyuan shilue* 白鹿洞书院史略 (Beijing: Education Science Press, 1989), 80.

89 See Bai, Xinliang 白新良. *Zhongguo guodai shuyun fazhan shi* 中国古代书院发展史 (Tianjin: Tianjin University Press, 1995), 19–20.

90 See Li, Caidong 李才栋. *Bailudong shuyuan shilue* 白鹿洞书院史略 (Beijing: Education Science Press, 1989), 81.

91 Zhang, Tingyu 张廷玉et al. "Xuexiao kao" 学校考. In *Xu wenxian tongkao* Vol. 50 续文献通考卷五十 (Hangzhou: Zhejiang Chinese Classics Publishing House, 1988), 3243.

92 Ke, Shaomin 柯绍忞. "Xuanju zhi" 选举志. In *Xin yuanshi* Vol. 64 新元史卷六十四 (Beijing: China Bookstore, 1988), 316.

93 "Huanfu lianxi shuyuan shenxiang" 还复濂溪书院神像. In *Siku quan shu* Vol. 648 四库全书第648册 (Shanghai: Shanghai Chinese Classics Publishing House, 1987), 373.

94 "Huanfu lianxi shuyuan shenxiang" 还复濂溪书院神像. In *Siku quan shu* Vol. 648 四库全书第648册 (Shanghai: Shanghai Chinese Classics Publishing House, 1987), 374.

46 *Academy, Society, and Politics*

95 See Bai, Xinliang 白新良. *Zhongguo gudai shuyuan fazhan shi* 中国古代书院发展史 (Tianjin: Tianjin University Press, 1995), 36–37.

96 Xu, Youren 许有壬. "Qingzhou shuyuan ji" 庆州书院记. In *Siku qun shu* Vol. 1211 四库全书第1211册 (Shanghai: Shanghai Chinese Classics Publishing House, 1987), 262.

97 Yu, Minzhong 于敏中. "Chengshi · neicheng nancheng" 城市·内城南城. In *Qinding rixia jiuwen* Vol. 49 钦定日下旧闻卷四十九 (Beijing: Beijing Chinese Classics Publishing House, 1983), 755.

98 See Xu, Zi 徐梓. *Yuandai shuyuan yanjiu* 元代书院研究 (Beijing: Social Sciences Literature Press, 2000), 54–125.

99 See Chen, Yuanhui 陈元晖, Yin, Dexin 尹德新, and Wang, Bingzhao 王炳照. *Zhongguo gudai de shuyuan zhidu*中国古代的书院制度 (Shanghai: Shanghai Education Publishing House, 1981), 63.

100 Zhang, Tingyu 张廷玉et al. "Xuanju zhi Vol. 1" 选举志一. In *Mingshi* Vol. 69 明史卷六十九 (Beijing: Zhonghua Book Company, 1974), 1686.

101 Zhang, Tingyu 张廷玉et al. "Xuexiao Vol. 4" 学校四. In *Xu wenxian tongkao* Vol. 50 续文献通考卷五十 (Hangzhou: Zhejiang Chinese Classics Publishing House, 1988), 3246.

102 Zhang, Tingyu 张廷玉et al. "Guxiancheng zhuan" 顾宪成传. In *Mingshi* Vol. 231 明史卷二百三十一 (Beijing: Zhonghua Book Company, 1974), 6053.

103 See Zhang, Liuquan 章柳泉. *Zhongguo shuyuanshi hua—songyuanmingqing shuyuan de yanbian*中国书院史话—宋元明清书院的演变 (Beijing: Education Science Press, 1981), 31–32. See Li, Caidong 李才栋. "Guanyu zhongguo shuyuan zhidu yanjiu de tongxun" 关于中国书院制度研究的通讯. In *Zhongguo shuyuan* Vol. 2 中国书院第二辑 (Changsha: Hunan Education Publishing House, 1998), 388–393. See Chen, YuanHui 陈元晖, Yin, Dexin 尹德新, and Wang, Bingzhao 王炳照. *Zhongguo gudai de shuyuan zhidu*中国古代的书院制度 (Shanghai: Shanghai Education Publishing House, 1981), 77–86.

104 Zhang, Tingyu 张廷玉et al. "Xuexiaokao Vol. 4" 学校考四. In *Xu wenxian tongkao* Vol. 50 续文献通考卷五十 (Hangzhou: Zhejiang Chinese Classics Publishing House, 1988), 3246.

105 Li, Fan 李汎. "Dongshan shuyuan jilüe" 东山书院记略. In *Zhongguo fangzhi congshu* 中国方志丛书 (Taibei: Chengwen Publishing House, 1985), 718.

106 Li, Fan 李汎. "Dongshan shuyuan jilüe" 东山书院记略. In *Zhongguo fangzhi congshu* 中国方志丛书 (Taibei: Chengwen Publishing House, 1985), 718.

107 Xia, Xie 夏燮. *Ming tongjian* Vol. 50 明通鉴卷五十 (Changsha: Yuelu Press, 1999), 1340.

108 Huang, Zongxi 黄宗羲. "Mingyi daifang lu · xuexiao" 明夷待访录·学校. In *Huangzongxi quanji* Vol. 1黄宗羲全集第一册 (Hangzhou: Zhejiang Chinese Classics Publishing House, 1988), 11.

109 Ding, Shanqing 丁善庆. "Shuyuan tiaogui" 书院条规. In *Zhongguo lidai shuyuan zhi*中国历代书院志 (Nanjing: Jiangsu Education Publishing House, 1995), 4, 434.

110 Fang, Qiyi 方其义. "Fanli binggui tiao Vol. 13" 凡例并规条十三. In *Zhongguo lidai shuyuan zhi*中国历代书院志 (Nanjing: Jiangsu Education Publishing House, 1995), 5, 459.

111 Dai, Fenyi 戴凤仪. "Kaoke" 考课. In *Shishan shuyuan zhi* Vol. 7 诗山书院志卷七 (Xiamen: Xiamen University Press, 1995), 130.

112 Jiang, Tingxi 蒋廷锡. "Fanli bing gutiao Vol. 11" 凡例并规条十三. In *Zhongguo lidai shuyuan zhi* Vol. 17 古今图书集成选举典卷十七 (Beijing: Zhonghua Book Company, 1986), 79884.

113 Li, Caidong李才栋. *Jiangxi gudai shuyuan yanjiu*江西古代书院研究 (Nanchang: Jiangxi Education Publishing House, 1993), 338.

114 Li, Caidong李才栋. "Xuexiaokao Vol. 7" 学校考七. In *Xu wenxian tongkao* Vol. 69 续文献通考卷六十九 (Hangzhou: Zhejiang Chinese Classics Publishing House, 1988), 5488.

115 See Bai, Xinliang白新良. "Shilun qingchu shuyuan de huifu he fazhan" 试论清初书院的恢复和发展. In *Zhongguo shuyuan* Vol. 5 中国书院第五辑 (Changsha: Hunan Education Publishing House, 2003), 388.

116 See Huang, Jinxing 黄进兴. *Youru shengyu—quanli、xinyang yu zhengdangxing*优入圣域—权力、信仰与正当性 (Xi'an: Shanxi Normal University Press, 1998), 99.

117 Xiong, Cilü 熊赐履. "Chongxiu donglin shuyuan ji" 重修东林书院记. In *Zhongguo lidai shuyuan zhi* Vol. 7中国历代书院志第七册 (Nanjing: Jiangsu Education Publishing House, 1995), 406.

118 See Bai, Xinliang白新良. "Shilun qingchu shuyuan de huifu he fazhan" 试论清初书院的恢复和发展. In *Zhongguo shuyuan* Vol. 5 中国书院第五辑 (Changsha: Hunan Education Publishing House, 2003), 326.

119 Elman 艾尔曼. *Cong lixue dao puxue-zhonghua diguo wanqi sixiang yu shehui bianhua mianmianguan*从理学到朴学—中华帝国晚期思想与社会变化面面观 (Nanjing: Jiangsu People's Publishing House, 1997), 95.

120 Xiong, Cilü 熊赐履. "Chongxiu donglin shuyuan ji" 重修东林书院记. In *Zhongguo lidai shuyuan zhi* Vol. 7中国历代书院志第七册 (Nanjing: Jiangsu Education Publishing House, 1995), 406.

121 Xiong, Cilü 熊赐履. "Wujinhua xiansheng shending donglin huiyue" 吴觐华先生申订东林会约. In *Zhongguo lidai shuyuan zhi* Vol. 7中国历代书院志第七册 (Nanjing: Jiangsu Education Publishing House, 1995), 201.

122 Li 李 . "Guanzhong shuyuan huiyue·xuecheng" 关中书院会约·学程. In *Erquji* Vol. 13 二曲集卷十三 (Beijing: Zhonghua Book Company, 1996), 118.

123 Shi, Huang 施璜. "Huangu shuyuan zhi" 还古书院志. In *Zhongguo lidai shuyuan zhi* Vol. 8中国历代书院志第8册 (Nanjing: Jiangsu Education Publishing House, 1995), 613.

124 See Gu, Weiying 古伟瀛. "Mingqing bianju xia de shuyuan" 明清变局下的书院. In *Zhongguo shuyuan* Vol. 5 中国书院第五辑 (Changsha: Hunan Education Publishing House, 2003), 272–320.

125 See Chen, Yuanhui 陈元晖, Yin, Dexin 尹德新, and Wang, Bingzhao 王炳照. *Zhongguo gudai de shuyuan zhidu*中国古代的书院制度 (Shanghai: Shanghai Education Publishing House, 1981), 93–94.

126 Chen, Yuanhui 陈元晖, Yin, Dexin 尹德新, and Wang, Bingzhao 王炳照. *Qing shilu gaozong shilu* Vol. 231 清实录·高宗实录卷二十 (Beijing: Zhonghua Book Company, 1985), 488.

2 Academy Sacrificial Rituals and Their Significance

Academies have a rather complicated sacrificial system. The sacrificial ritual is not only an indispensable part of the academy's regulations but also a good expression of its cultural and educational function. Together with teaching and book collection, it is considered "one of the three major undertakings of an academy."[1] Since the beginning of the Song dynasty, the sacrificial rituals of the academy had been developed and perfected and had shown uniqueness both in content and form that distinguishes themselves from other types of sacrificial rituals practiced somewhere else. A study on its cultural connotation will help us have a deeper understanding of the academy's features, roles, and position in the large social and cultural system.

Overview of Academy Sacrifice

Sacrifice is the offering of material possessions to the deities, deceased ancestors, sages, saints, or other important figures as an act of worship or for blessings. In the ancient social life of China, sacrificial activities occupied a very important position and were even considered to be a major event in the political life of a state. As is stated in the chapter "The Thirteenth Year of Duke Cheng" in *The Commentary of Zuo* (左传 · 成公十三年), "Sacrifices and wars are events of national importance."[2] A chapter titled "Discourses of Lu" in *Discourses of the States* (国语 · 鲁语上) also says, "Sacrifice is among the greatest rituals of the state." In a traditional Chinese society, as is known to all, rites work as an important means of social control and social governance.

> Only with rites can we discern evil from good, serve gods with full respect, establish rules, and distinguish benevolence and righteousness. In a word, only with rites can a nation be well-governed and the spirit of a nation be firmly upheld.

Therefore, the role of rites in social life cannot be overemphasized. Among rites of various kinds, rites of the sacrificial system hold the highest position. "Among the measures to govern the people, there is nothing more important than setting up the ritual system; among the five types of rituals in all, and there is nothing more important than sacrificing."[3]

DOI: 10.4324/9781003332305-2

Academy Sacrificial Rituals 49

Sacrificial rituals existed in ancient schools. The chapter "Spring Offices" in *Rites of Zhou* (周礼·春官·大宗伯) records, "When the school's opening ceremony is held in spring, it must be done together with a separate sacrificial ritual." Many a time does *The Book of Rites* (礼记) make several references to sacrificial rituals in ancient schools. As is recorded in the chapter "Records of Studies" in *The Book of Rites* (礼记·学记), "Every time School opens in spring (the emperor or an official of importance) will wear gowns designed for the specific occasion and offer sacrifices to their deceased teachers and sages as a token of respect." A chapter titled "The Meaning of Sacrifices" in *The Book of Rites* (礼记·祭义) states, "The purpose of worshiping sages of the former generations in Sixue (primary schools in the Zhou dynasty) is to educate federal lords to cultivate morality." The article "The Heir of King Wen" in *The Book of Rites* (礼记·文王世子) says about this as well:

> At the beginning of every school season, the ritual of Shidian (a kind of sacrificial ceremony) is performed to pay homage to the teachers of the former generations. The spring ceremony was conducted by the master teacher in the spring semester, and the same was done in the summer, autumn, and winter. All the schools established by federal lords on the emperor's order must perform the ritual of Shidian to Xiansheng (great Chinese kings include Shun, Yu, Tang, and Wen of the Zhou dynasty) and Xianshi (great teachers and thinkers who once assisted Xiansheng), and the offerings must be more expensive than usual, usually with shu bo (bundles of silk).

According to Li Shen (a scholar of the time), the rituals held in schools during the Zhou dynasty were mainly the kind dedicated to the venerable masters of some profession and the worshiped figures (or ritual targets) usually included Xiansheng, Xianshi, and Xianxian (great sages).[4] Since then, school sacrificial rituals began to make their presence gradually felt and have thus developed. With their content richer and form more diversified, an independent ritual space was gradually separated. Gao Mingshi, a Taiwanese scholar, examined the development of the sacrificial ritual space in ancient Chinese schools and concluded that the history of Chinese education could be described as the development process from "learning" to "temple learning." In the era of learning, except for the lecture hall, the main hall or the room of the main hall was used for sacrificial rituals. In the era of temple learning, there was a separate space for sacrificial rituals, and the campus consisted of two independent spaces for teaching and rituals, respectively. Before the Zhou dynasty, politics were closely integrated with sacrifice, and most of the educational activities were included in the sacrificial rituals. Learning was done in the same hall as the ritual of worshiping was practiced but in different rooms. Therefore, there were often occasions for students to attend worshiping rituals in the "school." The fusion of learning and sacrificial rituals had a great influence on education in the Han dynasty and thereafter. In the schools of the Han dynasty, the rituals of Shicai and Shidian were also held (Shicai is a sacrificial ritual performed when school opens, while Shidian, not held regularly, was another kind of sacrifice ceremony, the purpose of which was mainly to inform

50 *Academy Sacrificial Rituals*

ancestors of what had happened). In the tenth year of the Eastern Jin dynasty (ad 385), the Xiaowu Emperor built a Confucian temple in the west of the Imperial College, and thus, the temple-school system appeared for the first time. In the first year of the Tianbao period of the Northern Qi dynasty (ad 550), Emperor Wenxuan ordered a Confucian temple and a Yanhui temple to be established in county schools, which extended the temple-school system from the capital city to the local counties. In the fourth year of the Zhenguan period of the Tang dynasty (ad 630), the Taizong Emperor promoted the temple-school system further to schools in almost every corner of the country. By the Qing dynasty, the temple-school system had remained unchanged.[5] As is said by a scholar of the Qing dynasty, "Since the Tang and Song dynasties, all prefectures and counties have schools, and there are no schools without temples."[6] Ever since the Tang and Song dynasties, sacrificial rituals have always been an important part of educational activities in government schools.

Influenced by these government schools, the academy also performed sacrificial rituals in the process of its rise and growth. Many scholars even regard it as a distinctive feature of academies. For example, Sheng Langshi took sacrificial rituals as one of the "three major undertakings"[7] of the academy, and Zhang Liuquan regarded "offering sacrifices to ancient sages"[8] as one of the academy's characteristics. The specific origin of the academy sacrificial ritual, given scarce data, is not clearly verifiable, but it is certain that as early as the early Song dynasty, there were already rituals in the academy. For example, the practice of sacrificial rituals in Yuelu Academy started the moment Zhu Dong founded the academy in the ninth year of Kaibao in the Northern Song dynasty (ad 976).[9] In the third year of the Xianping period (ad 1000), Wang Yucheng (a scholar of the time) once talked about the reconstruction of Yuelu Academy by Li Yunze in his book *Records of Yuelu Academy in Tanzhou* (潭州岳麓山书院记):

> During the Kaibao reign, Zhu Dong, governor of Changsha City, and Sun Fengji, an official of one of the counties of Changsha, set up an academy by the Baohuang Cave at the foot of Mount Yuelu and began to recruit students from all over the country. However, after the two officials were removed from office and returned to their hometown, there was no successor to these affairs. All the students left the academy, and all the books were nowhere to be found, and there was no longer the sound of reading to be heard and rituals to be seen again. It was Li Yunze who repaired and expanded the academy, with a large number of houses built, quite a few lecture halls set up, and a library established. The statue of Confucius and those of his ten famous disciples were erected, and the pictures of the 72 wise disciples of Confucius were hung high up, all of whom were dressed neatly in formal attire and were extremely lifelike. Then he asked for more lands for the performance of sacrificial ceremonies in spring and autumn.[10]

From such words in the book as "all the things have been done in accordance with the old practice," it can be seen that there were already sacrificial rituals in

Yuelu Academy when Zhu Dong founded it. After Li Yunze rebuilt the academy in the second year of Xianping reign (ad 999), the rituals of the academy were not only restored to the old system but also further developed, with lands set aside for the ritual only. At the end of the Northern Song dynasty, when scholar Zhang Sunmin visited Yuelu Academy, he still saw that "inside Yuelu Academy, there were a shrine for Confucius to be worshiped and a room for books to be printed" and that "all the lecture halls together with their outer corridors were still intact."[11]

Bailudong Academy practiced sacrificial rituals as well in the early Song dynasty. In the fourth year of the Xianping reign (ad 1001), Emperor Zhenzong of the Song dynasty decreed that schools and academies throughout the country should be given copies of the classics printed by Directorate of Education (the highest educational administration in feudal China) and that Confucian temples should be repaired. In the fifth year of Xianping reign, Bailudong Academy was repaired, and "statues of the ten wise disciples of Confucius were erected for the worship."[12] In addition, during the Dazhongxiangfu period (ad 1008–1016), Yingtianfu Academy, which was established by a fellow countryman named Cao Cheng, had already a sacrificial area at the very beginning of its establishment. "In the front is the ancestral temple for sacrifice, and at the back is a lecture hall for teaching. There are altogether about a hundred rooms."[13] According to another scholar Gao Mingshi, the edict, issued in the fifth year of the Zhenzong reign (ad 1002), that ordered Confucian temples to be renovated in all the academies and schools across the country, can be regarded as "the beginning of the full implementation of the temple-school system (both in government schools and academies) in the Song dynasty."[14] At that time, sacrificial rituals in academies were actually quite common.

In the Yuan dynasty, it was a prevailing system for academies to have ancestral temples. Tang Su, a man of the Yuan dynasty, said, "In all academies, there are ancestral temples to worship the sages of the past and lecture halls to teach young readers, which is a unified system of the country."[15] In the Qing dynasty, there even appeared such a situation as Dai Junheng said that "now there are academies in every county across the country, and there are rules regulating the sacrificial rituals within every academy."[16]

In the process of the development of the academy, sacrifice is becoming an increasingly important element of the academy regulations. Most of the academies have been built with ancestral temples, and there have even been many academies in the later generations established mainly for sacrificial worship. For example, in the fourth year of the Jingding period of the Southern Song dynasty (ad 1263), in order to extol Zhou Dunyi's great contribution to Neo-Confucianism, Yang Yungong, the Tixing (title of officials whose duty was mainly to examine criminal cases and impeach corrupt officials) of Daozhou, built an ancestral temple in Zhou's former residence to pay homage to Zhou Dunyi and his son, "an ancestral hall is set up in the middle, with a Confucianism studio on its right side, to offer sacrifices to Zhou Dunyi and some other Confucian sages."[17] Lianxi Academy (Lianxi is Zhou Dunyi's alias) was thus founded. Actually, this academy was

52 *Academy Sacrificial Rituals*

established mainly for the worship of Zhou Dunyi. In addition, there were even some academies directly converted from ancestral temples. For instance, Master's Temple was built where Lü Zuqian (a great Neo-Confucianist of the Southern Song dynasty) once gave lectures, and later this temple "was transformed into an academy" in the early years of the Jiaxi period.[18] Another example is that Han Temple was transformed into an academy when Zheng Liangchen began to lecture there and renamed it later into Chengnan Academy during the Chunyou reign of the Southern Song dynasty (ad 1243). Han Temple was located in Haiyang County, Chaozhou. It was originally built to commemorate Han Yu (a great poet and philosopher of the Tang dynasty) during the Yuanyou period of the Northern Song dynasty. Later it was renamed for a third time into Hanshan Academy in the Zhishun period of the Yuan dynasty.[19]

The scale of worship at the academy has also been expanding. For example, according to *Annals of Bailudong Academy* (白鹿书院志), written by Mao Deqi in the 58th year of Kangxi of the Qing dynasty (ad 1719), the complex of ancestral buildings in Bailudong Academy is such a spectacle as include Dacheng Temple, Zongru Temple, Sages Temple, Loyalty Temple, Ziyang Temple, and some others. The figures of worship totaled more than 40 besides the most representative figures of the Confucian genealogy. In the 28th year of the Kangxi era (ad 1689), after the reconstruction of Daliang Academy in Henan Province, the rules and regulations of its sacrificial ritual got revised, and the number of worshiped figures thus determined reached 115.[20] During the reign of Qianlong of the Qing dynasty, Wenjin Academy, located in remote Huanggang County, Hubei Province, was not a large one in scale, but there was not only a temple dedicated to Confucius but also two more in the east and west, which were dedicated to Zhongzi and other hermits and to Zhuzi and other Confucian sages, respectively. There also stand Wen Chang Hall and Kui Pavilion around the Book Collection Building.[21] In the history of Yuelu Academy, a total of more than 100 people have been memorialized, and more than 20 shrines have been built. According to Vol. 48, titled "Rules and Regulations of Academies" (申明书院条规以励实学示), in *Collected Works of Chen Hongmou* (培远堂偶存稿), early in the 28th year of Qianlong reign in the Qing dynasty (ad 1763), out of the total expenses of 1,341.5 liang (a unit of weight for silver, 50 grams) of silver on Yuelu Academy, 28.4 liang was for sacrificial activities, accounting for only about 2%. But later, due to a growing number of figures of worship, the cost of sacrifice increased sharply, and even a possession of nearly 100 acres of sacrificial fields could not make ends meet. Therefore, the local government had to allocate a certain amount of silver every year to finance it, and social forces had to donate money to cover the expenses.[22] The aforementioned examples do say something about the scale, the prevalence, and the popularity of sacrificial activities in academies.

The academy sacrificial ritual mainly includes Shicai and Shidian. Shicai was also called Shecai in the chapter "Spring Offices" in *Rites of Zhou* (周礼·春官), which points out that "the school's opening ceremony was always held in spring with a specific sacrificial ritual." Zheng Xuan explains this passage: "Shecai means that the attendees will hold 'cai' (vegetables) with fragrant odors in their hands when attending sacrificial ceremonies" because it is recorded that ancient scholars always brought colored pheasants with them as a meeting gift when they visited the emperor and vegetables (cai) as a meeting gift when they visited their teachers. "Cai," in Chinese, refers to vegetables used for cooking. It is said that scholars were the noble subjects of the emperors, and therefore, their clothes were decorated colorfully. Shecai just means to reduce those colorful decorations by way of showing respect to their teachers ("she" in Chinese just means "to reduce or to give up," while "cai" refers to "vegetables"). Many records can be found about Shicai and Shidian in the academy sacrificial rituals in the past dynasties. For example, in the seventh year of the Chunxi period of the Southern Song dynasty (ad 1180), Zhu Xi, upon the completion of the reconstruction of Bailudong Academy, "offered sacrifices, together with both the teachers and students of the academy, to Xiansheng and Xianshi in the ritual of Shicai"[23]; in the fifth year of the Shaoxi period (ad 1194), when Zhulin Academy (later changed to Cangzhou Academy) was finished,[24] Zhu Xi held a grand sacrificial ritual of Shicai to inform Xiansheng and Xianshi of its completion and to show reverence for them; *Annals of Bailudong Academy* (白鹿洞志, 又名：白鹿洞书院志), a book written by Zheng Tinghu of the Ming dynasty, also had such a statement: "Shicai is held in the first month of spring every year, and Shidian somewhere in the months between spring and autumn every year"; Lumen Academy of Hubei Province in the Qing dynasty also stipulated that "on the first day of each month during the school days, sacrificial ceremonies should be held to pay homage to our great sages."[25]

The worshiped figures of the rituals of both Shicai and Shidian are Xiansheng and Xianshi, but the time and occasion will be different. The chapter "Records of Studies" in *The Book of Rites* (礼记·学记) says, "Shicai is generally held at the very beginning of school opening days, in which formal attire should be worn, and formal offerings should be made to show respect to Confucian orthodoxy." Zheng Xuan notes that "special sacrificial dishes are usually used in the ritual of Shicai to show respect for the deceased sages and teachers." In the chapter titled "Heir of King Wen" in *The Book of Rites* (礼记·文王世子), it is also recorded that

> at the beginning of every school season, the ritual of Shidian (another kind of sacrificial ceremony) is performed to pay homage to the teachers of the former generations. The spring ceremony was conducted by the master teacher, and the same was done in summer, autumn, and winter. All the schools established by federal lords on the emperor's order must perform the ritual of Shidian to Xiansheng and Xianshi, and the offerings must be more expensive than usual, usually with shu bo (bundles of silk). Whenever the ritual was practiced, there must be a joint performance of music and dance; if it happened that there was a war or a calamity in the country, then only the ritual was practiced, and the dancing and music performance would be canceled.

From these documents, it can be seen that the ritual of Shidian was rather more formal than that of Shicai and was usually held in spring, autumn, and winter

54 *Academy Sacrificial Rituals*

and at the very beginning of the establishment of the school. However, according to Zheng Xuan's statement, "Shidian is held in summer once in a while, which later has become an established routine"; it can be inferred that Shidian was performed in summer with the same grandeur as that held in spring, though there is no detailed account about its detailed procedures in that document (referring to *Liji · Wenwang shizi*).[26] Of course, Shidian was not exclusively performed in schools: "People in the past held rituals either in big mountains and rivers, or in clan temples and ancestral halls, or perhaps in schools."[27] Even in schools, there was still a difference between the rituals practiced when founding a school" and those performed in "spring, summer, autumn, and winter," as far as the worshiped figures were concerned. Sun Xidan gives more details about this in Vol. 20 of his monumental masterpiece titled *Annotations to the Book of Rites* (礼记集解). He explains that "establishing a school was an important event, so memorial rituals should be practiced to pay homage to Xiansheng on that occasion; the annual rituals of spring, summer, autumn, and winter were just regular ones, so only Xianshi were worshiped."[28] Shicai must be practiced when school opens, and the performance was confined to the school campus.

Academies followed the old practices in government schools and adopted the rituals of Shidian and Shicai as a way to show respect to sages and their ancestors, but in practice, they were slightly different from those practiced in government schools. For example, the specific date arrangement of Shidian in academies was often different from that in government schools. According to *Annals of Bailudong Academy* (白鹿洞志), written by Zheng Tinghu in the Ming dynasty, the date of Shidian of Bailudong Academy was Zhongding day (14th day) of Zhong month (February and August of the calendar used in the Spring and Autumn Period), which was different from Shangding day (fourth day) of Zhong month in government schools. It is recorded that the current practice is to hold the memorial ritual of worshiping Confucius on the fourth day of the second month in spring and autumn every year, with the governing officials of each prefecture, state, and county presiding over the ceremony and practicing the ritual of "Three Offerings" (三献礼, a kind of ceremony to show extra reverence for the worshiped by offering wine three times after the routine offerings were displayed), which is what we call "Shidian" of the old tradition. Bailudong Academy was under the jurisdiction of Nankang Prefecture where also stood a special Confucian school, so the ritual could not be held at the same time on that day. Therefore, it was decided that Bailudong Academy would hold sacrificial ritual on the 14th day of those two months, and the county sheriff presided over the ceremony.[29]

In the tenth year of Xianfeng reign of the Qing dynasty (ad 1860), *Statutes of Zhenyan Academy* (箴言书院章程), written by Hu Linyi, also says that

> the rituals dedicated to Xiansheng in Confucian schools are held on the fourth day of the second month in spring and autumn, which is the rule of the state. Academies dare not hold sacrificial ceremonies on the same day, so now they decide on the tenth day of February and the first day of September as their fixed ritual date.[30]

The worshiped figures in academies cover a very wide range, including Xiansheng, Xianshi, and Xianxian mentioned earlier. Xianxian—that is, the great Confucian masters, renowned officials, and some other celebrities of historical and cultural significance over the past dynasties—constitute a large portion of them. Huang Wenzhong, a native of the Yuan dynasty, says that "all academies were founded by people of virtue and wisdom in the past. They carried on the thoughts of the ancient sages to promote the education of the country, so they are examples for people to follow."[31] Dai Junheng, a native of the Qing dynasty, also says about the academies of the time, "the larger schools worshiped Confucius and his 72 wise disciples while smaller ones sacrificed to the sages who enjoyed fame in the locality."[32] As a matter of fact, in the official school system, there was also a tradition of ancestral halls being established to worship famous Confucian masters. For example, there were halls dedicated to Zhou Dunyi (Confucianist of the Northern Song dynasty) at the Municipal School of Shaozhou in the middle of the Southern Song dynasty, Chen Hao and Chen Yi (Confucianists and thinkers of the Northern Song dynasty, also referred to as "the Chengs" elsewhere) at the Municipal School of Huangzhou, and Gao Deng (a native of virtue in the neighborhood) at the Municipal School of Zhangzhou. Three-Master Hall at the Municipal School of Maoyuan was dedicated to Zhou Dunyi, Chen Hao, and Chen Yi; Lianxi Hall at the Municipal School of Longxing was dedicated to Zhou Dunyi, Mingdao Hall at the Municipal School of Jiankang was dedicated to Chen Hao (alias Mingdao); and so on. Zhu Xi wrote about that in quite a few articles, such as "Records of Cheng Hao Memorial Hall in Jiankang Prefectural School" (建康府学明道先生祠记), "Records of Zhou Dunyi Memorial Hall in Shaozhou State School" (韶州州学濂溪先生祠记), "Records of Yan Yan Memorial Hall in Changshu County School" (平江府常熟县学吴公祠记), and "Records of the Chengs Memorial Hall in Huangzhou State School" (黄州州学二程先生祠记). However, in comparison, sacrificial rituals in academies covered a more diverse and wider range of worshiped figures than those in government schools, which is also a striking feature of the academy sacrifice.

Sun Xidan, a Confucianist of the Qing dynasty, once explained Xiansheng and Xianshi:

> Those who set regulations about rituals for their descendants to follow are Xiansheng (great sages), such as Yao, Shun, Yu, Tang, King Wen of Zhou (named Ji Chang), King Wu of Zhou (named Ji Fa), and the Duke of Zhou (named Ji Dan); those who inherited the rituals set by those sages and used them to educate people are known as Xianshi (great teachers), such as Bo Yi and Hou Kui.[33]

However, Xiansheng and Xianshi do not mean the same in different historical periods. According to Li Shen's study, in the early Tang dynasty, the Duke of Zhou (a great thinker and statesman of the early Western Zhou dynasty and a forerunner of Confucianism) and Confucius alternated in the position of Xiansheng until the Gaozong reign in the Tang dynasty, when Confucius was universally

56 *Academy Sacrificial Rituals*

acknowledged as Xiansheng.[34] In the academy worship ritual, Xiansheng refers exclusively to Confucius, while Xianshi is often determined according to the specific circumstances of each academy. For example, as is recorded in Zhu Xi's "Homage to Sages on Completion of Bailudong Academy" (白鹿洞成告先圣文),[35] the worshiped figure honored as Xiansheng in Bailudong Academy was Confucius. In some other cases, Confucius was also addressed as Xianshi or Zhishengxianshi (sage of sages). For example, in Vol. 2 of *Annals of Xinjiang Academy* (信江书院志), compiled by Zhong Shizhen in the Qing dynasty, it is recorded that in the 20th year of Jiaqing (ad 1815), Xinjiang Academy "built Sanxi Temple for people to worship Xianshi and his disciples." What "Xianshi" here referred to is no other than Confucius.[36] In addition, according to *Annals of Bailudong Academy* (白鹿洞志), authored by Zheng Tinghu, a scholar of the Ming dynasty, Bailudong Academy performed the ritual of Shidian every spring and autumn, and the main figure they worshiped was also Confucius, accompanied by his four disciples "Yan Hui, Zeng Shen, Zi Si, and Meng Ke."[37] From these documents, it can be seen that what are called Xiansheng and Xianshi in the academy sacrificial ritual are, generally speaking, Confucius and his famous disciples and descendants.

The academy also paid tribute to Confucian masters of all ages who were related to the academic tradition and scholarly interests of the academy. As mentioned earlier, in the third year of Shaoxi reign in the Southern Song dynasty (ad 1192), Zhu Xi built Zhulin Academy in Kaoting to commemorate the seven scholars, Zhou Dunyi, the Chengs, Zhang Zai, Shao Yong, Si Maguang, and Li Dong, among whom the first six were Neo-Confucian scholars in the Northern Song dynasty. Zhu Xi held them in high esteem and spoke highly of their contribution to the development of Neo-Confucianism in his essay titled "Portraits of Six Great Masters" (六先生画像赞).[38] Li Dong was Zhu Xi's teacher. In another instance, in the first year of Chunyou of the Song dynasty (ad 1241), Jiang Wanli, a general of an army, built Bailuzhou Academy. He "set up King Wenxuan Temple, Lingxing Gate (the outer gate of the Confucian temples in the past)" and later "built a shrine named 'Six Gentlemen Temple' for the worship of Chen Hao and Cheng Yi, along with another four Neo-Confucianists (Zhou, Zhang, Shao, Zhu, etc.)."[39] In the first year of Yanyou of the Yuan dynasty (ad 1314), Yuelu Academy began to hold ceremonies to worship Zhu Xi and Zhang Shi, and during the Hongzhi era of the Ming dynasty, Chongdao Temple was built to offer sacrifices to Zhu Xi and Zhang Shi.[40] For hundreds of years thereafter, Yuelu Academy continued to keep memorial rituals for the two great masters.[41] In the reign of Kangxi, Chongzheng Academy was established in Yunnan Province to worship the following five Neo-Confucian scholars: Zhou Dunyi, Cheng Hao, Cheng Yi, Zhang Zai, and Zhu Xi. In the fifth year of Jiaqing reign (ad 1800), Ruan Yuan built Gujing Academy by the West Lake of Hangzhou, as a base for the research and teaching of the theory of Han learning. Gujing Academy was set up to worship Xu Shen and Zheng Xuan, scholars of the Eastern Han dynasty, and "the memorial tablets of Mr. Xu and Mr. Zheng are enshrined in the middle of the house, and people would bow down before the tablets." The reason was that "Mr. Xu and Mr. Zheng's study on the Han dynasty is the most authoritative, so they deserve to be worshiped."[42] Zhan Ruoshui, a scholar of the Ming dynasty and a follower of Baisha Xin Xue (a school of psychology named after his founder Chen Baisha, the doctrine of which shares some similarities with that of Yangmingism), even said that "wherever you go, you should establish an academy and then offer sacrifices to Chen Xianzhang (alias Chen Baisha) in it."[43] Among the figures of worship in Bailudong Academy, Zhou Dunyi, Cheng Hao, Cheng Yi, Shao Yong, Zhang Zai, Zhu Xi, Lu Jiuyuan, Huang Gan, Cai Shen, Lin Zizhi, and some other Confucian masters occupied a large proportion.

It is worth noting that after the Yuan dynasty, among the numerous Confucian masters worshiped in academies around the country, Zhu Xi was the most prominent, and the worship of Zhu Xi and his disciples was the most common. For example, Gong Shitai, a scholar of the Yuan dynasty, said that

> academies are scattered all over the country, with the largest number in Fujian Province. Most of them are dedicated to Zhu Xi and his disciples, such as those in places like Yanping, Wuyi Mountain, Jian'an, Sanshan, Quanshan, Youxi, Shuangfeng, and Beishan.[44]

Zhu Xi was born in Youxi, Fujian Province, where he made great contributions. The construction of his ideological system was also mainly accomplished in the academies around Fujian, so it is natural that the offerings of the academies in central Fujian give special prominence to Zhu Xi and his disciples. But in fact, in academies of other regions, Zhu Xi is also the most important figure of worship. According to Xu Zi's research, in the Yuan dynasty, Zhu Xi was widely worshiped in academies. Out of the 50 randomly selected Yuan dynasty academies, 33 were dedicated to the Song and Yuan scholars, and among the 33 academies, 67% of them sacrificed to Zhu Xi.[45] It can be said for sure that Zhu Xi was the main figure of worship in the academy sacrificial rituals of the time.

Moreover, the academy paid homage to the officials who once contributed a great deal to its establishment and development. For example, in the history of Yuelu Academy, there were several local officials who contributed greatly to its evolution. In addition to the aforementioned Zhu Dong (governor of Tanzhou), who founded Yuelu Academy in the ninth year of the Northern Song dynasty (ad 976), and Li Yunze (governor of Tanzhou), who presided over the expansion of the academy in the second year of Xianping (ad 999), Liu Gong, governor of Hunan province, rebuilt Yuelu Academy in the first year of Qiandao in the Southern Song dynasty (ad 1165), which made Yuelu Academy flourish again for a while. Besides, Chen Gang and Yang Maoyuan, commanders of Changsha, reconstructed Yuelu Academy later, making it thrive again after a hundred years of oblivion. These officials, who have contributed considerably to Yuelu Academy, are the constant worshiped figures of the academy. During the Jiajing period, Six Gentlemen Hall was set up in Yuelu Academy to worship the five aforementioned officials, as well as the superintendent of the academy, Zhou Shi.[46] In 1590, Wu Daoxing, governor of Changsha, rebuilt the academy. Later, his descendants, who

58 *Academy Sacrificial Rituals*

thought that "Mr. Wu has contributed a great deal to the education of this region, and that the continuity of the Confucian tradition all depends on him,"[47] enshrined Wu Daoxing in Six Gentlemen Hall, and thus, Six Gentlemen Hall was renamed Seven Gentlemen Hall. In addition, in the first year of Jiaqing reign (ad 1796), Li Zhongcheng Temple was built in Yuelu Academy as a shrine dedicated to Li Faga, accompanied by Ding Si-kong, Li Hu, and Chen Hongmou (governors of different counties), all of whom were instrumental in the construction and development of Yuelu Academy.[48]

Among the worshiped figures of Bailudong Academy, there are also many officials who have made outstanding contributions to the history of the academy. For example, during the reign of Hongzhi of the Ming dynasty, Shao Bao, deputy director of the Education Department of Jiangxi Province, built a temple in Bailudong Academy, where he gave lectures, wrote books, and conducted research. During the reign of Zhengde, Li Mengyang, deputy director of the Education Department, lectured in the academy often, built pavilions, wrote records for the academy, and rewrote *Annals of Bailudong Academy* (白鹿书院志), contributing greatly to the academy. These great officials were later all enshrined in Sages Temple of Bailudong Academy.[49] According to Mao Deqi's *Annals of Bailudong Academy* (白鹿书院志), in the 57th year of Kangxi (ad 1718), many famous officials of the Ming dynasty were set as figures of worship in Sages Temple of Bailudong Academy, such as Li Ling, Sukui, Chen Kuen, Shao Bao, Cai Qing, and Shi Tanglong, all of whom contributed a great deal to the development of Bailudong Academy in different ways during their tenure.[50] In the second year of Song Xiangxing (ad 1279), Jiang Wenzhong Gong Temple was set up in Bailuzhou Academy to worship Jiang Wanli (posthumous title, Wenzhong Gong), an official of Jizhou who founded the academy during the reign of Chunyou. Yingshan Academy in Zhejiang was once rebuilt by Zhou Ke, a county magistrate, in the third year of Longqing of the Ming dynasty (ad 1569) and rebuilt for a second time by Gao Erxiu, also a county magistrate, in the reign of Shunzhi of the Qing dynasty. As a result, Zhou Ke and Gao Erxiu were worshiped in this academy.[51]

In addition, the academy also worshiped historical and cultural celebrities who made contributions to the local area or who had a national influence. This trend was especially evident in the Yuan academies. The Yuan government had stipulated that "academies should be established where Confucian masters and influential cultural figures had once stayed or where there were people who were enthusiastic about public welfare and provided generous subsidies to education."[52] Therefore, many local historical and cultural celebrities were worshiped by more than an academy at the time. Huang Xianglong talks about rituals in academies at that time in his article titled "Restoration of Cihu Academy" (重修慈湖书院本末记), saying, "academies must be established where Confucian masters of the past generations have once stayed or lived so that students are more willing to learn their thoughts."[53] Similar situations were common in other dynasties. According to *A Sequel to Yuelu Academy Annals in Changsha* (长沙岳麓书院续志), by Ding Shanqing, Yuelu Academy, in the reign of Wanli of the

Ming dynasty, began to worship Zou Hao, a famous loyal minister during the reign of Chongning in the Northern Song dynasty. Zou Hao had some connections with Changsha since he had once been exiled to Mount Yuelu for offending the powerful Cai Jing due to his outspokenness. In another instance, in the first year of Jiaqing (ad 1796), Sanlu Temple was built in Yuelu Academy in memory of Qu Yuan (a great national hero drowning himself in the Miluo River by way of a protest against realpolitik).[54] In addition, Yuelu Academy also built Jia Taifu Temple for the worship Jia Yi, a scholar of the Western Han dynasty and a government official of Changsha. In the Ming dynasty, Loyalty Temple was set up in Bailudong Academy to worship Tao Yuanming (a poet of the Jin dynasty who lived at the foot of Lushan Mountain) and Yan Zhenqing (a renowned governor of the Tang dynasty whose residence was located in the local Yan Mountain).[55] The 115 figures worshiped in Daliang Academy of Henan following its reconstruction in the 28th year of Kangxi in the Qing dynasty (ad 1689) "were all scholars who were either born here, or once served as local officials here, or once lived in seclusion here. They all have made great contributions to this region, making Daliang a splendid place."[56] In the 34th year of Kangxi (ad 1695), Seven-Sage Academy, located in Jiaying Prefecture in Guangdong Province, expanded its ancestral temple, adding Zhou Dunyi and Wang Yangming to their memorial list, as the two both once lived there.[57] And for this, it was renamed Nine-Sage Academy. Shigu Academy of Hengshan in the Qing dynasty built Zhuge Temple to pay tribute to Zhuge Liang, who had once lived in Hengyang.[58] In the 19th year of Guangxu (1893), Shishan Academy, upon its completion, began to worship Ouyang De and Zhu Xi, since Shishan was not only the birthplace of Ouyang De (a Tang dynasty official in charge of education of the children) but also where Zhu Xi started his official career.[59] In a word, historical and cultural celebrities who were worshiped in academies were all people of importance who once had some connections with the academy. Some scholars even argue that "some celebrities become famous just because they are related to academies in one way or another."[60]

In addition to the groups of figures mentioned, the academy also worshiped a variety of gods and spirits. Since the late Song dynasty, some academies began to build the Kui Pavilion, the Wen Chang Hall, or sacrificial temples like that, worshiping Wen Chang (a god in charge of one's academic performance in traditional Chinese legends) and Kui (a god in charge of exams in traditional Chinese legends).[61] For example, during the Song dynasty, Kui was worshiped in Xijian Academy in Gao'an, Jiangxi Province. People offered sacrifices to Kui in the hope of "asking the god to bless them with excellent writings" so that "the students will get good luck in imperial examinations and then have a smooth political career." Since the Southern Song dynasty, Yuzhang Academy in Nanchang, Jiangxi, also had the Wen Chang Hall built to pay homage to Wen Chang.[62] In the later stage of academy development, the worship of Wen Chang and Kui became more common in different types of academies around the country.[63] The Kui Pavilion and the Wen Chang Hall were built in some of the more influential academies. For example, according to *A Sequel to Yuelu Academy Annals*

60   *Academy Sacrificial Rituals*

in Changsha (长沙岳麓书院续志), Yuelu Academy built the Wen Chang Hall behind the lecture hall in the seventh year of Kangxi to enshrine Wen Chang. In the 57th year of Qianlong (ad 1792), Bi Yuan, governor of Hu-guang, donated 100 liang of gold to establish the Kui Pavilion in the academy to deify Kui, and it is said that the worship rituals were of considerable grandeur.[64] Yingyuan Academy, founded in the eighth year of Tongzhi (ad 1869), enjoyed a high prestige in Guangdong Province at that time, but from the provisions of the academy's sacrificial expenditure, the worshiped figures included no other than Wen Chang and Kui. In some less well-known academies, it was more common to worship Wen Chang and Kui in order to get better academic results.[65] According to Dong Guifu's *Annals of Ziyang Academy* (紫阳书院志略, Vol. 3), in the 11th year of Jiaqing (ad 1806), Ziyang Academy in Hankow also had the Kui Pavilion and the Wen Chang Hall built.[66] Dai Junheng, a scholar of the Qing dynasty, criticized the phenomenon of the academy at that time, saying, "Folks worship Wen Chang and Kui, set up special buildings to set up statues inside, and hold worship activities, believing that Wen Chang and Kui can help them with the imperial examinations."[67] From these historical records, it can be easily seen that the practice of worshiping Wen Chang and Kui in the academy at that time was long-standing and quite common.

Guan Yu (a god of martial arts) and the God of Lands were common figures for people to worship as well. As mentioned earlier, Shishan Academy in Nan'an, Fujian Province, enshrined both Guan Yu and the God of Lands during the Guangxu era of the Qing dynasty,[68] while Bailudong Academy had been keeping the God of Lands for worship ever since it was set up in the Ming dynasty.[69] In the early years of the Kangxi period, there were both Guan Yu Hall and Lu Yue Temple[70] dedicated to gods of Guan Yue and Lu Yue, respectively. In addition, based on what was recorded in the Vol. 8 of *Annals of Ziyang Academy* (紫阳书院志略),[71] in the 12th year of the Yongzheng era (ad 1734), there were also temples set up in Ziyang Academy of Hankow for the worship of the God of Lands.[72] In the Qing dynasty, Virtue Temple was built in Duanxi Academy of Zhaoqing, Guangdong Province, to enshrine the God of Lands.[73]

Functionality of Academy Sacrifice

Sacrifice is an important way of educating scholars and carrying out social edification activities in the academy. According to the chapter "Summary Account of Sacrifices" in *The Book of Rites* (礼记·祭统), the sacrificial ritual was a magnificent spectacle, and the offerings presented at the ritual were rich enough. The heart of filial piety, coupled with rich offerings, may be the foundation of edification. So a gentleman's education must start from the fundamentals, which can only be achieved through the sacrificial ritual. The sacrificial rituals discussed here that serve as the "fundamentals of edification and enlightenment" undoubtedly include sacrifices held in academies. In this section, the social edification function of academy sacrifice will be discussed in more detail from the following four aspects.

To Establish and Enhance Scholars' Identity with Confucianism

As far as the ritual targets are concerned, the academy sacrifice is a large compound of different classes of worshiped figures. These figures include Xiansheng, Xianshi, great Confucian sages, eminent officials, and so on. The selection of these figures is undoubtedly a reflection of ethics and indicates a certain value orientation. For example, Sun Xidan once defined Xiansheng as "those who develop rituals and compose ritual music for future generations" and Xianshi as "those who inherit what sages established in the past to educate future generations."[74] Actually, this explanation was made from the perspective of constructing, promoting, and spreading the core values of Confucianism. As the main sacrificial figure in the academy, Xiansheng Confucius is the founder of the Confucian school. He redacted rules formulated by King Wen and King Wu of the Zhou dynasty, elaborated on Six Classics, and eventually established a solid values system of Confucianism (featured by Ren and Li) by integrating and innovating the thoughts of the three ancient dynasties and by proposing a set of political and ethical principles and codes of conduct. Taking Confucius as the main target of the sacrificial ritual was a recognition of Confucius' founding role in the history of Confucianism.

The great Confucian masters and Xianshi enshrined in academies are often those who made significant contributions to the creation of Confucian theory or the promotion of Confucian values in different eras. For example, after the Song dynasty, many academies began to offer worship to Zhou Dunyi. The main reason is that Zhou Dunyi accomplished the continuance of the Confucian tradition, breaking through the thousand-year darkness after Confucius and Mencius, clarifying the essence of spirituality and righteousness, opening up a new road for the development of Confucianism in the early Song dynasty, and thus playing a "pioneering" role in the history of the development of Neo-Confucianism. Zhu Xi is worshiped mainly for his remarkable contribution to the development of Confucianism. On the basis of integrating the great achievements of Confucianism in the Northern Song dynasty, Zhu Xi constructed a whole set of large-scale, exquisite, and detailed ideological and theoretical systems that earned him a solid position in the Confucian system. The worship of such masters of Confucianism is undoubtedly for the promotion, dissemination, and advancement of Confucianism. As Jiang Yi of the Yuan dynasty said when talking about the reason for the worship of the sages and Confucian masters in the academy,

> They inherited the theories of great Confucian masters of various academic schools—mainly Lian, Luo, Guan, and Min—and, from the remarks of Confucius and Mencius, drew values, rules, and principles for people to follow and for the sovereign to govern the world. With these values and rules, the folks got well-educated. Everyone followed the Confucian ethics, which made the cultural undertakings of the Song dynasty more prosperous than those of the Tang and Han dynasties. This prosperity chiefly resulted from

62 Academy Sacrificial Rituals

these Confucian masters' promotion to Confucian tradition. In view of this, the supreme rulers wanted to honor these sages and Confucians, so they set up official positions for and offered worship to those great Confucian masters from the four academic schools mentioned earlier, setting role models for teachers of a hundred generations.[75]

Some other figures are deified mainly because they embody some ethical qualities of Confucianism or show sound character and uplift minds. For example, Bailudong Academy set up Loyalty Temple for Zhuge Liang and Tao Yuanming and sacrificed to them as they possessed the highly lauded virtue of loyalty, as indicated by the name of the shrine. The sacrifice to them was out of people's respect for their loyalty and integrity. Tao Yuanming, whose "clear and noble spirit shines brightly both in the past and present," was worshiped in this academy so as to "teach his students how to be a man and a government official."[76] "The two gentlemen, who both served their country faithfully, are recorded in the list of national meritocrats and can be thought of as figures of extraordinary brilliance for a hundred generations."[77]

There are also certain rules to be followed when selecting the worshiped figures from among the eminent officials, famous superintendents, and lecturers related to the academy. Li Qi from the Yuan dynasty, when talking about the reason the academy was dedicated to Fan Zhongyan, said,

> Ever since the Six Classics were restricted from spreading, the passing on of the Confucian tradition has been stranded. Rulers who govern the world do not respect and follow the traditional Confucian values. This situation continued until Fan Zhongyan started to establish schools and renewed the respect for teachers. He hoped to educate people with Confucian teachings, consciously assuming the responsibility to inherit Confucian values and principles. His contribution to the governance of the country and the spread of Confucian ethics is marvelous! Since he has done so much for the country, then it is fully justified that later generations would worship him as the advocate of Confucian orthodoxy and promoter of education. Now, we set up academies and honored him to expand his influence and to pass on the Confucian thoughts and philosophies.[78]

"The reason for worshiping Fan Zhongyan was actually out of consideration for inheritance and continuance of Confucian thoughts."[79] In an address on the sacrificial ceremony held in Bailudong, it is also stated that the target figures of these rituals are

> noble in character, respectful of humanity, devoted in studies, well-versed in the six classics, and whether they are serving as officials or living in seclusion, they all want to improve their learning of the humanities and to enhance their virtue. Although they differ in their way of life, their merit and moral influence on the country are completely the same.

It can be said that the purpose of worshiping these figures is certainly to express our respect and admiration for them as a person and, more importantly, to respect the spiritual values they embodied and advocated. Jiang Yi, a scholar of the Yuan dynasty, says more about this:

> Taking pains to hold grand ceremonies in the spring and autumn of each year, set up special official position in charge of them, and follow every detail of the rules and regulations is not just to honor a certain figure but to show respect for the values he sticks to.[80]

Consequently, the choice of Xiansheng and Xianshi as the ritual targets shows the respect for and affirmation of the values they created, advocated, and embodied.

Obviously, the selection of target figures has a clear guiding role. It highlights the values and principles these figures advocated and the shining qualities they embodied and represented. Their pictures, their statues, and the shrines built for them are actually an unpronounced expression of their academic views and values of life. Their existence in the academy has become an important part of the environment where the students live and study and, thus, will produce a vital influence on them in a quiet and unconscious way. "Looking at the statues of sages, the beholders will be inspired with awe by the statues. If he does not change his arrogant attitude yet while admiring the icon, can he still be considered a scholar?"[81] Furthermore, academicians who were deeply lost in this environment for a long time would naturally produce a sense of identity with them and eventually grow into Confucian scholars who met the requirements. During the Hongzhi reign of the Ming dynasty, Yang Lian writes in "Records of Shrine of Confucian Ancestors" (宗儒祠记) of Bailudong Academy,

> The students in the academy live, study, and communicate with each other. They are thirsty for knowledge and devote themselves to the study of Confucianism, just as an archer always expects to hit the bull's-eye and just as a wanderer on a trip longs to return home. At the beginning and in the middle of each month, I will gaze up at the icons of the sages with humble reverence, and as it is said in *Annotations with Illustrations* (图说), "I will be peaceful in mind with the benevolence of the sages," and in *Cave Poetry* (洞赋), "I will try to be close enough to the sages by understanding and feeling their sincerity." Thus, I will develop a keenness for knowledge and study hard every day. In addition, I also read and research on the articles of Zhiqing (Huang Gan) and other Confucian masters and grow gradually insightful by reading and studying more. I do not believe that I cannot reach the level of those Confucian masters if I study carefully and repeatedly.[82]

It is just on the basis of this understanding that Yang emphasizes the persuasive, guiding effect of academy rituals on scholars: "This is the original purpose of founding the ancestral hall." In fact, it was of vital importance for a person to

64 *Academy Sacrificial Rituals*

set up goals in the process of seeking learning and enhancing virtue. Building ancestral temples in academies was to set up role models for academy students and make it clear where to go. When talking about the role of worshiping rituals, Zhu Xi said, "The rituals do not only mean to set up statues of sages and to provide gorgeous artifacts and clothing for sages but to set examples for students to follow."[83] It can be said that the academy rituals mainly provided an orientation, a norm, by which students should determine the direction of their own cultivation. What is more important about the practice of worship is to inherit and carry forward Confucian learning rather than to make believe. As Huang Wenzhong, a Confucian scholar of the Yuan dynasty, says in an essay titled "Records of Construction of Four Worthies Hall in Shuangfeng Academy" (顺昌双峰书院新建四贤堂记),

> When you enter the hall of the school and see the statues of these sages, if you know well about their deeds and achievements, you will know why they should be respected and what to learn from them, and thus, you will gain all the more reason for inheriting and continuing their thoughts.[84]

During the Wanli period of the Ming dynasty, Fang Xuejian also says in "Records of Reconstruction of Daonan Sacrificial Hall" (重建道南祠记), "I hope that those who enter this temple will not only stay solemn and reverent in the worshiping ceremony but will also strive to pursue their learning."[85] Peng Shi, a Confucian of the Ming dynasty, also talks about the educational role of the rituals: "Throwing worshiping ceremonies in the academy is to make the scholars hold up their heads to see his (Confucius') statue, bend down to read and study the books he wrote, and try to learn from him."[86] In the Ming dynasty, when Bailudong had the Two-Sage Shrine rebuilt to worship Zhou Dunyi and Zhu Xi, Jiang Guoxiang, a local official in Nankang, writes in "Notes on Reconstruction of Shines of Two Worthies" (蜀府同知蒋国祥重建二贤祠记),

> I renovate a room for the two sages. Is it just for the purpose of holding a ritual? No! Only by reading his books and following his example, by living and studying in his shrine and reflecting on Confucianism, and by using his standards to discipline oneself can one strictly distinguish ethics from desires; only by using Confucian morality to govern the people of the country can one strictly distinguish kingship from hegemony; and only by using Confucian morality to educate people can one distinguish Confucianism from Buddhism.[87]

The ultimate goal of worshiping sages is to imitate their (the sages') person, study their scholarly ideas, reflect on their teachings, follow their examples, and strive to learn from them. If what the scholars studied in the academy were mostly abstract principles and norms, then they would become more concrete in the case of these figures of worship. By familiarizing himself with what these worshiped figures did in different historical, social, and ethical situations, one could have a more sincere and profound comprehension of and identification with the ethical principles and norms of Confucianism. This effect could hardly be achieved by mere lecturing and indoctrination. As some scholars have pointed out, the ritual is a visualization of the educational ideal.[88] Through a shrine, a statue, or a painting, Confucian values and academic philosophy are accentuated. In daily academy life, these values and academic concepts will live in people's memories with more vividness, occupying their memory space and producing a stronger sense of identity.

To Trigger Scholars' Faith in Confucianism

Faith is a deeper and more solid sense of spiritual and psychological identity beyond reason, which has a strong and lasting effect on the shaping of moral characters. The creation of faith often requires a certain occasion, atmosphere, or situation, while the academy's sacrificial activity is just such an occasion where a certain situation and atmosphere can be created to trigger the scholars' faith in Confucianism.

As is said in the chapter "Summary of the Rules of Propriety" in *The Book of Rites* (礼记·曲礼), "The routine worshiping activity itself cannot bring senses of piety and awe without rites for people to follow. When offering sacrifices to ancestors, sages, gods, and spirits, respect cannot be inspired if people do not conform to the norms of the ritual system." Academy sacrifice included a series of rites. These rites, together with the furnishings and offerings, created a solemn scene that sublimated people's reverence for Xiansheng, Xianshi, sages, and other target figures into a sacred experience. For instance, in the Saints' Hall of Bailudong Academy, the ceremony of Shicai was held every year when the county sheriff sent all the students to the academy, while the ritual of Shidian was practiced on the Zhongding day (14th day) of the Zhong month (February and August of the calendar used in the Spring and Autumn Period). Before the ritual, the attendees needed to "fast for three days with prohibitions of alcohol and meat. During the first two fasting days, they needed to stay alone in a separate room, clean their bodies, with sex, amusement, and mourning forbidden; on the third day, they were further required to stay out in a quiet place, away from their house, so that their soul would be cleansed." Maxim Academy of Yichahng, Hunan Province, also had similar provisions: "three days before the ritual was held, the supervisor would ask the superintendent to tell all students to fast." Fasting was actually a removal of worldly distractions and a purification of their minds. It was a process of urging people to be away from the worldly and concentrating their thoughts more on the target figures of sacrifice. Many other historical documents also recorded such details of these rites. Through this set of prescribed rules and regulations, the worshiper could generate a strong feeling of reverence for the ritual targets from within.

66 Academy Sacrificial Rituals

The prayers read in the worshiping ceremony are the finishing touch in the whole sacrificial activities, which bring out the main purpose and significance of the ritual, thus making the attendees sublimate their admiration for the worshiped figures to a profound recognition of the academic theories they advocate, the principles and norms they practice, and the moral character they embody. For example, in the psalm to Confucius memorialized in Bailudong Academy, Confucius is praised as

> a man whose virtue is the same as that of heaven and earth and the same as that of the sun and the moon, whose doctrines have been passed down to all generations, a great educator who first compiled the Six Classics and used them as textbooks for his teaching, and whose classics have become the model for all generations.[89]

In a word, these psalms or prayers, while illustrating the reason why the ritual figures are memorialized and honored, have furthered the significance of sacrifice from the worship of the specific figure itself to the faith in Confucian values and principles.

To Stimulate Scholars' Sense of Moral Mission and Social Responsibility

As mentioned earlier, some sacrificial target figures of the academy are Confucian masters who have made great contributions to the creation, development, and transmission of Confucianism, represented by Confucius and his disciples (including Zhou Dunyi, Cheng Yi, Cheng Hao, Zhang Zai, Shao Yong in the Northern Song dynasty, and Zhu Xi and his followers in the Southern Song dynasty); some are sages who practice in person and embody Confucian moral principles, represented by Zhu Geliang, Tao Yuanming, and Yan Zhenqing, worshiped in Bailudong Academy, as well as Zou Hao in Yuelu Academy. The worship of these figures can naturally stimulate a sense of mission in the hearts of the scholars. As the saying goes, "When understand the reason why Shun is worshiped, you will know what Shun deserves to be learned by future generations."[90] Then the scholars will follow the example of these target figures and take their noble qualities and great achievements as the goal for self-expectation and role model for the cultivation of their own moral character. The scholar Zhan Li of the Ming dynasty says in "Biographies of Three Masters" (三先生祠行状) that the significance of such practices as rebuilding Yingshan Academy and offering worship to Zhu Xi, who once engaged in academic research there, is that "hence, many scholars will hold in great respect his person and learning and thus aspire to be saints (learn from saints) like him."[91] Dai Junheng, a scholar of the Qing dynasty, also says that the worship of sages and teachers was "not only to show admiration for sages and display respect for Confucian values but also to enable future scholars to truly look up to the role models and thus to cultivate their own moral character and enrich their own learning." "Entering the ancestral hall and looking up to the worshiped sage with reverence, you will spontaneously envision his way of being a man, develop an keenness to learn from him, and then determine to further your study on his works and thoughts."[92] Some other scholars even point out in a direct way that the rituals of the academy are actually intended to inspire a sense of longing and mission through setting up examples and models.

Chen Jixin points out,

> The reason the academy pays homage to masters and sages is to set an example for sound character and rich learning to the students as they can feel the inculcation and influence of the sages every day. Entering the ancestral hall where the sages are worshiped is really like encountering them in person, and while reading and studying their books, the students can truly experience their state of mind, thus creating a longing to learn from them, to be true men like them.[93]

Li Guojun also remarks in *History of the Chinese Academy* (中国书院史) that "one of the main goals of the academy sacrificial ritual is to set examples of learning, inspire scholars to learn from him, and let them 'enter the ancestral hall where he is worshiped, as if they were really seeing him in person.'"[94] These words are quite insightful. Actually, what the academy rituals provide is a paradigm of an ideal personality presented in a sensual, visual form. The scholars, by osmosis, will unconsciously develop feelings of admiration and aspiration. In the process of setting their own life goals, their admiration and awe for the worshiped figures will be transformed into a strong sense of mission, firmly believing that they can, like the figures of worship, carry forward Confucianism, can put Confucian ethics into practice, and "will not cause humiliation to the sages of the past." This sense of mission is undoubtedly a powerful driving force in the process of one's moral character cultivation.

Academy sacrificial rituals can also inspire a sense of social responsibility among scholars. Many of the ritual target figures, as mentioned earlier, are Confucian masters, eminent officials who have contributed substantially to the creation and development of the academy, as well as superintendents or learned teachers of the academies. It is with their efforts that the academy is founded and developed despite varieties of disasters and calamities. The Six Gentlemen Hall of Yuelu Academy was dedicated to such sages. The scholars studying here, as the main beneficiaries of the business started by these sages, they will be naturally reminded of the pains that these sages have taken and the contribution they have made to the evolution of the academy. It will dawn on them that the current good learning environment is not easy to come by, and thus their thankfulness will be generated. More importantly, with these sacrificial activities, scholars will gain a better understanding of the fact that what these predecessors have been taking pains to do is just to cultivate talents for the country. Early in the Qiandao reign of the Southern Song dynasty, after Liu Gong restored Yuelu Academy, Zhang Shiba said, "Mr. Liu's main reason for doing this . . . is to cultivate talents and to improve the lives of the people by spreading and promoting

68 *Academy Sacrificial Rituals*

Confucian values and principles."[95] Yuan Xie also remarks in "Records of Donghu Academy" (东湖书院记),

> Is the purpose of a gentleman engaging in learning just to memorize and recite such minutiae? It is supposed to seek and inherit Confucianism . . . Scholars work together to study, discuss, and devote themselves to seeking and passing on the Confucian academic and thought system. Through these efforts, they can improve their moral quality so that their own character can be formed, and then Confucianism will be further strengthened and promoted. This was originally the goal of setting up academies.[96]

Obviously, the academy memorial rituals to the sages actually put such questions in front of the scholars: How could a scholar live up to the ardent expectations placed on him by the sages in creating and developing the academy so that he could become a person capable of shouldering the important task of governing the people? How could the academy be further developed? If the development of the academy was an undertaking passed on from generation to generation, then the worship of the sages who contributed to the academy was to strengthen this sense of social responsibility of the scholars.

In addition, it is worth mentioning that academy's worship to local eminent officials and Confucians can give scholars a sense of closeness, thereby enhancing their confidence to be sages. Many of the honored figures are the ones who are related, in one way or another, to the academy or grow up in the locality, which is just what we mean by saying, "whoever has no connection with the academy will not be involved."[97] In this light, superintendents, erudite teachers, and successful students who once governed, lectured, and studied there are also often included in the list of the ritual targets of the academy.

"When chopping wood with an ax, one should adjust the chopping method according to the length of the ax handle." This close association between the figure of worship and the locality tends to make scholars feel a sense of intimacy, which is evidently apt to inspire them to follow their model. At the same time, for many aspiring scholars, at the thought of the fact that the worshiped figure used to live in the same place where they are now living, the seemingly unreachable saint will become at once so close to them that they naturally produce a sense of affection. Just as Dai Junheng of the Qing dynasty says when talking about offering sacrifices to local celebrities in Tongxiang Academy, "with this closeness, these worshiped figures will be easily regarded as the kinsfolk, and the sense of alienation from the role models can thus be avoided."[98]

To Edify and Enlighten the General Public

Academy sacrificial rituals not only played a role in the cultivation of talents but also had a far-reaching influence beyond the academy itself on the whole society, performing a social edification function.

The academy, through the selection of the worshiped figures, reflects a certain value orientation. Based on this understanding, academy sacrificial ceremonies are often held with the purpose to improve the academic atmosphere and folk custom of the local area. For instance, Jiang Guoxiang of the Ming Dynasty, after restoring the two ancestral halls of Bailudong Academy dedicated to Zhou Dunyi and Zhu Xi, spoke of his hope that the move would be beneficial to the indoctrination of the local community: "I modified and created a new ancestral hall room. Is it only for the purpose of holding rituals? Read the books they wrote and emulate them as a person, live and communicate inside their shrines, and reflect on their teachings. . . . I hope to be able to encourage each other and learn together with the people of the same county." As far as social edification is concerned, some academy ancestral halls, originally built outside the academy, have actually the nature of local public buildings. For example, Six Gentlemen Hall of Yuelu Academy, which is dedicated to the sages who have contributed to the academy, was first built on the highland not far from the academy, and Qu Zi Temple of the academy was also built outside a few hundred meters away. They are practically an integral part of the cultural life of the local community. Even some of the shrines built inside are not completely isolated from the outside world, easily accessible to ordinary members of the local community. As a result, their existence, as a cultural symbol, clearly expresses the value orientation of the academy, and their openness and public nature in turn allow the values advocated by the academy to radiate to the surrounding areas and play an edifying role in the local community.

The process of the sacrificial rituals is also a process in which the academy interacts with the local community, members of the local community come into the academy, and the academy's influence permeates the community. Some important sacrificial rituals of the academy are often presided over and attended by local officials. Local gentry and ordinary people also had the opportunity to participate in the sacrificial activities of the academy. For example, in December of the fifth year of Shaoxi reign (ad 1193) of the Southern Song dynasty, Zhu Xi held a grand ceremony of Shicai upon the completion of Cangzhou Jingshe Academy (located where Confucians used to give lectures). The attendees came from all parts of the county, as is recorded in *The Analects of Zhu Xi* (朱子语类): "people living in the neighborhood, young and old, all came to attend the ritual."[99] It can be said that a ritual is an extensive social indoctrination activity. Members of different social classes attending the rituals from all parts of the locality will be educated and baptized by Confucianism, and thereby, the values embodied in the ritual will reach a wider audience.

In particular, Banzuo is of vital importance in strengthening the edifying function of sacrificial rituals in their unique form. The so-called Banzuo is a special sacrificial activity of awarding meat to the worshipers in accordance with certain regulations at the end of a sacrificial ritual. The custom of Banzuo has a long history and is recorded in *Rites of Zhou* (周礼) and *The Commentary of Zuo* (左传). In many academies, Banzuo is included in the sacrificial ritual. For example, in the 22nd year of Jiaqing reign in the Qing dynasty (ad 1817), Yuelu Academy made regulations stipulating that at the end of a sacrificial ritual, the main priest, the attendees, and attendants of all kinds could all receive Banzuo (the award of sacrificial meat). And a chapter titled "On Banzuo" in *Records of Shishan Academy* (诗山书院志· 颁胙说) also elaborates on Banzuo:

70 *Academy Sacrificial Rituals*

When the ritual is finished, the meat used as offerings to deities will be distributed.

> Any scholar who has got scholarly title from Dingjia (an umbrella term for Zhuangyuan, Bangyan, and Tanhua, who come first, second, and third in the highest imperial examination) to Xiucai (one who has passed the imperial examination at the county level), and any official from the first to the ninth rank, regardless of whether they are civil officials or military officers, can get the sacrificial meat. Jiansheng (student of the Imperial College) who have passed the examination at the county level can also get it.[100]

The purpose of Banzuo was undoubtedly to strengthen the effect of social educational effect of the memorial ritual and extend the influence of the ritual beyond the academy to the general public, giving full play to its social edification function. Here, the zuo (the meat awarded) is no longer sacrificial meat in the ordinary sense but a cultural symbol with a profound symbolic meaning that is shrouded in a halo of sanctity. It transmits the sacredness of the activity to the attendees and tries to make them experience and understand its profound connotation.[101]

Some of the academy worship rituals, due to their grander scale, often drew much attention from the public and naturally became events of cultural significance in the local area, generating a greater social impact. For example, in the autumn of the 60th year of Qianlong reign of the Qing dynasty (ad 1795), Yuelu Academy held a grand ceremony of Dingji (memorial ritual worshiping Confucius), where they

> prepared four lamp posts, all several feet in height, with a square bucket placed on them like the Big Dipper, and placed two lamp posts directly opposite the Kui Pavilion, while the other two were arranged on the left and right sides of the entrance to the academy. The sound of drums and music reverberated for three days and nights, and the sound of firecrackers echoed in the valley, going off more than tens of thousands of times. From the first day to the fifteenth, the ceremony lasted half a month. People from all parts of the country came to visit, and they were all very happy and joyful.[102]

The reason for such a grand and spectacular event was to expand its social influence. These fanfare rituals actually turned the academy sacrificial rituals into a remarkable local cultural event with strong symbolic significance. With a kind of social orientation of reverence for Confucianism, these worshiped figures, as role models, went beyond the academy and reached the local community.

To sum up, the academy, in essence, is an integral part of a larger social system that was connected with the locality in a variety of ways, and the role the sacrificial rituals played in society extend far beyond the academy itself and could be seen as an important means of social indoctrination.

Academy Sacrifice and Confucian Daotong

Origin and Essence of Confucian Daotong

Confucian Daotong (or Confucian orthodoxy) has been a hot research topic for many Confucian scholars since the Tang and Song dynasties. Many Confucian scholars have studied the origin and development of Daotong and have put forward various enlightening views. It is generally believed that early Confucian ideas about Daotong sprouted in Mencius' (371–289 bc) thought and that the Confucian Daotong theory was firstly proposed by Han Yu (768–824).[103]

In the final chapter of *Mencius* (孟子), "Devotion" (尽心下), there is a passage in which Mencius describes how Confucian doctrine was passed on through ancient sages Yao, Shun, Yu (2123–2025 bc), Tang (1675–1646 bc), King Wen of Zhou (1152–1056 bc), and Confucius (551–479 bc). He points out the Confucian doctrine came down in one continuous line and that a great sage would emerge about every 500 years to bring the doctrine to a greater height of development. He argues that some ancient sages directly inherited the doctrine from their predecessors, but some revived it according to legends or historical records about the past sages. At the same time, Mencius also expresses his worry about whether there would be a successor after Confucius and pays close attention to when the great inheritor of Confucius would appear to develop the doctrine to a higher stage. His exact words are as follows.[104]

> During the 500-plus years from the reign of Yao and Shun to the reign of Tang (1675–1646 B.C.), Yu (2123–2025 B.C.), and Gao Yao (2220–2113 B.C.) inherited the Confucian doctrine directly from the sages. As to Tang, he learned it through legends. In the more than 500 years between the reign of Tang and the reign of King Wen of Zhou (1152–1056 B.C.), Yi Yin (1648–1549 B.C.) and Lai Zhu (1152–1056 B.C.) learned it directly from Tang, and King Wen of Zhou knew it only through historical records. During the over 500 years from the reign of King Wen of Zhou to Confucius, Jiang Ziya (1156–1015 B.C.) and San Yisheng (11th cent. B.C.) inherited the teachings directly from King Wen of Zhou, while Confucius learned it only through historical records. Now, about 100 plus years after the death of Confucius, we still live close to the sage's hometown and under his influence. If we do not carry forward his thought, no one else will engage in this endeavor.

Mencius repeatedly emphasized the importance of "thoroughly understanding and resolutely carrying forward the teachings of the past sages" and made it his mission to defend and inherit the teachings of the sages. He says,

> I feel worried about this, so I want to familiarize myself with the teachings of the past sages, to resist the theories of Yang Zhu (ca. 395–335 B.C.) and Mo Di (ca. 476–390 B.C.), and to refute false and exaggerated statements so that heresy and fallacies can no longer prevail.[105]

72 Academy Sacrificial Rituals

He also notes,

> I also want to purify people's minds, stop heretical ideas, criticize excessive indulgence, resist biased behaviors, and refute absurd remarks so as to inherit the thoughts of the three sages (Yu, King Wen of Zhou, and Confucius) and carry forward their great cause.[106]

According to Zhu Xi (1130–1200), what the book *Mencius* (孟子) explicitly shows is an affirmation of Daotong and an expression of sense of self-responsibility to carry on Confucian doctrine. Zhu Xi says,

> Although Mencius never claimed himself to be an inheritor of Confucian doctrine, he felt worried about losing it in the future because he found few people really understand its meaning. So he himself voluntarily shouldered the responsibility of advocating and spreading the teachings in the hope that future generations will inherit and promote them. He left his words in the book to tell people how Confucian doctrine was passed on through sages and what it was. By doing this, he made it possible for future generations to understand and inherit these teachings. His words exerted a far-reaching influence.[107]

Obviously, here in *Mencius* (孟子), the idea about Daotong had already been in embryo.

When Yang Zhu's and Mo Di's thoughts prevailed, Mencius took it as his duty to criticize excessive indulgence and biased behaviors and refute absurd remarks. To achieve this goal, he traced the lineage of Confucian doctrine directly back to its origin and thus elevated himself to the level of "becoming familiar with the teachings of the sages of the past." He hailed his own studies as an exploration of the teachings of the past sages and to the wisdom of Yu, King Wen of Zhou, and Confucius. Mencius' studies were undoubtedly of great significance in clarifying the origin of Confucianism, correcting misconceptions, and providing directions for Neo-Confucianism that emerged more than 1,000 years later. Mencius' action was a great inspiration to Han Yu, who refuted Buddhist and Taoist thoughts but advocated Confucianism in the mid-Tang dynasty. Han Yu lived in an era when Buddhism and Taoism prevailed in society. To compete with Buddhist and Taoist thoughts and strengthen the authority of Confucianism, Han Yu created a fictitious line of inheritance depicting how Confucian doctrine came down in one continuous line from Yao, Shun, Yu, Tang, King Wen of Zhou, King Wu of Zhou (1110–1043 bc), and the Duke of Zhou, named Ji Dan (11th cent. bc), to Confucius and Mencius, and argued that Confucian Daotong was on the wane after Mencius' death.

> Confucian doctrine was passed from Yao to Shun; from Shun to Yu; from Yu to Tang; from Tang to King Wen, King Wu, and the Duke of Zhou; from King Wen, King Wu, and the Duke of Zhou to Confucius; and from Confucius to Mencius, and after the death of Mencius, there was no successor.[108]

Academy Sacrificial Rituals 73

Han Yu's theory on the transmission of the Confucian doctrine directly inspired the creation of the Confucian Daotong theory in the mid–Northern Song dynasty.

During the Confucian revival movement in the mid–Northern Song dynasty, Confucian scholars enthusiastically discussed Confucian Daotong, and every Confucian school claimed to be the inheritor of the Confucian orthodoxy, striving to acquire the orthodox position in Confucianism. However, each school differed from the other in terms of the genealogy of the Confucian doctrine. The theory of Daotong of Sun Fu (992–1057) and Shi Jie (1005–1045) was based on Han Yu's belief, adding to the transmission line six more legendary sages before Yao—Fuxi, Shennong, the Huang Emperor (2717–2599 bc), Shaohao (2422–2322 bc), Zhuanxu (2342–2245 bc), and Gaoxin (2275–2176 bc)—and another four outstanding Confucian scholars after Mencius—Xun Kuang (third cent. bc), Yang Xiong (53–18 bc), Wang Tong (584–617), and Han Yu. Su Shi (1037–1101), on the other hand, proposed a new transmission line of Confucian orthodoxy in the lineage from Confucius and Mencius to Han Yu and Ouyang Xiu (1007–1072). He held that after the death of Confucius and Mencius,

> Han Yu appeared more than 500 years later, whose academic contribution was as outstanding as that of Mencius; 300 years after Han Yu's death, Ouyang Xiu appeared, whose achievement surpassed Han Yu and Mencius and thus could be placed on a par with Confucius.[109]

Cheng Yi (1033–1107) and Cheng Hao (1032–1085), representative scholars of the Confucian Luo School of the Northern Song dynasty, devoted their lives to promoting the teachings of sages and were remembered as inheritors of Confucian doctrine. After Cheng Hao's death, Cheng Yi composed a complimentary epitaph for him titled "Tomb Inscription" (墓表), saying,

> After the death of the Duke of Zhou, Ji Dan, teachings of the sages stopped being implemented. After the death of Mencius, they declined in influence . . . Cheng Hao was born about 1,400 years after Mencius but was determined to influence the people with the Confucian doctrine that he successfully deciphered by studying ancient classics . . . Thanks to Cheng Hao's efforts, the Confucian doctrine was clarified again. This was a great contribution.[110]

In this epitaph, Cheng Yi describes Cheng Hao as the successor of Confucian doctrine in the Song dynasty, officially establishing the Daotong's origin for Neo-Confucianism.

Zhu Xi made a significant contribution to the development of the Neo-Confucian theory of Daotong. First of all, he attached great importance to Daotong and made his Daotong theory a key component of his ideological and academic system. He not only gave a clear account of the genealogy of Confucian doctrine but also elaborated on its specific connotations, thus making the theoretical development of Daotong more complete and profound. Second, Zhu Xi had great influence in the academic circles of his time, and his teachings were respected and gradually

74 *Academy Sacrificial Rituals*

elevated to official academic status since the late Southern Song dynasty, which made his Daotong theory rather popular and widely spread.

On the basis of inheriting and summarizing the previous Confucian Daotong theories, Zhu Xi further expounded upon the transmission line of Confucian doctrine. According to him, the Confucian doctrine was handed down from sage to sage in early prehistoric China: from Yao to Shun and from Shun to Yu. He notes,

> Since then, it was passed on from sage to sage. Some sages had the chance to rule the country, such as Tang, King Wen of Zhou, and King Wu of Zhou, and some had the chance to serve the country as high-ranking officials, such as Gao Yao, Yi Yin, Fu Yue (12th cent. B.C.), Ji Dan (the Duke of Zhou), and Ji Shi (the Duke of Zhao; 11th cent. B.C.), all of whom have been the inheritors of Confucian doctrine. Later appeared our respected Confucius. Even though he did not have such title as a monarch, he could continue the teachings of the previous sages and make pioneering undertakings for the learning of future generations, so he achieved more than Yao or Shun did. Unfortunately, back then, only Yan Hui (521–481 B.C.) and Zeng Shen (505–435 B.C.) inherited the Confucian doctrine directly from Confucius. Zeng Shen imparted the teachings to his disciple who later taught them to Confucius' grandson Kong Ji (483–402 B.C.).

Zhu Xi also observes, "Later, Mencius interpreted Kong Ji's book and succeeded in inheriting Confucian doctrine. Nevertheless, after the death of Mencius, Confucian doctrine found no successor and was thus discontinued."[111] To fill in the gap between Mencius' time and his day, Zhu Xi took Cheng Yi and Cheng Hao as inheritors of the Confucian doctrine after Mencius, stressing that they constituted an indispensable link in Confucian orthodoxy. He says,

> The brothers Cheng Yi and Cheng Hao's studies that were based on textual research revived the lost knowledge about Daotong. Kong Ji's contribution was remarkable, but without the Cheng brothers, his book could not be explained and his thought could not be understood.[112]

In this way, Zhu Xi further improved the genealogy of Confucian orthodoxy on the basis of the theory of his predecessors and clarified how Neo-Confucian doctrine had been handed down from Yao, Shun, Confucius, and Mencius to the Cheng brothers.

Zhu Xi not only discussed the genealogy of Confucian orthodoxy but also gave a clear exposition of the connotation of the Confucian doctrine. In the general prologue to *Syntactic and Semantic Analysis of the Doctrine of the Mean* (中庸章句序), Zhu Xi writes,

> The origin of Confucian doctrine can be traced back to prehistoric China, when the country was ruled by sages. Daotong is presented in classical

writings. It is the impartial and just way that Shun inherited from Yao. It is the governance guidance that Shun offered to Yu, which required Yu to remain devoted to the great cause and implement the impartial and just way. Yao's interpretation of Daotong was complete enough, but Shun still further elaborated it. Nevertheless, Yao's interpretation is always the most founding principle.[113]

In the preface, Zhu Xi (1130–1200) explicitly proposes the theory of two hearts. (In Chinese culture, a man's heart can be divided into two parts: the heart of a biological being and the heart of a moral being. That is to say, man as a biological being is dangerous and unpredictable, while he as a moral being is subtle and difficult to understand. Therefore, man should combine the two hearts into one, practice the "mean" principle, and try to be sincere and focused enough.) This theory was the very essence of the Confucian doctrine that was passed down through Yao, Shun, Yu, Tang, King Wen of Zhou, King Wu of Zhou, the Duke of Zhou, and Confucius. Zhu Xi made a very detailed interpretation of the two-hearts theory from a rather Neo-Confucian perspective so that it was later incorporated into the track of Neo-Confucianism, and became an important theoretical basis and spiritual core for the construction of its theoretical system.

The philosophical connotation of Confucian orthodoxy can be concluded in the following three aspects: sense of identity, sense of orthodoxy, and sense of responsibility to expand teachings.[114] Accordingly, we can understand the essence of Confucian Daotong from the following three aspects.

First, scholars' concern about Daotong shows their identification with Confucian thoughts. Confucian scholars generally shared the following beliefs: There is a universal, eternal existence called the Way (roughly referring to the law of the heaven, the earth, and the human society) existing beyond the limits of time and space. The Way, ever since prehistoric times, has been repeatedly challenged and obscured by various heresies in its development, but none of the heresies succeeded in defeating the Way. The prosperity or the decline of the Way determines the destiny of the secular world. The success of achieving historical progress and realizing academic prosperity is based on the premise that the Way is widely advocated and thoroughly implemented.

For these beliefs, Confucian scholars usually exerted a great effort to promote Confucian Daotong on the one hand and resist Buddhism and Taoism on the other, trying their best to maintain the authority of Confucianism and seeing that it would play a leading role in all aspects of social life.

Second, Confucians often talked about Daotong as a way of demonstrating their understanding of the essence of Confucianism. They tended to interpret the connotation of Daotong according to their own understanding, set their own standards to select figures to file into the genealogy, and predicted the direction of Confucianism, on the basis of which they boasted their inheritance of the Confucian doctrine and thus established their orthodox status in Confucianism. This sense of orthodoxy usually led to many academic disagreements and even disputes among

76 *Academy Sacrificial Rituals*

Confucian scholars and among Confucian schools. Based on its own understanding of and standards of Confucianism, a Confucian school often criticized other schools of scholars for their impurity and even boldly declared that other Confucian schools were not orthodox enough.

Third, Confucian scholars who talked about Daotong often demonstrated a strong sense of responsibility. They took it as their own mission to inherit, carry forward, and advocate Confucian doctrine, or the Way of the sages. This was true of all Confucian scholars, from Han Yu in the Tang dynasty to Shi Jie, Cheng Yi, and Zhu Xi in the Song dynasty.

It is worth noting that, as Chen Rongjie, a historian, says, "The controversy over Daotong is more philosophical than historical or textual."[115] The so-called Daotong is not a reflection of some historical reality. For example, the two-hearts theory that Zhu Xi claimed to be the essence of Confucian doctrine was actually quoted from "Counsels of Yu" (大禹谟), a chapter from *Documents of Antiquity* (古文尚书), which had once been considered a version of the Confucian classic *Shang Shu* but later identified as a forged ancient document created in the Eastern Jin dynasty (317–420). According to a textual analysis essay titled "Commentaries and Explanations to Documents of Antiquity" (尚书古文疏证), written by Yan Ruoqu (1638–1704) of the Qing dynasty, the fake record in the forged copy of *Gu Wen Shang Shu* was plagiarized from *Xunzi* (荀子), a book recording the teachings of Xun Kuang, and the sentence being plagiarized was quoted from "Dao" (道经) (one part in *Classic of the Way and Virtue,* authored by Laozi) and *The Analects of Confucius* (论语).[116]

Therefore, there is no historical basis for Zhu Xi's use of it as the spiritual core of Confucian orthodoxy, and the genealogy of Confucian doctrine that he drew up was also largely fictional. In fact, scholars put forward the theory of Daotong mainly to express their understanding of the essence of Confucianism by elaborating on the so-called connotation of the Confucian Way and selecting certain figures into the genealogy. It was also out of a need to respond to the issues of the time and construct an academic theory. In the case of Han Yu, Shi Jie, and other early Song scholars, the Daotong theory was probably put forward to show their identification with Confucianism, to respond to the challenges of Buddhism and Taoism, which were flourishing while Confucianism was declining. In the case of Cheng Yi, Cheng Hao, Zhu Xi, and many later scholars, things were different. At a time when Confucianism prevailed and many Confucian schools argued with each other, the theory of Daotong was proposed mainly to establish a spiritual core among the various systems of Confucian thought that were advancing in parallel and to prescribe the direction of the development of Confucianism.

The establishment of Confucian Daotong theory underpinned the process of constructing a Confucian theoretical system. Given this, generations of Confucian scholars made great efforts to promote and strengthen their sense of Daotong when imparting Confucian teachings. As the ritual space of the academy was an important place to educate scholars, the awareness of Confucian Daotong was very clearly reflected in the academy sacrificial rituals.

Confucian Daotong and Academy Sacrifice

In December of the fifth year of Shaoxi reign in the Southern Song dynasty (1194), Zhu Xi decided to retreat to the mountains and take in students, teaching them to read and write. He then built Zhulin Academy (later renamed Cangzhou Academy). After the completion of the academy, Zhu Xi held a grand sacrificial ceremony. A disciple of Zhu Xi, Ye Hesun gave a detailed account of this activity. He claimed,

> Now that the academy has been completed, a ritual of Shicai will be held to offer worship to our ancestors and sages. We read *New Ceremonies of the Five Rites from the Zhenghe Reign-Period* (五礼新仪) carefully for the rules to follow until every detail of the sacrificial ritual is worked out.

Zhu Xi, who was responsible for this activity personally, worked hard all the way. He "rose with the crow of the rooster every day, rushed to the academy before dawn" and discussed all the minutiae of the ritual with his disciples. The ceremony was held in the lecture hall, for the ancestral hall was not yet fully refurbished. The statue of Confucius was in the middle. Duke Yan of the Yan clan, Marquis Cheng of the Zeng clan, Marquis Yishui of the Kong clan, and Duke Zou of the Meng clan were placed one by one (paper cards of them) from west to north. Zhou Dunyi, Cheng Yi, Cheng Hao, Shao Yong, Wenguo, Zhang Zi, and Li Tong were also worshiped here. As the venue for the ritual was not spacious enough, parts of this event did not meet the requirements, but both the host and attendees of the ceremony were full of sincerity all the way.[117]

From these descriptions, we can see the importance Zhu Xi attached to this sacrifice. On the one hand, every detail of the ritual was deliberated over and over again, and on the other hand, the ceremony was held with great sincerity and reverence. The most striking about this sacrifice activity was the figures worshiped. Besides Confucius, Yan Hui, Ceng Can, Kong Ji, Mencius, and other pre-Qin Confucian masters, such as Zhou Dunyi, Cheng Yi, and Cheng Hao, Shao Yong, Sima Guang, Zhang Zai, Li Tong (Zhu Xi's teacher), and several other founding scholars of Neo-Confucianism were also included in the list of the worshiped figures in this ritual.

Actually, prior to the building of Zhulin Academy, there had been some cases where some provincial, state, and county academies built shrines to worship Zhou Dunyi, Cheng Yi, Cheng Hao, Hu Anguo, and other scholars of Neo-Confucianism. For example, in the third year of the Chunxi reign (1176), Pan Ciming and Lü Sheng (local officials of Jiangzhou) repaired Lianxi Academy for the worship of Zhou Dunyi. Zhu Xi composed an essay titled "Reconstruction of Lian Xi Study Hall in Jiangzhou" (江州重建濂溪先生书堂记) in the fourth year of Chunxi, taking notes on this event. In March of the seventh year of Chunxi (1180), following the restoration of Bailudong Academy, Zhu Xi personally led the military and county officials of Nankang and the students and teachers of the academy to hold a grand worshiping ceremony, sacrificing to great teachers and great sages,

78 *Academy Sacrificial Rituals*

with Confucius, Duke Yan, and Duke Zou as the main figures of worship.[118] More than a decade later, Zhu Xi again busied himself offering worship to some other famous Neo-Confucianists at Zhulin Academy. However, at that time, it was not common for academies to pay tribute to Neo-Confucianists. So what did Zhu Xi mean by this?

If the worship of Zhou Dunyi at Lianxi Academy in Jiangzhou in the third year of Chunxi can be interpreted as restoring the old site and commemorating the local sages, the several sages worshiped at Zhulin Academy, however, had no direct connection with the academy. Some researchers examined the significance of this sacrificial ritual from the perspective of highlighting the origin of the school.[119] They believe that the worship at Zhulin Academy was the beginning of the worship of sages from a certain school of thought by academies. However, this is not enough to reveal the essence of the sacrificial ceremony at Zhulin Academy. Among the several Neo-Confucianist scholars worshiped, only Li Tong was Zhu Xi's teacher and had a direct relationship with the academy. While the other six scholars were pioneers of Confucianism with the same academic pursuits, the differences in their scholarly interests and theories were also rather obvious, and surely, they did not constitute a definite academic school. From the perspective of academic origin, through Li Tong, Luo Congyan, and Yang Shi, Zhu Xi inherited Cheng Yi and Cheng Hao's school of thought and was considered the fourth-generation disciple of the Chengs; however, building shrines for Zhou Dunyi, Cheng Yi and Cheng Hao, Shao Yong, Zhang Zai, and Sima Guang was obviously not out of this academic inheritance. Instead, it was quite a spiritual expression of their identification with Neo-Confucian teachings. It could be said that the ritual was done out of a sense of Daotong. Zhu Xi once said, "The state arranges sacrificial activities in accordance with traditions. In school, we worship sages and teachers. This is to manifest the existence of Daotong and to continue it."[120] Academic inheritance is mainly to organize and sort out the relationship between teachers and students, which is an expression of historical facts, while talking about Daotong was an expression of one's identification with thoughts of a certain school. This identification was based on a kind of value judgment rather than sheer facts.

From "Reconstruction of Lian Xi Study Hall in Jiangzhou" (江州重建濂溪先生书堂记), one can see that Zhu Xi worshiped Zhou Dunyi out of his intention to promote and continue Daotong. He had a strong sense of Daotong and understood well the significance of sacrificing to Zhou. He says,

> The Way of the world has never disappeared. The question is whether it has advocates and inheritors or not. It cannot be changed by human intellect, although it is sometimes seen and sometimes hidden when it is transmitted in the world.

Combined with what Zhu Xi said in his essay titled "Homage to Sages on Construction of Cangzhou Academy" (沧州精舍告先圣文), we can say for sure that

Zhu Xi's worship of Zhou Dunyi, Cheng Yi, Cheng Hao, Shao Yong, Zhang Zai, and Sima Guang in Zhulin (Cangzhou) Academy was the very reflection of his strong sense of Daotong:

> Daotong has been established ever since Fu Xi and Xuan Yuan's time, and it is to the credit of the Great Sage (Confucius) that Daotong was in its greatness. Confucius explained the thoughts of ancient sages and offered guidance to future generations, setting an example for all generations to come. He taught more than 3,000 students in all, and his education was like a timely rain. Among the many students, only Yan Hui and Zeng Shen grasped the essence of Daotong, and later they passed it on to Mencius, who was to further promote it. But after Mencius, Daotong fell into silence for a time. More than a thousand years had passed before Zhou Dunyi, Cheng Hao, and Cheng Yi appeared, who inherited Daotong.[121]

Here, Zhu Xi firmly upheld Daotong, taking the inheritance of Daotong as a yard by which figures of worship, was chosen, treating them as Daotong's successors at its different stages of development in different periods. By so doing, what Zhu Xi wanted to stress was the inheritance of Confucian orthodoxy from generation to generation rather than the academic teacher-student relationship. He hoped to take the academy as a base for advocating and prospering Confucian orthodoxy and the academy sacrificial ritual as a means to promote it. The choice of the figures of worship in the academy was undoubtedly an expression of his attitude toward Daotong. He hoped that Daotong would be deeply rooted in people's hearts through the rituals.

It is worth noting that Zhu Xi, by promoting Daotong through sacrificial activities at Cangzhou Academy, actually claimed a vacancy for himself in the genealogy of Daotong and gave a clue to the orthodox status of his teachings in the Confucian school of the time. This can be clearly seen when he put his teacher Li Tong on the list of the figures of worship. As early as when he retired to Kaoting, Zhu Xi expressed his desire to continue writing and teaching, saying that "Confucian ethics will continue to be taught in Cangzhou Academy."[122] He took it as his duty to inherit and promote Confucian Daotong, declaring,

> I, Zhu Xi, was born ordinary, with scanty knowledge, and have been educated in Confucian doctrine since I was young. I did not have a fixed teacher in my studies but was fortunate enough to learn about Daotong in my later years. I studied hard and kept in mind all the time inheriting and transmitting Daotong and never dared to go against my original intention . . . Daotong is sure to be passed on.[123]

However, at a time when the imperial court's ban on "pseudoscience" was increasingly serious and in a situation where Confucianism was denounced, Zhu Xi could not but hope to find himself by inheriting and diffusing Daotong.

80 *Academy Sacrificial Rituals*

Zhu Xi's way of propagating Daotong through academy sacrificial rituals was recognized by scholars of the Zhu Xi School. They all consciously linked the building of academies, worshipping sages, and the mission to adhere to Daotong. Xiong He, a late Song and early Yuan Neo-Confucian scholar, says in "On Restruction of Tongwen Academy on the Site of Jiangyang Study Hall" (建阳书坊同文书院疏) that the construction of Tongwen Academy was "to honor ancient sages of Daotong and cultivate talents who promote it."[124] In the second year of Duanping in the Song dynasty (1235), a local official surnamed Cao from Pingjiang, Jiangsu Province, "built an ancestral hall and rooms and collected the writings of Lin Bu for students to read."[125] Huqiu Academy was built to worship the Neo-Confucian scholar Yin Tun (Lin Bu). Liu Zai claimed that the building of the ancestral hall in this academy was of great significance. "It is the continuation of the Confucian thoughts of Lin Bu." In the fifth year of Baoyou (1257), Lianxi Academy was built in Hunan Province to worship Zhou Dunyi, "the middle of which is the ancestral hall for worshiping Mr. Zhou, while in the east and west corridors are rooms for worshiping the other sages." The scholar Gao Side spoke highly of Zhou Dunyi, claiming that "he bravely assumed the task of continuing Daotong after it was temporarily halted. He inherited the legacy of Daotong."[126] One can see from the statement that the academy sacrificial ritual, in the view of the scholars of the Zhu Xi School, was closely related to the propagation of Daotong.

This practice of promoting Daotong through worshiping rituals in academies was inherited by future generations and even became a generally accepted consensus at the time. As mentioned earlier, the widespread worship of Zhu Xi in academies in the Yuan dynasty was related to the recognition of Zhu Xi's important position in Daotong.[127] Wang Yun, a scholar of the Yuan dynasty, writes in "On Reconstruction of Academy in Raozhou Lu" (饶州路创建书院疏),

> We decided to select a scenic spot on Raozhou Road and set up an academy there, with an ancestral hall built to worship Zhu Xi. Children of the clan will be taught there so that they can continue the legacy of Daotong (referring to the teachings advocated by Zhu Xi at Kaoting).[128]

Jiang Yi of the Yuan dynasty writes in the preface to "When We Parted: to Superintendent of Kaoting Chen Yanxi" (送考亭山长陈彦西序),

> Through the writings of Zhou Dunyi, Cheng Hao, Cheng Yi, Zhang Zai, Shao Yong, and so on, Daotong can be traced back to Yao, Shun, the Duke of Zhou, and Confucius. It is also possible to explore the views of other scholars by examining these writings, and through cross-reference and mutual stimulation, academic study prospers and gradually comes closer to the essence of Daotong. Hence, the teachings of Yao, Shun, the Duke of Zhou, and Confucius were once again reproduced in Zhu Xi . . . We choose him as the figure of worship so that he may enjoy the same glory as Confucius enjoys in ancestral halls and clan temples. Let there be no end to this veneration for his merits.[129]

During the Hongzhi reign in the Ming dynasty, Bailudong Academy changed the name of Three Sages Temple (Sanxian Temple) into Confucian Ancestral Hall, dedicated to Zhou Dunyi and Zhu Xi. Li Mengyang, in his "Notes on Shrine of Confucian Ancestors of Bailudong Academy" (白鹿洞书院宗儒祠记), expounds on the meaning of the name "Ancestral Confucian" and the status of Zhou Dunyi and Zhu Xi in the Confucian Daotong.

> After the death of Confucius, the tradition of Daotong was cut off. More than a hundred years after the death of Confucius, it was fortunate that Mencius succeeded him. More than a thousand years after the death of Mencius, it was fortunate that Zhou Dunyi and Zhu Xi assumed the responsibility of continuing Daotong. It was only after the death of Zhou and Zhu that people of the world began to clearly understand Confucius and Mencius were great masters of Daotong and then quickly subscribed to the Confucian doctrine with sincerity.
>
> After that, Daotong rose to the highest prestige in the whole country, like Mount Tai in the mountains, the sea in the waters, and the eldest son of the family. Everyone respects them from the bottom of their hearts, and that is why Zhou Dunyi and Zhu Xi are considered great masters of Daotong.[130]

Later, Lu Jiuyuan was added to the list of figures of worship in Confucian Ancestral Hall beside Zhou Dunyi and Zhu Xi, which was also mainly out of consideration for the continuation of Daotong. "The three sages of the Song dynasty are the proper lineage of Daotong and used to conduct lecturing activities in the cave (Bailudong Academy), acting as role models for all generations."[131] In the 31st year of Kangxi in the Qing dynasty (1692), Wang Jinzheng states more clearly in "On Homage to Zhu Xi in Huangu Academy" (还古书院祀朱文公议), "The Academy sacrifices to these great sages who have passed on the Confucian teachings just in order to further confirm the status of Daotong."[132] "Zhu Xi should be worshiped in all places of teaching to strengthen his prestige as a great master of Daotong." Ziyang Academy of Hankou was built in the 60th year of Kangxi (1721) mainly for the purpose of worshiping Zhu Xi and disseminating Daotong.[133] In "Rituals" (祀典), Vol. 4 of *Annals of Huangu Academy* (还古书院志), compiled in the early years of the Qianlong reign, it is stated that "the first thing to do when establishing an academy is to sacrifice to ancient sages. The reason we chose Confucius and Zhu Xi as figures of worship is just to show our respect for Daotong."[134]

Although many scholars over the past dynasties have viewed academy sacrificial activities as a means of "honoring and clarifying the lineage of Daotong," their understanding of the content of Daotong quite differs. Connected with this divergence were different views on the genealogy of Daotong by scholars of different schools. In the case of the academy rituals, the differences were demonstrated as the different figures that scholars of different schools chose to worship. In other words, the choice of different figures of worship reflected the different understanding of Daotong by the worshiper.

82 *Academy Sacrificial Rituals*

As mentioned earlier, Zhu Xi took upon himself the responsibility of continuing and disseminating Daotong. After Zhu Xi's death, his position in Daotong was determined and affirmed by his disciples and later scholars. Huang Gan, a follower of the Zhu Xi School, says in "Biography of Zhu Xi" (行状), an essay written in memory of Zhu Xi,

> I think the continuation of Daotong needs to be undertaken by a special person. Since the Zhou dynasty, there were few people who assumed the responsibility of inheriting and disseminating Daotong and even fewer who could make Daotong understandable to the public . . . Zhu Xi just appeared in time. He made Daotong, which had been transmitted from sage to sage since the Zhou dynasty, at once clear up, just like the sun clearing the clouds and shining on the earth.[135]

In the first month of the first year of Chunyou (1241), Emperor Lizong of the Song dynasty issued an edict praising Zhu Xi for making "Daotong clearer and more explicit." He ordered Zhu Xi's shrine to be placed for worship side by side with those of Zhou Dunyi, Zhang Zai, Cheng Yi, and Cheng Hao in Confucian temples. Therefore, in this case, if we say Huang Gan's "Xing zhuang" (行状) was nothing but a personal recognition of Zhu Xi's role in "inheriting and disseminating Daotong" by his disciples, then the edict issued by the Lizong Emperor was no other than an official affirmation of Zhu Xi's high status in Daotong.

Since then, Zhu Xi was held in higher esteem. According to Xiong He, a scholar of the late Song dynasty, "for the 1,500 years after Confucius and Mencius, Confucian Daotong had never been revered as much as it was during Zhu Xi's time."[136]; "There is no one who does not respect Confucianism throughout the country and whoever has eyes and ears knows the existence of Daotong . . . . Wherever boats and chariots can reach, there are books on Confucianism."[137] In the second year of Renzong of the Yuan dynasty (1313), Zhu Xi's annotations to *Four Books* (四书) were set as the main content of the imperial examination. "Zhu Xi's theory is popularized and highly respected. All lectures must be based on his discourses, and all learning originates from his writings."[138] "The various writings of Zhu Xi were determined by the state as guidelines that learners must respect, and no one dared to raise any doubts."[139] This was a sign that Zhu Xi's studies earned an official academic position and that his position as a successor of Daotong was even more secure. At the same time, Tuotuo (a Yuan dynasty historian) and others compiled *History of Song* (宋史) and *Neo-Confucian Scholars* (道学传), setting Xi, Zhou Dunyi, Cheng Hao, and Cheng Yi as the core figures of Daotong in the Song dynasty. This move further enhanced Zhu Xi's status in the evolution of Daotong from a historical perspective. When talking about Zhu Xi's position, Song Lian, a scholar of the Yuan dynasty, points out,

> Since the death of Mencius, the lineage of Daotong had been no longer clear until Lian (Zhou Dunyi), Luo (Cheng Hao, Cheng Yi), Guan (Zhang Zai), and Min (Zhu Xi) were born, and then Daotong was renewed. Therefore, Zhu

Xi's appearance was just like a bright sun rising all of a sudden in the sky, making Daotong shine again. The four had all made great contributions in diffusing Daotong, among whom Zhu Xi was the most eminent, of course.[140]

From these words, one can see that Song Lian's resect for Zhu Xi was shown between the lines.

In the 13th year of the Yongle reign in the Ming dynasty (1415), *Complete Works of Four Books* (四书大全), *Complete Collection of the Five Classics* (五经大全), and *Complete Collection on Neo-Confucian Teachings* (性理大全) were compiled under the auspices of the government. These three books were much influenced by Zhu Xi's teachings,[141] and *Complete Works of Four Books* (四书大全) is even a similar version of Zhu Xi's *Interlinear Analysis of and Collected Commentaries on the Four Books* (四书集注). The three collections "traced back to the origin of Confucianism and converged multiple doctrines in one system, sweeping away the sluggishness of the academic field," which further established Zhu Xi's position in the evolution of Daotong from the aspect of canonical works of the Confucian culture. Later in the Qing dynasty, the Kangxi Emperor issued an edict requiring Zhu Xi to be worshiped as one of the Ten Philosophers in Confucian temples, and meanwhile, he ordered Li Guangdi to compile *Complete Collection of Zhu Xi* (朱子全书) and *A Compendium on Neo-Confucian Teachings* (性理精义), both of which were asked to be issued nationwide. In the prefaces to the two books, Kangxi highly praised Zhu Xi for his "bringing thousands of theories together into a large theoretical system, continuing the once-interrupted Confucian doctrine and establishing norms and principles which can be used for tens of thousands of years." Zhu Xi's position in Daotong peaked.

The affirmation of Zhu Xi's position in Confucian Daotong was directly reflected in the sacrificial rituals of the academy in different periods. This reflection was consistent with the changes in his status in Daotong. Soon after he died, he was enshrined and worshiped in quite a few academies. For example, in the fifth year after his death (in 1205), Zhu Xi was worshiped in the lecture hall of Bailudong Academy together with Zhou Dunyi, Cheng Hao, and Cheng Yi. As Fang Yanshou pointed out in *Textual Research on Academies Related to Zhu Xi and His Disciples* (朱熹书院与门人考), there had already been large numbers of academies sacrificing to Zhu Xi by the end of the Song dynasty.[142] He argued further that, especially after Zhu Xi was posthumously ennobled as the Duke of Huiguo in the late Southern Song dynasty and thus enjoyed as much esteem as Zhou, Zhang, Cheng Hao, and Cheng Yi, there were even more academies offering sacrifices to Zhu Xi.[143]

After the Song dynasty, it became more common to worship Zhu Xi in academies. Xu Zi, when studying the sacrificial rituals of the Yuan dynasty, said that Zhu Xi was worshiped in many academies. Whether it was at his birthplace, the place where he once worked, or where he had taught, there were always academies dedicated to him. Even academies with no direct relationship with him offered sacrifices to him out of respect for his teachings. Besides, there were also some other academies that worshiped his disciples or mentors. All in all, it

84 *Academy Sacrificial Rituals*

became a general trend to pay tribute to Zhu Xi in most academies of the time. In "Reconstruction of Zhu Xi Memorial Hall in Kaoting Academy" (考亭书院重建朱文公祠堂制), Yu Ji says,

> Among the many academies that have been set up to provide places of learning for students, most of them were established under the influence of Zhu Xi, while some others were built for his mentors, friends, and disciples. For example, in the county of Jianning alone, there are as many as seven academies, all of which are set up where Zhu Xi had once been.[144]

In this view, it is safe to say that Zhu Xi and his followers were the key figures of worship in academies in the Yuan dynasty.[145]

Zhu Xi's position became increasingly prominent in the sacrificial rituals held in academies of the Ming dynasty. For example, when Shigu Academy (located in Hengxiang) was just completed, a large hall was reserved to offer sacrifice to Confucius, Yan, Zeng, Si, and Mencius, while another one behind it was for the worship to Han Yu and Zhang Jingfu. Zhu Xi was not worshiped at all at that time. Actually, he had not been worshiped until the 18th year of Chenghua in the Ming dynasty (1428), when He Xun (local governor) began to "enshrine Zhu Xi, as he had once taught at Hengxiang, in the same ancestral hall as Han and Zhang (Han Changli and Zhang Nanxuan) had been sacrificed." He Xun also set up a three-room building behind the ancestral hall and hung a sign on it that said "Look upward," which meant looking up to upright moral values."[146] Afterward, Zhu Xi not only became one of the worshiped figures, but he also became the core of it. Yuelu Academy had a ceremonial hall dedicated to Confucius and his disciples in the Yuan dynasty and another one to Zhang Shi, Zhu Xi, Zhou Shi, and Liu Gong. At that time, Zhu Xi was only among the many figures enshrined. However, after the Ming dynasty, Yuelu Academy set up Chongdao Ancestral Hall, sacrificing exclusively to Zhu Xi and Zhang Shi. In the 38th year of Jiajing (1559), a plaque saying "Successor of Daotong" was hung at the front of Chongdao Ancestral Hall gate, and in the 18th year of Wanli (1590), the plaque was changed to say "Authentic Successor of Daotong." These initiatives were just an expression of Zhu Xi's increasing position in worship rituals held in Yuelu Academy. In Bailudong Academy, Zhu Xi was worshiped together with Zhou Dunyi, Cheng Hao, and Cheng Yi during the reign of Kaixi of the Song dynasty; during the reign of Zhengtong of the Ming dynasty, Zhu Xi was enshrined in Three-Sage Temple together with Li Binke and Zhou Dunyi; during the Hongzhi reign of the Ming dynasty, Li Binke was moved away from Three-Sage Temple, and only Zhou Dunyi and Zhu Xi were left for worship, but later another 14 people who once traveled with Zhu Xi were added to the sacrificial list.[147] Hence, Zhu Xi has become a central character in the worship rituals at Bailudong Academy.

Zhu Xi continued to occupy a central position in academy worship ceremonies in the Qing dynasty. During the reign of Kangxi, some scholars even believed that it was a must to worship him in academies. In "On Homage to Zhu Xi in Huangu Academy" (还古书院祀朱文公议), Wang Jinzheng says,

Zhu Xi should be worshiped in all places where knowledge is imparted, and only by doing so can the authentic transmission of Daotong be established. The scholars nowadays must respect Zhu Xi, which is actually an expression of their genuine reverence for Confucius. It is quite true that Confucius integrated the teachings of ancient sages while Zhu Xi integrated the teachings of all Confucian scholars. As Confucius was revered in ancient times, so Zhu Xi must now be respected.[148]

At Bailudong Academy, Zhu Xi featured in the ancestral Confucian shrine. During the 48th year of Kangxi (1709), Bailudong Academy built Ziyang Temple dedicated to Zhu Xi, where another 15 figures were also worshiped, including Lin Zezhi, Cai Shen, Huang Gan, and so on.[149] Ziyang Temple carried out special worship rituals for Zhu Xi, and the specifications of these rituals were significantly higher than those held in Ancestral Confucian Temple (Zongru Ci), Sages Temple, and Loyalty Temple. Obviously, as Zhu Xi's status in Daotong rose, his importance in the academy sacrificial rituals also increased considerably.

The importance of Zhu Xi in the sacrificial rituals of the ancient academies just reflected the recognition of his status in the Confucian genealogy. However, it is worth noting that, as discussed earlier, the proposal of the Daotong theory indicates people's careful deliberation on the essence and spiritual core of Confucianism. When scholars of different schools put forward their understanding of Daotong, they specified its connotation based on their own understanding and then picked out what they thought were important figures. Therefore, scholars with different theoretical inclinations and academic interests were often of quite different opinions in their understanding of Daotong. While many Confucians agreed with Zhu Xi's understanding of Daotong and respected him as its successor, many Confucians also put forward different views on it. For example, Lu Jiuyuan, the representative of Xin Xue in the Song dynasty, had a different understanding of Daotong from that of Zhu Xi. In Lu Jiuyuan's view, Mencius was an important figure who inherited the Way from Confucius, Ceng Can, and Kong Ji. At the same time, he believed that "for more than 1,500 years from the time of Mencius to the present, there were many scholars who were renowned for being proficient in Confucianism." Among them, Xun, Yang, Wang, and Han are the best-known. However, theirs is only a "superficial resemblance" rather a real understanding of its essence. "There is no room for any vagueness and ambiguity in the inheritance of orthodoxy from Yao, Shun, Confucius, and Mencius." In this light, there are no significant differences between Lu Jiuyuan and Zhu Xi. However, contrary to Zhu Xi's advocacy of Zhou Dunyi, Cheng Yi, and Cheng Hao as heirs of Daotong, Lu Jiuyuan denied the importance of the Northern Song Neo-Confucianists in Daotong. He argues,

Wise figures such as Zhou Dunyi, Cheng Hao, and Cheng Yi have studied Daotong in great depth, showing extensive research and dedicated aspirations. They were loyal in their practice of Daotong, and this was something that was not found in the Han and Tang dynasties.

86 *Academy Sacrificial Rituals*

These figures have achieved a lot, but they are still far from being comparable with Mencius, Ceng Can, and Kong Ji; thus, they have no qualifications to be the inheritors of Daotong. Meanwhile, he regarded himself as a sage and took it as his mission to inherit and pass on the teachings of Confucius and Mencius.

> Daotong is about to decline. This trend has already started from the time of Confucius and Mencius. We can do nothing to change the laws of nature. Nevertheless, would a sage or a wise man give up his career and aspirations due to the declining moral order of that time?[150]

In Lu Jiuyuan's view, he had already surpassed the Confucian scholars of the Han, Tang, and Northern Song dynasties and had inherited the untold teachings that was gone for 1,500 years. "I might be thinking too highly of myself, but despite my limited wisdom, I shall be the first one to make Daotong clear again since the time of Mencius."[151]

Lu Jiuyuan was very influential in the ideological and academic circles of the mid–Southern Song dynasty. His ideological scholarship attracted many students and was widely disseminated. His school of thought occupied almost the same position as Zhu Xi's. In the process of disseminating his thoughts and academic ideas, Lu Jiuyuan's theory won great popularity. Some disciples, out of sectarian awareness or the need to build school lineages, even promoted Lu's views through various methods in an attempt to establish Lu Jiuyuan's position in the Confucian lineage. Under such circumstances, the worship rituals in academies naturally became an effective way for scholars from the Lu school to promote Xin Xue.

Lu Jiuyuan had once started to lecture in the reign of Qiandao at Huetang, and in the Chunxi period, he went up to Guixi to lecture at Yingtian Mountain. Later on, his disciples built a temple there, and due to the mountain's resemblance to an elephant, it was later renamed Xiangshan (Elephant Mountain). Lu Jiuyuan's teaching activities in Xiangshan Academy had a tremendous impact. Many scholars and students came from all over the nation, brought their food supplies, built facilities at the mountain, and lived together. They discussed and exchanged views, making Xiangshan Academy the base of academic research for Xin Xue. After Lu Jiuyuan's death, Xiangshan Academy continued to serve as the base camp of Xin Xue, attracting and gathering scholars from all over. At the same time, Xiangshan Academy also began to worship Lu Jiuyuan to unveil the quintessence of the School of Mind; thus, "after the death of Mr. Wen'an (Lu Jiuyuan), scholars respected him and erected an ancestral hall to worship him." In the second year of Qingyuan (1196), Liu Qihui, the governor of Guixi County, set up a shrine in Xiangshan Academy and paid tribute to Lu Jiuyuan in spring and autumn. In the third year of Shaoding (1230), Zhao Yanxian, an official of Jiangdong, rebuilt Xiangshan Academy and worshiped Lu too.[152] In the fourth year of Shaoding, Yuan Fu, an official of Jiangdong, asked the court to move the academy to the bottom of Sanfeng Mountain and got the name "Xiangshan Academy" from the imperial court. And Lu Jiuzhou, Lu Jiushao, Lu Jiuling, Yang Jian, and Yuan

Xie were worshiped there ever since. In the sixth year of Shaoding, the governor of Jinxi built Huaitang Academy for the worship of Lu Jiuyuan and Lu Jiuling. In "Xiangshan shuyuan ji" (象山书院记), Yuan Fu talks about Lu Jiuyuan's contribution to the dissemination of Confucianism and the purpose of establishing academies and temples:

> Mr. Lu Jiuyuan of Xiangshan founded the theory of Mind, which has made a great contribution to the country's education. Intellectuals all over the world would like to see his demeanor in person, learn from him, and seek the source of his wisdom so that they may carry forward his doctrine.
>
> I cannot help but lament that the evils of the secular world are becoming increasingly obvious, and the students haven't got the essence of the Way. Those who follow what is written think that they are right, and those who indulge in pointless debates think they are smart. The two kinds of inadequate learning tendencies are mixed, making the inheritance and passing on of the Way increasingly ambiguous. The establishment of the academy is just to clarify the Way.[153]

In an essay titled "Homage to Lu Xiangshan" (祭陆象山先生文), Yuan Fu writes, "Mr. Lu's theories are a legacy of Mencius, so much so that, when the academy was first established, he personally participated in the foundation-laying ceremony."[154] It can be seen that the worship of Lu Jiuyuan in academies was a decisive act toward Daotong. Scholars then sought to proclaim Lu Jiuyuan's philosophies as the essential and right doctrine of Daotong and tried to establish him as a direct successor of Mencius and heir to Confucianism.

After Lu Jiuyuan, there were also some representatives of Xin Xue among his disciples who became figures of worship in the academy. Yang Jian, for example, was an influential scholar who inherited and spread Lu's school of thought. He was called "Lu's meritorious servant" by Quan Zuwang. After the death of Yang Jian, "the officials of Yili were the first to start building ancestral shrines on the shores of lakes for his worship."[155] After that, they "created some other sacred buildings to worship him." During the ninth year of Xianchun (1273), Wen Jiweng explained the significance of this move mainly from the perspective of propagating the Way in "Records of Cihu Academy" (慈湖书院记), saying,

> Mr. Cihu, who is also known as Yang Wenyuan, practices a doctrine that is a part of Xin Xue . . . The essence of Mind (Xin "心") is the root of everything. This Mind is the foundation of Taiji and Huang Ji as well as the bases of Yao's and Shun's great causes. King Yu based his conscientious work on this Mind, as did King Tang, King Wen of Zhou, King Wu of Zhou, the Duke of Zhou, Confucius, and Mencius. Zeng Zi and Zi Si did so as well."[156]

88 *Academy Sacrificial Rituals*

This concretized Lu Jiuling's theory that "the essence of what is passed down by ancient sages is the mind." He believed that the mind is what sages passed on to the later generations. So it was evident here that Yang Jian was regarded as the heir of Daotong, who had grasped and faithfully practiced the gist of Xin Xue.

By the Ming dynasty, Yangmingism (Wang Yangming's Theory of Mind) emerged. In the academic environment where Zhu Xi's school of thought dominated, Yangming's theory "set up another set of teachings, obviously contrary to Zhu Xi's theoretical doctrine." However, it was quite compatible with Lu Jiuyuan's theory in terms of spirituality and methodology, so later scholars called it Lu-Wang Xin Xue. Followers of Yangmingism "are all over the world, and Yangmingism will continue beyond centuries."[157] It is thus clear that Yangmingism had a tremendous impact on the ideological and academic circles at that time.

Scholars of Xin Xue, represented by Wang Yangming, gave much importance to the academy and used it as an important base for the creation and dissemination of their thoughts.

The establishment, development, and widespread dissemination of the Yangming School were closely related to the academy lecture activities of Wang Yangming and his disciples. It is said that "there are 72 Yangming academies in the whole world, and six of them are in central Zhejiang."[158] After the death of Wang Yangming, followers of the Yangming School continued to use academies as their base for academic development and dissemination, and lectures in academies flourished. Wang Yangming was, therefore, worshiped in many academies. According to "The Annals" (年谱) in Appendix 1 to *The Complete Works of Wang Yangming* (王阳明全集卷·年谱附录一), during the reign of Jiajing (1522–1566), although the Yangming School was still regarded as "pseudoscience" by the imperial court and was cracked down on, many scholars and Yangming's followers continued to build academies to worship him.

For example, in the ninth year of Jiajing, Xue Kan, one of the followers, built an academy in Tianzhen Mountain to worship Yangming. In the first month of the 13th year of Jiajing, another follower named, Zou Shouyi, built Fugu Academy in Anfu to worship Yangming; in November of the 16th year of Jiajing, Xue Kan (also a follower) built an academy in Wenhu, Xiushui County, under the auspices of a local official, Shen Mi, to worship Yangming; in the 19th year of Jiajing, Zhou Tong, Ying Dian, and some others, built an academy in Shouyan, Yongkang County, to worship Yangming; in the 21st year of Jiajing, Fan Yinnian (a follower) built the Hunyuan Academy in Qingtian County to worship Yangming; in the 23rd year of Jiajing, Xu Shan (a follower) built Huxi Academy in Chenzhou to commemorate Yangming; in August of the 27th year of Jiajing, scholars from Wan'an County jointly built Yunxing Academy to pay tribute to Yangming; in September, Chen Dalun built the Mingjing Academy in Shaozhou in memory of him. In addition to Yangming's followers, many government officials also joined in the efforts of worshiping him. In the first month of the 29th year of Jiajing, the head of the Ministry of Personnel built Jiayi Academy in Liyang for Yangming's worship; in the 30th year of Jiajing, Zhao Jin, an imperial censor of Guizhou, built Yangming Temple for Yangming's worship in Longgang Academy of Guiyang; in the 33rd year of Jiajing, another imperial censor built Shuixi Academy to sacrifice to Yangming; in August of the 42nd year of Jiajing, Luo Rufang, a local official, established Zhixue Academy in Xuancheng to pay tribute to Yangming.[159] In short, a quite large number of disciples and government officials who were followers of his doctrine built various temples and academies to worship Wang Yangming throughout the reign of Jiajing.

The worship of Yangming was not only an expression of admiration for Xin Xue but also an affirmation of Yangming as the successor to the Confucian Daotong. Shortly after Yangming's death in November of the seventh year of Jiajing (1528)—in fact, shortly after Wang Yangming's death in November 1528—"there had been different opinions among the court, so various graces such as titles, gifts, and awards were no longer practiced, and an imperial decree was issued to ban it as pseudoscience." Under such circumstances, there were still scholars who stood out to defend Wang Yangming, and Huang Wan was just one of them. He spoke highly of Yangming, saying that Wang Yangming was "the true legacy of Confucianism."[160] This can represent the awareness of some scholars at that time about the higher status of Wang Yangming among the Confucianists and the sacrificial rituals to Yangming practiced in academies during the Jiajing period are just a good expression of this awareness. In May of the first year of Longqing (1567), after Muzong of the Ming dynasty succeeded to the throne, he granted Wang Yangming the posthumous title of Marquis Wencheng. In the imperial edict, Wang Yangming was praised for his "dedication to inheriting the Way of Yao and Confucius, explaining it in simple terms, and advocating the teachings of Zhou Dunyi, Cheng Hao, and Cheng Yi for the benefit of later learners."[161] This represented the supreme rulers' approval of Wang Yangming's position in Daotong, as well as an acknowledgment of the efforts of Yangming's disciples and later scholars in the Jiajing years to enhance Wang Yangming's prestige in Daotong.

Since then, the intention to honor Daotong became more pronounced when Wang Yangming was worshiped in academies, which could be seen quite clearly from the process of the establishment of Yaojiang Academy. In the 12th year of Chongzhen (1639), Shen Guomo, Shi Xiaoxian, and some others built Yaojiang Academy to worship Wang Yangming. The portrait of Confucius was originally hung high up on the front wall of the sacrificial hall. But later, that of the great master of the Yaojiang School (referring to Wang Yangming) occupied the central position, and the ritual of Shidian was practiced to pay tribute to him both in spring and autumn.[162] The reason for this change is that, in their view,

> during the reign of Zhengde and that of Jiajing, Wang Yangming occupied a significant position in Daotong. While superficially, Wang's transmission of Daotong is similar to that of Mencius and Cheng Mingdao, it is often closer to that of Yi Yin in terms of his meritorious service to the country, his seclusive lifestyle, and his understanding of the wishes of the ancestors.[163]

In other words, Yaojiang Academy's tribute to Wang Yangming was based on the recognition of Wang's position in the process of passing on the Confucian

90 *Academy Sacrificial Rituals*

Daotong. Similar expressions can be found repeatedly in the various recording texts of Yaojiang Academy.

> The succession of Daotong relies on the sages, the most outstanding of whom are Wang Yangming, Zhu Xi, Cheng Hao, Cheng Yi, Confucius, Yan Hui, Ceng Can, and Mencius. Wang Yangming was a sage of previous generations of the Yao Jiang School, so there are always academies dedicated exclusively to him.[164]
>
> There is no one in the world who is as good at learning as Mr. Yang, and there is no one who is as good at educating as Mr. Yang. As the doctrine of Cheng Yi, Cheng Hao, and Zhu Xi was once interrupted, he tried to save it and worked hard to learn from the former sages. No one is as wise as Mr. Yang, and he is the very person who has to be regarded as a representative of Confucianism.[165]
>
> Mr. Zhu Xi studied Confucian doctrines, but his talent was not up to the level of Confucius, so his learning was only limited to the level of Mr. Cheng. That is why his achievements are no greater than that of Mr. Cheng, let alone reach the level of Confucius. Mr. Wencheng (Wang Yangming) learned from Mencius, and as his talent is similar to Mencius, he thus can achieve achievements greater than Yi Yin.[166]

In their opinion, Wang Yangming's "moral cultivation and achievements were close to those of Mencius and higher than those of Yiyin, and therefore, he was justifiably the successor of the Confucian Daotong after Confucius, Yan Hui, Ceng Can, and Mencius."[167] Obviously, the worship of Wang Yangming in Yaojiang Academy was, to a large extent, a concretization of the recognition of Wang Yangming's status as the inheritor of the Confucian Daotong.

It was precisely because the sacrificial rituals held in academies were closely related to the promotion of Daotong that academies always took into careful consideration their influence on the propagation of Daotong when choosing figures of worship. For example, during the Jingding reign in the Song dynasty, Xuancheng Academy was established to enshrine Zhang Shi and Lü Zuqian. The academy was later destroyed by fire during the Song and Yuan dynasties and remained utterly dilapidated until a winter of the Yuan dynasty in the third year of Zhizheng (1343), when the constitutional envoy "inspected the academy and found that the worship to Mr. Zhang and Lü was not up to standard." He hence ordered it be rebuilt. In "Restoration of Xuancheng Academy" (重修宣成书院记), Guangzu mentions the reasons Zhang and Lü were determined as the idols for worship:

> I heard that after the death of Mencius, Daotong would no longer be passed on. God takes special care of Confucianism. Masters of Confucianism, such as Lian, Luo Zhou Dunyi, Cheng Hao, and Cheng Yi, emerged, who took great pains to clarify the meaning of the Confucian doctrine. Later, Master Zhu Xi consolidated what his predecessors achieved, and still later, Zhang

and Lü further enriched it. With the efforts of Zhang and Lü, the gist of the Six Classics and the Four Books was ultimately unveiled and known to the public. Their achievements are really marvelous! People with great insights and brilliant wisdom all showed respect and admiration for the two gentlemen. Why is that so? Because they played an important role in the transmission of Confucianism.[168]

Although Zhang Shi and Lü Zuqian were not considered to be successors to Daotong, they were credited with the transmission of Daotong because of their academic connection with Zhu Xi, the core figure in the lineage of Neo-Confucianism. This kind of academic connection showed itself as mutual inspiration, reference, integration, absorption, and so on. From the perspective of academic development, the development of Zhu Xi's school of thought could not have been possible without the help of Zhang Shi and Lü Zuqian. Of course, Zhang and Lü became the figures of academy worship mainly because they had once aided Zhu Xi in consolidating and promoting Confucianism. To put it simply, they were worshiped undoubtedly out of a sense of Daotong.

Take Wei Liaoweng as another example, who was worshiped in *Records of Heshan Academy* (鹤山书院记). Wei Liaoweng was one of the representative figures of Neo-Confucianism in the late Southern Song dynasty. Alongside Zhen Dexiu and other scholars, he actively promoted and spread Neo-Confucianism, expanded its influence, and contributed greatly to the rise of Neo-Confucianism and the improvement of its social status in the late Southern Song dynasty. In the first year of Zhishun in the Yuan dynasty, Wei Qi, the great-grandson of Wei Liaoweng, requested the imperial court to set up a shrine in Wei Liaoweng's former residence in Wuzhong. The request was approved by the emperor, and Yu Jifeng, a renowned scholar at that time, was ordered to inscribe four Chinese characters, "Heshan Shuyuan" (which means "Heshan Academy"), on its plaque. In "Heshan Shuyuan Ji" ("Records of Heshan Academy"), Yu Ji elaborated on the reasons for the establishment of the shrine. He first argued for the true existence of the Confucian Daotong and then, on this basis, affirmed the substantial contribution Wei Liaoweng made in advocating the teachings of Cheng and Zhu and in ensuring the continuity of the Confucian Daotong at a time when the Confucian Way was obscure, and the Confucian doctrine was being banned. This dedication itself exuded a strong sense of Daotong.

As the sacrificial rituals held in academies were often associated with respect for Daotong, some scholars even projected such inclinations on certain idols of worship who were not originally identified with advocating Daotong. For example, Yang Shi, a Neo-Confucian scholar during the reign of Zhenghe Confucianism, lived in Wuxi, Jiangsu, where he had gathered disciples to teach for 18 years. "After his death, the respect and reverence that scholars had for him did not die away, so an ancestral hall was established there to worship him." Donglin Academy was thus built. When the academy first worshiped Yang Shi, it was more of a memorial. There was no obvious hint to suggest that the worship was conducted to disseminate Confucianism. However, after the rise and fall of academies, in

92 *Academy Sacrificial Rituals*

the 32nd year of Wanli in the Ming dynasty (1604), when Gu Xiancheng and some others rebuilt academies, a shrine named Daonan Temple was built on the left side of the courtyard to worship Yang. In the 39th year of Wanli (1611), Fang Xuejian wrote about the worship of Yang at Donglin Academy from the perspective of spreading Confucianism in "Notes on Reconstruction of Daonan Memorial Hall in Donglin Academy" (重建东林书院道南祠记), saying that Yang Shi's theory revealed the essence of Confucianism, and it played a transitional role in the transmission of Daotong and acted as a bridge between Zhou Dunyi, Cheng Hao, and Zhu Xi. In Fang Xuejian's view, people talked more about Yang Shi's political affairs and papers but "did not know his Confucian thoughts were also forceful enough." In this way, Fang propagated Confucianism through his morally rich interpretation of the event of consecrating Yang Shi in the academy, making Daonan Temple more of a place that embodies the Confucian Daotong.

Academy Sacrifice and Shift of Learning Mindset

Academy sacrificial rituals, to some extent, reflect a certain sense of Daotong and the then prevailing academic trends. The selection of different worshiped figures suggested different academic pursuits of scholars who came from different schools and had different academic preferences. Through a diachronic investigation of figures worshiped by academies in different periods, it is possible to understand the change in academic style and the shift in learning mindset. Hu Shi (1891–1962) once observed, "The spirits of an era can be best represented by the figures worshiped in academies of that time."[169]

For a long period of time, worships in academies followed systems of government schools that took Confucius and his disciples as the main worshiped figures. For example, in the Northern Song dynasty (960–1127), when Li Yunze (953–1028) rebuilt Yuelu Academy in the second year of the Xianping reign (999), he "built statues for the ten most outstanding disciples and the 72 virtuous disciples of Confucius";[170] when Bailudong Academy was renovated in the fifth year of the Xianping reign (1002), the academy also "built statues for the 10 most outstanding disciples of Confucius."[171] In the Southern Song dynasty (1127–1279), Lianxi Academy of Jiangzhou Prefecture, which was built in the third year of the Chunxi reign (1176), worshiped Zhou Dunyi (1017–1073), the earliest founder of Neo-Confucianism;[172] but Bailudong Academy, which was renovated under the guidance of Zhu Xi (1130–1200) in the eighth year of the Chunxi reign (1181), still only worshiped Confucius and his disciples.[173] This shows that during this period of time, academies mainly worshiped Confucius and other pre-Qin Confucian masters and venerated Confucius as the founder and symbol of Confucianism. Generations of Confucian scholars, different in research methods, theoretical perspectives, and academic viewpoints, though, all considered Confucius as their common symbol. It can be seen that until the early Southern Song dynasty, Confucian schools' distinctions in learning approaches, purposes, and academic pursuits among different Confucian schools were not manifested in academy sacrificial rituals. During that period of time, academies had not yet highlighted and marked their own preferences in academic interests and methods of learning through worship.

Such a situation started changing in the late Southern Song dynasty. As mentioned previously, in the sacrificial ceremony held by Zhu Xi in Zhulin Academy in the fifth year of the Shaoxi reign (1194), the worshiped figures included not only Confucius (551–479 bc), Yan Hui (521–481 bc), Zeng Shen (505–435 bc), Kong Ji (483–402 bc), and Mencius (371–289 bc) but also several Song dynasty pioneers of Neo-Confucianism, such as Zhou Dunyi (1017–1073), Cheng Yi (1033–1107), Cheng Hao (1032–1085), Shao Yong (1012–1077), Sima Guang (1019–1086), Zhang Zai (1020–1077), and Li Dong (1093–1163), Zhu Xi's teacher. Although Zhu Xi's intention was to promote Confucianism and highlight the concept of Confucian Daotong through this sacrificial ritual, the choice of worshiped figures in Zhulin Academy actually greatly facilitated our understanding of academic trends of academies at that time. Since the middle of the Northern Song dynasty, Confucian scholars such as Zhou Dunyi, Ercheng, and Zhang Zai had been committed to reviving Confucianism in view of the decline of it and the flourishing of Buddhism and Taoism since the Han and Tang dynasties. They renewed their approaches to Confucianism, abandoning the study of exegesis since the Han and Tang dynasties and replacing them with Neo-Confucian studies featuring philosophical thinking. At the same time, by absorbing theoretical achievements of Buddhism and Taoism and discussing theoretical issues such as destiny, disposition, rationalism, and so on, they constructed an ideological system of Neo-Confucianism that was theoretically different from traditions. From its inception to the mid–Southern Song dynasty, Neo-Confucianism remained to be a non-official Confucian school that had limited influences and suffered repeated setbacks and even bans in the process of its spreading, but its innate vitality ensured its steady development and helped it to become increasingly influential. The formation and establishment of Zhu Xi's system of doctrines, which is both extensive and refined, was inseparable from the succession and development of academic achievements of Neo-Confucian predecessors in the middle of the Northern Song dynasty. Zhou Dunyi, Ercheng, Shao Yong, Zhang Zai, Sima Guang, Li Dong, and so on were all representative figures that influenced the rise and growth of Zhu Xi's theory, though they lived in different eras and proposed distinctive viewpoints. Compared with traditional Confucian scholars, they represent a new academic paradigm featuring the exploration of morality, human nature, and law of the objective world and the study of the interactions among these three factors. Worships of these scholars in academies show that Neo-Confucian theory that explores the principles of heaven and life has been much revered and pursued by many scholars.

As mentioned earlier, shortly after his death, Zhu Xi became the key figure worshiped by academies. From the perspective of ideological and academic development, Zhu Xi epitomized Neo-Confucianism in the Song dynasty. It was through Zhu Xi's efforts that the theoretical system of Neo-Confucianism matured and was widely accepted by many scholars at that time. Besides, as Zhu Xi attached great importance to education, he built schools and academies, gave lectures

94 *Academy Sacrificial Rituals*

wherever he lived, and thus attracted many students, which greatly expanded his academic influence. His theory was once denounced as pseudo-Confucianism and prohibited from spreading, but shortly after his death, he became increasingly respected. Many Confucian scholars even study only Zhu Xi's Neo-Confucianism or Zhu Xue (learning of the Neo-Confucian principles) and reject other Confucian schools. Chen Zhu (1214–1297), a Confucian scholar in the Song dynasty, once commented, "Zhu Xi expounded and exerted himself to the extreme in the work *The Doctrine of the Mean* (中庸), making any efforts of the others unnecessary."[174] Xiong He (1247–1312), a scholar of the Song and Yuan dynasties and a descendant of Zhu Xi, once said of the reverence for Zhu Xue in the academic world at that time, *Four Books* (四书) directly continued the teachings of Confucius, and *The Compendium* (纲目) directly followed the writing style of *The Spring and Autumn Annals* (春秋). Now in the whole world, almost everyone reads Mr. Zhu Xi's books." To conclude, Zhu Xi's thought prevailed at that time, and the numerous memorial rituals dedicated to him revealed the respect of the entire society for his thought and academic achievements.

Of course, Zhu Xi was not the only key figure worshiped in academies in the late Song dynasty and throughout the Yuan dynasty. Some academies also worshiped representative scholars of Xin Xue (School of Mind, 心学), such as Lu Jiuyuan (1139–1192). Lu Jiuyuan and other outstanding scholars of the school were mainly worshiped in Xin Xue academies that these scholars built or in the academies where they once gave lectures, such as the aforementioned Huaitang Academy of Jinxi County, Xiangshan Academy of Guixi City, Donghu Academy (which worshiped Lu Jiuyuan), and Cihu Academy of Cixi County (which worshiped Yang Jian; 1141–1226). These memorial rituals reflected the status and influence of Lu Jiuyuan's Xin Xue. Both Lu Jiuyuan's Lu Xue (the Lu School) and Zhu Xi's Zhu Xue (the Zhu School) belonged to Neo-Confucianism theories, but there were huge differences in their research methods and ontology theory. Lu Jiuyuan put forward the ontological thought: since xin (mind) creates the world, which means the world where human being lives and everything in it are created by the human mind, it is essential to clear your mind, highlight morality, and respect your heart. This thought quite differs from Zhu Xi's thought that knowledge is acquired through experience and studies. In the second year of the Chunxi reign of the Southern Song dynasty (1175), Zhu and Lu had a heated debate over this disparity when they met at Goose Lake in Lingshan, Xinshou, but ended with disagreement. In the following years, the two battled back and forth through letters to discuss and debate but never reached agreement. The scholar Zhu Hengdao, who had participated in the meeting of Goose Lake, commented on the meeting of Goose Lake in a letter to a friend,

> In the debate of Goose Lake discussing the issue of how to educate people, Zhu Xi advocates more reading and more observation of things based on experience, analysis, synthesis, and induction before coming to a conclusion. Lu's brothers believe that if the mind is clear, then all things will be naturally transparent. You do not have to read more and be busy examining external

things. Respecting virtue and nourishing the heart and mind are the most important things as opposed to doing more reading and poor reasoning work. Zhu Xi thinks that the Lu brothers' education methods are too crude, but the Lu brothers refute that Zhu Xi's education is not systematic. Thus, there is a wide gap between the two sides.[175]

As both Zhu Xi and Lu Jiuyuan were influential figures in the academic circle at that time, their students and inheritors gradually set up academic divergences and firmly stuck to their own views, gradually forming two opposite Confucian schools. In the academic confrontation between the two schools of thought, when the influence and power of Lu were inferior to that of Zhu, academies actually functioned as an academic base to inherit the path of Lu's scholarship. They held memorial activities for Lu Jiuyuan to manifest their own academic purposes and tendencies. Thus, the figure of worship is both a sign of academic style and a banner to attract scholars. For example, in the ninth year of the Xianchun reign of the Southern Song dynasty (1273), in his book *Records of Cihu Academy* (慈湖书院记), Wen Jiweng (12th cent.) explains the significance and purpose of the academy's memorial rituals for Yang Jian:

> The doctrine of Yang Wenyuan Gong (Yang Jian) of Cihu is a kind of Xin Xue. What he considers to be the most important in learning is the mind. The highest state of mind is called a sage. If one cannot reach the degree of saintliness, one is not learning properly; if one cannot learn about the cultivation of the mind, one is not learning deeply. One's inner emptiness will have no limitations; the mind can immediately reach beyond the universe thousands of generations ago or millions of years later, and all can be unified by the mind. If one does not know the mind, then it will be meaningless to learn.

Here, the Xin Xue ideology was strongly advocated, which stressed the importance of understanding "Xin" (Mind) and studying through "Xin."

Academies worshiping Zhu Xi or Lu Jiuyuan demonstrated two different and mutually exclusive Confucian thoughts, but there were still some other academies worshiping both Zhu Xi and Lu Jiuyuan. Such academies include the Four Gentlemen Memorial Hall dedicated to Zhu Xi, Lü Zuqian, Lu Jiuyuan, and Lu Jiuling, which was built by Xinzhou Prefecture governor Yang Ruli and renamed Wenzong Academy later in the tenth year of the Chunyou reign (1250);[176] Daoyi Academy, which was built during the early years of the Yuan dynasty by Cheng Shaokai (1212–1281), first a follower of Lu Jiuyuan, but later hoped to combine the thoughts of Zhu Xi and Lu Jiuyuan;[177] and Bailudong Academy, which worshiped Zhou Dunyi, Zhu Xi, and Lu Jiuyuan during the Ming dynasty. These academies reflected a historical fact that the academic circle gradually agreed on a compromise between Zhu Xi's and Lu Jiuyuan's thoughts: Zhu Xi and Lu Jiuyuan both upheld the Confucian principles and ideology, which had been passed down from Confucius and Mencius; there was no fundamental difference in their theories, as they were based on the same ethical value orientation, and differed only

96 *Academy Sacrificial Rituals*

in study and research methods. The debates between these two schools showed that both sides had theoretical strengths and advantages and that both of them had shortcomings and defects. On this basis, some scholars attempted to integrate the two theories by combining their strengths and avoiding their weaknesses, thus giving rise to the tendency to harmonize Zhu and Lu's theories. In the fourth year of Shaoding of the Southern Song dynasty (ad 1231), Yuan Fu, a famous scholar who was a judge and a provincial magistrate in Jiangdong with a deep connection with the School of Mind, built Xiangshan Academy in Guixi, advocating that "the method that Mr. Wang Yangming used in doing scholarship which focuses on concentration and revelation of the original mind is the most important part of his contribution."[178] It is apparent to see that Yuan Fu wanted to make Xiangshan Academy the center for the development and dissemination of Lu's learning. Meanwhile, Yuan Fu also presided over the renovation of Bailudong Academy, a major base for Zhu Xi's thought, and successively hired Zhu Xi's students Zhang Qia and Tang Jin, a scholar who originally preferred Lu Xue and then wanted to combine Zhu Xi's and Lu Jiuyuan's thoughts after learning from Zhu Xi, to take charge of the academy's educational activities. What Yuan Fu did for Bailudong Academy could be explained as an effort to promote Xin Xue, as Lu Jiuyuan once gave lectures at Bailudong Academy at the invitation of Zhu Xi and achieved great success there. The academy even had the contents of his lectures carved in stone and well-preserved inside Bailu Cave. However, this move also embodied the tendency to harmonize Zhu and Lu in the academic community at that time, and Yuan Fu, who was a devout follower of Lu, was also influenced by this trend and showed his respect for Zhu. In the late Song and early Yuan dynasties, Wu Cheng (1249–1333), a scholar of Neo-Confucianism, was more obvious in his synthesis of Zhu Xi's and Lu Jiuyuan's theories. He even argued that there was no contradiction between Zhu and Lu and that the so-called disparities were created by the disciples of the two schools, saying,

> Zhu Xi and Lu Jiuyuan teach the same general principle, but the mediocre and stubborn students, each boasting their own correctness while denigrating each other's errors, create barriers and conflicts between the two schools, which still confuse today's scholars.[179]

Zheng Yu (1298–1358), a Yuan dynasty Neo-Confucian scholar, further pointed out that Zhu Xi and Lu Jiuyuan "have no difference in their basic views and goals." He said,

> All scholars of the two schools honor what they have heard and practice what they know, thus not being able to unify the two for more than 200 years. In my opinion, however, it is the personality that causes the differences between the two schools. Lu Jiuyuan is a quick thinker and thus prefers simplicity and effectiveness. Zhu Xi is a down-to-earth doer, so he emphasizes the importance of experience and studies. Because of differences in innate temperament, they hold different ways of thinking and expression. But for

the goal of learning the so-called three principles and five rules, benevolence and morality, there is no distinction at all. Besides, they both think that Yao and Shun are right and that Xia Jie and Shang Zhou are wrong. Meanwhile, they both advocate Confucianism while rejecting Buddhism and Taoism. Furthermore, they commonly hold that the Divine Principle is public and that human desires are private. They obviously intend to achieve the same goal.[180]

These views had a great influence on the then academic circle. Under this influence, some scholars of Xin Xue started studying Zhu Xi's theory; some followers of Zhu Xi began learning Xin Xue; some scholars decided to adopt both. The merging of Zhu and Lu became an important feature of the development of Neo-Confucianism from the late Song till the early Ming dynasties.[181] Under such circumstances, it was quite natural for some academies to worship both Zhu Xi and Lu Jiuyuan.

After the Jiajing reign (1507–1567) of the Ming dynasty, many academies began worshiping Wang Yangming (1472–1529), including the aforementioned academies set up by his students and inheritors during the Jiajing reign, as well as many other academies. One example is Fuli Academy, which was located in Lianhua County, Jiangxi Province, and was built by Liu Yuanqing (1544–1609) in the sixth year of the Longqing reign (1572). Another example was the memorial temple dedicated to four outstanding Confucian scholars, including Wang Yangming, and Zou Shouyi (1491–1562), which was built in the 17th year of the Wanli reign (1589). This new worshiping trend was closely related to the rise and wide spreading of Wang Yangming's theory. After the Song dynasty, as Zhu Xue was favored and promoted by the rulers, its dominant position continued to rise and became the standard for the imperial examinations during the Yangyou period of the Yuan dynasty. It is even established as the guiding ideology for governing the country at the beginning of the Ming dynasty. In line with this, Zhu Xue occupied a mainstream position in the academic world. Some scholars even held that "Zhu Xi explains Confucian classics and principles so clearly that and that there is no need for further interpretations." Some proposed, "Zhu Xue is profound, inclusive, precise, and refined. It clearly and thoroughly interprets past sages' teachings, and all Confucian scholars have to adopt and carefully study his interpretations so as to improve themselves."[182] Some even said, "Only with Zhu Xi's guidance can you correctly understand Confucianism. Only by visiting Mount Lu can you understand the beauty of a mountain."[183] This academic atmosphere made scholars follow Zhu Xi's teachings without proposing any challenge. They only focused on reciting and practicing old principles, worked to regulate daily human relations, and were cautious enough to ensure that their speeches and deeds were correct. Gradually, Zhu Xi's teachings became dull doctrines with a lack of vitality and progress. To a large extent, Zhu Xue actually became a rigid dogma. Although its ideas still quickly spread to nearly every corner of the country, given their political status, they did not actually provide guidance for social life and exemplify the role of the people.

98 *Academy Sacrificial Rituals*

This weakness of Zhu Xi's school stimulated the emergence of a new academic trend. After the middle of the Ming dynasty, Wang Yangming (1472–1529) and others, with the aim of "driving the thief out of the mind," came up with Xin Xue, a new academic theory that differed drastically from that of Zhu Xi. Yangming's Xin Xue advocated the innate moral goodness of human beings, the unity of inner knowledge and practice, and the necessity of acquiring knowledge through the mind or heart, thus elevating subjective spirit to a higher status.[184] The theory on humans' innate moral goodness breathed life into the conservative and dull academic world of the time, prompting scholars to shake off the shackles and free themselves of the rigid dogmas, and as a result, the academic culture got changed dramatically. Wang Yangming once said, "I'm engaging myself all my life in giving lectures to explain humans' innate moral goodness."[185] His theory on humans' innate moral goodness won wide support from scholars. Compared with the complexities and pedantry of Zhu Xi's school, Wang Yangming's doctrine was remarkably concise and straightforward. Quan Zuwang (1705–1755) once commented, "Wang Yangming's teachings can shake up the fragmented and philological scholarly methods, and thus, it may be an excellent remedy to correct academic ills."[186] This strength of Yangming's doctrine facilitated the spreading of Wang's theory. In addition, Yangming's disciples interpreted the doctrines of their teacher from different perspectives and kept spreading them by means of lectures in the academy, thus leading to a sharp rise of Xin Xue in popularity across the country. Yangming's theory gradually gained a higher position in the middle and late Ming dynasty, attracting a large number of enthusiastic followers. Quan Zuwang said about the then situation in the following words:

> During the years of Zhengde and Jiajing in the Ming dynasty, the theory of Wang Yangming and that of Zhan Ruoshui became very popular. Although the doctrines of the two were slightly different, the general ideas were very similar, and the scholars of the time usually chose to follow one or the other.[187]

Obviously, despite being a Confucian school officially recognized by the government, Zhu Xi's school was still challenged by Wang Yangming's theory in many aspects. Thus, although Zhu Xue was still officially in the dominant position, the rise and popularity of Wang Xue (Yangming School of Mind) had shaken Zhu Xue's position fundamentally in many ways. The academy's worship of Wang Yangming was actually an acknowledgment of his achievement of successfully changing the academic trend and shifting the learning mindset. Scholars from Yaojiang Academy, where Wang Yangming was worshiped, expressed almost the same views as mentioned earlier: "Yangming's concise and to-the-point teachings enabled scholars to easily grasp the essence of Confucianism."[188] "In the reign of Zhengde's (1506–1521) and that of Jiajing (1522–1566), Wang Yangming required a correct and deeper understanding of Confucianism, which helped him win support from many of the outstanding scholars."[189] Yangming was worshiped in many academies during this period of time, which was a symptom of the rising popularity of Wang Yangming's doctrine.

Some academies were offering worship to both Zhu Xi and Wang Yangming. One example is Rixin Academy, set up during the Wanli reign (1573–1620) of the Ming dynasty. "Confucius, Zhu Xi, and Wang Yangming were worshiped in this academy, with the statue of Confucius located in the central position, while the statues of the other two were on its left and right, respectively."[190] During the Wanli reign, academies announced their different academic pursuits by worshiping either Zhu Xi or Wang Yangming, which made Rixin Academy exceptional. Regarding the unusual practice of the academy, Gu Xiancheng (1550–1612) gave an analysis based on the change in the academic trend in his book *Records of Rixin Academy* (日新书院记). He notes,

> Before the Hongzhi reign (1488–1505) and the Zhengde reign (1491–1521), Zhu Xi was more respected than Confucius, which led to the nasty stagnation of thinking, and thus, the radical viewpoints of Wang Yangming won wide support. After the Zhengde reign (1491–1521) and the Jiajing reign (1522–1566), Wang Yangming gained more recognition than Confucius, which led to a radical tendency hated by lots of people, and thus, they began to miss the benefits of Zhu Xi's teachings. When people were attracted by the radical viewpoints of Wang Yangming, they neglected Zhu Xi's wisdom; when they began pursuing Zhu Xi, they paid little attention to Wang Yangming's wisdom. They tended to go to extremes, to either overestimate or belittle the two masters, as they were unable to figure out the relations and similarities between the thoughts of the two. How can they achieve anything by doing so?[191]

Gu Xiancheng's analysis is logical and profound. He summarized the change in the academic trend and pointed out the unnecessary extreme attitudes of Zhu Xi's and Wang Yangming's followers. He grasped a clear picture of how extreme attitudes caused the conflicts between the two Confucian schools. Gu Xiancheng further points out, "Zhu Xi relied on studies and experiences to gain spiritual enlightenment, but Wang Yangming proposed that spiritual enlightenment occurred before the academic studies and experiences. They were just two different sequences." In his opinion, it was totally acceptable for Rixin Academy to worship both Confucian masters simultaneously. He said that "by adopting and integrating Zhu Xi's and Wang Yangming's theories, scholars can better understand and promote Confucianism."[192] Gu Xiancheng's viewpoint reflected an academic trend that emphasized the integration of Zhu Xi's and Wang Yangming's theories instead of the disparities and differences between the two schools. This trend was evident in the memorial activities of Yushan Academy, which was renovated by Geng Ju, the magistrate of Changshu County, in the 34th year of the Wanli reign (1606). The academy mainly worshiped Ziyou (506–443 bc), a student of Confucius, but it also worshiped the traditional five sages and 16 virtuous Confucian masters, which included not only traditional sages, such as Fuxi, Yao, Shun, King Wen of Zhou, and Confucius, but also Neo-Confucian masters, such as Zhou Dunyi, Cheng Yi, Cheng Hao, Shao Yong,

100   *Academy Sacrificial Rituals*

Zhang Zai, Zhu Xi, Lu Jiuyuan, Xue Xuan (1389–1464, a representative follower of Zhu Xi living in the early Ming dynasty), Wang Yangming, and Chen Xianzhang (1428–1500, the founder of Jiangmen Xin Xue).[193] The selection of the figures of worship reflected an all-embracing and unbiased attitude of Confucian scholars. In the early Qing dynasty, Yaojiang Academy, a major base of Wang Yangming's school, also began to embrace the idea of integrating Zhu Xi's or Wang Yangming's theories. In the 41st year of the Kangxi reign (1702), Shao Yancai, who presided over the educational work of the academy, discusses the pursuit of the academy in his book *Records of Yaojiang Academy* (姚江书院记): "We adopt the theories proposed by Zhou Dunyi, Cheng Yi, Cheng Hao, Zhu Xi, and Lu Jiuyuan, accept both their similarities and differences, and let them play an important role in our practice."[194] Quan Zuwang's book *Records of Six Great Masters Academy* (杜洲六先生书院记) also records such a trend of integrating the theories of Zhu Xi and Wang Yangming. Duzhou Academy, located in Zhejiang Province's Cixi County, was built in the second year of Zhida (1309) of the Yuan dynasty, and it worshiped six outstanding scholars who had once given lectures in the county, such as Tong Juyi (12th cent.) and Huang Zhen (1213–1280). Tong Juyi, a student of Yang Jian and widely known as Master Duzhou, advocated the theory of "learning through heart or mind, and inherited the theory of Lu Jiuyuan. Huang Zhen (courtesy name Huang Dongfa) was an inheritor of Zhu Xi's theory, and Quan Zuwang once praised him as the most steadfast follower of Zhu Xi.[195] Despite the fact that Tong Juyi and Huang Zhen were representatives of two quite different Confucian schools, they were both chosen to be worshiped in Duzhou Academy. Quan Zuwang thought highly of this choice and observed,

> Yang Jian and Tong Juyi are inheritors of Lu Jiuyuan's Xin Xue, but Huang Dongfa (courtesy name of Huang Zhen) is an inheritor of Zhu Xi's theory. They came from two nearly opposite schools. Huang Dongfa, in his book *Richao* (日钞), seemed to belittle Xin Xue. Focusing only on the disparities and differences between different Confucian schools is what confines one's thinking most. The past sages and virtuous scholars emphasized practice instead of empty words, so Huang Dongfa, who somewhat resisted Xin Xue, still recognized Yang Jian's effort to advocate the importance of practice. Duzhou Academy decided to worship both of them, showing that it respected the disparities between the two schools and enhanced itself academically by integrating the thoughts proposed by both schools.[196]

Quan Zuwang's comment reflected the early Qing dynasty's academic trend of shelving academic differences and focusing on promoting academic development.

In the mid and late Qing dynasty, Han learning that emerged during the reign of Qianlong and Jiaqing (1736–1820) thrived, adding new names to the academies' list of worshiping figures, and many outstanding textual scholars or scholars focusing on Han learning became new figures of worship. According to historical records, in the second year of the Jiaqing reign (1797), Ruan Yuan (1764–1849), a well-known Han-learning scholar, brought a group of Confucian scholars to Mount Gu in Hangzhou City to compile a book titled *Commentary Collections on Confucian Classics* (经籍纂诂), and after finishing the book, he built Gujing Academy on the spot and selected scholars from Zhejiang Province to teach Confucian classics, history, and poems there.

Back then,

> as some students, including Lu Yaochun from Renhe County, Yan Jie from Qiantang County, and Zhou Zhongfu from Wucheng County, requested to worship early pioneers of Han learning, the head teacher Sun Xingyan (1753–1818) turned the academy's Yongsu Hall into a memorial hall for Xu Shen (58–147) and Zheng Xuan (127–200) after obtaining the consent from Ruan Yuan.

In his book[197] *Records of Gujing Academy* (西湖诂经精舍记), Ruan Yuan records how the academy started worshiping Zheng Xuan and Xu Shen:

> The students requested to trace back to the origin of Han learning and wanted to worship Zheng Xuan in the academy. Sun Xingyan agreed with them and expressed that Xu Shen also made a great contribution to Han learning and needed to be worshiped together with Zheng Xuan. In the fifth month of the fifth year of the Jiaqing reign, we respectfully placed memorial tablets of Xu Shen and Zheng Xuan in the hall and sacrificed to them to demonstrate our academic pursuit.[198]

From then on, Gujing Academy started the tradition of worshiping renowned scholars on Han learning in academies.

After Gujing Academy began worshiping Zheng Xuan and Xu Shen, many other academies also made some Han dynasty (202 bc–ad 220) scholars focusing on Han learning and historians their figures of worship. For example, Xuehai Academy in Guangzhou City and Nanjing Academy in Jiangsu Province worshiped Zheng Xuan (127–200);[199] Yuelu Academy worshiped the famous historian Sima Qian (145–86 bc) during the early years of the Jiaqing era (1760–1820).[200] These sacrificial rituals reflected the then prevailing academic trend and advocated the research methods concerning Han learning. When discussing why Gujing Academy began worshiping Xu Shen and Zheng Xuan, Ruan Yuan said,

> The past sages and virtuous scholars imparted their knowledge through ancient classics, and only by carefully studying the ancient classics can we correctly understand them. In this process, the research methods concerning Han learning are the most reliable study methods . . . Han learning, done in the Han dynasty, is reliable guidance for us to understand ancient classics because, chronologically speaking, Han dynasty scholars were closest to the time they were studying on. Xu Shen and Zheng Xuan are outstanding Han-learning scholars and worth being worshiped.[201]

102 *Academy Sacrificial Rituals*

Xu Shen and Zheng Xuan are the most representative Han dynasty scholars focusing on Han learning. By worshiping them, Gujing Academy demonstrated that it gave great importance to ancient classics and focused on Han learning. Scholars of Gujing Academy said,

> The academy worships the two Han-learning scholars not just to make up for what had been neglected previously in academic study but also to emphasize the necessity of carefully studying the ancient classics by following the example of the two. Studies on the ancient classics should be carried out in a down-to-the-earth way instead of through some subjective assumption.[202]

Yu Yue (1821–1907), another well-known Han-learning scholar, also agreed on this point. In the fifth year of Tongzhi (1866), when writing the book *Restoration of Gujing Academy* (重修诂经精舍记), he notes,

> The reason that Ruan Yuan decided to worship the two Han dynasty Confucian scholars, Xu Shen and Zheng Xuan, in Gujing Academy was that he wanted his students to acquire a good knowledge of ancient languages and ancient institutions so as to correctly understand the ancient classics.[203]

Gradually, some famous Han-learning scholars at the time became figures of worship by academies. The first example is Qian Daxin (1728–1804), a famous Han-learning scholar who lived during the reign of Qianlong and Jiaqing. Qian Daxin had a profound understanding of ancient classics, especially historical classics, and was proficient in Chinese character-making methods, ancient arithmetic, astronomy, geography, clans, inscriptions, bureaucratic systems, and the languages of the Jin kingdom and Yuan dynasty. He wrote 35 books, a total of more than 300 volumes, including *Collection of Qian Daxin* (潜研堂文集), a treatise on Han learning titled "A Record of Studies in Shijia Study" (十驾斋养新录), and another treatise of historical textual research titled "Critique of the Twenty-Two Dynastic Histories" (廿二史考异). His research on Han learning solved age-old puzzles in Confucian studies, and his historical textual research became important referential materials for history students.[204] He also gave lectures and presided over educational activities at Zhongshan Academy, Loudong Academy, and Ziyang Academy. During the Daoguang reign (1782–1850), Zhongshan Academy began to worship Qian Daxin. Apart from that, Xuehai Academy and Jupo Academy in Guangdong Province, also started worshiping Ruan Yuan and Chen Li (1810–1882), respectively; Yuelu Academy added some famous Han-learning scholars to its list of worship figures, such as Wang Wenqing (1696–1787), Kuang Minben (1700–1784), and Luo Dian (1719–1808). It seemed that some academies of that time simply chose to worship their founders or head teachers, but the fundamental reason that they chose to worship these Han-learning scholars was that they wanted to announce their academic pursuit and set those Han-learning scholars up as academic role models. Hu Peihui (1782–1849), another famous Han-learning scholar that once served as the head teacher of Zhongshan Academy during the Daoguang reign (1782–1850), discussed this issue in his book *Records of Qian Zhuting Being Worshiped in Zhongshan Academy* (钱竹汀先生入祀钟山书院记), saying,

> The academy holds memorial rituals for Qian Daxin, worshiping him along with other sages and other outstanding Confucian scholars, not only because he is qualified to enjoy these ceremonies but also because the academy wants to promote Han learning.[205]

By paying homage to Han-learning scholars like Qian Daxin through memorial rituals, Zhongshan Academy set them up as role models for its students and encouraged them to engage in Han learning. As a number of Han-learning scholars are worshiped in academies in the Qianlong and Jiaqing reign, it is fair to say that at that time, the learning mindset of emphasizing textual research and understanding ancient classics under the guidance of textual studies is widely embodied in the academies' sacrificial rituals, and academic pursuit and studying methods of Han-learning scholars are widely recognized and adopted.

Notes

1 Sheng, Langxi 盛朗西. *Zhongguo shuyuan zhidu* 中国书院制度 (Beijing: Zhonghua Book Company, 1934), 47.
2 Ruan, Yuan 阮元. "Li yun" 礼运. In *Shisanjing zhushu* 十三经注疏 (Beijing: Zhonghua Book Company, 1980), 1418.
3 Ruan, Yuan 阮元. "Ji tong" 祭统. In *Shisan jing zhushu* 十三经注疏 (Beijing: Zhonghua Book Company, 1980), 1602.
4 Li, Shen 李申. *Zhongguo rujiao shi* 中国儒教史 (Shanghai: Shanghai People's Publishing House, 1999), 27–39.
5 See Gao, Mingshi 高明士. "Shuyuan jisi kongjian de jiaoyu zuoyong" 书院祭祀空间的教育作用. In *Zhongguo shuyuan* Vol. 1 中国书院第一辑 (Changsha: Hunan Education Press, 1997), 27–39.
6 Wu, Shengqin 吴省钦. "Shifang xian fangting shuyuan xinjian shengxiang loubei" 什邡县方亭书院新建圣像楼碑. In *Xuxiu siku quan shu* Vol. 1147 续修四库全书第1147册 (Shanhai: Shanghai Chinese Classics Publishing House, 2002), 623–633.
7 See Sheng, Langxi 盛朗西. *Zhongguo shuyuan zhidu* 中国书院制度 (Beijing: Zhonghua Book Company, 1934), 47.
8 See Zhang, Liuquan 章柳泉. *Zhongguo shuyuan shi hua—song yuan ming qing shuyuan de yuanbian jiqi neirong* 中国书院史话—宋元明清书院的演变及其内容 (Beijing: Educational Science Publishing House, 1981), 13–15.
9 See Chen, Chinese Classicsa 陈谷嘉, and Deng Hongbo 邓洪波. "Yuelu shuyuan jisi shulue" 岳麓书院祭祀述略. In *Zhongguo shuyuan zhidu yanjiu* Appendix 1 中国书院制度研究附录一 (Hangzhou: Zhejiang Education Publishing House, 1997), 585–594.
10 Wang, Yucheng 王禹偁. "Tanzhou yuelushan shuyuan ji" 潭州岳麓山书院记. In *Siku quan shu* Vol. 1086 四库全书第1086册 (Shanghai: Shanghai Chinese Classics Publishing House, 1987), 164.
11 Zhang, Shunmin 张舜民. "Chen xing lu" 郴行录. In *Siku quan shu* Vol. 1117 四库全书第1117册 (Shanghai: Shanghai Chinese Classics Publishing House, 1987), 52.
12 Wang, Yinglin 王应麟. "Songchao sishuyuan" 宋朝四书院. In *Siku quan shu* Vol. 947 四库全书第947册 (Shanghai: Shanghai Chinese Classics Publishing House, 1987), 353.

104 *Academy Sacrificial Rituals*

13 Xu, Du 徐度. "Caocheng juanjian yingtianfu shuyuan" 曹诚捐建应天府书院. In *Siku quan shu* Vol. 863四库全书第863册 (Shanghai: Shanghai Chinese Classics Publishing House, 1987), 753.

14 Gao, Mingshi 高明士. "Shuyuan jisi kongjian de jiaoyu zuoyong" 书院祭祀空间的教育作用. In *Zhongguo shuyuan* Vol. 1中国书院第1辑 (Changsha: Hunan Education Press, 1997), 72.

15 Tang, Su 唐肃. "Huanggang shuyuan wugou xiansheng citing ji" 皇冈书院无垢先生祠堂记. In *Xuxiu siku quan shu* Vol. 1326 续修四库全书第1326册 (Shanghai: Shanghai Chinese Classics Publishing House, 2002), 148.

16 Dai, Junheng 戴钧衡. "Shuyuan zayi sishou" 书院杂议四首. In *Zhongguo lidai shuyuan zhi* Vol. 9 中国历代书院志第9册 (Nanjing: Jiangsu Education Publishing House, 1995), 766.

17 See Teng, Xunzhen 滕巽真. "Panfu tixing gaofeng xiansheng shouci zhi ji" 判府提刑高峰先生寿祠之记. In *Hunan tongzhi* Vol. 279 湖南通志卷二百七十九 (Shanghai: Shanghai Chinese Classics Publishing House, 2002), 352.

18 Yuan, Fu 袁甫. "Donglai shuyuan zhuxuan ji" 东莱书院竹轩记. In *Siku quan shu* Vol. 1175. 四库全书第1175册 (Shanghai: Shanghai Chinese Classics Publishing House, 1987), 500.

19 See Lu, Weiyou 卢蔚猷. "Haiyang xian zhi" Vol. 19 海阳县志卷十九. In *Zhongguo fangzhi congshu*中国方志丛书 (Taibei: Chengwen Publishing House, 1985), 173.

20 See Yan, Xingbang 阎兴邦. "Chongjian dajiang shuyuan lizheng sidian ji" 重建大梁书院厘正祀典记. In *Siku quan shu* Vol. 536 四库全书第536册 (Shanghai: Shanghai Chinese Classics Publishing House, 1987), 516–517.

21 See "Huanggang xian zhi" Vol. 5 黄冈县志卷五. In *Zhongguo defang zhi jicheng* 中国地方志集成 (Nanjing: Jiangsu Chinese Classics Publishing House, 2001), 180.

22 See Yang, Shenchu 杨慎初. *Yuelu shuyuan shi lue* 岳麓书院史略 (Changsha: Yuelu Press, 1986), 132–136.

23 Zhu, Xi 朱熹. "Bailudong cheng gao xiansheng wen" 白鹿洞成告先圣文. In *Zhuzi quan shu*朱子全书 (Shanghai: Shanghai Chinese Classics Publishing House, 2002), 4037.

24 Zhu, Xi 朱熹. "Cangzhou jingshe gao xiansheng wen" 沧州精舍告先圣文. In *Zhuzi quan shu*朱子全书 (Shanghai: Shanghai Chinese Classics Publishing House, 2002), 4051.

25 Chen, Dawen 陈大文. "Chongxiu lumen shuyuan ji tianjian shengxian yixiangdian ji" 重修鹿门书院暨添建圣贤遗像殿记. In *Zhongguo Fangzhi Congshu* 中国方志丛书 (Taibei: Chengwen Publishing House, 1985), 776.

26 Ma, Duanlin 马端临. "Xuexiao kao si" 学校考四. In *Wenxian tongkao* Vol. 43 文献通考 (Beijing: Zhonghua Book Company, 1986), 403.

27 Ma, Duanlin 马端临. "Xuexiao kao si" 学校考四. In *Wenxian tongkao* Vol. 43 文献通考 (Beijing: Zhonghua Book Company, 1986), 403.

28 Sun, Xidan 孙希旦. "Wenwang shizi" 文王世子. In *Liji ji jie* Vol. 20 礼记集解卷二十 (Beijing: Zhonghua Book Company, 1989), 560.

29 Zheng, Tinghu 郑廷鹄. "Shi dian" 释奠. In *Zhongguo lidai shuyuan zhi* 中国历代书院志 (Nanjing: Jiangsu Education Publishing House, 1995), 353.

30 Hu, Linyi 胡林翼. "Jisi"祭祀. In *Zhengyan shuyuan zhi* 箴言书院志 (Nanjing: Jiangsu Education Publishing House, 1995), 195.

31 Huang, Wenzhong 黄文仲. "Shunchang shuangfeng shuyuan xinjian sixiantang ji" 顺昌双峰书院新建四贤堂记. In *Quanyuan wen* Vol. 1421全元文卷一四二一 (Nanjing: Jiangsu Chinese Classics Publishing House, 1999), 144.

32 Dai, Junheng 戴钧衡. "Shuyuan zayi si shou" 书院杂议四首. In *Zhongguo lidai shuyuan zhi* Vol. 9中国历代书院志第9册 (Nanjing: Jiangsu Education Publishing House, 1995), 766.

33 Sun, Xidan 孙希旦. "Wenwang shizi" 文王世子. In *Liji jijie* Vol. 20礼记集解卷二十 (Beijing: Zhonghua Book Company, 1989), 560.

34 Li, Shen 李申. *Zhongguo rujiao shi* 中国儒教史 (Shanghai: Shanghai People's Publishing House, 1999), 812–819.

35 Zhu, Xi 朱熹. "Bailudong cheng gao xiansheng wen" 白鹿洞成告先圣文. In *Zhuzi quan shu*朱子全书 (Shanghai: Shanghai Chinese Classics Publishing House, 2002), 4037.

36 Zhong, Shizhen钟世桢. "Xinjiang shuyuan zhi" 信江书院志. In *Zhongguo lidai shuyuan zhi* Vol. 2 (Nanjing: Jiangsu Education Publishing House, 1995), 369.

37 Zheng, Tinghu 郑廷鹄. "Shi dian" 释奠. In *Zhongguo lidai shuyuan zhi* 中国历代书院志 (Nanjing: Jiangsu Education Publishing House, 1995), 354.

38 See Zhu, Xi 朱熹. "Liuxinasheng huaxiang zan" 六先生画像赞. In *Zhuzi quan shu* 朱子全书 (Shanghai: Shanghai Chinese Classics Publishing House, 2002), 4001–4003.

39 Liu, Yi 刘绎. "Jianzhi" 建置. In *Zhongguo lidai shuyuan zhi* 中国历代书院志 (Nanjing: Jiangsu Education Publishing House, 1995), 568.

40 Ding, Shanqing 丁善庆. "Miaosi" 庙祀In *Zhongguo lidai shuyuan zhi* Vol. 4中国历代书院志第4册 (Nanjing: Jiangsu Education Publishing House, 1995), 414.

41 See Zheng, Gongxun 郑功勋. "Chongxiu chongzheng shuyuan wuxianci ji" 重修崇正书院五贤祠记. In *Jianshui zhou zhi* Vol. 11建水州志卷十一.

42 Ruan, Yuan 阮元. "Xihu gujing jingshe ji" 西湖诂经精舍记. In *Congshu jicheng*丛书集成 (Beijing: The commercial Press, 1936), 61.

43 Zhang, Tingyu 张廷玉 et al. "Zhanruoshui zhuan" 湛若水传. In *Mingshi* 明史 (Beijing: Zhonghua Book Company, 1974), 7266.

44 Gong, Shitai 贡师泰. "Mianzhai shuyuan ji" 勉斋书院记. In *Fuzhou fu zhi* 福州府志 (Fuzhou: Haifeng Press, 2001), 357.

45 See Xu, Zi 徐梓. *Yuandai Shuyuan yanjiu*元代书院研究 (Beijing: China Social Sciences Publishing House, 2000), 158.

46 Ding, Shanqing 丁善庆. "Miaosi" 庙祀. In *Zhongguo lidai shuyuan zhi* Vol. 4中国历代书院志第4册 (Nanjing: Jiangsu Education Publishing House, 1995), 414.

47 See Li, Tengfang 李腾芳. "Chongxiu yuelu shuyuan beiji" 重修岳麓书院碑记. In *Zhongguo lidai shuyuan zhi* 中国历代书院志 (Nanjing: Jiangsu Education Publishing House, 1995), 476.

48 Ding, Shanqing 丁善庆. "Miaosi"庙祀. In *Zhongguo lidai shuyuan zhi* Vol. 4 中国历代书院志第4册 (Nanjing: Jiangsu Education Publishing House, 1995), 415.

49 See Mao, Deqi 毛德琦. "Xian xian"先献. In *Zhongguo lidai shuyuan zhi* Vol. 2中国历代书院志第2册 (Nanjing: Jiangsu Education Publishing House, 1995), 88–89.

50 See Mao, Deqi 毛德琦. "Xian xian" 先献. In *Zhongguo lidai shuyuan zhi* Vol. 2中国历代书院志第2册 (Nanjing: Jiangsu Education Publishing House, 1995), 88–89.

51 See Fang, Zude 方祖德. "Si xiansheng citang ji" 四先生祠堂记. In *Zhongguo lidai shuyuan zhi* 中国历代书院志 (Nanjing: Jiangsu Education Publishing House, 1995), 420.

52 Song, Lian 宋濂. "Xuanju zhi" 选举志. In *Yuanshi* 元史 (Beijing: Zhonghua Book Company, 1976), 2032.

53 Huang, Xianglong 黄翔龙. "Chongxiu cihu shuyuan benmo ji" 重修慈湖书院本末记. In *Songyuan fangzhi congkan* 宋元方志丛刊 (Beijing: Zhonghua Book Company, 1990), 6340.

54 Ding, Shanqing 丁善庆. "Miaosi" 庙祀. In *Zhongguo lidai shuyuan zhi* 中国历代书院志 (Nanjing: Jiangsu Education Publishing House, 1995), 414–415.

55 See Zhou, Wei 周伟. et al. "Zhongjie ci jili" 忠节祠祭礼. In *Zhongguo lidai shuyuan zhi*中国历代书院志 (Nanjing: Jiangsu Education Publishing House, 1995), 554.

56 See Yan, Xingbang 阎兴邦. "Chongjian dajiang shuyuan lizheng sidian ji" 重建大梁书院厘正祀典记. In *Siku quan shu* Vol. 536四库全书第536册 (Shanghai: Shanghai Chinese Classics Publishing House, 1987), 517.

57 See Cao, Yanyi 曹延懿. "Zengjian zhou wang er xiansheng ci genge jiuxian shuyuan ji" 增建周、王二先生祠更额九贤书院. 记. In *Zhongguo fangzhi congshu*中国方志丛书 (Taibei: Taibei Chengwen Publishing House, 1985), 259.

106 *Academy Sacrificial Rituals*

58 See "Shuyuan er"书院二. In *Xuxiu siku quan shu* Vol. 663续修四库全书第663册 (Shanhai: Shanghai Chinese Classics Publishing House, 2002), 100.

59 Dai, Fengyi 戴凤仪. "Sidian" 祀典. In *Shishan shuyuan zhi* 诗山书院志. Vol. 6 (Xiamen: Xiamen University Press, 1995), 117.

60 Yang, Lian 杨廉. "Bailudong shuyuan zongru ci ji" 白鹿洞书院宗儒祠记. In *Bailudong shuyuan guzhi wuzhong* 白鹿洞书院古志五种, 108.

61 Ding, Gang 丁钢. *Shuyuan yu zhonguo wenhua* 书院与中国文化 (Shanghai: Shanghai Education Press, 1992), 41–42.

62 Yao, Mian 姚勉. "Xijian shuyuan ji kuixing zhuwen" 西涧书院祭魁星祝文. In *Siku quan shu* Vol. 1184四库全书第1184册 (Shanhai: Shanghai Chinese Classics Publishing House, 1987), 329.

63 See Zhao, Yuhong 赵与鸿. "Yuzhang shuyuan wenchangge ji" 豫章书院文昌阁记. In *Nanchang yi chengwen zheng* Vol. 18 南昌邑乘文征卷十八.

64 Ding, Shanqing 丁善庆. "Miaosi" 庙祀. In *Zhongguo lidai shuyuan zhi* 中国历代书院志 (Nanjing: Jiangsu Education Publishing House, 1995), 414.

65 See Wang, Kaitai 王凯泰. "Yingyuan shuyuan zhi lue zhangcheng" 应元书院志略章程. In *Zhongguo lidai shuyuan zhi* Vol. 3中国历代书院志第3册 (Nanjing: Jiangsu Education Publishing House, 1995), 271.

66 See Dong, Guifu 董桂敷. "Ziyang shuyuan zhi lue" 紫阳书院志略. In *Zhongguo lidai shuyuan zhi* 中国历代书院志 (Nanjing: Jiangsu Education Publishing House, 1995), 519–521.

67 Dai, Junheng 戴钧衡. "Shuyuan zayi si shou · si xiangxian" 书院杂议四首·祀乡贤. In *Zhongguo lidai shuyuan zhi* Vol. 9中国历代书院志 (Nanjing: Jiangsu Education Publishing House, 1995), 766.

68 Dai, Fengyi 戴凤仪. "Sidian" 祀典. In *Shishan shuyuan zhi* Vol. 6诗山书院志卷六 (Xiamen: Xiamen University Press, 1995), 118.

69 See Wang, Qin 王溱. "Xinpi shidong gao houtu wen" 新辟石洞告后土文. In *Zhongguo lidai shuyuan zhi* Vol. 1中国历代书院志第1册 (Nanjing: Jiangsu Education Publishing House, 1995), 819.

70 See Mao, Deqi 毛德琦. "Zhifu Liao Wenying shenxiang jianzu wen" 知府廖文英申详减租文. In *Zhongguo lidai shuyuan zhi* Vol. 2中国历代书院志第2册 (Nanjing: Jiangsu Education Publishing House, 1995), 142.

71 Ding, Shanqing 丁善庆. "Miaosi" 庙祀. In *Zhongguo lidai shuyuan zhi* Vol. 4中国历代书院志第4册 (Nanjing: Jiangsu Education Publishing House, 1995), 414.

72 See Dong, Guifu 董桂敷. "Si houtu wen" 祀后土文. In *Zhongguo lidai shuyuan zhi* Vol. 3中国历代书院志第3册 (Nanjing: Jiangsu Education Publishing House, 1995), 627.

73 Fu, Weisen 傅维森. "Sidian"祀典. In *Zhongguo lidai shuyuan zhi* Vol. 3中国历代书院志第3册 (Nanjing: Jiangsu Education Publishing House, 1995), 368.

74 Sun, Xidan孙希旦. "Wenwang Shizi" 文王世子. In *Liji jijie* Vol. 20礼记集解卷二十 (Beijing: Zhonghua Book Company, 1989), 560.

75 Jiang, Yi 蒋易. "Song yunzhuangshan chang zhang xiaoya xu" 送云庄山长张小雅序. In *Quanyuan wen* 全元文 (Nanjing: Jiangsu Chinese Classics Publishing House, 1999), 77.

76 Zheng, Tinghu 郑廷鹄. "Zhongjieci jili" 忠节祠祭礼. In *Zhongguo lidai shuyuan zhi* Vol. 1中国历代书院志第1册 (Nanjing: Jiangsu Education Publishing House, 1995), 355–356.

77 Zhou, Wei 周伟. "Zhifu tianguan zhongjie ciji" 知府田琯忠节祠记. In *Zhongguo lidai shuyuan zhi* Vol. 1中国历代书院志第1册 (Nanjing: Jiangsu Education Publishing House, 1995), 650.

78 Li, Qi 李祁. "Fanwenzheng gong shuyuan ji" 范文正公书院记. In *Siku quan shu* Vol. 1四库全书第1219册 (Shanghai: Shanghai Chinese Classics Publishing House, 1987), 717.

79 Zheng, Tinghu 郑廷鹄. "Xianxianci jili" 先贤祠祭礼. In *Zhongguo lidai shuyuan zhi* Vol. 1 中国历代书院志第1册 (Nanjing: Jiangsu Education Publishing House, 1995), 356.

80 Jiang, Yi 蒋易. "Lufengshan chang huangyuchen xu songbie" 庐峰山长黄禹臣序送别. In *Quanyuan wen* Vol. 48 全元文第48册 (Nanjing: Jiangsu Chinese Classics Publishing House, 1999), 77.

81 Kuai, Demo 蒯德模. "Gaijian pingjiang shuyuan bing siwen chenegxiang shixiang ji" 改建平江书院并祀文丞相石像记. In *Zhongguo fangzhi congshu* 中国方志丛书 (Taibei: Taibei Chengwen Publishing House, 1985), 622.

82 Yang, Lian 杨廉. "Zongru ci ji" 宗儒祠记. In *Zhongguo lidai shuyuan zhi* Vol. 2 中国历代书院志第2册 (Nanjing: Jiangsu Education Publishing House, 1995), 175.

83 Zhu, Xi 朱熹. "Xinzhou zhouxue dacheng dian ji" 信州州学大成殿记. In *Zhuzi quan shu* 朱子全书 (Shanghai: Shanghai Chinese Classics Publishing House, 2002), 3806.

84 Huang, Wenzhong 黄文仲. "Shunchang shuangfeng shuyuan xinjian sixiantang ji" 顺昌双峰书院新建四贤堂记. In *Quanyuan wen* Vol. 46 全元文第46册 (Nanjing: Jiangsu Chinese Classics Publishing House, 1999), 144.

85 Gao, Long 高隆 et al. "Donglin shuyuan zhi" 东林书院志. In *Zhongguo lidai shuyuan zhi* Vol. 7 中国历代书院志第7册 (Nanjing: Jiangsu Education Publishing House, 1995), 400.

86 Peng, Shi 彭时. "Chongxiu huwending gong shuyuan ji" 重修胡文定公书院记. In *Ming wen zai* 明文在 (Changchun: Jinlin People's Publishing House, 1998), 348.

87 Jiang, Guoxiang 蒋国祥. "Shufu tongzhi jiangguoxiang chongjian erxianci ji" 蜀府同知蒋国祥重建二贤祠记. In *Zhongguo lidai shuyuan zhi* Vol. 2 中国历代书院志第2册 (Nanjing: Jiangsu Education Publishing House, 1995), 353.

88 See Gao, Mingshi 高明士. "Shuyuan jisi kongjian de jiaoyu zuoyong" 书院祭祀空间的教育作用. In *Zhongguo shuyuan* Vol. 1 中国书院第一辑 (Changsha: Hunan Education Press, 1997), 27–39.

89 Zhou, Wei 周伟. "Sidian" 祀典. In *Zhongguo lidai shuyuan zhi* Vol. 1 中国历代书院志第1册 (Nanjing: Jiangsu Education Publishing House, 1995), 550.

90 Cheng, Jufu 程钜夫. "Lishan shuyuan ji" 历山书院记. In *Siku quan shu* Vol. 1202 四库全书第1202册 (Shanghai: Shanghai Chinese Classics Publishing House, 1987), 157.

91 Zhan, Li 詹理. "San xianshengci xing zhuang" 三先生祠行状. In *Zhongguo Lidai shuyuan zhi* Vol. 8 中国历代书院志第8册 (Nanjing: Jiangsu Education Publishing House, 1995), 417.

92 Dai, Junheng 戴钧衡. "Si xiangxian" 祀乡贤. In *Zhongguo Lidai shuyuan zhi* Vol. 9 中国历代书院志第9册 (Nanjing: Jiangsu Education Publishing House, 1995), 766.

93 See Chen, Jixin 陈继新. "Cong jiaoyu guandian xilun songdai shuyuan zhidu" 从教育观点析论宋代书院制度. In *Songdai shuyuan yu songdai xueshu zhi guánxi* 宋代书院与宋代学术之关系 (Taibei: Wenshizhe Publishing House, 1991), 85.

94 Li, Guojun 李国钧. *Zhongguo shuyuan shi* 中国书院史 (Changsha: Hunan Education Publishing House, 1994), 164.

95 Zhang, Shi 张栻. "Tanzhou chongxiu yuelu shuyuan ji" 潭州重修岳麓书院记. In *Siku quan shu* Vol. 1167 四库全书第1167册 (Shanghai: Shanghai Chinese Classics Publishing House, 1987), 506.

96 Yuan, Xie 袁燮. "Donghu shuyuan ji" 东湖书院记. In *Siku quan shu* Vol. 1157 四库全书第1157册 (Shanghai: Shanghai Chinese Classics Publishing House, 1987), 122.

97 Yan, Lian 杨廉. "Zongru ci ji" 宗儒祠记. In *Zhongguo lidai shuyuan zhi* Vol. 2 中国历代书院志第2册 (Nanjing: Jiangsu Education Publishing House, 1995), 174.

98 Dai, Junheng 戴钧衡. "Si xiangxian" 祀乡贤. In *Zhongguo Lidai shuyuan zhi* Vol. 9 中国历代书院志第9册 (Nanjing: Jiangsu Education Publishing House, 1995), 767.

99 Li, Jingde 黎靖德. *Zhuzi yu lei* Vol. 90 朱子语类卷九十 (Beijing: Zhonghua Book Company, 1986), 2295.

108   *Academy Sacrificial Rituals*

100 Dai, Fengyi 戴凤仪. "Shi cai shuo" 释菜说. In *Shi shan shuyuan zhi* Vol. 7 诗山书院卷七 (Xiamen: Xiamen University Press, 1995), 125.

101 Wen, Tianxiang 文天祥. *Wen Tianxiang quanji* Vol. 9 文天祥全集卷九 (Beijing: Zhonghua Book Company, 1985), 219.

102 Dai, Fengyi 戴凤仪. "Shi cai shuo" 释菜说. In *Shishan shuyuan zhi* Vol. 7 诗山书院卷七 (Xiamen: Xiamen University Press, 1995), 125.

103 See Li, Junxiu 李峻岫. "Shilun Han Yu de daotongshuo jiqi mengxue si xiang" 试论韩愈的道统说及其孟学思想. In *Kongzi yanjiu*孔子研究 Vol. 6 (2004).

104 Zhu, Xi 朱熹. "Jin xin zhangju xia" 尽心章句下. In *Mengzi jizhu* Vol. 14孟子集注卷十四 (Beijing: Zhonghua Book Company, 1983), 376–377.

105 Zhu, Xi 朱熹. "Teng wengong zhangju xia" 滕文公章句下. In *Mengzi jizhu* Vol. 6孟子集注卷六 (Beijing: Zhonghua Book Company, 1983), 272.

106 Zhu, Xi 朱熹. "Teng wengong zhangju xia" 滕文公章句下. In *Mengzi jizhu* Vol. 6孟子集注卷六 (Beijing: Zhonghua Book Company, 1983), 273.

107 Zhu, Xi 朱熹. "Jin xin zhangju xia" 尽心章句下. In *Mengzi jizhu* Vol. 14孟子集注卷十四 (Beijing: Zhonghua Book Company, 1983), 377.

108 Han, Yu 韩愈. "Yuan dao" 原道. In *Han Yu wenji* Vol. 1韩愈文集卷一 (Shanghai: Shanghai Chinese Classics Publishing House, 1997), 122.

109 Sun, Shi 苏轼. "Jushi ji xu" 居士集叙. In *Su Dongpo qianji* Vol. 24 苏东坡前集卷二十四 (Beijing: Zhonghua Book Company, 1986), 315.

110 Cheng, Hao 程颢, and Cheng, Yi 程颐. *Er cheng ji* 二程集 (Beijing: Zhonghua Book Company, 1981), 640.

111 Zhu, Xi 朱熹. *Zhongyong zhangju xu* 中庸章句序 (Beijing: Zhonghua Book Company, 1983), 14–15.

112 Zhu, Xi 朱熹. *Zhongyong zhangju xu* 中庸章句序 (Beijing: Zhonghua Book Company, 1983), 15.

113 Zhu, Xi 朱熹. *Zhongyong zhangju xu* 中庸章句序 (Beijing: Zhonghua Book Company, 1983), 14.

114 See Peng, Yongjie 彭永捷. "Lun rujia daotong ji songdai lixue de daotong zhi zheng" 论儒家道统及宋代理学的道统之争. In *Wen shi zhe* 文史哲 Vol. 2 (2001).

115 Chen, Rongjie 陈荣捷. *Zhuxue lun ji* 朱学论集 (Taibei: Student Book Company, 1982), 17.

116 Liu, Qiding 刘起釪. *Shangshu xue shi* 尚书学史 (Beijing: Zhonghua Book Company, 1989), 274.

117 Li, Jingde 黎靖德. *Zhuzi yu lei* Vol. 90 朱子语类卷九十 (Beijing: Zhonghua Book Company, 1986), 2295.

118 See Zhu, Xi 朱熹. "Bailudong chenggao xiansheng wen" 白鹿洞成告先圣文. In *Zhuzi quan shu* 朱子全书 (Shanghai: Shanghai Chinese Classics Publishing House; Hefei: Anhui Education Publishing House, 2002), 4037.

119 See Zhang, Liuquan 章柳泉. *Zhongguo shuyuan shihua-songyuan mingqing shuyuan de yanbian jiqi neirong* 中国书院史话—宋元明清书院的演变及其内容 (Beijing: Educational Science Press, 1981), 13.

120 See Zhu, Xi 朱熹. "Xinzhou zhouxue dacheng dian ji" 信州州学大成殿记. In *Zhuzi quan shu* 朱子全书 (Shanghai: Shanghai Chinese Classics Publishing House; Hefei: Anhui Education Publishing House, 2002), 3806.

121 See Zhu, Xi 朱熹. "Cangzhou jingshe gao xiansheng wen" 沧州精舍告先圣文. In *Zhuzi quan shu* 朱子全书 (Shanghai: Shanghai Chinese Classics Publishing House; Hefei: Anhui Education Publishing House, 2002), 4050.

122 See Zhu, Xi 朱熹. "Shui diao ge tou" 水调歌头. In *Zhuzi quan shu* 朱子全书 (Shanghai: Shanghai Chinese Classics Publishing House; Hefei: Anhui Education Publishing House, 2002), 560.

123 See Zhu, Xi 朱熹. "Cangzhou jingshe gao xiansheng wen" 沧州精舍告先圣文. In *Zhuzi quan shu* 朱子全书 (Shanghai: Shanghai Chinese Classics Publishing House; Hefei: Anhui Education Publishing House, 2002), 4050–4051.

Academy Sacrificial Rituals 109

124 Qiong, He 熊禾. "Jianyang shufang tongwen shuyuan shu" 建阳书坊同文书院疏. In *Siku quan shu* Vol. 1188 四库全书第1188册 (Shanghai: Shanghai Chinese Classics Publishing House, 1987), 800.

125 Liu, Zai 刘宰. "Pingjiang fu huqiu shan shuyuan ji" 平江府虎丘山书院记. In *Siku quan shu* Vol. 1170 四库全书第1170册 (Shanghai: Shanghai Chinese Classics Publishing House, 1987), 612.

126 Gao, Side 高斯得. "Baoqing fu lianxi shutang ji" 宝庆府濂溪书堂记. In *Siku quan shu* Vol. 1170 四库全书第1182册 (Shanghai: Shanghai Chinese Classics Publishing House, 1987), 54.

127 See Xu, Zi 徐梓. *Yuandai shuyuan yanjiu* 元代书院研究 (Beijing: Social Sciences Academic Press, 2000), 158–159.

128 Wang, Yun 王恽. "Raozhoulu chuangjian shuyuan shu" 饶州路创建书院疏. In *Siku quan shu* Vol. 1201 四库全书第1201册 (Shanghai: Shanghai Chinese Classics Publishing House, 1987), 63.

129 Jiang, Yi 蒋易. "Songkaoting shanzhang chen yanxi xu" 送考亭山长陈彦西序. In *Quanyuan wen* Vol. 48 全元文第48册 (Nanjing: Jiangsu Chinese Classics Publishing House, 1999), 75.

130 Yang, Lian 杨廉. "Bailudong shuyuan zongru ci ji" 白鹿洞书院宗儒祠记. In *Bailudong shuyuan guzhi wuzhong* 白鹿洞书院古志五种, 108.

131 Zhou, Wei 周伟. "Zongru ci ji li" 宗儒祠祭礼. In *Zhongguo Lidai shuyuan zhi*. Vol. 1 中国历代书院志第1册 (Nanjing: Jiangsu Education Publishing House, 1995), 553.

132 Wang, Jinzheng 汪晋征. "Huaigu shuyuan si zhu wengong yi" 还古书院祀朱文公议. In *Zhongguo fangzhi congshu* 中国方志丛书 (Taibei: Taibei Chengwen Publishing House, 1985), 1299.

133 Dong, Guifu 董桂敷. "Dao Tong" 道统. In *Zhongguo lidai shuyuan zhi*. Vol. 3 中国历代书院志第3册 (Nanjing: Jiangsu Education Publishing House, 1995), 419–482.

134 Shi, Huang 施璜. "Huaigu shuyuan zhi Vol. 4" 还古书院志卷四. In *Zhongguo lidai shuyuan zhi* Vol. 8 中国历代书院志第8册 (Nanjing: Jiangsu Education Publishing House, 1995), 559.

135 Huang, Gan 黄榦. "Xing zhuang" 行状. In *Zhuanji ziliao* 传记资料 (Beijing: Zhonghua Book Company, 1998), 523.

136 Qiong, He 熊禾. "Chongxiu wuji shuyuan shu" 重修武夷书院疏. In *Siku quan shu* Vol. 1188 四库全书第1188册 (Shanghai: Shanghai Chinese Classics Publishing House, 1987), 800.

137 Qiong, He 熊禾. "Shufang tongwen shuyuan shangliang wen" 书坊同文书院上梁文. In *Siku quan shu* Vol. 1188 四库全书第1188册 (Shanghai: Shanghai Chinese Classics Publishing House, 1987), 804.

138 Yu, Ji 虞集. "Kaoting shuyuan chongjian wengong citang ji" 考亭书院重建文公祠堂记. In *Quanyuan wen* Vol. 26 全元文第26册 (Nanjing: Jiangsu Chinese Classics Publishing House, 1999), 524–525.

139 Yu, Ji 虞集. "Ba ji ning lizhang suoke jiujing sishu" 跋济宁李璋所刻九经四书. In *Quanyuan wen* Vol. 26 全元文第26册 (Nanjing: Jiangsu Chinese Classics Publishing House, 1999), 333.

140 Song, Lian 宋濂. "Lixue zuanyan xu" 理学纂言序. In *Siku quan shu* Vol. 1223 四库全书第1223册 (Shanghai: Shanghai Chinese Classics Publishing House, 1987), 368.

141 Hou, Wailu 侯外庐, Qiu, Hansheng 邱汉生, and Zhang, Qizhi 张岂之. *Songming lixue shi.* 宋明理学史 (Beijing: People's Publishing House, 1997), 21.

142 Li, Mengyang 李梦阳. "Bailudong shuyuan xinzhi" 白鹿洞书院新志. In *Bailudong shuyuan guzhi wuzhong* 白鹿洞书院古志五种, 23.

143 See Fang, Yanshou 方彦寿. *Zhuxi shuyuan yu menren kao* 朱熹书院与门人考 (Shanghai: East China Normal University Press, 2000), 6–35.

144 Yu, Ji 虞集. "Kaoting shuyuan chongjian zhuwengong citang zhi" 考亭书院重建朱文公祠堂制. In *Quanyuan wen* Vol. 26 全元文第26册 (Nanjing: Jiangsu Classics Publishing House, 1999), 525.

110 *Academy Sacrificial Rituals*

145 See Xu Zi 徐梓. *Yuandai shuyuan yanjiu*元代书院研究 (Beijing: Social Sciences Academic Press, 2000), 151–159.

146 Zhou, Hongmo 周洪谟. "Chongxiu shuyuan ji" 重修书院记. In *Zhongguo lidai shuyuan zhi* Vol. 4 中国历代书院志第4册 (Nanjing: Jiangsu Education Publishing House, 1995), 84.

147 See Li, Yingsheng 李应升. "Yange" 沿革. In *Zhongguo lidai shuyuan zhi* Vol. 1 中国历代书院志第1册 (Nanjing: Jiangsu Education Publishing House, 1995), 732.

148 Wang, Jinzheng 汪晋征. "Huangu shuyuan si zhuwengong yi" 还古书院祀朱文公议. In *Zhongguo fangzhi congshu huazhong* Vol. 181 中国方志丛书华中第181号 (Taibei: Taibei Chengwen Publishing House, 1985), 1299–1300.

149 See Mao, Deqi 毛德琦. "Yange" 沿革. In *Zhongguo lidai shuyuan zhi* Vol. 2 中国历代书院志第2册 (Nanjing: Jiangsu Education Publishing House, 1995), 46.

150 Lu, Jiuyuan 陆九渊. "Yu zhisun xun" 与侄孙濬. In *Lu Jiuyuan ji* Vol. 1 陆九渊集卷一 (Beijing: Zhonghua Book Company, 1980), 12.

151 Lu, Jiuyuan 陆九渊. "Yu lu yanbin" 与路彦彬. In *Lu Jiuyuan ji* Vol. 10 陆九渊集卷十 (Beijing: Zhonghua Book Company, 1980), 134.

152 Huang, Xianglong 黄翔龙. "Chongxiu cihu shuyuan benmo ji" 重修慈湖书院本末记. In *Songyuan fangzhi congkan* 宋元方志丛刊 (Beijing: Zhonghua Book Company, 1990), 6340.

153 See Li, Guo jun 李国钧, et al. *Zhongguo shuyuan shi* 中国书院史 (Changsha: Hunan Education Publishing House, 1994), 325.

154 Yuan, Fu 袁甫. "Xiangshan shuyuan ji" 象山书院记. In *Siku quan shu* Vol. 1175 四库全书第1175册 (Shanghai: Shanghai Chinese Classics Publishing House, 1987), 486–487.

155 Yuan, Fu 袁甫. "Ji lu xiangshan xiansheng wen" 祭陆象山先生文. In *Siku quan shu* Vol. 1175 四库全书第1175册 (Shanghai: Shanghai Chinese Classics Publishing House, 1987), 532.

156 Huang, Xianglong 黄翔龙. "Chongxiu cihu shuyuan benmo ji" 重修慈湖书院本末记. In *Songyuan fangzhi congkan* 宋元方志丛刊 (Beijing: Zhonghua Book Company, 1990), 6340.

157 Wen, Jiweng 文及翁. "Cihu shuyuan ji" 慈湖书院记. In *Songyuan fangzhi congkan* 宋元方志丛刊 (Beijing: Zhonghua Book Company, 1990), 6337.

158 Zhang, Tingyu 张廷玉 et al. "Rulin zhuanxu" 儒林传序. In *Mingshi* Vol. 282 明史卷二百八十二 (Beijing: Zhonghua Book Company, 1974), 7222.

159 See Wang, Shouren 王守仁. "Nianpu" Appendix 1 年谱附录一. In *Wang Yangming quanji* Vol. 36 王阳明全集卷三十六 (Shanghai: Shanghai Chinese Classics Publishing House, 1992), 1328–1355.

160 Wang, Shouren 王守仁. "Nianpu san" 年谱三. In *Wang Yangming quanji* Vol. 35 王阳明全集卷三十五 (Shanghai: Shanghai Chinese Classics Publishing House, 1992), 1326.

161 Wang, Shouren 王守仁. "Nianpu"Appendix 1 年谱附录一. In *Wang Yangming quanji* Vol. 36 王阳明全集卷三十六 (Shanghai: Shanghai Chinese Classics Publishing House, 1992), 1353.

162 Dong, Chang 董玚. "Yaojiang shuyuan fuji" 姚江书院附记. In *Zhongguo lidai shuyuan zhi* Vol. 9 中国历代书院志第9册 (Nanjing: Jiangsu Education Publishing House, 1995), 276.

163 Shao, Tingcai 邵廷采. "Yaojiang shuyuan zhuan" 姚江书院传. In *Zhongguo lidai shuyuan zhi* Vol. 9 中国历代书院志第9册 (Nanjing: Jiangsu Education Publishing House, 1995), 315.

164 Shao, Tingcai 邵廷采. "Yaojiang shuyuan ji" 姚江书院记. In *Zhongguo lidai shuyuan zhi* Vol. 9 中国历代书院志第9册 (Nanjing: Jiangsu Education Publishing House, 1995), 279.

165 Dong, Chang 董玚. "Yaojiang shuyuan fuji" 姚江书院附记. In *Zhongguo lidai shuyuan zhi* Vol. 9 中国历代书院志第9册 (Nanjing: Jiangsu Education Publishing House, 1995), 277.

166 Dong, Chang 董玚. "Yaojiang shuyuan fuji" 姚江书院附记. In *Zhongguo lidai shuyuan zhi* Vol. 9 中国历代书院志第9册 (Nanjing: Jiangsu Education Publishing House, 1995), 277.

167 Shao, Tingcai 邵廷采. "Yaojiang shuyuan houji" 姚江书院后记. In *Zhongguo lidai shuyuan zhi* Vol. 9 中国历代书院志第9册 (Nanjing: Jiangsu Education Publishing House, 1995), 279.

168 Guang, Zu 光祖. "Chongxiu xuancheng shuyuan ji" 重修宣成书院记. In *Zhongguo fangzhi congshu huanan* Vol. 15 中国方志丛书华南第15号 (Taibei: Taibei Chengwen Publishing House, 1985), 225.

169 See Hu, Shi 胡适. "Shuyuan zhi shi lue" 书院制史略. In *Dongfang zazhi* Vol. 21 东方杂志第21卷. See Chen, Yuanhui 陈元晖, Yin, Dexin 尹德新, and Wang, Bingzhao 王炳照. *Zhongguo gudai de shuyuan zhidu* 中国古代的书院制度 (Shanghai: Shanghai Education Publishing House, 1981), 148.

170 Wang, Yucheng 王禹偁. "Tanzhou yuelushan shuyuan ji" 潭州岳麓山书院记. In *Siku quan shu* Vol. 1086 四库全书第1086册 (Shanghai: Shanghai Chinese Classics Publishing House, 1987), 164.

171 Wang, Yinglin 王应麟. "Gong shi · yuan" 宫室·院. In *Siku quan shu* Vol. 947 四库全书第947册 (Shanghai: Shanghai Chinese Classics Publishing House, 1987), 352.

172 See Zhu, Xi 朱熹. "Jiangzhou chongjian lianxi xiansheng shutang ji" 江州重建濂溪先生书堂记. In *Zhuzi quan shu* 朱子全书 (Shanghai: Shanghai Chinese Classics Publishing House; Hefei: Anhui Education Publishing House, 2002), 3739.

173 See Zhu, Xi 朱熹. "Bailudong chenggao xiansheng wen" 白鹿洞成告先圣文. In *Zhuzi quan shu* 朱子全书 (Shanghai: Shanghai Chinese Classics Publishing House; Hefei: Anhui Education Publishing House, 2002), 4037.

174 Chen, Zhu 陈著. "Jizhou bailuzhou shuyuan jiangyi" 吉州白鹭洲书院讲义. In *Siku quan shu* Vol. 1185 四库全书第1185册 (Shanghai: Shanghai Classics Publishing House, 1987), 520.

175 Lu, Jiuyuan 陆九渊. "Nianpu · chunxi ernian" 年谱·淳熙二年. In *Lu Jiuyuan ji* Vol. 36 陆九渊集卷三十六 (Beijing: Zhonghua Book Company, 1980), 491.

176 Lu, Jiuyuan 陆九渊. "Nianpu · chunxi ernian" 年谱·淳熙二年. In *Lu Jiuyuan ji* Vol. 36 陆九渊集卷三十六 (Beijing: Zhonghua Book Company, 1980), 490.

177 See Huang, Zongxi 黄宗羲, and Quan, Zuwang 全祖望. "Caolu xue'an" 草庐学案. In *Songyuan xue'an* Vol. 92 宋元学案卷九十二 (Beijing: Zhonghua Book Company, 1986), 3036.

178 Yuan, Fu 袁甫. "Chujian shuyuan gao luxiangshan xiansheng wen" 初建书院告陆象山先生文. In *Siku quan shu* Vol. 1175 四库全书第1175册 (Shanghai: Shanghai Chinese Classics Publishing House, 1987), 532.

179 Huang, Zongxi 黄宗羲, and Quan, Zuwang 全祖望. *Caolu xue'an* 草庐学案. *Songyuan xue'an* Vol. 92 宋元学案卷九十二 (Beijing: Zhonghua Book Company, 1986), 3046.

180 Zheng, Yu 郑玉. "Song Ge zixi zhi wuchang xuelu xu" 送葛子熙之武昌学录序. In *Quanyuan wen* Vol. 46 全元文第46册 (Nanjing: Jiangsu Chinese Classics Publishing House, 1999), 314.

181 See Hou, Wailu 侯外庐, Qiu, Hansheng 邱汉生, and Zhang, Qizhi 张岂之. *Songming lixue shi* 宋明理学史 (Beijing: People's Publishing House, 1997), 749–767.

182 Xue, Xuan 薛瑄. "Dushu lu" Vol. 1读书录卷一. In *Siku quan shu* Vol. 711 四库全书第711册 (Shanghai: Shanghai Chinese Classics Publishing House, 1987), 549.

183 Gao, Ruofeng 高若凤. "Songren dushu ludong" 送人读书鹿洞. In *Zhongguo Lidai shuyuan zhi* Vol. 2 中国历代书院志第2册 (Nanjing: Jiangsu Education Publishing House, 1995), 226.

184 Wang, Shouren 王守仁. "Waiji san · da xu chengzhi zhier" 外集三·答徐成之之二. In *Wang Yangming quanji* Vol. 31 王阳明全集卷三十一 (Shanghai: Shanghai Chinese Classics Publishing House, 1992), 808–809.

185 Wang, Shouren 王守仁. "Xubian yi · ji zheng xiannan shoumo erjuan" 续编一·寄正宪男手墨二卷. In *Wang Yangming quanji* Vol. 26 王阳明全集卷二十六 (Shanghai: Shanghai Chinese Classics Publishing House, 1992), 990.

186 Quan, Zuwang 全祖望. "Chahu shuyuan ji" 槎湖书院记. In *Xuxiu siku quan shu* Vol. 1429 续修四库全书第 1429册 (Shanghai: Shanghai Chinese Classics Publishing House, 2002), 615.

187 Quan, Zuwang 全祖望. "Chahu shuyuan ji" 槎湖书院记. In *Xuxiu siku quan shu* Vol. 1429 续修四库全书第 1429册 (Shanghai: Shanghai Chinese Classics Publishing House, 2002), 615.

188 Dong, Chang 董场. "Yaojiang shuyuan fuji" 姚江书院附记. In *Zhongguo lidai shuyuan zhi* Vol. 9 中国历代书院志第9册 (Nanjing: Jiangsu Education Publishing House, 1995), 277.

189 Shao, Tingcai 邵廷采. "Yaojiang shuyuan ji" 姚江书院记. In *Zhongguo lidai shuyuan zhi* Vol. 9 中国历代书院志第9册 (Nanjing: Jiangsu Education Publishing House, 1995), 278.

190 Gu, Xiancheng 顾宪成. "Rixin shuyuan ji" 日新书院记. In *Siku quan shu* Vol. 1292 四库全书第1292册 (Shanghai: Shanghai Chinese Classics Publishing House, 1987), 144.

191 Gu, Xiancheng 顾宪成. "Rixin shuyuan ji" 日新书院记. In *Siku quan shu* Vol. 1292 四库全书第1292册 (Shanghai: Shanghai Chinese Classics Publishing House, 1987), 144–145.

192 Gu, Xiancheng 顾宪成. "Rixin shuyuan ji" 日新书院记. In *Siku quan shu* Vol. 1292 四库全书第1292册 (Shanghai: Shanghai Chinese Classics Publishing House, 1987), 145.

193 See Zhang, Nai 张鼐et al. "Yushan shuyuan zhi" Vol. 3 虞山书院志卷三. In *Zhongguo lidai shuyuan zhi* Vol. 8 中国历代书院志第8册 (Nanjing: Jiangsu Education Publishing House, 1995), 57–68.

194 Shao, Tingcai 邵廷采. "Yaojiang shuyuan ji" 姚江书院记. In *Zhongguo lidai shuyuan zhi* Vol. 9 中国历代书院志第9册 (Nanjing: Jiangsu Education Publishing House, 1995), 278.

195 Huang, Zongxi 黄宗羲, and Quan, Zuwang 全祖望. *Dongfa xue'an* 东发学案, *Songyuan xue'an* Vol. 86 宋元学案卷八十六 (Beijing: Zhonghua Book Company, 1986), 2884.

196 Quan, Zuwang 全祖望. "Du zhou liuxiansheng shuyuan ji" 杜洲六先生书院记. In *Xuxiu siku quan shu* Vol. 1429 续修四库全书第 1429册 (Shanghai: Shanghai Chinese Classics Publishing House, 2002), 611.

197 Zhang, Yin 张釿. "Gujing jingshe zhi chugao" 诂经精舍志初稿. In *Wenlan xuebao* Vol. 2 文澜学报第2卷 (1936), 7.

198 Ruan, Yuan 阮元. "Xihu gujing jingshe ji" 西湖诂经精舍记. In *Congshu jicheng* 丛书集成 (Beijing: The Commercial Press, 1936), 61.

199 See Zhang, Liuquan 章柳泉. *Zhongguo shuyuan shihua—songyuan mingqing shuyuan de yanbian jiqi neirong* 中国书院史话—宋元明清书院的演变及其内容 (Beijing: Educational Science Publishing House, 1981), 15.

200 See Yang, Shenchu 杨慎初, Zhu, Hanmin 朱汉民, and Deng, Hongbo 邓洪波. *Yuelu shuyuan shilue* 岳麓书院史略 (Changsha: Yuelu Press, 1986), 130.

201 Ruan, Yuan 阮元. "Xihu gujing jingshe ji" 西湖诂经精舍记. In *Congshu jicheng* 丛书集成 (Beijing: The Commercial Press, 1936), 61.

202 Qian, Fulin 钱福林. "Gujing jingshe chongsi xu zheng liang xianshi ji" 诂经精舍崇祀许郑两先师记. In *Congshu jicheng* 丛书集成 (Beijing: The Commercial Press, 1936), 63.

203 Yu, Yue 俞樾. "Chongxiu Gujing jingshe ji" 重修诂经精舍记. In *Zhongguo fangzhi congshu huazhong* Vol. 199 中国方志丛书华中第199号 (Taibei: Taibei Chengwen Publishing House, 1985), 480.

204 Hu, Peihui 胡培翚. "Qian Zhuting xiansheng rusi zhongshan shuyuan ji" 钱竹汀先生入祀钟山书院记. In *Xuxiu siku quan shu* Vol. 1507 续修四库全书第1507册 (Shanghai: Shanghai Chinese Classics Publishing House, 2002), 453.

205 Hu, Peihui 胡培翚. "Qian zhuting xiansheng rusi zhongshan shuyuan ji" 钱竹汀先生入祀钟山书院记. In *Xuxiu siku quan shu* Vol. 1507 续修四库全书第1507册 (Shanghai: Shanghai Chinese Classics Publishing House, 2002), 453.

3 Academy and Regional Cultural Undertakings

In ancient China, for lack of efficient transportation and communication, different regions, separated by mountains and rivers, developed quite independently from one another and thus demonstrated different regional features. As bases for training Confucian scholars as well as innovating, developing, and disseminating Confucian thoughts, the academies, which were scattered all over the country, did not only greatly promote the development of regional education and culture, but also facilitated cultural communication among different regions.

Scholarly Activities and Regional Confucian Schools

Functions of academies changed over time, but, on the whole,[1] their major function—conducting academic research activities—remained unchanged. During the early years of these academies, they were places for book storage and individual studies. Gradually, as their educational role became increasingly prominent, they began recruiting students and giving lectures while maintaining the key function of conducting academic research. After the establishment of the Song dynasty (960–1279), the development of Confucianism varied regionally in China, and many regional Confucian schools emerged. In Vol. 6, "Annal of Confucian Scholars of Shi-Liu School" (士刘诸儒学案), in *Scholarly Annals of Song and Yuan Periods* (宋元学案), it is stated that "since the reign of Qingli (1041–1048), many Confucian schools have sprung up."[2] This is a reflection of the development trend of Confucianism during the Song and Yuan dynasties (960–1368). During this period of time, Confucian schools based in different regions of China disengaged themselves from the official-rigged interpretation of Confucianism and elaborated on its philosophy from different angles. Their interpretations of Confucianism boasted distinct regional characteristics. After the establishment of the Song dynasty (960–1279), unofficial Confucian schools thrived in different regions across the country, and they overturned the trend of accepting and disseminating the only officially recognized interpretation of Confucianism. This was the most remarkable change in the development of Confucianism at that time.[3] Over several hundred years, regional Confucian schools, such as the Lian School, the Luo School, the Guan School, the Min School, the Huxiang School, the Jinhua School,

DOI: 10.4324/9781003332305-3

Regional Cultural Undertakings 115

and the Yaojiang School, were active in China's ideological and academic circles, offering a diversified interpretation of Confucianism. These schools developed vigorously, showing strong vitality and creativity. Given that these non-official regional Confucian schools had to rely on the non-official academies to organize academic activities, the academies quickly became the bases for Confucian studies and innovations in different regions. Neo-Confucian researchers of the Song and Ming dynasties (960–1644) and the textology researchers of the Qing dynasty also had similar interactions with academies. There was a mutually fulfilling relationship between Confucian scholars and academies.

The Huxiang School was an important school of Song dynasty Neo-Confucianism, featuring a unique theoretical framework and characteristics. It was initiated by Hu Anguo (1074–1138) and his son Hu Hong (1105–1161) and carried forward by Hu Hong's disciple Zhang Shi (1133–1180). This school reached its heyday in the middle of the Southern Song dynasty (1127–1279) and had a great influence in academic circles. In "Annal of the Scholars of Nanxuan School" (南轩学案), Vol. 50 of *Scholarly Annals of Song and Yuan Periods* (宋元学案), Huang Zongxi, the author of the book, comments, "The Confucian school in Hunan Province was the most popular school at that time."[4] The Huxiang School conducted its academic activities in academies. During the early year of the Southern Song dynasty, Hu Anguo, who migrated from the Jingmen City of Hubei Province to the Xiangtan City of Hunan Province, purchased land and built a school there in a place named Biquan. This school was thus named Biquan School.[5] He built another school named Wending School at the foot of Ziyun Mount. At his schools, he furthered his studies, wrote books, and gave lectures. Later, his son, Hu Hong, expanded Biquan School and renamed it Biquan Academy. In his article dedicated to the academy titled "Records of Biquan Academy" (碧泉书院上梁文), he explained why he and his father built Confucian schools. He writes, "We hope to spread the thought of the sage by studying the Confucian classics and to enrich ourselves by studying the history. We want to discover the laws governing society. We aspire after truth instead of wealth."[6] Hu Hong was confident about the revival of Confucianism. He expressed such confidence in the following words: "The Confucian sages' great cause will be carried forward, and it will last forever."[7] Biquan School, Wending School, and Biquan Academy were Hu Hong and his father's research bases. Hu Anguo completed his representative work Commentaries on *The Spring and Autumn Annals* (春秋传) in Wending School, and Hu Hong completed his representative work *Words of Wisdom* (知言) when working as a teacher in his academy. In their research bases, they established their theoretical framework that highlighted the importance of human nature, which later became the theoretical foundation and characteristics of the Huxiang School. Their studies conducted on their research bases literally started the academic traditions of the Huxiang School.[8] Zhang Shi once described how his teacher Hu Hong taught and studied Confucian thought in Hunan Province for more than 20 years:

He spent more than 20 years at the foot of the mount, pondering over Confucian thought day and night and constantly putting the thought into practice.

116 *Regional Cultural Undertakings*

He analyzed every detail and thought about the governance issues . . . His words were concise but carried profound meaning. He mastered the essence of Confucian thought and governance wisdom.[9]

Zhang Shi used to teach *The Analects of Confucius* (论语) at Chengnan Academy and Yuelu Academy, and during this period of time,[10] he completed the following works to expound upon Confucian thought: Annotations to *The Analects of Confucius* (论语解) and *On Mencius* (孟子说). In the preface to *On Mencius* (孟子说), he writes, "This year, the fourth year of the Qiandao reign (1165–1173), I've studied together with several scholars in the academies in Changsha City. Please allow me to humbly record what I've learned in this book." In the following several years, he revised and edited the book again and again. In the ninth year of the Qiandao reign (1173), he finally finished the great work and shared it with other scholars.[11] In reality, in the Southern Song dynasty, the establishment, development, and success of the Huxiang School relied heavily on the thriving Biquan Academy, Chengnan Academy, and Yuelu Academy.[12]

The Min school, also known as the Zhuzi School or the Kaoting School, was initiated by Zhu Xi (1130–1200) and was regarded as one of the most famous Neo-Confucian schools, together with the Lian School, the Luo School, and the Guan School. Apart from Zhu Xi, representative scholars of the school also included Zhu Xi's students, such as Cai Shen (1167–1230), Huang Gan (1152–1221), and Chen Chun (1483–1544). Among all the Neo-Confucian schools, the Min School did the best in epitomizing the Song dynasty's Neo-Confucianism and had a far-reaching influence on the academic history of China. The academic activities of the Min School were usually carried out in academies, and such activities were a lifelong pursuit of Zhu Xi. Throughout his life, he traveled extensively, and wherever he went, he devoted energies to academic activities and the development of academies. Although he passed the imperial exam at the age of 19, his official career was not long. He worked as an official of a local government for only nine years and spent most of his time giving lectures in Jiangxi, Fujian, Zhejiang, and Hunan Provinces before he passed away at the age of 71. Even when he worked in the government, he also spent 40 days interpreting Confucian classics for the emperor. A researcher named Fang Yanshou wrote a treatise titled *Textual Research on Academies Related to Zhu Xi and His Disciples* (朱熹书院与门人考). In his treatise, he points out that the number of academies that Zhu Xi established, restored, or hosted reached several dozen.[13] These academic activities carried out in the academies were closely related to the establishment and development of Zhu Xi's academic thought. When working at these academies, Zhu Xi completed many of his Li Xue (Neo-Confucian) works. For example, in the sixth year of the Qiandao reign (1170), he built Hanquan Academy and worked there in the following several years. In those years, he completed a series of academic works such as the first draft of *Annotations to "Explanation of the Diagram of the Utmost Extreme"* (太极图说解), *Annotations to Zhangzai's Mottos* (西铭解), the 10-volume *A Compendium on The Analects of Confucius* (论语精义), the 14-volume *A Compendium on Mencius* (孟子精义), the 59-volume *Revised Version of Comprehensive Mirror in Aid of Governance* (资治通鉴纲目), and the 24-volume *Records of Words and Deeds of Eminent Persons of the Song Period* (八朝名臣言行录) and compiled quite a few academic works, including the 12-volume *Complete Writings of the Brothers Cheng* (程氏外书), the 14-volume *The Origins of the Yi-Luo School* (伊洛渊源录), the 16-volume *Family Rituals That Ever Existed* (古今家祭礼), and the single-volume *Textual Research on Yin Fu Jing* (阴符经考异). During this period of time, he also worked with Lü Zuqian (1137–1181) in compiling and editing the 14-volume *Close Thoughts* (近思录). For seven years, from the tenth year of the Chunxi reign (1183) to the first year of the Shaoxi reign (1190), Zhu Xi was all the time engaging himself in academic activities at Wuyi Academy. In those years, he finished the following works: the four-volume *A Interpretation of the Book of Changes* (易学启蒙), the single-volume *Amendment to the Classic of Filial Piety* (孝经刊误), the six-volume *Lexicography and Lesser Learning* (小学), *Syntactic and Semantic Analysis of the Great learning* (大学章句), and the single-volume *Syntactic and Semantic Analysis of the Doctrine of the Mean* (中庸章句). From the third year of the Shaoxi reign (1192) to the sixth year of the Qingyuan reign (1200), Zhu Xi spent most of his time giving lectures and writing academic works at Kaoting Academy. The works that he finished during this period of time included *Essential Ideas of Mencius* (孟子要略), *Critical Investigations of Han Yu's Essays* (韩文考异), the six-volume *The Commentary on Book of Documents* (书集传), the eight-volume *Interpretation on Chuci* (楚辞集注), the two-volume *Arguments on Chuci* (楚辞辨证), the 37-volume *General Explanation on Etiquettes and Rites* (仪礼经传通解), and the single-volume *Critical Investigations of the Kinship of the Three and the Book of Changes* (周易参同契考异).[14] In the third month of the sixth year of the Qingyuan reign, Zhu Xi continued working on the notes to "Self-Restraint" (诚意章), a chapter of the Confucian classic *The Great learning* (大学), in his sickbed. Zhu Xi's most representative work, *Interlinear Analysis of and Collected Commentaries on the Four Books* (四书章句集注), was also completed during the years when he gave lectures at different academies.[15] His students wrote a 140-volume book titled *The Analects of Zhuzi* (朱子语类), which included all the lectures that Zhu Xi gave at different academies across the country. The book also demonstrated that it was a daily routine of Zhu Xi to have discussions on a wide range of subjects with his students, such as universal principles, human nature, and laws of the world. In this process, his Li Xue (Neo-Confucian) studies became increasingly profound.

In the Song and Ming dynasties (960–1644), almost all Neo-Confucian schools relied on academies to conduct academic activities such as lectures and academic research. The Wu School, represented by Lü Zuqian, gave lectures at Mount Mingzhao and built an academy there, which was named Lize Academy. The Xin Xue School (School of Mind), which emphasized the learning of the mind and was represented by Lu Jiuyuan (1139–1192), took Xiangshan Academy and Donghu Academy as its research bases. Wang Yangming (1472–1529) and his students set up academies wherever they went to spread their philosophy that highlighted the importance of one's innate moral goodness. On the whole, the mutually fulfilling relationship between Neo-Confucian research and the academies was apparent.

118   *Regional Cultural Undertakings*

With the help of academies, Neo-Confucian scholars spread their thoughts and ideas, and with the help of the scholars, the academies developed vigorously. When discussing the development of Neo-Confucianism in the Song dynasty, scholars tend to recognize such a fact, "During the last years of and after the collapse of the Northern Song dynasty (960–1127), the development of academies and that of Neo-Confucianism were closely bounded: they thrived together and declined together."[16]

After the establishment of the Qing dynasty (1616–1912), given the change in the academic atmosphere, the studies on the connotations and essence of the Confucian classics were replaced by textual studies in the academies. During the Qianlong and Jiaqing reign (1711–1820), some scholars who had different opinions about academic studies began propagating "reliable studies" and highlighted the importance of conducting textual studies on classical works. A well-known Han-learning scholar named Wang Mingsheng (1722–1797) expressed the following ideas in the preface to his book *Critique on the Seventeen Dynastic Histories* (十七史商榷).

> The focus of studying is better placed on reliable facts rather than unreliable interpretations and comments. The historical records are reliable, and scholars are supposed to adopt reliable methods to study history. In this way, reliable knowledge can be achieved.[17]
>
> The classics were created to explain laws and principles. It is unnecessary to interpret them. We should carefully study the very writing, pronunciation, and meaning of the original text. In this way, we can clearly understand the laws and principles described in the classics.[18]

Dai Zhen (1724–1777) notes, "The classics are about laws and principles, and they resort to characters to express them. We shall carefully study the characters, the words, the sentences so as to correctly understand the meaning of the classics."[19] These scholars tried to dig out the essence of Confucianism by studying the ancient characters and the original texts and thus engaged themselves in textual studies. Back then, most academies still focused on training for imperial exams and stuck to their tradition of interpreting classics for practical purposes.[20] They were still good at the imperial exam training but could not adapt to the changing academic atmosphere. Given this, many textual research scholars, who wanted to train textual researchers, build their own research bases, and boost the development of textology, began reforming academies. In the middle of the 18th century, many academies in areas south of the lower reaches of the Yangtze River began shifting their focus from imperial exam training to textual studies on classics, trying to turn themselves into textology research bases. American scholar Benjamin A. Elman observed that Han learning rose in Suzhou City in China in the middle of the 18th century and exerted an immediate influence on the local academies and that its influence quickly expanded to other areas south of the lower reaches of the Yangtze River, where the academies replaced their traditional Confucian studies that had been passed on from the Song dynasty with Han learning.[21] During this period of time, many academies were closely bonded with textology: Wuxing's (now Wuxing District of Zhejiang Province's Huzhou City) Longcheng Academy, Jiangyin County's Ziyang Academy and Jiyang Academy, Suzhou City's Ziyang Academy, Yangzhou City's Anding Academy and Meihua Academy, Nanjing City's Zhongshan Academy, and Hangzhou City's Fuwen Academy, Chongwen Academy, and Ziyang Academy. Well-known textologists of that time, such as Lu Wenchao (1717–1795), Li Zhaoluo (1769–1841), Qian Daxin (1728–1804), Wang Mingsheng (1722–1797), Wang Chang (1725–1806), Chen Zude (1841–1914), Hang Shijun (1695–1773), Zhao Yi (1727–1814), and Qi Zhaonan (1703–1768), worked as teachers in these academies or ran some of these academies, making these academies research bases for Han learning.[22]

Some textologists also built their new academies that specialized in Han learning research and education. In the sixth year of the Jiaqing reign (1801), Ruan Yuan (1764–1849), who served as the governor of Zhejiang Province, built an academy advocating Han learning named Gujing Academy at the foot of an isolated hill near the West Lake in Hangzhou City, and invited famous Han-learning scholars Sun Xingyan (1753–1818) and Wang Chang (1725–1806) to preside over the research work of the academy. During the early years of the Daoguang reign (1782–1850), Ruan Yuan became the governor of Guangdong and Guangxi Provinces and built another Han-learning academy named Xuehai Academy on top of Mount Yuexiu in Guangzhou City. He explicitly pointed out that this academy should be specialized in "reliable studies"—namely, textual studies on Confucian classics. To promote the development of textual studies on Confucian classics, Ruan Yuan organized teachers and students of the two academies to collate different explanations of Confucian classics and compiled the following books: *Commentaries on Thirteen Classics* (十三经注疏) and *Research on Classics Conducted in the Qing Dynasty* (皇清精解).[23] Duan Yucai (1735–1815) once described how Ruan Yuan presided over the editorial work of *Commentaries on Thirteen Classics* (十三经注疏) at Gujing Academy:

> He invited famous scholars to Gujing Academy, which was situated near the West Lake, and asked them to collate the documents and edit the book there. At night, when he returned from his work, Ruan Yuan would light a candle and proofread the work.[24]

Because of Ruan Yuan's efforts, these two academies became the most prestigious Han-learning research and training bases of that time. A researcher named Li Guojun commented that Gujing Academy and Xuehai Academy best represented the Qing dynasty academies, as they inherited the academic tradition of studying the original texts and accelerated the development of the Qianjia School.[25]

Under the influence of Gujing Academy and Xuehai Academy, a number of Han-learning academies were built across the country: Ronghu Academy of Guilin City, which was built by the head of the Guangxi provincial government in the 14th year of the Daoguang reign (1834); Xiyin Academy of Nanjing City, which

120 *Regional Cultural Undertakings*

was built by Tao Shu, governor of the Liangjiang Region (Jiangsu, Jiangxi, and Anhui Provinces) and governor of Jiangsu Province, in the 18th year of the Daoguang reign (1838); Jingxun Academy of Nanchang City, which was built by Liu Banzhong, attorney general of Jiangxi Province in the 20th year of the Daoguang reign (1840); Longmen Academy of Shanghai City, which was built by Ding Richang (1823–1882), military commander of the Suzhou-Songjiang Region (now Suzhou City and Shanghai City), in the fourth year of the Tongzhi reign (1865); Gujing Academy of Shanghai City, which was built by Shen Bingcheng (1823–1895), head of the local government, in the 12th year of the Tongzhi reign (1873).[26] Although they boasted their own unique features, these academies all focused on textual studies of ancient classics. *Statutes of Xiyin Academy* (惜阴书院章程), formulated by Tao Shu, clearly stipulated that the purpose of the academy was to study ancient classics for practical uses. Wu Rongguang (1773–1843) built Xiangshui Jiaojingtang Academy, when he worked as the governor of Hunan Province. When he built the academy, he mentions the academic pursuit of the academy in his poem "Parting in the South of Hunan" (湘南述别), which was to seek the real meaning of Confucian classics and the essence of Confucian thought.[27]

Regional cultures in China were tightly associated with the territories they inhabited. Given this, when a region's academic activities thrived, the corresponding regional culture became increasingly academic. A regional culture usually covered multiple levels and a wide range of contents, but its core was always the prevailing academic theory in the region. Academic theories that prevailed in different regions represented these regions' highest academic achievements and influenced the trends in the development of the corresponding regional cultures. Now some scholars even hold that there was an isomorphic relationship between some regional Confucian schools and the corresponding regional cultures: Academically active Confucian academies of a region usually conducted cutting-edge theoretical studies of the relevant social phenomena so as to respond to the needs of society and the time;[28] in this process, they effectively improved their Confucian thought and established their unique academic theory that would become the core and the development trend of their regional culture and would enhance the culture academically. Regional Confucian schools such as the Huxiang School and the Min School of the Song dynasty and the textology school represented by Xuehai Academy in the Qing dynasty were the best examples in this regard.

In the Southern Song dynasty, scholars of the Huxiang School, represented by Hu Hong and Zhang Shi, took academies as their research bases and the exploration of the way to achieve a harmonious society as their duty. They inherited the Neo-Confucian thought of the Northern Song dynasty scholars and further developed the Confucian thoughts regarding the human inner world and the pursuit of the goodness of the human inner world. Hu Hong highlighted the importance of human nature and regarded it as the foundation of the world. On this basis, he proposed his theory about the human inner world, stating that human nature was the underlying law of the world and governed all the other laws and principles in the world.[29] This was his conclusion and sublimation of the Song dynasty

Neo-Confucian thought. His thought, which was remarkably different from Zhu Xi's thought and that of Lu Jiuyuan, had unique theoretical features and made a contribution to the development of Confucian thought about the human inner world. As to how to pursue the goodness of the human inner world, the Huxiang School advocated one's intentional efforts to observe and improve oneself. The school highlighted the importance of self-awareness and self-correction. Zhu Xi once agreed with this theory, but later he began to criticize it.[30] Many influential academic arguments and debates between Zhu Xi and Zhang Shi evolved around this theory. Given its academic achievement, the Huxiang School attracted the entire Chinese academic circle's attention, and its theory was once venerated as the most advanced Confucian theory of its time. Lü Zuqian, a famous Southern Song dynasty scholar, thought highly of the Huxiang School, and Quan Zuwang (1705–1755), a famous Qing dynasty historian, also praised the school in a chapter titled "Annal of the Confucian Scholar Hu Hong" (五峰学案) of his book *Scholarly Annals of Song and Yuan Periods* (宋元学案). Quan Zuwang (1705–1755) writes, "Hu Hong outshone his peers, and the Donglai School even thought that his work *Words of Wisdom* (知言) surpassed Zhang Zai's (1020–1077) *Enlightenment* (正蒙)." Present-day representative Neo-Confucian scholar Mou Zongsan observes,[31]

> Hu Hong's thought focuses on human nature and how to achieve the goodness of the human inner world through human nature. His method is different from Cheng Yi and Zhu Xi's heteronomous method, but it is not exactly the same as Mencius' ethical self-discipline theory. His theory has its unique significance.[32]

Mou Zongsan puts the Confucian schools of the Song and Ming dynasties into three categories: the first one is represented by Hu Hong, the second one by Wang Yangming, and the third one by Zhu Xi. He also emphasizes the importance and uniqueness of Hu Hong's thought.[33] The previously mentioned comments on the Huxiang School are not completely uncontroversial, but they can prove that the Huxiang School did play an irreplaceable role in the development of Neo-Confucianism in Song and Ming dynasties.

The Min School represented by Zhu Xi had a more far-reaching impact on the ideological history of the Song and Ming dynasties. Zhu Xi conducted an in-depth study on the way to achieve a harmonious society and read extensively to conclude the previous Neo-Confucian thoughts. With these efforts, he established a profound, detailed Neo-Confucian academic system that included theories about human nature, moral cultivation, and the essential principles of the world, covering all aspects of Neo-Confucian studies. He inherited Zhang Zai's (1020–1077), Cheng Yi's (1033–1107), and Cheng Hao's (1032–1085) theories about the essential principles of the world, and after rigorous step-by-step reasoning, he concluded that the essential principles of the world generated everything in the world, and things in this world were materialized embodiment of the principles.[34] This conclusion was a key concept in Zhu Xi's Neo-Confucian thought.

122 *Regional Cultural Undertakings*

Later, Zhu Xi developed his predecessors' theories and proposed two kinds of human nature: innate human goodness and secular human character. According to him, innate human goodness, which was pure and perfect, was produced and shaped by the essential principles of the world, and secular human character, which was materialized embodiment, could be good or bad. On this basis, he advocated that knowledge was improved through experience, and so was one's morality. Zhu Xi's Neo-Confucian academic system integrates contents regarding nature, human society, and human life. It is metaphysical and highly abstract and can be regarded as a peak in the ideological development of ancient China. Li Daochuan (1170–1217), a Neo-Confucian scholar of the late Song dynasty, made the following comment on Zhu Xi's thought: "Zhu Xi's thought is conducive to self-improvement. It expounds upon the ways to serve the monarch and govern the people."[35] In the third year of the Baoqing reign of the Song dynasty (1227), the emperor of the time spoke highly of Zhu Xi's thought in his imperial edict, stating that Zhu Xi's explanatory notes to Confucian classics, such as *The Analects of Confucius* (论语), *The Doctrine of the Mean* (中庸), *The Great Learning* (大学), and *Mencius* (孟子), were precise, refined, and practical. In his *Scholarly Annals of Song and Yuan Periods* (宋元学案),[36] Quan Zuwang (1705–1755) gave the following comment on Zhu Xi: "Zhu Xi's thought covers a wide field, goes into details, and concludes the previous thoughts."[37] Zhu Xi's thought prevailed during the late Southern Song dynasty in China, and in the Yuan dynasty (1271–1368), his explanatory notes to the four Confucian classics mentioned earlier were used as teaching materials for imperial examinations. In other words, Zhu Xi's thought became official Confucian thought for several hundred years. In Ming and Qing dynasties, it was even venerated as the guiding governance philosophy. Complicated reasons contributed to the fact that Zhu Xi's Min School was promoted from a regional Confucian school based in private academies to the nation's mainstream ideology. Some of these reasons were historical, and some were social. Nevertheless, the most important reason was that Zhu Xi's academic system was nearly impeccable.

In the Qing dynasty, textological research prevailed in academies across the country, and considerable academic achievements were made in this regard. According to a treatise by a contemporary scholar named Li Xubai, titled *Research on Simple and Plain Learning Conducted in the Qing Dynasty in Guangdong Province* (清代广东朴学研究), in the late Qing dynasty, textology thrived in Guangdong Province, and this was because the then academic leader, Ruan Yuan (1764–1849), actively promoted the development of textology by building textology academies, recruiting textology students, and offering awards for outstanding textology experts. The most famous academic base of Guangdong textology was Xuehai Academy. Under the guidance of Ruan Yuan, the academy was devoted to textological studies and compiling textological works. Xuehai Academy boasted scholars with different fields of expertise: there were experts in ancient classics, textual studies, logical reasoning, history, politics, and literature.[38] These scholars made different contributions that complemented one another. Together, they created many academic works. *County Annals of Nanhai* (南海县志), which was produced during the Tongzhi reign (1862–1874), contains the following record about a famous Xuehai Academy scholar named Zeng Zhao (1793–1854):

> Zeng Zhao remains dedicated to studies on ancient classics. With the help of ancient dictionaries, such as *Explaining Simple and Analyzing Compound Characters* (说文解字), *Jade Book* (玉篇), *Topolect Dictionary* (方言), and *Approach to Correct [Expressions]* (尔雅), he carefully studies the texts of the ancient classics and offers a well-founded explanation of these texts.

His academic works include the seven-volume *Notes of Yu on the Book of Changes* (周易虞氏义笺), the four-volume *Annotations to Rites of Zhou* (周礼注疏小笺), the two-volume *On Poetry* (诗说), and the single-volume *Similarities and Differences of Mao Xiang's and Zheng Xuan's Annotations to the Book of Songs* (诗毛郑异同辨). Some scholars of that time commented that Guangdong's academic achievements began to be acknowledged throughout the country during the Xianfeng and Tongzhi reigns (1831–1874).[39] This comment may not be completely correct, but no one can deny the fact that when Ruan Yuan, the founder of the academy, taught in Xuehai Academy during those years of the Jiaqing and Daoguang reigns (1760–1850), Guangdong Province did outshine its peers in terms of academic achievements.[40]

Geographical Distribution and Regional Culture

The development of a regional culture was not only about the improvement of theoretical thinking and academic research in the region but also about its increasing influence on its surrounding areas and even the entire country. Academies were not only institutes where Confucian scholars passed on knowledge, carried on innovations, and enriched and spread Confucian thoughts, but they were also of great symbolic importance. To fulfill their ambition of educating the public and propagating Confucian culture, academies actively expanded to cover more areas that were far away from prosperous cities. Some academies were even based in remote areas.[41] The influence of a Confucian school was extended when its academies increased in number and coverage, and the thriving academies were regarded as symbols of culture and civilization. Once an academy was established in a locality, the Confucian culture could penetrate deeply into the local people's life. In a word, the expansion of academies embodied the development of a regional culture.

On the whole, after their inception in the Tang dynasty (618–907), academies continued increasing in number and coverage. During their heyday in the Qing dynasty (1616–1912), there were several thousand academies across China, and academies thrived in every locality, except for ethnic minority areas such as Tibet. *The County Annals of Laoting* (乐亭县志), which was produced during the Guangxu reign (1871–1908), comments, "Academies are all over the place." Across the country, the number of academies grew continuously and reached a peak during the Qing dynasty. They also quickly expanded to counties and even

124 *Regional Cultural Undertakings*

many remote areas. This section will explain this phenomenon by analyzing the expansion of academies in Hunan and Jiangxi Provinces.

Academies appeared quite early in Hunan Province. According to relevant research, as early as the Tang dynasty, the province already had seven academies.[42] During the early years of the Northern Song dynasty (960–1127), when the country and its economy had just recovered from the recent national unrest, Yuelu Academy was established in Changsha City and quickly became an important influence in the country.[43] In the Song and Yuan dynasties (960–1368), Ma Duanlin (1245–1322) listed four top academies of the early Song dynasty: Shigu Academy of Hengyang City, Yuelu Academy of Changsha City, Bailudong Academy of Jiangxi Province, and Yingtianfu Academy of Henan Province, among which two were located in Hunan Province. Throughout the Northern Song dynasty, there were 12 academies established in different places of Hunan Province, such as Changsha City, Xiangyin County, Hengshan County, Linwu County, Yongzhou City, Xingning County (now Zixing County), and so on. During the Southern Song dynasty (1127–1279), academies developed rapidly in the province, and their total number quickly surpassed 44: academies were established in 12 of the province's 15 prefectures, cities, and military regions and in 27 of its 59 counties. In the Yuan dynasty (1271–1368), given the government's protection policy for academies, there were 41 academies established in Hunan Province, of which 22 were new academies and 19 were restored old academies. Compared with the Southern Song dynasty (1127–1279), the Yuan dynasty (1271–1368) actually saw a decline in the number of academies in Hunan Province, but given the short lifespan of the Yuan dynasty, which lasted for merely several decades, this decrease in number could not be interpreted as a decline in the development of the academies. During the Yuan dynasty, academies developed vigorously in Hunan Province, and most prefectures and counties of the province had academies. During the Ming dynasty (1368–1644), as many as 124 academies were based in Hunan Province, including 25 restored academies and 99 new academies. This number was equal to the sum of the numbers of Hunan academies of the Tang, Song, and Yuan dynasties. Back then, 53 out of the 56 counties of the province had academies, including many counties located in its relatively backward western and southern regions. For example, Chenzhou County (now the northern region of Hunan Province's Huaihua City) had five academies; Yuanling County, Xupu County, and Yuanzhou County each had three academies; and Qianyang County (now a district of Hunan Province's Huaihua City) and Yongshun County each had one academy. The number of Hunan academies surged after the middle of the Qing dynasty (1644–1911), reaching a remarkable number of 286 and covering every county of the province. Some counties even had more than ten academies, such as Liuyang County, Hengshan County, You County, Chaling County, Xintian County, Xupu County, Ling County (now Yanling County), Xingning County, and Yizhang County. As most of these counties were located in relatively remote areas, it was fair to say that academies were universalized in Hunan Province during the Qing dynasty.

Like the situation in Hunan Province, Jiangxi Province's earliest academy was also built during the Tang dynasty. According to Li Caidong's research, seven academies were based in Jiangxi Province in the Tang dynasty, including Gao'an City's Guiyan Academy, Nanchang City's Cheng Family Feilin Academy, Luling County's (now Ji'an City) Huangliao Academy and Dengdong Academy, and Xunyang County's (now Jiujiang City) Dongjia Academy, Jingxing Academy, and Li Bo Academy, of which three academies were located in Jiangzhou Prefecture, two in Hongzhou Prefecture, and another two in Jizhou Prefecture. During the Five Dynasties period (907–960), six new academies were established in the province, including four in Hongzhou Prefecture and two in Jizhou Prefecture. During the Northern Song dynasty, academies thrived in the province, and about 50 academies were built there, including eight academies in Hongzhou Prefecture, 11 in Jiangzhou Prefecture, five in Nankang Military Region, six in Fuzhou Prefecture, six in Jianchang Military Region, five in Jizhou Prefecture, two in Ruizhou Prefecture, one in Yuanzhou Prefecture, one in Linjiang Military Region, one in Raozhou Prefecture, one in Xinzhou Prefecture, one in Qianzhou Prefecture, and one in Nan'an Military Region. Compared with the situation in the Tang dynasty and that in the Five Dynasties period, academies apparently covered more parts of the province. The Southern Song dynasty was the heyday of academies, and this was especially true in Jiangxi Province. During this period of time, 160-plus new academies were built in the province, covering all the 12 prefectures and military regions of the province: 21 new academies were established in Longxing Prefecture (formerly known as Hongzhou Prefecture), seven in Ruizhou Prefecture, nine in Linjiang Military Region, five in Yuanzhou Prefecture, 17 in Fuzhou Prefecture, two in Jianchang Military Region, 37 in Raozhou Prefecture, 26 in Xinzhou Prefecture, 20 in Jizhou Prefecture, five in Ganzhou Prefecture, three in Nan'an Military Region, and nine in Nankang Military Region. During the Yuan dynasty, 95 new academies were built in the province, including eight in Longxing Prefecture, eight in Linjiang Prefecture, 19 in Ji'an Prefecture, four in Jianchang Prefecture, one in Nanfeng Prefecture, 14 in Raozhou Prefecture, 12 in Xinzhou Prefecture, two in Nankang Prefecture, two in Jiangzhou Prefecture, one in Nan'an Prefecture, 14 in Fuzhou Prefecture, four in Ruizhou Prefecture, and six in Wuyuan Prefecture. Reliable written records of the Ming dynasty clearly showed the founding dates of 265 new academies built in the province during this period of time, and in the Qing dynasty, 399 academies, including 74 restored academies, were rooted in the province, covering every county of the province. During the Qing dynasty, the prosperous Nanchang City had 19 new academies built, and a relatively remote prefecture named Yining Prefecture (now Xiushui County and Tonggu County) also had 18 new academies established. Nevertheless, the most startling example was Wanzai County. This county initiated 25 academies during the Qing dynasty, with 12 of them built during the Guangxu reign (1871–1908). These academies that were great in number and located extensively across the province reflected the thriving regional culture and the popularity of Confucianism in this region.

126 Regional Cultural Undertakings

The establishment and expansion of these academies effectively increased the influence of Confucianism in different regions of China and helped Confucianism to spread to many remote, uncivilized places that had been ignored by the country's mainstream culture. Linda Walton, a US scholar, once gave such a comment on Song dynasty academies: academies located in "uncivilized" inland regions, such as the academies in Ganzhou City, were like messengers of civilization.[44] The establishment of academies in such regions exerted a civilizing influence. Hunan Province has endless hills and turbulent rivers, and it is the home of many ethnic minority groups. Given this, this province was generally considered a place featuring inconvenient traffic, closed environment, and backward culture in ancient China.[45] Its natural conditions, to some extent, did constitute a blockade of information dissemination back then. Even in Song and Yuan dynasties, some remote areas of the province were still out of the reach of Confucian culture. For example, in the Yuan dynasty, when Guangde Academy was built in Huitong County, Jingzhou Prefecture, Hunan Province, there was hardly any local culture there. Ancient records about this region were usually as follows: "Jingzhou Prefecture is located in the most remote part of Hunan Province, surrounded by Dongting Lake, the mountainous region of Sichuan Province, and the habitats of some cave people and hermits, and many people there are rowdy and aggressive." "This place (Jingzhou Prefecture) is far away from the developed regions, and the local people were uncivilized." Guangde Academy brought education to Jingzhou Prefecture. Similar things happened to Mount Meng, situated in Ruizhou Prefecture's Shanggao County.[46] According to historical records, "People there were greedy as they were often exposed to expensive goods, but they were vulgar, uneducated, and uncivilized." In the 27th year of the Zhiyuan reign (1290), an officer in charge of the silver field of Mount Meng built Zhengde Academy to teach Confucian thought to the local people, and in the second year of the Yanyou reign (1315), the academy was expanded to recruit more students. Years of Confucian education successfully changed the local people's behaviors.[47] In the Ming dynasty, when Yunshan Academy was built in Hubei Province's Yun County, a place featuring high mountains and torrential rivers, people there began to pay attention to education.[48] In the 28th year of the Qianlong reign (1763), the magistrate of Sichuan Province's Gong County, which was located in a remote, mountainous region, built Nanguang Academy to satisfy the local people's needs for education. During the Yuan dynasty, when Tianmen Academy was founded in Hunan Province's Cili Prefecture near the Dong ethnic group's habitation, Confucian culture quickly influenced the local people's life and became a prevailing culture: "The local people attached great importance to education, devoted to their work and enjoyed their social life, and this place became civilized."[49] In the second year of the Huangqing reign of the Yuan dynasty (1313), when Rulin Academy was built in Wugang City, a remote, mountainous city and the home to many ethnic minority groups, Confucian culture successfully spread to the region, and the local people became civilized and valued education.[50] These mentioned facts showed that *academies* played a significant role in spreading

Confucianism to underdeveloped and even uncivilized places in China and in promoting the development of regional cultures.

Academies not only facilitated the geospatial spread of regional cultures but also helped the cultures to penetrate deeper into the localities through various kinds of lectures. In the third year of the Qiandao reign of the Southern Song dynasty (1167), Zhu Xi (1130–1200) and Zhang Shi (1133–1180) started giving lectures at Yuelu Academy. Since then, such lectures had gotten increasingly popular and gradually became a tradition in the late Ming dynasty. Lectures became an indispensable part of academic activities, through which academies realized their goal of educating the public and spreading their culture. Lectures of the academies directly facilitated the dissemination of regional cultures. According to historical records, in the third year of the Qiandao reign (1167), Zhu Xi's and Zhang Shi's lectures attracted so many people to Yuelu Academy that wagon-dragging horses drank up all the water in the pool there. Apparently, their lectures did help to spread Huxiang Neo-Confucian thought. Lectures were also popular during the mid-Ming dynasty. During the Jiajing reign (1507–1567), Zou Shouyi (1491–1562), a Jiangxi-Province scholar, inherited Wang Yangming's (1472–1529) thought, built Fugu Academy, and organized Xiyin Meetings to give lectures in Jiangxi and Anhui Provinces, exerting widespread influence: "Everyone in the region, including peasants living in poor villages and deep valleys, heard about those lectures and lived and worked in peace."[51] Zou Shouyi's student Qian Dehong (1496–1574) observed, "My teacher was devoted to public education, guiding them to learn and practice the Confucian principles."[52] This showed that Wang Yangming's education in cultivating inner goodness was widely recognized in the region, which provided a solid foundation for the development of Wang Yangming's school in Jiangxi Province. These academic activities were of positive significance to the development and dissemination of culture. Because of these academic activities, many regional cultures extended their influence to the entire country. For example, in the third year of the Song dynasty's Xianping reign (1000), when Li Yunze (953–1028) restored Yuelu Academy, a scholar named Wang Yucheng (954–1001) said, "Hunan Province is as civilized as Confucius and Mencius' hometown." Academies turned Hunan Province into a civilized region that enjoyed a high cultural reputation in China.

The establishment of academies and cultural promotion events such as public lectures also generated an academic environment that further fostered the Confucian culture. Such an environment shaped the dynamics between the Confucian culture and other cultures and gradually changed the regional cultural scene.

The establishment of some academies implied the power struggle between Confucianism and Taoism. Hualin Mountain in Fengxin, Jiangxi was where Li Babai and Mr. Taoqiu practiced Taoism and made elixir in the Jin dynasty.[53] It later transformed into a religious center for Taoists. In his article "Records of the Hu Family Academy in Huashan" (洪州华山胡氏书堂记), Xu Xuan writes, "Both Mr. Taoqiu and Li Babai used to practice Taoism here."[54] However, in the early Northern Song dynasty, Hu Zhongyao founded Hushi Academy at the mountain. He built over 100 rooms and archived 5,000 volumes of books in the

128 *Regional Cultural Undertakings*

academy, which attracted dozens of scholars and students from other parts of the country.[55] Public lectures and academic communication were conducted all year round. The academy thus became a headquarters for the promotion of Confucianism, which could be evidenced by poems written by people of that age. The Right Grand Master of Remonstrance Yao Mi wrote a poem, which reads, "The landscapes in Nanji are the prettiest. Confucianists wander about forests and springs on this fairyland." The official of the Academy of Scholarly Worthies in the Court of Imperial Entertainments, Yang Yi, wrote a poem, which says, "Students carried the profile of those from Eastern Lu. Books exceeded those in a scholarly room. The Confucian culture prevails in this academy, and music is performed in harmony." The vice director of the Ministry of Rites Yan Shu writes in his poem, "Students not only gain proficiency in the *Four Books*, but they also often practice singing and perform music." The poem by Chen Kang of the Institute for the Glorification of Literature Auxiliary in the Court of Imperial Sacrifices reads,

> A gateway tower has been erected outside the thatched house of the institution, where Confucian officials conduct academic communication. Scholars observe Confucian traditions, and students view Yanzi and Zengzi as their role models. Townspeople reside in simple dwellings among clouds and boulders. They draw water from streams and rivers. A large number of books have been stored away at Hualin Academy, and this place is elevated to an esteemed academic mountain.[56]

Hualin Mountain was thus transformed from an immortal mountain of Taoism into an "esteemed academic mountain" for Confucianism. Apparently, the establishment of Hualin Academy changed the local cultures in a fundamental way and secured the dominant position of Confucianism in the local regions. In fact, many academies were transformed from Taoist temples. Shigu Academy in Hengyang, for instance, used to be Xunzhen Temple, according to historical documents. In the Yuanhe reign of the Tang dynasty, the scholar Li Kuan "converted the Taoist temple to an academy where he worshiped Confucius and taught students Confucianism."[57] The Taoist temple at Bishan in Yi County in Huizhou, Anhui was transformed into Biyang Academy by the magistrate Xie Tingjie in the 42nd year of the Jiajing reign (1563). Xie Tingjie "converted the Taoist temple to an academy to promote Confucianism instead of Taoism." Jindieshan at Puqi County in Hubei used to be where the county school was located in the Tang dynasty.[58] "Later, some Taoists gathered construction materials and built a memorial temple to worship loyal government officials. They thus settled down and expanded their family here." In the Zhengde reign of the Ming dynasty, local officials "encouraged the public to study Confucianism" and therefore "relocated the temple to the southern suburb." Fengshan Academy was then established at Jindieshan.[59] Jupo Academy in Guangzhou was transformed from a former temple in this area. In Chen Li's article "Records of Jupo Academy" (菊坡精舍记), he writes,

There was a Taoist temple at Yuexiu Mountain earlier called Yingyuan Palace. On either side of the temple stood trees and a pavilion named Yinfeng Pavilion, which was later renamed Changchun Immortal House. The building was destroyed when barbarians invaded China. The censor-in-chief Jiang Xiangquan and local officials discussed converting this place into an academy. After extensive renovations, the academy was refurbished and named Jupo Academy.[60]

Also, for many academies, their establishment reflected the power alternation between Confucianism and Buddhism in that certain area. Lushan, Jiangxi, used to be a world-famous Buddhist religious center. In the Eastern Jin dynasty, the notable monk Huiyuan built a temple here, and in the late Tang dynasty, Li Bo used to live a scholarly life in reclusion. During the Shengyuan reign of the Southern Tang dynasty, Lushan Academy was established. By the early Song dynasty, the academy had been renamed Bailudong Academy. These events changed the cultural appearance around Lushan and made this place an important hub for promoting Confucianism. In the Northern Song dynasty, "hundreds of students used to congregate" at Bailudong Academy.[61] At one time, it was one of the "Four Great Academies in the early Song dynasty." Later, the academy was abandoned due to constant wars. In the sixth year of the Chunxi reign of the Southern Song dynasty (1179), Zhu Xi, who served as the Military Prefect of Nankang then, planned to reestablish the academy. Zhu Xi's goal was very clear. He decided to use the academy as a base to promote Confucianism, diminish the influences of Buddhism, and alter the local cultural and geographic patterns. During his reasoning with the government, Zhu Xi repeatedly stressed the necessity and urgency of rejuvenation of Confucianism by comparing the thriving of Buddhism and Taoism to the declining Confucianism. He claimed,

> There are over 100 Buddhist and Taoist temples around Lushan, many of which are constantly being renovated and refurbished. Nevertheless, there is only one Confucian academy there, which has been abandoned for years. The decline of Confucianism is strikingly sad and horrific. Emperor Taizong's wish to cultivate talents and correct social customs has not been passed down to this area. It is local officials' obligation to promote Confucianism throughout the public.[62]

In another memorial, he writes,

> Over 100 Taoist and Buddhist temples were built and renovated despite constant wars, but the sole Confucian academy here has been left to abandonment . . . Besides, tolling bells in these temples can be heard everywhere. People ignore secular moral principles but throw themselves into a world of emptiness and illusions, never being tired of religious practice. In contrast, Confucian academies advocated by previous emperors, which are the

130 *Regional Cultural Undertakings*

foundations of mass education and cultural promotion, are hardly available. Only three remain in the prefecture and the county. We just need to put a little bit of effort into reviving this academy.[63]

Obviously, Zhu Xi was discontent with and concerned about the blooming Taoism and Buddhism in Lushan. In the end, after strenuous work, Zhu Xi successfully reestablished Bailudong Academy and started to purchase books and farmlands, recruit teachers and students, and design curriculums. After that, he assumed the positions of both military prefect and academy headmaster while giving lectures and teaching students in person. His friends Liu Qingzhi and disciples Lin Zezhi and Huang Gan all taught in Bailudong Academy. In the eighth year of the Chunxi reign (1181), the great scholar of Xin Xue, Lu Jiuyuan, traveled from Jinxi to Bailudong Academy with his students as a guest speaker. For a very long period after that, Bailudong Academy flourished. Instead of only hearing tolling bells in the temples with few academies in view, one would notice that Lushan had acquired a completely new outlook. Zhu Xi finally achieved his goal of making Confucianism equivalently influential to Buddhism and Taoism.

Another example was Mount Jiuhua in Anhui, which was also a popular tourist designation like Wuyishan and Lushan after the Tang dynasty. At Mount Jiuhua, "poets, hermits, Taoists, and Buddhists interacted with each other while nobody advocated for Confucianism." It thus can be seen that Buddhism and Taoism overshadowed Confucianism for a long time in this region. During the Hongzhi reign of the Ming dynasty, Wang Yangming visited Mount Jiuhua and favored this place. In the Zhengde reign, when Wang Yangming paid Mount Jiuhua a second visit with his Confucian students, he attempted to revive Confucianism here.[64] Hence, Wang Yangming resolved to build an academy to the west of Huacheng Temple for students to study and collect books. It was obvious that Wang Yangming planned to promote the Confucian culture to compete against Taoism and Buddhism by building an academy next to the temple, but he was unable to fulfill his wish. It was not until the seventh year of the Jiajing reign (1528) that local officials finally finished Wang Yangming's uncompleted work and built an academy at Mount Jiuhua. The academy was named Yangming Academy. Wang Yangming's student Zou Shouyi writes in his article "Records of Yangming Academy in Jiuhuashan" (九华山阳明书院记), "The establishment of the academy relied on the joint efforts of generations of scholars. In this way, we could lead students away from unorthodox doctrines of heresy while guiding them toward Confucian principles."[65] This statement elucidated the mission of Yangming Academy, which was to repudiate Buddhism and Taoism. Further to the founding of Yangming Academy, the power dynamics between Confucianism and Buddhism/Taoism changed, and the cultural appearance at Mount Jiuhua, correspondingly, altered.

In the history of academy development, academies and Buddhist and Taoist temples always had an acrimonious relationship, which directly mirrored the balance of power between the Confucian and Buddhist cultures. A number of academies were established for the purpose of competing against Buddhism and Taoism. In the first year of the Jiatai reign of the Song dynasty (1201), the magistrate of Taihe County, Jiangxi, Zhao Rumo, built Longzhou Academy, and the scholar Zhou Bida wrote a commemorative article for it. When he broached the balance of power between Confucianism and Buddhism/Taoism in this area, he said,

> Taihe used to be a vassal's fief. As I looked at the map, I found that there are 100 Buddhist temples and 15 Taoist temples, not including those destroyed or abandoned . . . These days, old schools have all been converted to Buddhist and Taoist temples.[66]

In Zhou Bida's opinion, as a result of a decline in Confucianism, the Confucian culture had lost its battle to Buddhism and Taoism in Taihe. Given such circumstances, establishing Longzhou Academy to revive the Confucian culture in this region and change the cultural pattern of Taihe County became a pressing issue. In the 20th year of the Qianlong reign (1755), the magistrate of Taigu County, Shanxi, Lü Chongmi, restored Fengshan Academy as soon as he took office, primarily out of his concern about the decline in Confucianism in this region. He writes,

> In November of the Renshen year, I was appointed as the magistrate of Taigu County. After my arrival, I inspected the local landscapes and found the town bordered by beautiful Fengshan on the south while being connected by several rivers such as the Wuma River and Xiangyu River. People here are simple and honest, and educated literati carry an elegant profile. Magnificent Buddhist temples tower over the land in a serried formation. The only downside is that the local charity school only accepts a limited number of students. I really appreciate the customs and traditions here, but I'm concerned about how much Buddhism and Taoism take precedence over Confucianism.[67]

The establishment of some academies was achieved at directly the expense of temples. For example, in the eighth year of the Chenghua reign in the Ming dynasty (1472), Zhixue Academy, founded by Duan Jian, prefect of Nanyang, was formerly a Buddhist temple where "hundreds of monks used to reside." After Duan Jian arrived at Nanyang, as "mass education became his top priority," he requested assistance from local seniors and ordered monks to "enter marital unions" under the pretext that Buddhists did not observe the general ethical and moral principles governing society. Failure to do so would "be held legally accountable." In a couple of weeks, "all temples were empty."[68] Duan Jian then refurbished the buildings and founded Zhixue Academy. This was a typical example of dispelling Buddhists by force to promote Confucianism. Duan Jian's action revealed how Confucianists attempted to defend their culture and preserve their cultural territories by establishing academies.

Building academies at the expense of temples was quite common in the history of academy development, one example of which was Sichuan Province. In the Jiajing reign of the Ming dynasty, to memorize Wei Liaoweng, Heshan Academy was built in Meizhou, Sichuan, to which end, "the temple at the southwest of the city was demolished."[69] In the 12th year of the Jiajing reign (1533), the Touring Inspector of Jiading, Sichuan, Xiong Juechang, built Jiufeng Academy, also for the purpose of prioritizing Confucianism over Buddhism. According to Peng Rushi's article "Records of Jiufeng Academy" (九峰书院记), when Wei Gao administrated Shu, a monk from Guizhou carved a colossal Buddhist statue on the cliff and built a ten-story Buddhist temple. An increasing number of believers thus came to worship the Buddha, and the temple had been prospering ever since. An academy was built to the south of Gaobiao Mountain, which was occupied by Taoists for a long time. Mr. Jia first engraved the text of "Words of Encouragement and Exhortation" (敬一箴), composed by the emperor, on it, and then Mr. Xiong reestablished the academy. The two mountains were, subsequently, under the administration of the academy. It is commendable that both gentlemen encouraged orthodox doctrines of Confucianism while dismissing heretic sayings of Taoism and Buddhism.[70] In the 19th year of the Qianlong reign (1754), the prefect of Tongchuan, Sichuan, Fei Yuanlong, converted half of Caotang Temple in the east of the city to Wenfeng Academy.[71] Later, as Du Fu used to take up his abode here, the academy was renamed Caotang Academy. Ziyun Academy in Pi County in Sichuan, initially built in the Chenghua reign of the Ming dynasty, later transformed into Shuiyue Temple.[72] It was not until the townsman Li Changfu "decided to convert the temple back to an academy" in the Qing dynasty that the Confucian culture was revived there.

Some Confucianists often granted farmlands and properties attached to temples in their official capacity as a way of supporting academies while they were in power. For example, the government official Li Ba, during the Qianlong reign, "divided temple farmlands several times to support academies" during his administration. When he governed Funing, Fujian Province, as a prefect, "after seeing temple properties were constantly stolen and illegally sold, he suggested that instead of providing farmlands to temples for monks to squander, it would be better to grant them to academy students as a way of supporting them to pursue their academic career." At that time, some monks at Xiapu County had a dispute over temple properties. Li Ba thus expelled the monks and "instructed his men to guard the temple. Half of the rent of the temple, which was 40 piculs of food per annum, was used to fund the academy."[73] In the 15th (1750) and 18th (1753) years of the Qianlong reign, the two magistrates of Fu'an County, Funing Prefecture, Qin Shiwang and Xia Hu, both granted 200 acres of temple farmlands to Ziyang Academy in succession.[74]

Apart from economic considerations such as taking advantage of original foundations, residences, and properties, another reason for converting temples to academies or granting temple farmlands to academies was to achieve a balance of power between Confucianism and Buddhism or Taoism. In fact, local power struggles between Confucianists and Taoists/Buddhists for a dominant cultural position were fairly prevalent. Competition for farmlands and properties was simply one aspect of such cultural contention. During the game of power between academies and temples, not only could temples be transformed into academies, as mentioned

Regional Cultural Undertakings 133

earlier, but many academies and academy farmlands could also be occupied by monks or Taoists. One example was Hejing Academy in the memorial of the Neo-Confucianist Yin Tun. The academy was first built in Huqiu, Suzhou, and it was occupied by monks in the early Yuan dynasty. In the second year of the Jiajing reign of the Ming dynasty (1523), the governor Hu Zuanzong finally reestablished the academy at the site of the temple. In his article "Restoration of Diaotai Academy" (重修钓台书院记),[75] the scholar Huang Jin in the Yuan dynasty mentioned that Diaotai Academy's properties were once seized by monks. He writes, "Monks in the neighboring area took the properties from the academy. A lawsuit was made, but only half of them were recovered. Students sustained themselves by only 50 acres of lands."[76] In his article "Records of Farmlands of Mingzheng Academy" (明正书院田记), Huang Jin even states that "following the Yuan dynasty, 70% to 80% of farmlands attached to Mingzheng Academy, dated back to the late years of Jingding reign of the Song dynasty, were seized by Buddhists and Taoists and the government paid little attention to it."[77] In *Prefectural Annals of Funing* (福宁府志) in the Qianlong reign, there are records of some officials like Li Ba distributing temple farmlands to support academies in Funing, Fujian, as discussed earlier, but there are also records of academies being transformed into temples. For instance, Lingxi Academy in Ningde County, at the foot of Baiyan Peak, situated in a reclusive and quiet surrounding, was transformed into a temple. On the right side of Lingxi Academy, there was a well with incessant fresh drinking water even during a severe drought. Guangfu Academy, located at Lianhua Peak, for which the townsman Gong Dao wrote a commemorative article, was also converted into a temple.[78] Perhaps, from these incidents, we can gain a more profound understanding of the purpose of Confucianists converting temples to academies.[79]

Apart from Buddhism and Taoism, rituals to local deities and cult practices also exerted a deep impact among folks and shaped the local cultural patterns. They could even elevate to the dominant culture of that region in a short period of time. Under such circumstances, the establishment of academies could serve as an effective way for Confucianists to secure their dominant cultural position in the local community. For example, during the Zhengde reign in the Ming dynasty,

a local deity was worshiped at Weixian Temple by citizens in Qiongzhou, Sichuan. Every year on the deity's birthday, the first day of the fifth moon, the natives worshiped him while wearing colorful clothes. Some of them cut their skins with swords, and others offered farmlands and properties as sacrifices. Men and women mingled with each other. Such obscene and costly rituals gradually became local customs.

In September of the 13th year of the Zhengde reign (1518), the touring censorial inspector, Lu Yong, and the governor of Qiongzhou, Wu Xiang, "removed the statue of the deity and transformed the front hall of the temple into a memorial hall," where they built Heshan Academy to "provide townsmen education." Yang Tingyi, a scholar of that age, writes in his article "Tablet Inscription of Heshan Academy" (鹤山书院碑记),

134 *Regional Cultural Undertakings*

Unrestricted and unorthodox worship stems from blind belief in Taoism and Buddhism. Without these illegal rituals, believers in Taoism and Buddhism would decrease . . . Establishing academies and promoting orthodox Confucian doctrines were remarkable contributions to the development of Confucianism.[80]

The contributions to the development of Confucianism refers to procurement of a dominant cultural position for Confucianists.

A similar situation occurred in the Yongzheng reign of the Qing dynasty. In Chaoyang, Guangdong, cult leaders such as Lin Miaogui and Hu Aqiu wrecked local communities and caused social commotions. For years, hundreds of their followers, who were all scoundrels from different parts of the town, claimed that they could cure diseases with talismans, treat infertility, and summon widows' late husbands at night. As a result, people from Chengzhou, Jieyang, Huizhou, and Fengzhou all came to worship them. After suppressing this organization, the magistrate Lan Dingyuan asserted that "local officials should take full responsibility for such an upheaval." He "attributed the emergence of the cult to the diminishing of Confucian influences" and believed that "it was the optimal time for the public to study Confucianism when they were just awakened from illusions of heresy." Hence, he founded Mianyang Academy to "offer mass education to townspeople." Following the establishment of the academy, cults and frauds disappeared. The public adhered to Confucian principles again, and traditions and customs were thus corrected. Then music and rites could be performed.[81] Another example was Fengyi (current Tianyang), Guangxi. It was a small border prefecture formerly under the rule of barbarians on the Western Plain. Subsequent to the Yuan and Ming dynasties, due to constant wars, citizens there were dispersed. In the Guangxu reign of the Qing dynasty, "over 100 men and women assembled at Yuhuang Pavilion in Dongmuzhou and practiced witchcraft as the White Lotus Sect used to do. Some women stuck to a vegetarian diet and resolved to remain single for their whole life." As Confucianism encountered such a challenge from a "cult," in the 14th year of the Guangxu reign (1888), the chief administrator Li Zhanchun transformed Yuhuang Pavilion at Dongmuzhou into Chongzheng Academy, in order to defend the Confucian culture and prevent further expansion of the heretic sect. Li Zhanchun states,

The cult these days encourages heretic religions and customs. Their influences have extended to border towns. If we do not stop it, the cult will disturb the social order and mislead the public. Our society will then fall apart, and our people won't be able to live a peaceful life while being correctly educated.[82]

Li Zhanchun held that orthodox Confucianism was the natural enemy of cults. Only by promoting orthodox Confucian doctrines could the heresy be refuted. This was the only way to eliminate the negative impact of the cult. Apparently, the founding of Chongzheng Academy quashed the rampant local cult and established the dominant cultural position of Confucianism.

Book Collecting and Engraving Activities in Academy and Regional Culture Undertakings

One of the important features of an academy was book collection and book engraving. In its early days, an academy primarily served as a place for people to collect, write, and read books. The term "书院" (lit. "book institution") is directly associated with book collection. In the next thousand years, academies continued to function as libraries and developed a unique system for collecting books. It became an essential aspect of the book collection system in ancient China. During the development of academies, many institutions also engraved books and formed an influential book engraving industry. Many ancient books engraved and edited by academies, due to their high quality and good reputations, had been passed down through generations.

Book collection and book engraving events held by various academies were a part of the local book collection and engraving industry in virtue. The development of regional book collection and engraving industries, as a reflection of the development of the local cultural industry, could foster rich regional cultures. Apart from that, academies printed books not only for their own research and teaching activities but also for the general public. Book collection in academies could also be divided into three categories based on its audience: for the government, for individuals, and for temples. They offered this service to people of different socio-economic status, including academy students and teachers as well as literati and civilians. As a consequence, book collection and printing events held by academies played an indispensable role in regional cultural promotion and development. In this light, we can have an insightful look at how academies facilitated regional cultural development by examining book collection and engraving events in academies and their social impact in general.

Book Collection in Academies

Founders and superintendents of academies attached great importance to book collection and viewed it as a fundamental aspect of an academy. The scholar in the Qing dynasty, Dai Junheng, said, "The institution is called '书院' (which literally means a place closely bound up with 'book') in Chinese because it is a place for collecting books so that students can further their education."[83] In his opinion, an academy would not have been regarded as an academy had there been no books in it. Some scholars also held that books were a necessity for talent cultivation. They stated,

> Under-age students studying in an academy are usually from an impoverished family who have no financial means to purchase books. Even if they seized the opportunity to study classics and pursued their education with dedication, it would be hard for them to become accomplished without a book collection for reference or research, and their views would still be limited. Therefore, classics and history books were essential tools for talent cultivation.[84]

136 *Regional Cultural Undertakings*

This insightful and eloquent argument reveals the relationship between an academy and its book collection, as well as how crucial book collection was in academy education. We know that books are the physical concretion of cultures. Academic research and teaching activities in an academy relied on books. Without the support of books, academic research will ultimately fail. Meanwhile, students in academies were expected to be independent. They usually conducted research on Confucian classics by themselves under the guidance of their teachers. Given such, book collection was undeniably pivotal to academies. Without a broad selection of books, an academy would not function properly.

Because of this universal understanding of book collection, book collection was often viewed as an important part of the founding or reestablishment of an academy. We can see a substantial amount of documentation pertaining to book collection events during the founding of academies in the early Northern Song dynasty. Dou Yujun from Fanyang "built an academy to the south of his residence composed of 40 rooms and collected 5,000 books."[85] Hu Zhongyao from Hongzhou founded an academy at the foot of Xuanxiu Peak to the south of his mansion at Mount Hua, "which consisted of 100 rooms, where he stored 1,000 volumes of books."[86] Sun Fu established Taishan Academy to the south of Mount Tai, which he filled with Confucian classics and resided there with his students.[87] Yuelu Academy had already possessed a significant number of books before its founding in the ninth year of the Kaibao reign (976), but all of its books were "scattered and lost later."[88] It was not until the early Xianping reign, when Li Yun "collected all the lost books, built a lecture hall at the center, and established a library" that the academy was finally restored. Cao Cheng, a wealthy man from Songcheng, funded the construction of Yingtianfu Academy and "purchased farmlands and books to attract students and teachers."[89] According to the scholar in the Qing dynasty, Dai Junheng, during the reign of Taizong and Zhenzong of the Song dynasty, academies proliferated. Officials would submit a request for books to the government when a new academy was built.[90] From these records, we can see that book collection was fairly common during the early stage of an academy. It had become a vital part of academy construction and restoration.

During the development of the academy system, book collection accompanied the founding and restoration of an academy, no matter where the academy was located, what kind of academy it was, or who the founder was. For example, when Da Ke, a Mongolian, who lived in Sichuan for his whole life, retired from his position as eunuch director in the Yuan dynasty, he privately funded the construction of Shishi Academy in Sichuan and "stored books, both ancient classics and those recently published, and musical instruments in it."[91] In the fifth year of the Yanyou reign of the Yuan dynasty (1318), Qian Nu, the Duke of Lishan, built Lishan Academy after he retired to Pushang. Qian Nu "collected thousands of books and hired celebrated scholars to teach townsmen."[92] In the Chunxi reign of the Southern Song dynasty, when Zhu Xi assumed the post of military prefect of Nankang and restored Bailudong Academy, one important thing he did was

Regional Cultural Undertakings 137

collect books strenuously. In the eighth year of the Chunxi reign (1181), Zhu Xi submitted a memorial to the emperor, requesting for the "*Stone Classics* copied by the Retired Emperor and printed copies of *Annotations to Nine Classics* (九经注疏), *The Analects of Confucius* (论语), and *Mencius* (孟子) so that students in the academy could read them."[93]

In the meantime, Zhu Xi also collected books from local literati and government bodies to the south of the Yangtze River for "the benefit of scholars."[94] He donated his own books as well. In the "Postscript to Book of Han Collected in Bailudong Academy" (跋白鹿洞书院所藏〈汉书〉), Zhu Xi writes,

> I wrote a biography for Liu Zihe, and his son Liu Renji donated his books, including 44 volumes of *The Book of Han* (汉书) collected by his ancestors, to express his gratitude. At that time, Bailudong Academy was just reestablished. I accepted the books for future use of scholars.[95]

We can say that book collection, as an important function of an academy, came hand in hand with the establishment and restoration of the institution. Had there been no books in an academy, the academy would not have been a real one. "If there were no books in an academy, the academy would not be worthy of its name. What could scholars rely on?"[96]

The sizes of book collections in different academies could vary drastically, and many academies had large book collections. In the early stage of the academy system, when printing technologies were still relatively limited, it was not easy to search for books. Some academies housed thousands of books. In the Southern Tang dynasty during the Five Dynasties period, for instance, Dongjia Academy in Jiangxi had dozens of rooms and housed thousands of volumes of books.[97] Yingtianfu Academy, established in the second year of the Dazhong Xiangfu reign in the early Song dynasty (1009), also "held thousands of books."[98] In the Southern Song dynasty, as a result of booming printing technologies and flourishing cultures, book collection became a popular trend. Under such social influences, academies started to collect an increasing number of books. Compared to the size of academy book collections in the Northern Song dynasty, which was merely thousands of volumes, this number surged to tens of thousands and even exceeded 100,000 in the Southern Song dynasty. For example, in the late years of the Chunyou reign of the Song dynasty (1241–1252), Shilin Academy in Guixi, Jiangxi, founded by Ye Mengde, a scholar of Xin Xue, contained "tens of thousands of ancient and contemporary books."[99] Heshan Academy in Pujiang, Qiongzhou, Sichuan, initially built in the second year of the Kaixi reign (1206) by Wei Liaoweng, housed 100,000 volumes. In "Detailed Records of Heshan Academy" (书鹤山书院始末), Wei Liaoweng writes,

> In addition to my private book collection at home, I also procured copies of some rare books and transcribed them. Together with the books privately or publicly published, I have acquired a book collection of 100,000, and I stored them away with my old books in the academy with reverence.[100]

138 *Regional Cultural Undertakings*

According to Deng Hongbo's research, aside from Heshan Academy and Shilin Academy, which held a collection of tens of thousands of books in the Song dynasty, Liangshan Academy in Zhangpu, Fujian, and Nanyuan Academy in Dongyang, Zhejiang, also housed an immense book collection. Among all, Heshan Academy was the institution with the largest book collection in the Song dynasty.[101]

Following the Song dynasty, the number of academies with a book collection of thousands of volumes and even tens of thousands of volumes increased significantly. Lishan Academy in the Yuan dynasty, which we mentioned earlier, housed a collection of tens of thousands of books. Xie Jieheng from Bohai in the Yuan dynasty "possessed thousands of volumes of books at his home."[102] In the first year of the Yanyou reign (1314), he founded Dong'an Academy "in the east of his residence, with a towering building at the center to house his collection."[103] Feng Mengzhou from Xuchang, Henan, in the Yuan dynasty, built an academy at Yingchang. As he often purchased books, he accumulated a massive book collection, from Confucian classics and history books all the way to records of unofficial anecdote, with a total number of tens of thousands in his academy.[104] Further, based on the "Contents of Books Donated to Yuelu Academy" (岳麓书院新捐官书目录), printed and published in the sixth year of the Tongzhi reign (1867), following the restoration of the library of Yuelu Academy, local officials and academy students and staff members donated over 220 sets of books, including more than 5,720 titles, in a total of 14,130 volumes.[105] According to "Annals of Classics in Zhenyan Academy" (箴言书院典籍志), published in the fifth year of the Tongzhi reign (1866) and compiled by Hu Linyi, the academy housed 1,337 books in a total of 36,261 volumes at that time.[106] In the fourth year of the Guangxu reign (1878), Huang Pengnian claims in his article "Tablet Inscription of Book Collection in Wanjuan Library" (万卷楼藏书碑记) that "Lianchi Academy in Baoding contained a total of 33,711 volumes of books, not including those with missing pages."[107] Not did only prominent academies have an enormous book collection, but a great many smaller and less known academies also possessed a considerable number of books. For instance, according to Hu Zhaoxi's research, Laifeng Academy in Jingyan County and Fengming Academy in Dazhu County in Sichuan both housed a collection of 10,000 books each. Although it is now hard to find out the exact number of books held by Longzhou Academy in Yiyang, Hunan, in the Ming dynasty, we can roughly judge its book collection size based on the building of its library. In Jiang Xin's article "Records of Longzhou Academy" (龙洲书院记), the author states that the "library of Longzhou Academy consisted of three stories, with a height of 50 feet, built at a standard specification in terms of depth and width."[108] Such a colossal library must have contained a huge number of books.

Immense book collections in academies, undoubtedly, carried great significance to regional cultural development. Academy book collections, government book collections, individual book collections, and temple book collections were seen as the four pillars that supported the book collection industry in ancient China. Academy book collection formed a pivotal part of ancient book collections, as it was a salient indicator of regional cultural development. A remarkable academy book collection not only increased local cultural resources but also laid a solid foundation for further cultural development in that region. Consequently, the region would then procure a more dominant cultural position throughout the nation.

Apart from that, in areas relatively not culturally developed, academy book collections could, to a large extent, remedy the situation. In the Yuan dynasty, since Chengdu was a remote and inaccessible city "confined to a corner," there were insufficient books for the smooth running of Caotang Academy. It was also not easy to procure new books. In the end, for the development of the academy, staff members searched for books strenuously across the south and north of the country and finally obtained 270,000 volumes. In "Ode to Books in Caotang Academy" (草堂书院藏书铭), its author, Li Qi, writes,

> It is very important to understand that book collections are crucial for the development of the academy. After referring to documentation already published, we searched for books around the country. Our expedition extended to Yan in the north, Yue in the south, Shaan in the west, and Wu in the east. We purchased all books available on the market and transported them by carriages. The number of our books thus increased rapidly, and now we have successfully acquired 270,000 volumes.

Both the quantity and quality of the books in the academies improved significantly, for new books that the academy had not owned before were added to the collections, and those old copies were replaced by new ones. The expansion of the book collection, which was considered a major cultural event that "benefited the entire Sichuan province," promoted local cultural development.[109] Another similar case was Qianjiang County in Sichuan. Since "the county was remote and underdeveloped, there were very few book collectors in the town . . . Many scholars felt frustrated about being financially incapable of purchasing books."[110] During the Guangxu reign, staff members from Moxiang Academy in this county purchased books and classics from Zunjing Academy and Jinzhou Academy in Chengdu and Hubei Wuchang Bookstore during the establishment of the academy for students and teachers. The huge influx of books boosted the local culture.

Compared to book collections owned by the government, individuals, and temples, academy book collections were typically more practical, and the contents of their books usually reflected societal needs in that era, particularly when the state was undergoing a social transformation or ideological change. According to the research of some scholars, in the Guangxu reign, there were 171 types of books in Longmen Academy in Shanghai, among which more than 110 were books related to "Modern" or "Western" subjects. At the same time, Longmen Academy also housed imported foreign books.[111] Further, Daliang Academy in Kaifeng, Henan, held books on mathematics, geography, military, and political affairs of foreign countries, business, railway, engineering, chemistry, physics, coal mining, astronomy, herbology, English, French, and Japanese, aside from traditional Chinese classics and history books. According to "Contents of Books

Collected in Daliang Academy" (大梁书院续藏书目录), books in the academy were divided into seven categories: classics, history, philosophy, literature, series, mathematics, and social and political study, out of which 44% were in the latter two categories.[112] It thus can be seen that academies adjusted their selections of books according to social needs, and a lot of times, they played a pioneering role in the cultural industry. Changes in the contents of academy books also altered the structure of local book collections and brought in new blood to the local culture.

Book collections in academies predominantly served students and teachers in the institutions. The government's book collections, which normally served a few rulers of the upper class only, were inaccessible to ordinary scholars. Individual book collections typically had little practical value, as collectors focused solely on accumulating rare copies. Many collectors' books were locked up in the depth of their libraries, never shown to the public. Unlike government and individual book collections, academy books were collected for practical use. The purpose of collecting books was to provide students and teachers in academies with access to various books for their academic research and benefits. This was the fundamental object of academy book collections. For example, in the 12th year of the Daoguang reign (1832), Huang Jing writes in his article "On Book Collection in Xianti Academy" (仙堤书院藏书说),

> One would not have a well-regulated mind without reading classics and works of previous scholars. Only when a person possesses extensive knowledge can he become academically achieved. Now, we have added a dozen types of books to our library to allow students to study them while broadening their views.[113]

In his article "Records of Library in Zhaoyi Academy" (昭义书院藏书楼记), the author Hou Shaoying says,

> One could only gain a profound understanding of what a book mainly tries to convey after he reads a considerable number of ancient classics. We acquired a few books to add to our book collection . . . Scholars could read these books during their breaks from academic research. After immersing themselves in the library and spending their time reading day and night, they would, naturally, have a thorough understanding of the books and write good articles.[114]

These records show that academy libraries were open to students and teachers. Both students and teachers could borrow books to read. In the 28th year of the Qianlong reign in the Qing dynasty (1763), for instance, Chen Hongmou, governor of Hunan, composed "Rules and Regulations of Academies" (申明书院条规以励实学示) at Yuelu Academy and Chengnan Academy. He writes, "Classics, histories, and works of ancient and contemporary scholars, as well as annals of the province, were collected by the academy over time. Students could borrow them at will for academic purposes."[115] These policies indicated the openness and accessibility of academy book collections.[116] Hence, scholars without financial means had an easy access to a substantial number of books. Therefore, in comparison with the other book collection types, academy book collections were available to a larger audience. Since many students in academies were local townsmen, academy book collections also played a crucial role in exploiting collective intelligence, creating an academic environment, and enhancing the cultural competence of the masses. In fact, research work and teaching activities in academies all relied on a large selection of books. In this light, academy book collections also constituted an essential part of the development of local academic research, talent cultivation in academies, and thereby regional cultural prosperity.

Nevertheless, it is particularly worth noting that although most academy books were "only available to students, forbidden to loan to outsiders,"[117] still, many academies were open to the public in the time of history, serving directly as a public library in the local community. Historical documents are strewn with such records. According to some academic research, during the Tang dynasty, at the early stage of the academy system, Dongjia Academy, established by the Chens in Jiangxi, was open to the general public. "Not only could the kin of the Chens read books, but visitors also had the same entitlement as well."[118] In the Yuan dynasty, after Feng Mengzhou founded Yingchang Academy, all books in the academy were available to the local community. Feng Mengzhou stated that he "purchased thousands of books and stored them away in the library to serve those who did not own such a huge collection." Feng made the following rules:

> I've purchased thousands of books and offered them to people who do not own books. Those who came to borrow books just need to put their names and the names of the books they borrowed. When he returns the book, his name will be struck out from the records.[119]

In the Ming dynasty, a significant number of books in Bailudong Academy were also loaned to visitors as a way of supporting Jiangxi scholars in the imperial examinations. Later, Shao Rui composed "Prohibitions of Bailudong Academy" (白鹿洞学禁约), which specifically says,

> The book collections in the academy are provided to scholars for education and academic purposes. In recent years, scholars in Jiangxi have borrowed our books to prepare themselves for the imperial examinations. However, when those books are returned, they are either missing pages or lost, and book borrowers do not disclose this information. This is the biggest reason that many academy books are missing pages or lost. From now on, all books for the imperial examination in Jiangxi will be distributed by Provincial Administration Commission.[120] To prevent further loss, books at Bailudong Academy will no longer be available for borrowing.

There are more records of academy books being available to the public in the Qing dynasty. For example, Zhao Yingchen, magistrate of Julu County, Hebei in the Qing dynasty, donated 36 books in 142 cases, in a total of 980 volumes,

142   *Regional Cultural Undertakings*

to Guangze Academy, in an attempt to help students who struggled to be academically accomplished. Local scholars could borrow or copy these books. The record reads, "If a local scholar has the ambition to be academically achieved, he is allowed to borrow, read, and copy books to conduct extensive academic research and examine the patterns of histories."[121] Book borrowing policies were also made for visitors to Zhenyan Academy in Yiyang, which was founded by Hu Linyi in the Xianfeng reign of the Qing dynasty. The policies said,

> For visitors who would like to borrow a certain book, he must bring fagot, vegetable, and lantern oil to the academy and submit an application to the supervisor. A deadline to return the book will be given, and the person cannot take the book out of the academy.[122]

In the Tongzhi reign, a book loaning office was built at Xiyin Academy in Jiangning, whose staff members procured books specifically for local scholars who did not own a private book collection. "Local scholars could go to the academy to read books."[123] Some scholars believe that the book loaning office at Xiyin Academy was indeed a "typical public library."[124]

As academy book collections were available to local communities, scholars had access to these public cultural resources. In the meantime, academy books were made full use of and thereby contributed significantly to the local cultural industry. During this process, academies, as the key to regional cultural development, furthered regional cultural interaction and integration.

Book Engraving in Academies

Many academies throughout history engaged in book engraving business. Following the mid–Southern Song dynasty, with the development of printing technology, the publishing industry bloomed, and records of book engraving in academies could be found everywhere in historical documents. For example, when Zhu Xi taught at Wuyi Academy, he was quite passionate about engraving books. Zhu Xi engraved and published the book *Lexicography and Lesser Learning* (小学), with the words "Engraved by Wuyi Academy" on its cover. In his letter to Cai Jitong, Zhu Xi mentioned book engraving several times. When he found that *Collected Works of the Chen Brothers* (二程文集), published by Liu Gong earlier in Changsha, which contains "numberless errors and typos,"[125] was republished in Sichuan, he felt quite agitated. Hence, he decided to conduct proofreading himself to prevent the book from misleading readers further.[126] In the third year of the Jiaxi era during the reign of Emperor Lizong of Southern Song (1239), Wang Ye engraved and published 100 volumes of collected works of Zhu Xi at Jian'an Academy. Some scholars point out that this was the earliest edition of Zhu Xi's collected works, composed of 100 volumes, engraved in the Song dynasty.[127] Other scholars conducted research based on current existing documentation and books engraved and published by academies in the Song dynasty and found that numerous academies once engraved books in the Southern Song dynasty, such as Wengong Academy in Chaozhou, Mingdao Academy in Jiankang, Shigu Academy in Hengyang, Ziyang Academy and Meiyin Academy in Huizhou, Lize Academy in Wuzhou, Bailuzhou Academy in Jizhou, Hushan Academy in Ezhou, Huanxi Academy in Fu'an, Fujian, Longxi Academy and Zhuxi Academy in Zhangzhou, and Xiangshan Academy, Longshan Academy, and Yongze Academy in Guixi, Xinzhou.[128] Although there is a very limited number of historical records pertaining to academy book engraving in the Song dynasty, it is certain that book engraving was quite popular among academies in the Song dynasty. Gu Yanwu, a scholar in the Ming and Qing dynasties, states, "For book engraving in academies in the Song and Yuan dynasties, the superintendent oversaw the whole event, prominent Confucian scholars edited books, and students exchanged copies to further distribute them."[129] Liu Guangye, another scholar in the late Qing dynasty, asserts, "Book engraving boomed in the Song dynasty. Most books printed by academies were called academy copies."[130] After the Yuan dynasty, book engraving in academies was even more common. Some scholars found through research and statistical reports that there were 32 academies engaging in book engraving business in the Yuan dynasty and 40 in the Ming dynasty at least. In the Qing dynasty, academy book engraving became even more prevalent. For academies that engraved and published *Annals of Academies* (书院志), which usually reflected the development and teaching quality of the institution, lecture handouts, and research works, based on current administrative divisions, there were 14 in Jiangxi, 9 in Anhui, 11 in Fujian and 21 in Hunan. There were also countless academies that engraved and published books on arts, literature, collected works and compilations, and massive academic publications. Book engraving in academies reached its pinnacle in the Qing dynasty.[131]

As for some academies, they engraved books on a massive scale. For example, Xihu Academy in the Yuan dynasty, which was developed from the Imperial College of the Southern Song dynasty, inherited engraving plates originally carved by Directorate of Education. One record states, "As Xihu Academy used to be administrated by Directorate of Education in the Song dynasty, it held more than 200,000 volumes of classics, history, literature, and philosophy books."[132] The total number of books exceeded 3,700. Xihu Academy successively repaired the engraving plates previously carved by Directorate of Education and also produced new ones several times. The most extensive book engraving event occurred in the 21st year of the Zhizheng era (1361), which started in October and ended in July the next year, during which time the academy reproduced 7,893 engraving plates for classics, history, philosophy, and literature books, in a total of 3,436,352 characters. They repaired 1,671 engraving plates, with a total of 201,162 characters.[133] In addition, from the first year of the Taiding era (1324) to the first year of the Zhiyuan era (1335), Xihu Academy engraved *History of Ancient Laws and Statutes* (文献通考), authored by Ma Ruilin, twice. This book, containing 348 volumes, is a gigantic publication describing institutions and regulations in ancient China. In the second year of the Zhizheng era (1342), Xihu Academy also engraved a compilation of all poems and essays in the Yuan dynasty and *Anthology of Literature in the Yuan Dynasty* (元文类), edited by Su Tianjue, comprising 70 volumes.

144 *Regional Cultural Undertakings*

These enormous engraving projects made Xihu Academy an influential publisher in Hangzhou.[134] In the Jiajing era of the Ming dynasty, Zheng Tinghu, vice director of the Provincial Surveillance Commission of Jiangxi, composed *The Annals of Bailudong Academy* (白鹿洞志), in which he wrote a chapter dedicated to engraving plates. According to his records, at that time in Bailudong Academy, there were 59 engraving plates for *The Book of Changes* (易经), 53 for *The Book of History* (书经), 68 for *Spring and Autumn Annals* (春秋), 197 for *The Book of Rites* (礼记), five for *Annotations to Five Rites with Illustrations* (五礼图), 2,000 for *The Book of History* (史记), 101 for *The Analects of Chen Hao* (尊道录), 235 for *Rites and Conducts* (仪教仪节), 49 for *On Virtue and Learning* (二业合一训), 160 for *The Origins of the Yi-Luo School* (伊洛渊源), and 224 for *Restoration of Bailudong Academy* (重修白鹿洞志).[135]

Book engraving in academies promoted regional cultural development in multiple aspects.

First, the large number of classics and documents produced by academies not only served as materials for academic research and teaching but were also circulated among the masses to benefit scholars and civilians. The distribution of these books facilitated cultural development of the local area.

Books engraved and published by academies were primarily Confucian classics and compilations of poems and essays of various writers. For instance, the engraving plates discussed previously in Bailudong Academy in the Ming dynasty were mostly used for engraving *The Book of Changes* (易经), *The Book of History* (书经), *Spring and Autumn Annals* (春秋), *The Book of Rites* (礼记), and *The Book of History* (史记).[136] Out of the 3,334 volumes of books engraved by Xuehai Academy, 1,400 belonged to *Research on Classics Conducted in the Qing Dynasty* (皇清精解), 416 to *Commentaries on Thirteen Classics* (十三经注疏), and 200 to *Collectanea of Lesser Learning* (古经解汇函小学汇函). Among the 5,746 volumes of books published by Guangya Bookstore, more than 260 volumes belonged to the *Thirteen Classics* (十三经), 1,000 to *The Whole Collection of Tang Period Literature* (全唐文), and 1,031 to *Collections of Confucian Classics* (聚珍丛书集部抽印). Engraving these documents and books normally supplied an academy with sufficient materials for academic research and teaching. In reality, many books engraved by the academy became one of the book resources of the institution. However, it should be noted that academy books were also distributed widely among the general public for the need for regional cultural development. When Weijing Academy in Shaanxi engraved *Thirteen Classics* (十三经), *The Twenty-Four Histories* (二十四史), *General History of China* (通志), *Historic Cultural Establishment System of China* (通典), *Records of Ancient and Modern Laws* (通考), and *Comprehensive Mirror for Aid in Government* (通鉴) during the Guangxu era, they also foresaw some issues related to book sales and thereby took corresponding measures. "The publishing of these books significantly reduced book prices, prevented people from stocking up books, and thereby benefited all scholars."[137] As for Xuehai Academy in Guangzhou, they started an engraving-plate-renting business to allow the public to print books themselves. In *Annals of Xuehai*

Academy (学海堂志 • 藏板章程), the author writes, "For those who would like to print books, they first obtained permission, pay for renting the engraving plates, and then start printing according to the given schedule."[138] For Daliang Academy in Henan and Ruixi Academy in Guangdong, scholars who wished to print books just needed to bring ink and tools. In "Statutes of Book Printing" (印书章程) of Duanxi Academy, it is stated,

> Duanxi Academy printed 20 types of book series and possessed 596 engraving plates . . . If one would like to print additional books other than those already printed and distributed to students, he must bring tools and ink and submit an application to the student supervising the book printing matter. Only after the student reports to the headmaster and obtains printing permission could he start printing books. The student supervises the printing process, and copies shall not leave the academy.

Daliang Academy in Henan printed 25 types of ancient classics under the support of scholars in the local community, and the series was collectively titled *Jing Yuan* (经苑), with the words "in the custody of Daliang Academy" on its cover. Local scholars were allowed to distribute and copy them. One record states,

> In the spring of the Wuchen year, I discussed classics with my friends as all of us had the intention to revive the ancient culture. We raised funds and made an application to the superintendent of the academy, Mr. Pang Xingyuan, who generously printed the books for us without the slightest hesitation. In this way, more people have the opportunity to read classics.[139]

Book engraving in academies thus became a sort of public service, and academy books were no longer kept in the institutions only but became public cultural resources. This change definitely facilitated and supported regional cultural development. Therefore, scholars at that time viewed academy book engraving as a pivotal part of regional cultural construction. For example, scholars of that era described Daliang Academy sharing books with local literati as a glorious event that contributed to talent cultivation for the country and mass education. Liu Guangye illustrated the importance of book engraving in Weijing Academy to the cultural development in Shaanxi. He claims,

> Book engraving was an unprecedented event in the past hundreds of years. It carried great significance in a sense that the event benefited thousands of scholars . . . The fact that Shaanxi later produced so many talented men was possibly because of book engraving.[140]

Xie Guozhen, a scholar in modern China, also mentioned the profound impact of book engraving in Guangya Academy on cultural development in Guangdong: "The Guangdong culture thus prospered and exerted a lasting influence that still perpetuates today."[141]

146 *Regional Cultural Undertakings*

Second, engraving a great variety of books and documents in academies boosted the development of the local cultural industry.

Local documents engraved and published by academies could be roughly divided into three categories. The first type was the annals of provinces, prefectures, and counties. Li Jingwen's research on academies in Henan in the Qing dynasty provides us with a glimpse of annals printed and published by academies. Li Jingwen mentioned that superintendents of many academies in Henan in the Qing dynasty actively participated in the editing of local annals. Sun Qifeng edited *Textual Research on Eminent Persons* (中州人物考) and *County Annals of Xin'an* (新安县志). Zhang Mu edited *County Annals of Shangcai* (上蔡县志), *Prefectural Annals of Kaifeng* (开封府志), and *Annals of Henan* (河南通志). Huang Shubing was the editor-in-chief for *County Annals of Xiangfu* (祥符县志). At that time, Henan academies printed and published a great number of regional annals. For example, in the 17th year of the Qianlong era (1752), Huanghua Academy in Linxian County printed and published *County Annals of Lin* (林县志), edited by Yang Chao, and Zhenyuan Academy in Luyi County printed and published *County Annals of Luyi* (鹿邑县志), edited by Xu Tan. Baiquan Academy in Huixian County printed and published *County Annals of Hui* (辉县志), edited by Zhou Jihua and Dai Ming, in the 15th year of the Daoguang era (1835), whereas Lechang Academy in Nanle County printed and published *County Annals of Nanle* (南乐县志), edited by Wu Xunchao and others, in the 29th year of the Guangxu era (1903). Dacheng Academy in Fugou County printed and published *County Annals of Fugou* (扶沟县志), edited by Geng Wenkai and Xiong Can, in the 19th year of the Guangxu era (1893).[142]

The second type included poems and essays of local scholars and literati. In *Research on Chinese Academy System* (中国书院制度研究), the authors Chen Gujia and Deng Hongbo stated that some academies in the Qing dynasty published compilations of poems and essays that displayed local cultures. For instance, Jinyang Academy in Yangqu County, Shanxi engraved ten volumes of *Collections of Works of Four Literary Schools* (国初山右四家文钞); Xihe Academy in Chaoyi County, Shaanxi, published *Collections of Ancient Classical Works in Xihe* (西河古文录), composed of eight volumes, in the Daoguang era; Lanshan Academy in Gansu engraved and published *Series of Books of Eryou Hall* (二酉堂丛书), edited by Zhang Shu, which included 21 "publications from Guanlong," in a total of 27 volumes, in the first year of the Daoguang era (1821); during the Daoguang era, Xuehai Academy in Guangzhou engraved and published *Collections of Important Works About Lingnan* (国朝岭南文钞), composed of 18 volumes, written by Chen Zaiqian, one volume of *A Hundred Poems About Lingnan* (南海百咏), written by Fang Xinru in the Song dynasty, and *A Sequel to A Hundred Poems About Lingnan* (南海百咏续编), consisting of four volumes, composed by Fan Feng in the Qing dynasty; in the ninth year of the Jiaqing era (1804), Wuhua Academy in Kunming engraved and published four books—*Collection of Yunnan Poems* (滇明诗略), *Collection of Yunnan Poems Composed in the Current Dynasty* (滇国朝诗略), *A Sequel to Collection of Yunnan Poetry* (续刻滇南诗略), and *Collection of Yunnan Essays* (滇南文略)—all of which were poems and essays about Yunnan created by different writers throughout history.[143]

The third type was the annals of academies edited by staff members themselves. For example, Songyang Academy in Henan Province printed and published *Annals of Songyang Academy* (嵩阳书院志) in the early Qing dynasty. Yunan Academy printed and published *Map of Yunan Academy* (豫南书院图) in the tenth year of the Guangxu era (1884), and Ziyun Academy printed and published *Annals of Ziyun Academy* (敕赐紫云书院志), composed by Li Zhuoran, in the 30th year of the Kangxi era (1691). In the 13th year of the Tongzhi era (1874), Shenye Academy printed and published *Annals of Shenye Academy* (莘野书院四斋说), and in the 21st year of the Guangxu era (1895), Mingdao Academy printed and published *Annals of Mingdao Academy* (明道书院志).[144]

Engraving and publishing the aforementioned regional historical documents facilitated regional cultural preservation and development. First of all, editing, printing, and publishing provincial, prefectural, and county annals, which normally describe local geography and landscapes, histories, stories of prominent local figures, transformation of administration systems, cultural and education industries, and customs and traditions, can help demonstrate local cultural characteristics, increase cultural recognition, and thus establish cultural identities. These engraving activities are actually an important method of regional cultural construction. Second, literary works and academic publications of various scholars and literati about local communities in ancient times manifested how culturally developed a certain region was in terms of literature, art, and philosophical theories. Compiling, engraving, and publishing regional historical documents not only displayed and promoted local cultures but also preserved historical records of regional cultural development for later generations. It thereby provided ideological resources and spiritual power for the further development of local culture. Third, academies, as a concretion of the Confucian culture, produced, promoted, and developed the Confucian culture over time. The establishment and development of academies in different areas constituted a significant part of regional cultures. Academy annals, which record the history and current situation of an academy, preserve a great variety of documentation regarding the development of the institution. In a way, engraving and publishing academy annals not only portrayed regional cultural development but also had a positive impact on regional cultural construction. Overall, book engraving and publishing in academies was an important strategy that academies used to directly serve society, promote local cultures, and achieve cultural accumulation. It was a driving force for continuous regional cultural development.

Academy and the Cultivation of Regional Talents

As an organizational part of a large social system, the academy has a multifaceted role to play, including talent cultivation, intelligence development, cultural accumulation, academic research, and social edification. However, its core and most fundamental function lies in the first two aspects. As we examine the development history of academies, we would find that from the Song dynasty, when the academy system was initially established to the day this system matured into various

148 *Regional Cultural Undertakings*

stages, most academies place great emphasis on talent cultivation, although their geographic locations, teaching qualities, types, organizers, missions, guiding principles, and objectives might vary. Overall, academies started to focus on talent cultivation in the Tang dynasty. Following the early Song dynasty, giving lectures and cultivating talents became its underlying function, which underpinned the development of the institutions.

As early as the late eighth century and early ninth century, academies that functioned like schools, engaging in education and some academic work, appeared, such as Zhang Jiuzong Academy in Suining, Sichuan; Guiyan Academy in Gao'an, Jiangxi; and Shigu Academy in Hengyang, Hunan.[145] Since then, giving lectures and teaching students have become the most distinguished function of academies. Many scholars have talked about the cultivation of talents in the academy at that time. For instance, subsequent to the establishment of Hushi Academy in Hongzhou, Xu Xuan said, "Dozens of students, including clansmen and those from other parts of the town, assembled here to attend academic seminars and lectures, which lasted all year round."[146] Wang Yucheng also mentioned that Hualin Academy in Hongzhou "built a great many houses and provided food to accommodate students."[147] Subsequent to the founding of Yuelu Academy,[148] "a large number of students were admitted into the institution."[149] Yingtianfu Academy "invited numerous students to their lectures." Some scholars typically viewed these academies as supplementary education resources to formal schooling, believing that academies could replace the official schools in cultivating talents when the school system collapsed during wars. They held that "when government-funded schools were destroyed, and no places were available for the literati to pursue their academic work, they normally built an elegant cottage at a place with beautiful natural surroundings to give lectures to the public."[150] As discussed in Chapter 3 of this book, one important reason why sovereigns advocated, encouraged, and supported academies in the early Song dynasty was that they believed these institutions could provide an enormous number of talented and educated elites at a turbulent political moment. Some scholars even thought there were no significant differences between an academy and a school, maintaining that prefectural schools and academies should merge. The scholar in the Southern Song dynasty, Hong Mai, said,

> During the Qingli era, an imperial decree was issued that schools should be established in every prefecture and professors appointed. The so-called academies should merge with schools, as from the perspective of state affairs management, it was inappropriate to have two education systems in one country.[151]

This argument was made from the perspective of talent cultivation.

During the Southern Song dynasty, academies formed a close tie with Neo-Confucianism. Many academies became research centers for the promotion and study of Neo-Confucianism. Despite the increasing role that academies played in research, talent cultivation was still one of the most important parts of the institutional operation. In fact, great academic scholars, such as Zhu Xi, Zhang Shi, and Lü Zuqian, all upheld that academic research and talent cultivation came hand in hand. They all, invariably, paid much attention to talent development. Zhu Xi and Lü Zuqian both made detailed rules and regulations in "Statutes of Bailudong Academy" (白鹿洞书院揭示) and *Rules and Regulations of Lize Academy* (丽泽书院学规) as to the objective of talent cultivation, research contents, and the fundamental way to conduct academic research, to realize self-cultivation, and to manage affairs and perceive things. Zhang Shi specifically pointed out that the mission of an academy was to "cultivate talents, promote Confucian philosophies and benefit the populace."[152] In this light, although academies at that time were multifunctional, the core mission of an academy was to provide mass education and cultivate talents.

In the Yuan dynasty, as an increasing number of academies became government-funded, academies were institutionalized. Some scholars asserted academies in the Yuan dynasty shifted from research centers to education institutions. At that time, like all local government-funded schools of different levels, academies were also viewed as education organizations controlled and supervised by local governments.[153] Under such circumstances, talent cultivation, without a shadow of doubt, became the top priority for academies. Therefore, as some scholars stated, although academies only occupied a small portion of education institutions in the country in the Yuan dynasty and their role in education continuously declined due to abandonment,[154] academies were still indispensable in talent cultivation for the state.

During the mid and late Ming dynasty, academies flourished. At that time, one important phenomenon that marked the pinnacle of the development of academies was proliferating public lectures, which we have discussed previously. These public lectures held by academies were open to not only students but also people from the general public of different socio-economic status. As a result, academies in that period played an immense role in democratizing Confucianism, exploiting collective intelligence and educating the masses. Nevertheless, even in such an atmosphere, talent cultivation was still the main goal of academies. We can tell how people perceived academies from their commemorative articles. "Scholars conducted their research and spent leisurely hours in academies rather than schools."[155]

> Currently, only a specific number of staff members is allowed in government-funded schools, so chances of having extensive academic communication in these schools are slim for scholars. Policies in terms of admission and curriculums in academies, on the other hand, are relatively flexible. As a consequence, scholars prefer to receive their education in local private academies to cultivate themselves or attend prefectural schools to broaden their views through research.

These statements show that, in their opinions, academies were essential organizations for talent cultivation. Even the goal of Shuixi Academy in Jing County,

Anhui, which served as the main venue for academic communication for scholars of Xin Xue, was still talent cultivation. "Scholars in this academy supervised and educated students from six towns."[156] In the fourth year of the Jiajing era (1525), Wang Shouren made it clear in his article "Annals of Wansong Academy" (万松书院记) after the academy was renovated that the main purpose of this institution was to cultivate learned men. He writes, "Modelled after the system implemented in Bailudong Academy, we select talented students and allow them to study and exchange ideas here as a way of encouraging and guiding townsmen." Wang Yangming stressed that the fundamental goal for opening academies was to "motivate literati to study by managing and operating academies."[157]

In the Qing dynasty, academies were further institutionalized, and academies gradually played a dominant part in talent cultivation. In the 11th year of the Yongzheng era (1733), the Yongzheng Emperor issued an imperial decree that clearly specified the purpose of founding provincial academies by regional governors. The decree was as follows:

> The purpose of founding an academy is to elect a cultivated and honorable man in this province to educate the general public. This man shall give lectures during daytime and in evenings, set himself as an example for townspeople, and become academically accomplished. In this way, scholars in other parts of the province will be encouraged and inspired. This is also an approach to cultivating talents.[158]

In the first year of the Qianlong era (1736), the Qianlong Emperor issued an imperial order, which reads, "The purpose of establishing academies is to introduce and cultivate talents and provide what schools fail to fulfill."[159] The highest authority's perception and expectation of academies were thus widely acknowledged by many academy founders. For example, during the Qianlong era, the author of "Annals of Donglou Academy" (东娄书院记), writes, "The academy employs prominent scholars to teach students and implements a strict evaluation system to cultivate talented people for the state and supply what government-funded schools fail to provide."[160] In the 19th year of the Guangxu era (1893), Yang Jinkai writes in his article "Annals of Yuping Academy" (玉屏书院记), "Academies assist government-funded schools and cultivate talents for the nation."[161] Apparently, academies in the Qing dynasty attached great importance to talent cultivation. Some academies founded by eminent scholars in the Qing dynasty, however, were quite renowned for their academic research and indeed served as academic research centers. They facilitated the development of local research work and exerted a profound influence on scholars of that age and even later generations, but these academies only took up an insignificant portion of thousands of academies in the Qing dynasty. Most academies were still regarded as organizations for talent cultivation. Some scholars argue that by the mid and late Qing dynasty, prefectural and country schools had reduced to administrative education bodies that provided no teaching but only examinations and evaluations. The task of cultivating talents had been completely transferred to academies.[162]

Regional Cultural Undertakings   151

During the evolution of the academy system in the past 1,000 years, thanks to their unique teaching guidelines, methods, and contents, academies created numberless talented men, civilized local townspeople, and boosted the development of local cultures. Academies, different from both government-funded and private schools, carved themselves a glorious place in the history of Chinese education. On the one hand, the number of local government-funded education institutions was usually limited, often only one school in each administrative division, and it only accepted a small number of students. For instance, although government-funded schools burgeoned in the early Ming dynasty and "Confucian schools were founded in all prefectures, counties, and *weisuo*" far more than those in the Tang and Song dynasties, few students were admitted.[163] In the second year of the Hongwu era (1369), "only 40 students could be admitted into prefectural schools and this number reduced by ten each for county schools of lower levels."[164] Naturally, such scarce education resources could not meet the requirement of talent cultivation. On the other hand, some private institutions, such as community schools and charity schools, struggled to cultivate talents due to their small operation and low teaching qualities. Given that, academies scattered across the country became the dominant organizations responsible for talent cultivation.

In terms of the distribution and number of academies, we take the Qing dynasty when academies reached their prime, as an example. More than 4,000 academies were scattered across the nation, from metropolises all the way to remote towns. In terms of the size of academies, although it varied drastically among academies in different administrative divisions, the number of students in an academy usually ranged from several hundred to a thousand, according to various historical documents. For example, during the Shaoxing era in the Southern Song dynasty, Longguang Academy in Fengcheng, Jiangxi, "admitted over 300 people from all parts of the province."[165] Xuegu Academy in Sanyuan, Shaanxi, in the Yuan dynasty, "admitted more than 100 students from both neighboring and distant towns" when the scholar Cheng Yuegu gave lectures.[166] During the Qianlong era, Ziyang Academy in Suzhou "admitted no less than 2,000 students" during the 16 years when the esteemed scholar Qian Daxin served as the headmaster, "all of whom dedicated themselves to research on classics and endeavored to seek truth from facts."[167] In the Daoguang era (1821–1850), Ziyang Academy and Zhengyi Academy in Suzhou had "1,300 to 1,400 students."[168] Also, according to Liu Boji's book *Academy System of Guangdong* (广东书院制度), Yuexiu Academy in Guangzhou admitted 100 students of different types in the 20th year of the Qianlong era (1755) and 150 in the 14th year of the Jiaqing era (1809). Duanxi Academy in Zhaoqing accepted 320 students in the 16th year of the Jiaqing era and Rongjiang Academy in Jieyang 310 in the 42nd year of the Qianlong era. Nonetheless, only 36 students were allowed in prefectural schools and 40 subsidized and additional students each in Guangdong at that time. The maximum number of students for county school was 20, and 20 each for subsidized and additional students. Liu Boji thus argued that "the number of students admitted by academies constituted the majority of Confucian students, and it could be further inferred that academy education had a close relationship with literati back then."[169]

152 *Regional Cultural Undertakings*

In the Tang dynasty and the Five Dynasties period, most early academies did not offer lectures. Usually, they served as places for the literati to study and conduct research. In the Song dynasty, some academies also did not provide teaching services. For example, Qiaonan Academy, founded in the Jiading era in the Southern Song dynasty by Xu Zaishu from Xi'an, was simply a personal library.

By examining academies in different areas, we have a more profound understanding of how academies facilitated talent cultivation. For instance, in Hunan, the number, sizes, and influences of academies reached their peaks in the Southern Song and Qing dynasties. According to Bai Xinliang's research and statistical reports, the number of newly founded academies in Hunan in the Southern Song dynasty was fourth place in the country.[170] Yuelu Academy further extended its influences in the third year of the Qiandao era (1167) when Zhu Xi and Zhang Shi gave lectures to the public there. Among the 23 provincial academies established and funded by the government during the Yongzheng era of the Qing dynasty, two of them, Yuelu Academy and Chengnan Academy, were located in Hunan Province. Hunan Province was indeed one of the four provinces where two provincial academies were founded. Correspondingly, a number of talented people were from Hunan in the Southern Song and Qing dynasties. In the Southern Song dynasty, academies in Hunan, represented by Yuelu Academy, Biquan Academy, and Chengnan Academy, nurtured a great many prominent scholars. Some celebrated Neo-Confucianists of the Huxiang School, such as Peng Guinian, You Jiuyan, and Hu Dashi, were all graduates of Yuelu Academy. Even the renowned Neo-Confucianist Zhang Shi once learned from Hu Hong at Biquan Academy. Huang Zongxi and Quan Zuwang listed 33 Zhang Shi's students graduating from Yuelu Academy in the chapter "Annal of Confucian Scholars of Shi-Liu School" (士刘诸儒学案) in *Scholarly Annals of Song and Yuan Periods* (宋元学案) and compared them with Zhu Xi's students. They exclaimed, "Who said that Master Zhang's students could not compete against Master Zhu's?"[171] After the mid-Qing dynasty, Hunan nurtured more esteemed figures, including Tao Shu, Wei Yuan, Zeng Guofan, Zuo Zongtang, Hu Linyi, and Guo Songdao. These great men promoted the Hunan culture and exerted a lasting influence on the development of Chinese society. A popular proverb was circulated around the Tongzhi era, which says, "Among all the prominent political and military figures who contribute to the rejuvenation of the Chinese nation, most of them are from Hunan." These talented people were all, for the most part, closely associated with Yuelu Academy. The couplet hung on either side of the front gate of Yuelu Academy in the Jiaqing era of the Qing dynasty, which reads, "The Chu region fosters talented men, and the Academy nurtures learned scholars," gives the most precise and fairest comment on how Yuelu Academy cultivated talents in the Qing dynasty.

Another example was Guangdong in the Qing dynasty, where academies also proliferated. The number of new academies reached 482, which was the highest in the country, and it occupied 67% of all 719 academies in Guangdong founded in history.[172] In the Qing dynasty, particularly in the Jiaqing and Daoguang eras, Guangdong provided numerous talents to the state. According to Vol. 19 of *County Annals of Nanhai* (南海县志), published in the Xuantong era, "scholars

Regional Cultural Undertakings   153

dedicated to classics and poetry burgeoned,"[173] as well as those specialized in other areas. When Li Xupu conducted research on textology in Guangdong in the Qing dynasty, he affirmed that an enormous number of preeminent scholars appeared in Guangdong in the late Qing dynasty. These scholars, like dazzling stars, formed a remarkable scholar group. Members like Zeng Zhao, Chen Li, Li Wensi, Hou Kang, Wu Rongguang, Tan Ying, Zou Boqi, and Liang Tingnan all became first-class masters in textology in the Qing dynasty. The emergence of a substantial number of great scholars was an immediate result of the founding of Xuehai Academy when Ruan Yuan governed Guangdong in the Jiaqing and Daoguang eras. The founder of the Dongshu School and "master of textology for classics in the Qianlong and Jiaqing eras" during the Xianfeng and Tongzhi reigns, Chen Li was indeed one of the first graduates of Xuehai Academy. It is reasonable to say that Guangdong academies, represented by Xuehai Academy, Jupo Academy, and Guangya Academy, were the main venues for literati to study, conduct research, and attend cultural and academic events in the late Qing dynasty.[174]

On the role of the academy in the cultivation of local talents, the founders of academies also have many discussions. For example, when the magistrate of Taigu County in Shanxi, Lü Chongmi, founded Fengshan Academy in the Qianlong era, Wu Yihan explained the relationship between talent cultivation and the rise and fall of academies in his article "Records of Fengshan Academy" (新建凤山书院记). He writes,

> After some research, I found that academies reached their pinnacle in the Song dynasty. Bailudong Academy and Ehu Academy were both popular places for the literati to give lectures. As a result, a number of learned and noble Confucian scholars appeared. In the early Ming dynasty, the founding of Fengshan Academy in Guxian County inspired the general public and thereby generated a considerable number of talented people, such as Bai Junxu, Liu Junguan, and Liu Junsheng. Three people actually received the *xieyuan* degree, and Guxian County became the most culturally thriving county in the prefecture. In the late Ming dynasty, due to increasing restrictions on speech, academies were gradually abandoned, and townsmen were no longer as enthusiastic about learning as in the early years. After being ravaged by the peasant rebellion led by Li Zicheng, the county further declined, and few Confucian students participated in the imperial examinations or managed to receive their *jinshi* degree.[175]

Further to Wu Yihan's comments, Meng Shenghui also writes in his article "Tablet Inscription of Fengshan Academy" (凤山书院碑记), "Taigu is just a tiny county, but it has produced more successful candidates in the imperial examinations than any other counties. It is commonly believed that the academy is a big part of it."[176] In the 13th year of the Tongzhi era (1874), Ma Shengwu elaborated on the influence of academies in Tianjin on local talent cultivation in his article "Tablet Inscription of Creation of Chongzheng Academy" (建立会文书院碑记).[177] He says, "For the last few decades, there have been more successful candidates in the imperial examinations in this area than other parts of the country. This is largely ascribed to the academy." In the first year of the Daoguang era (1821), Xie Yun, magistrate of Yining, Guangxi, stated in his article "A Preface to Restoration of the Kui Pavilion in Yijiang Academy" (募修义江书院奎星阁桑山塔序) that following the establishment of Yijiang Academy, "local townsmen took pride in outstanding students who received good grades in the imperial examinations."[178] These arguments emphasized the crucial role that academies played in talent cultivation, and all the authors, invariably, attributed the success in the imperial examinations to academies. They failed to understand, however, that talent development was actually the product of various influences, such as local cultures, traditions, and social economy. In addition, these authors had a very narrow definition of talented people, including only those succeeding in the imperial examinations, which made their assertions less objective. Nevertheless, we should also realize that in an era when imperial examinations prevailed, almost all scholars had the ambition of participating in the examinations. Out of the sheer number of candidates, only a very few were fortunate enough to gain the ultimate victory in the examinations and climb up to the top of the pyramid. Therefore, the number of people succeeding in the imperial examinations could, in a way, reflect the size of the educated population and the local education level. Given that academies were widely scattered across the country and could accommodate a great number of students, academies constituted an essential part of the local education system. When we take these factors into consideration, we can reasonably be convinced that academies did have a positive impact on local talent development.

Talents are the main body of cultural innovations and promotion. Talent prosperity is an important indicator of whether a region is culturally developed. It is also the foundation of further development of the region's cultural undertakings. Academies civilized local townsmen by cultivating talents and local cultural elites, who further facilitated the continuous development of local cultures.

Academy and Regional Culture Exchange

The formation and development of a culture are, more or less, influenced by local geography and environment. With a certain geographical space as the background, culture always has regional characteristics and shows different traits in different regions. This territoriality is one of the essential attributes of culture, and it acts as a powerful force that constrains the nature, type, level, direction, and speed of the development of culture in that region. However, at the same time, culture is not entirely confined to the geographical environment.[179] It also breaks through the limitations of space and territory in various ways to spread and diffuse to other regions so that the cultures between different localities can be exchanged and integrated. In the process of cultural diffusion, talents, as important carriers of culture, played a dominant role. And as the academy is a place where talents gather, it is, therefore, of great importance in the process of cultural exchange and integration between regions.

Regional Cultural Undertakings 155

First, the tradition of giving lectures to the general public in academies made academies a public and open space. Through giving and attending lectures, scholars in different fields had the opportunity to discuss academic topics and exchange ideas with their peers and fellow students. These learned scholars introduced different theories, mindsets, and academic frameworks that reflected their regional cultures to academies. Consequently, the podiums in academies became crucial platforms for regional cultural and academic interaction. The Song and Ming dynasties were two eras when the trend of offering public lectures reached its peak. By examining the phenomenon of a number of scholars traveling to different parts of the country to give lectures and carry out academic communication, we can, in a way, gain a better understanding of how academies facilitated regional cultural interactions.

During the mid–Southern Song dynasty, Zhu Xi and Zhang Shi built and expanded their academic circles in Fujian and Hunan, respectively. In terms of academic background, Zhu Xi was one of the two Chengs' disciples (the two Chengs are Cheng Yi and Cheng Hao, who are great masters of Neo-Confucianism in the Song dynasty; see Volume 1, Chapter 4]) in the fourth generation, preceded by Yang Shi, Luo Congyan, and Li Dong. Yang Shi, a scholar from Jiangle, Nanjian, in Fujian, who advocated the philosophies of the Yiluo School in the southeast, was an important Neo-Confucianist in the south. Later, his successor Luo Congyan passed down the same philosophies to Li Dong, who then passed them down to Zhu Xi. All four scholars shared the same philosophical ideology. As they all rose to fame in Nanjian Prefecture in the north of Fujian, and as Nanjian was called Yanping following the Yuan dynasty, later generations regarded them as the Four Great Sages of Yanping.[180] Apparently, after generations of hard work and development in Fujian, the southern Yiluo School had formed its own distinct character. Although Zhu Xi's philosophies were largely drawn from theories of multiple Neo-Confucian schools established in the Northern Song dynasty, a majority of his principles were developed in Fujian, under the deep influence of Yang Shi, Luo Congyan, and Li Dong. Therefore, his school was also known as the Min (abbreviation of Fujian) school. Zhang Shi, on the other hand, was Hu Hong's (Hu Hong has been generally regarded to be founder of the Huxiang School) eldest disciple, who learned Confucianism from Hu Hong at Biquan Academy and was highly spoken of by his teacher. During the seven years he taught at Yuelu Academy, Zhang Shi cultivated a large number of scholars. He was thus referred to as a representative figure of the Huxiang School. During the process of developing their own respective theoretical frameworks, Zhu Xi and Zhang Shi wrote to each other to explore and discuss academic topics that they both had an interest in. As their discussions extended further, Zhu Xi found it necessary to meet in person and have a face-to-face conversation. He wrote in his letter, "I recently found that we should meet. It is not easy to figure things out without a personal meeting."[181] Therefore, in the fall of the third year of the Qiandao era (1167), Zhu Xi and his students traveled 600 miles all the way to Changsha from Chong'an, Fujian. At Yuelue Academy and Chengnan Academy, the two scholars had an in-depth debate on some academic issues. This meeting

156 *Regional Cultural Undertakings*

lasted for over two months. Their discussions became so intense that they "could not reach a mutual agreement until three days later."[182] The academic communication between Zhu and Zhang was later described as the Zhu and Zhang Conference, which was a direct interaction between the Min School, represented by Zhu Xi, and the Huxiang School, represented by Zhang Shi. After this conference, the Huxiang School influenced Zhu Xi to some degree, for in a poem Zhu Xi wrote upon their partings: "I was ignorant of many theories in the past. After the meeting with you, I came to understand patterns of nature at last. Now I began to see the beauty of Tai Chi. It is so ineffable, in fact."[183] The following year, Zhu Xi wrote in his letter to Cheng Yunfu,[184] "Last winter when I traveled to Hunan, I learned a lot from the discussions." Likewise, Zhang Shi was also somewhat influenced by Zhu Xi's ideas. We are confident to say that Yuelu Academy and Chengnan Academy provided platforms for the communication and interaction between the Min school and the Huxiang school. The academic exchange had mutual impact on both of them.[185]

Many scholars of that age indeed used academies to conduct academic communication with different schools. Lü Zuqian and Lu Xiangshan, the representative figures of the Wu School and the Xiangshan School, respectively, were as academically achieved as Zhu Xi, but they both had formed their own distinct theories. Quan Zuwang states,

> Following the Qiandao and Chunxi eras of the Song dynasty, three schools came into existence, which were the Zhu school, the Lü school and the Lu school. The three schools were formed in the same era, but they were all different from each other. The Zhu school focused on obtaining knowledge through research, Lu's emphasized spiritual enlightenment, and the Lü school drew the strengths of the former two schools while further refining them by using the classics dominating the Central Plains.[186]

Lü Zuqian and Lu Jiuyuan had extensive academic communication and discussions with Zhu Xi in academies. In the spring of the second year of the Chunxi era (1175), Lü Zuqian traveled from Wuzhou to Fujian, where he met Zhu Xi at Hanquan Academy. They read the works of Zhou Dunyi, Zhang Zai, and the two Cheng brothers together and compiled over 600 chapters, classified them into 14 categories, and included them in the book *Close Thoughts* (近思录). This book then became the introductory book for Neo-Confucianism. In the meantime, the two also jointly edited *Remnant Books of the Cheng Brothers* (二程遗书) and composed an edited version titled "Maxim of the Cheng Brothers" (程子格言). During their one-month meeting at Hanquan Academy, Zhu Xi and Lü Zuqian explored many topics and reached mutual understandings on various issues. This meeting had a direct impact on Zhu's and Lü's thoughts and philosophies, respectively. It was, in fact, an in-depth interaction between the Wu School and the Min School.[187]

During the mid and late Ming dynasty, as public lectures in academies thrived, scholars in different fields often traveled back and forth between different academies to promote their theories. For example, Zhan Ruoshui, founder of the Ganquan School in Zengcheng, Guangdong Province, dedicated his whole life to delivering lectures in academies. During his middle age, he spared no efforts to give lectures in academies of Nanjing and its suburban districts, including Xinquan Academy in Jinling, Xinjiang Academy in Jiangpu, Ganquan Academy in Chizhou, Doushan Academy in Huizhou, Fushan Academy in Wuyuan, and Tianquan Academy in Xiuning. In his late years, he came a long way from Guangdong to Hengshan of Hunan seven times and lectured there at Shigu Academy.[188] Another example is Qian Dehong, a disciple of Wang Yangming's and a representative of Xin-Xue, who spent his whole life giving lectures all over the southern parts of the Yangtze River. "In the 30 years after his retirement, there was not a day when he did not engage in lecturing activities, and everywhere his lecture halls could be found throughout the southern regions."[189] Wang Ji, another disciple of Wang Yangming's in the central region of Guangdong Province, also lectured in various places. "For more than 40 years of his retirement, he traveled across a large area and was indefatigable in giving lectures every single day, and until his eighties, he did not stop."[190] It should be noted that during the Song and Ming dynasties, it was fairly common for scholars to travel to different academies to deliver lectures there. For example, apart from Zhu Xi, who usually gave lectures during the Qiandao era in the Song dynasty at Yuelu Academy, Chen Fuliang of the Zhedong School also lectured often at academies during the Chunxi era in the Song dynasty. Besides, many other scholars, such as Ji Ben, Luo Hongxian, Zhang Yuanbian, and Zou Yuanbiao from the Yangming School and Gao Shitai from the Donglin school, all promoted their own theories by giving lectures in academies.[191] Donglin Academy was just such a favorite place that had once attracted "quite a number of well-known and erudite scholars in other parts of the country to come here from afar to lecture."[192] Such large-scale academic gatherings greatly facilitated academic communication and cultural interaction between scholars of different schools and regions.

Second, students in academies could select their teachers according to their own preferences. There were hardly any admission requirements on where students came from. Students from different parts of the country could live and study together in academies to further their education. Academies, as a consequence, became places where different cultures clashed and integrated with each other. As a non-official cultural and education organization different from government-funded schools, an academy distinguished itself in various aspects. In terms of admission, government-funded schools of different levels usually accept students from a certain administrative division only. They did not accept those living outside the town. For instance, one record in *Draft to Institutional History of the Song Dynasty* (宋会要辑稿) says, "In March of the fifth year of the Qingli era, an imperial decree was issued that all government-funded schools shall only accept local students. All students traveling from other provinces shall be deported to their native towns."[193] In glaring contrast, for many academies, there were no restrictions on where students should come from when it came to admission. This was one big difference between an academy and a prefectural or county school.

158 *Regional Cultural Undertakings*

Zhu Xi writes in his article "Measures to Promote Learning at Yuelu Academy" (潭州委教授措置岳麓书院牒), "After examining the prefectural school, it is decided to reestablish Yuelu Academy. The initial purpose of founding the academy is to provide accommodations and education to students who travel to the town for academic communication and pursuits."[194] During the Yuanzhen era in the Yuan dynasty, Ji Hou, the pacification commissioner of Jiangdong, in his commemorative article written for Changxiang Academy of Fuliang (current Jingde Town in Sichuan Province), specified the difference in admission requirements between academies and schools. He pointed out that "only local townspeople were allowed to study in schools," whereas this was not the case for academies. In fact, "people from either neighboring or distant towns assembled at academies to study."[195] Li Yuanzhen, a scholar in the Kangxi era of the Qing dynasty, writes in his article "Records of Nanyang Academy" (南阳书院记),

> Students from government-funded schools must be selected for the schools, as they have been under the administration of these government-funded schools and classified by administrative division level. Students have to meet these admission requirements to be accepted. However, anyone who is passionate about academic research is allowed to study at academies, no matter where they come from.[196]

When we examine the history of academy development, we find that many academies accepted students from out of province. For instance, when Zhang Shi, an honorable and knowledgeable scholar, taught at Yuelu Academy in the Southern Song dynasty, a significant number of students traveled from Sichuan and other provinces near Hunan to the academy out of pure admiration. According to historical records, "when Mr. Nanxuan taught at Hunan, many Sichuan students followed."[197] Scholars of the Huxiang School who carried out their academic activities mainly at Yuelu Academy, apart from learning from Zhang Shi, also often visited academies in Jiangxi, Zhejiang, and Fujian to take lectures of other masters, such as Zhu Xi, Lu Jiuyuan, and Lü Zuqian. For example, Hu Dashi, a celebrated disciple of Zhang Shi and prominent scholar of the Huxiang School graduating from Yuelu Academy, studied Neo-Confucianism from Zhang Shi first before he learned from Zhu Xi and Lu Jiuyuan. Jiang Yuanfu used to be Zhang Shi's student, but he later learned from Lu Jiuyuan. Shen Youkai learned from Lü Zuqian and Xu Jixuan in addition to Zhang Shi. Zhu Shen became Lü Zuqian's student after he graduated from Zhang Shi. Zhang Xun "traveled to Wuyi to study the Huiweng School" established by Zhu Xi after learning from Zhang Shi.[198] From the fact that scholars of the Huxiang School furthered their academic pursuits through learning from different teachers in different academies, we judge that it was quite frequent for scholars to conduct academic communication with peers in other areas. What was more worth noting was that among those eminent scholars of the Huxiang School from Yuelu Academy listed in the *Scholarly Annals of Song and Yuan Periods* (宋元学案), Peng Guinian, was from Qingjiang, Jiangxi; the brothers You Jiuyan and You Jiugong were from Jianyang,

Fujian; and Chen Qi was from Linjiang, Jiangxi. All of them were out-of-province students at Yuelu Academy.

At that time, some academies specified in their admission requirements that no restrictions were placed on students' places of birth. For example, "Rules and Regulations of Mingdao Academies" (明道书院规程) says, "Students passionate for academic research can be admitted after they discuss their situations with the headmaster in person and submit a well-written, articulate essay, no matter where they come from."[199] This statement actually ensured that students from all parts of the country could be admitted to academies in a written format. According to *Research on Academies of the Yuan Dynasty System* (元代书院研究), authored by Xu Zi, academies in the Yuan dynasty, mostly founded by eminent families, mainly accepted kin or children in the local community. However, some of them also accepted students from other regions, such as Mingjing Academy in Wuyuan, Heming Academy in Chongyang, Hubei, Qingjie Academy in Taihe, Jiangxi, and Yuxi Academy in Yuxi, Poyang. In their admission requirements, there was always an article saying "regardless of where students come from" or "to hire teachers to teach students from all parts of the country."[200] When the Neo-Confucianist in the early Yuan dynasty, Xu Qian, retired to Mount Bahua in Dongyang and established Sixian Academy, scholars from both distant prefectures, such as You, Ji, Qi, and Lu, and provinces close by, such as Jing, Yang, Wu, and Yue, all came to study.[201] During the Jiajing era of the Ming dynasty, Wang Yangming founded Jishan Academy to "teach and supervise students from various towns." His students traveled from numerous provinces, covering a vast expanse of territories, such as Guangdong, Huguang, Zhili, Jiangxi, and Zhejiang. For instance,

> Xiao Qiu, Yang Rusen, and Yang Shaofang were from Huguang; Yang Shiming, Xue Zongkai, and Huang Mengxing were from Guangdong; Wang Gen, Meng Yuan, and Zhou Chong were from Zhili; He Qin and Huang Honggang were from Nangan; Liu Bangcai and Liu Wenmin were from Anfu; Wei Liangzheng and Wei Liangqi were from Xinjian; and Zeng Bian was from Taihe.[202]

These incidents showcase that academies, by that time, had become places where scholars from different parts of the country congregated.

In the Qing dynasty, it was also very common for academies to accept students from other parts of the country. For example, Cai Shiying, governor of Jiangxi during the Shunzhi era in the Qing dynasty, once added one more entry of "assembling Confucianists from other regions" to the stipulations of Bailudong Academy. He mandated that the academy should admit students from different parts of the country if they passed the entrance examination. This entry reads,

> The academy shall accept talented students from all parts of the nation rather than confine admission to one certain area only. It is morally inappropriate to reject fellows who are attracted to our academy and attempt to study and conduct academic research here. The vice superintendent of the academy

160 *Regional Cultural Undertakings*

shall first have a meeting with such persons to evaluate whether they are truly talented and achieved. If so, he could introduce the subject student to the superintendent for further assessment. If the subject student is really an honorable and learned man, we shall retain him for future academic research.[203]

In the 21st year of the Kangxi era (1682), Gao Huang stipulated in "Long-term Plan of Bailudong Academy" (经久规模议) that

students from other provinces must clearly set forth such personal information as their names, places of birth, and family backgrounds in their applications for approval by the government of Xingzi County before they can be admitted. This policy is to protect the academy from people harboring ill designs or intentions. Nevertheless, those who are well acquainted with academy teachers or students and in possession of referral letters from these acquaintances are exempted from this rule.[204]

During the Xianfeng era, "Statutes of Enrolling Students in Zhenyan Academy" (箴言书院选士章程) also states, "For all under-age students from other provinces that are attracted to the academy to study, the academy will accept them if there is capacity."[205] From what was previously discussed, we can see that academy students in the Qing dynasty were typically classified by their places of birth. However, some provincial academies or institutions with abundant funds admitted quite a few under-age students from other provinces or prefectures as well. Zhongshan Academy in Jiangning has 50 boarding students, 70 day students, and many guest students from other regions; Anding Academy and Meihua Academy of Yangzhou have altogether 20 students from other prefectures and ten from other provinces, to give only a few. In general, the admission of students from other parts of the country provides a platform for regional cultural exchanges.

Third, superintendents and teachers in academies were usually from different regions. As a scholar's way of thinking and living was inevitably shaped by the culture where he was raised, his academic works naturally reflected the culture of that specific region. By teaching students and conducting academic research in academies, they carried out a sort of inter-territorial cultural communication. The influences of such communication and cultural promotion could extend from the academy further to its surrounding areas and impact the local culture. Meanwhile, scholars themselves would also learn from new cultures and thereby develop new theories that mirrored an integrated culture.

As a cultural and educational organization, the superintendent and teachers play a significant role in the operation of an academy. Every academy had detailed rules as to the election of its superintendent and staff members. Some academies would select their superintendents based on where they came from and confined the candidates to local townsmen. For instance, Xihu Academy in Xiaogan, Hubei, during the Guangxu era of the Qing dynasty stipulated in its policies,

For the election of the academy superintendent, the most respected gentleman in the town shall select a local *juren* or a *jinshi* of noble character with extensive knowledge for public election. The elected *juren* or *jinshi* will then be employed by the academy to oversee and supervise affairs within the academy. People without a *juren* or a *jinshi* degree are not qualified for the teaching position. In the event that the elected person failed to meet the expectation of the general public in terms of academic achievement and moral standing, or he is not a native, the gentry could report the case and request his resignation.[206]

In the policies made by the government of Guangnan Prefecture, Yunnan, titled "Rules and Regulations of Gongyi Academy" (广南绅士公议书院条规), it was stipulated that "the superintendent of the academy should hire people who had received a degree in an imperial examination and should not employ anyone who had a bad reputation among the public."[207] Nevertheless, most academies were quite lenient with the selection of their superintendent and teachers, with few restrictions on their places of birth. This practice particularly pervaded the Song and Ming dynasties. For example, Zhang Shi, the superintendent of Yuelu Academy in the early year of the Qiandao era of the Southern Song dynasty, was from Sichuan, Mianzhu. The renowned scholar Ouyang Shoudao, who assumed the superintendent position of Yuelu Academy in the tenth year of the Chunyou era (1250), was from Jizhou, Jiangxi. When Zhu Xi revived Bailudong Academy, he took office as the headmaster of the academy. Later, he hired a man named Wu from Hefei as the superintendent. Zhu Xi's coworkers at Bailudong Academy also included his two disciples, Lin Yongzhong from Gutian, Fujian, and Huang Gan from Minxian County, Fujian. Afterward, their students Lin Kuisun from Gutian, Fujian, and Chen Mi from Putian both taught at Bailudong Academy.[208] It thus can be seen that scholars from other parts of the country not only stayed at an academy for a short period of time for academic conferences and communication, but they also took long-term teaching positions. At that age, it was commonly accepted that there were no restrictions on where superintendents or teachers came from.

In the Qing dynasty, although some academies did place restrictions on places of birth for their superintendents and teachers, most of them paid more attention to their characters, academic achievement, and educational backgrounds. For example, in the first year of the Qianlong era (1736), the Qianlong Emperor issued an imperial decree to provincial educational commissioners regarding the employment of superintendents. The decree reads, "All academy superintendents shall possess extensive knowledge in classics and have a high moral standing. They shall be role models for local townsmen."[209] The policies of Jingxiu Academy in Fenghuang, Hunan, during the Jiaqing era stipulated, "Academy teachers must be morally righteous and academically accomplished. The practice of favoritism or abuse of power is strictly forbidden."[210] As was stated in "Statutes of Fenghu Academy" (丰湖书院章程) in the Jiaqing era,

> The academy superintendent must be selected from candidates successful in the imperial examinations who have obtained academic achievement while adhering to their moral principles. The selected candidate must be publicly elected by the gentry and approved by the local government before being hired.[211]

162 *Regional Cultural Undertakings*

Apparently, these rules specified requirements on personal characters, academic accomplishment, and education backgrounds of academy superintendents and teachers, but nothing was mentioned regarding their places of birth. Some academies even made clear rules that geography was not considered an employment requirement for superintendents. One example was "Rules and Regulations of Fenghu Academy" (丰湖书院规制), written by Hu Linyi, in the tenth year of the Xianfeng era (1860), which says,

> The superintendent of the academy is responsible for guiding students and providing them with moral education. He does not participate in the management of administrative affairs of the academy. There are no requirements on his academic degree, age, or place of birth. Whether he is a local or from another county, he must be honorable in personal character and knowledgeable in classics. He must have an impeccable reputation. After deliberation and discussion of the academy director, executives, and the gentry, then he will be employed.[212]

In fact, it was fairly common for scholars to teach in academies outside their native towns at that time. For instance, during the Kangxi era, Chen Jiding from Huanggang, Hubei and Li Zhongsu from Macheng, Hubei, both assumed the superintendent position of Yuelu Academy. According to Bai Xinliang's research, in the Qianlong era, many academies employed scholars who excelled in classics and histories as their superintendents. Some of the most famed ones included Sang Tiaoyuan teaching at Daliang Academy in Kaifeng, Henan, Lianxi Academy in Jiujiang; Jiangxi and Luoyuan Academy at Jinan, Shandong; Hang Shijun at Yuexiu Academy in Guangzhou and Anding Academy in Yangzhou; Quan Zuwang at Jishan Academy in Shaoxing and Ruixi Academy in Zhaoqing, Guangdong; Shen Tingfang at Aofeng Academy in Fuzhou, Fujian and Leyi Academy in Yizheng, Jiangsu; Dai Zhen at Jinhua Academy in Zhejiang and Shouyang Academy in Shanxi; and Yao Nai at Zhongshan Academy in Jiangning, Jiangsu, and Ziyang Academy in Suzhou.[213] Evidently, these scholars were hired by academies in different parts of the country. This phenomenon provided us with a glimpse of the geographic diversity among academy teachers.

As the leading body of an academy, the superintendent and teachers played a considerable role in determining the characteristics and development direction of the academy's teaching and academic research. By presiding over the teaching and research activities held in different academies, these academy leaders and teachers from different regions added new elements and vitality to the local culture, and thus, in the process of integration and mutual communication, regional culture got continuously promoted.

Notes

1 Some scholars believe that the nature of the Yuan dynasty academy as a research institution faded out while its nature as a teaching institution became more

prominent, which shows a schooling trend of academies at the time. See Xu, Zi徐梓. "Lun yuandai shuyuan de xuexiaohua" 论元代书院的学校化. In *Zhongguo shuyuan* Vol. 2 中国书院第二辑 (Changsha: Hunan Education Press, 1998), 102–110. In addition, Hu Zhaoxi also pointed out that almost all of the Sichuan academies in the Qing dynasty were teaching-oriented, and "there are not enough records to show that among the Sichuan academies in the Qing dynasty, there existed academically oriented research academies." See Hu, Zhaoxi胡昭曦. *Sichuan shuyuan shi*四川书院史 (Chengdu: Prachuap Khiri Khan Book Club, 2000), 194.

2　Huang, Zongxi 黄宗羲, and Quan, Zuwang 全祖望. "Shiliu zhuru xue'an" 士刘诸儒学案. In *Songyuan xue'an* Vol. 6宋元学案卷六 (Beijing: Zhonghua Book Company, 1986), 252.

3　The discourse on the locality of Confucianism in the Song dynasty. See Yang, Nianqun杨念群. *Ruxue diyuhua de jindai xingtai-sanda zhishi qunti hudong de bijiao yanjiu*儒学地域化的近代形态——三大知识群体互动的比较研究 (Beijing: Beijing Sanlian Bookstore, 1997), 47–64; See also Cheng, Minsheng程民生. *Songdai diyu wenhua*宋代地域文化 (Kaifeng: Henan University Press, 1997), 312–315.

4　Huang, Zongxi 黄宗羲, and Quan, Zuwang 全祖望. "Nanxuan xue'an" 南轩学案. In *Songyuan xue'an* Vol. 50宋元学案卷五十 (Beijing: Zhonghua Book Company, 1986), 1611.

5　See Li, Jingde 黎靖德. *Zhuzi yulei* Vol. 101朱子语类卷一百零一 (Beijing: Zhonghua Book Company, 1986), 2581.

6　Hu, Hong 胡宏. "Biquan shuyuan shangliangwen" 碧泉书院上梁文. In *Huhongji*胡宏集 (Beijing: Zhonghua Book Company, 1987), 202.

7　Hu, Hong 胡宏. "Biquan shuyuan shangliangwen" 碧泉书院上梁文. In *Huhongji*胡宏集 (Beijing: Zhonghua Book Company, 1987), 202.

8　Huang, Zongxi 黄宗羲, Quan, Zuwang 全祖望. "Xulu" 序录. In *Songyuan xue'an* Vol. 42宋元学案卷四十二 (Beijing: Zhonghua Book Company, 1986), 1366.

9　Zhang, Shi 张栻. "Huzi zhiyan xu" 胡子知言序. In *Huhongji*胡宏集 (Beijing: Zhonghua Book Company, 1987), 338.

10　See Zhu, Xi 朱熹. "Yu caoshu jinshu" 与曹叔晋书. In *Zhuzi quan shu*朱子全书 (Shanghai: Shanghai Chinese Classics Publishing House), (Hefei: Anhui Education Publishing House, 2002), 1089.

11　See Zhu, Xi 朱熹. "Yu caoshu jinshu" 与曹叔晋书. In *Zhuzi quan shu*朱子全书 (Shanghai: Shanghai Chinese Classics Publishing House; Hefei: Anhui Education Publishing House, 2002), 1089.

12　See Zhu, Hanmi 朱汉民, and Chen, Gujia 陈谷嘉.*Xiangxiang xuepai yuanliu*湘湘学派源流 (Changsha: Hunan Education Press, 1992), 30–40.

13　See Fang, Yanshou 方彦寿. *Zhuxi shuyuan yu menren kao*朱熹书院与门人考 (Shanghai: East China Normal University Press, 2000), 1.

14　See Fang, Yanshou 方彦寿. *Zhuxi shuyuan yu menrenkao*朱熹书院与门人考 (Shanghai: East China Normal University Press, 2000), 1–7.

15　See Wang, Maohong 王懋竑. *Zhuzi nianpu* Vol. 4朱子年谱卷四 (Beijing: Zhonghua Book Company, 1998), 265.

16　See Wu, Wanju 吴万居. *Songdai shuyuan yu songdai xueshu zhi guanxi*宋代书院与宋代学术之关系 (Taibei: Wenshizhe Publishing House, 1991), 245. See Zhu, Hanmin 朱汉民. "Nansong lixue yu shuyuan jiaoyu" 南宋理学与书院教育. In *Zhongguo zhexue* Vol. 16中国哲学第十六辑, 495–518.

17　Wang, Mingsheng王鸣盛. "Xu" 序. In *Xuxiu siku quan shu* Vol. 452续修四库全书第452册 (Shanghai: Shanghai Chinese Classics Publishing House, 2002), 138.

18　Wang, Mingsheng 王鸣盛. "Xu" 序. In *Xuxiu siku quan shu* Vol. 452续修四库全书第452册 (Shanghai: Shanghai Chinese Classics Publishing House, 2002), 138.

19　Dai, Zhen戴震. *Gujing jiegou chenxu* Vol. 10古经解钩沉序卷十 (Beijing: Zhonghua Book Company, 1980), 146.

20 Cheng, Yanzuo 程廷祚. "Shang limutang xiansheng lun shuyuan shuxu" 上李穆堂先生论书院书序. In *Congshu jicheng xubian* Vol. 190丛书集成续编第190册 (Taibei: Xinwenfeng Publishing Company, 1988), 766.

21 Ehrman (美)艾尔曼. *Cong lixue dao puxue-zhonghua diguo wanqi sixiang yu shehui bianhua mianmianguan*从理学到朴学—中华帝国晚期思想与社会变化面面观, Trans. Zhao, Gang 赵刚 (Nanjing: Jiangsu People's Publishing House, 1997), 86.

22 See Ehrman (美)艾尔曼. *Cong lixue dao puxue-zhonghua diguo wanqi sixiang yu shehui bianhua mianmianguan*从理学到朴学—中华帝国晚期思想与社会变化面面观, Trans. Zhao, Gang 赵刚 (Nanjing: Jiangsu People's Publishing House, 1997), 86–89.

23 Ma, Xinyi 马新贻. "Xinjian xuehaitang ji" 新建学海堂记. In *Zhongguo fangzhi congshu Central China* No. 199中国方志丛书华中第199号 (Taibei: Chengwen Publishing House, 1985), 480.

24 Duan, Yucai 段玉裁. "Shisanjing zhushu shiwen jiaokanji xu" 十三经注疏释文校勘记序. In *Xuxiu siku quan shu* Vol. 1434 续修四库全书第1434册 (Shanghai: Shanghai Chinese Classics Publishing House, 2002), 571.

25 Li, Guojun 李国钧. *Zhongguo shuyuan shi*中国书院史 (Changsha: Hunan Education Press, 1994), 906–910.

26 See Li, Guojun 李国钧. *Zhongguo shuyuan shi* 中国书院史 (Changsha: Hunan Education Press, 1994), 911–912.

27 See Liu, Qi 刘琪, and Zhu, Hanmin 朱汉民. "Xiangshui jiaojingtang shuping" 湘水校经堂述评. In *Yuelu shuyuan yi qian ling yi shi zhounian jinian wenji*岳麓书院一千零一十周年纪念文集第1辑 (Changsha: Hunan University Press, 1986), 26–34.

28 See Zhu, Hanmi 朱汉民, Chen, Gujia 陈谷嘉. *Xiangxiang xuepai yuanliu* 湘湘学派源流 (Changsha: Hunan Education Press, 1992), 336–344.

29 Zhu, Xi朱熹. "Huzi zhiyan yiyi" 胡子知言疑义. In *Huhongji*胡宏集 (Beijing: Zhonghua Book Company, 1987), 328.

30 See Zhu, Hanmi 朱汉民, and Chen, Gujia 陈谷嘉. *Xiangxiang xuepai yuanliu* 湘湘学派源流 (Changsha: Hunan Education Press, 1992), 395–398.

31 Huang, Zongxi 黄宗羲, and Quan, Zuwang 全祖望. "Xulu" 序录. In *Songyuan xue'an* Vol. 42 宋元学案卷四十二 (Beijing: Zhonghua Book Company, 1986), 1366.

32 Mou, Zongsan 牟宗三. *Xinti yu xingti*心体与性体中册 (Shanghai: Shanghai Chinese Classics Publishing House, 1999), 335.

33 Mou, Zongsan 牟宗三. *Xinti yu xingti*心体与性体上册 (Shanghai: Shanghai Chinese Classics Publishing House, 1999), 42–46.

34 Zhu, Xi 朱熹. "Da hanngdaofu" 答黄道夫. In *Zhuzi quan shu* 朱子全书 (Shanghai: Shanghai Chinese Classics Publishing House; Hefei: Anhui Education Publishing House, 2002), 2755.

35 Chen, Bangzhan 陈邦瞻. "Daoxue chongchu" 道学崇黜. In *Songshi jishi benmo* Vol. 80 宋史纪事本末卷八十 (Beijing: Zhonghua Book Company, 1977), 877.

36 Bi, Yuan 毕沅. *Xu zizhi tongjian* Vol. 164 续资治通鉴一百六十四 (Beijing: Zhonghua Book Company, 1957), 4458.

37 Huang, Zongxi 黄宗羲, and Quan, Zuwang 全祖望. "Huiweng xue'an" 晦翁学案. In *Songyuan xue'an* Vol. 48 宋元学案卷四十八 (Beijing: Zhonghua Book Company, 1986), 1495.

38 Ruan, Yuan 阮元. "Xuehaitang jixu, Xuehaitang ji" 学海堂集序, 学海堂集. In *Zhongguo lidai shuyuan zhi* Vol. 8 中国历代书院志第8册 (Nangjing: Jiangsu Education Press, 1995), 1.

39 Liang, Zhiwen 梁志文. "Sanshui liangtaigong chongyou fengshui zhenglei wenqi" 三水梁太公重游沣水征涞文启. In *Guangdong wenzheng xubian* Vol. 1, 338广东文征续编第1册, 第338页.

40 On the study of park science in Guangdong during the Qing dynasty, with Xuehai-Tang as the main base. Li, Xubai 李绪柏. *Qingdai guangdong puxue yanjiu* 清代

广东朴学研究 (Guangzhou: Guangdong Provincial Map Publishing House, 2001), 37–50, 132.

41 Liu, Zhaijun 刘宅俊 "Tongxiang shuyuan ji" 桐乡书院记. In *zhongguo lidai shuyuan zhi* 中国历代书院志Vol. 9 (Nanjing: Jiangsu Education Publishing House, 1995), 667.

42 See Zhang, Chuting 张楚廷, and Zhang, Chuansui 张传遂. *Hunan jiaoyu shi* 湖南教育史 (Changsha: Yuelu Publishing House, 2002), 107–113.

43 See Ma, Duanlin 马端临. "Zhiguan kao· jiaoshou" 职官考·教授 In W*enxian tongkao* 文献通考Vol. 63 (Beijing: Zhonghua Book Company, 1986), 571.

44 Linda, Wall 琳达·沃尔顿. "Nansong shuyuan de dili fenbu" 南宋书院的地理分布. In *Journal of Hunan University* Vol. 1 (1993).

45 Qian, Jibo 钱基博. *Hunan jin bainian xuefeng· daoyan* 湖南近百年学风·导言 (Beijing: China Renmin University Press, 2004), 3.

46 Jie, Xisi 揭傒斯. "Jingzhou guagde shuyuan ji." In *siku quan shu* Vol. 1208 四库全书第1208册 (Shanghai: Shanghai Chinese Classics Publishing House, 1987), 245.

47 Wu, Cheng 吴澄. "Ruizhoulu zhengde shuyuan ji" 瑞州路正德书院记. In Q*uanyuan wen* Vol. 502 全元文卷五〇二 (Nanjing: Jiangsu Chinese Classics Publishing House, 1999), 140.

48 Ai, Junmei 艾浚美. "Yunshan shuyuan ji" 郧山书院记. In *Zhongguo difang zhi jicheng· Hubei fuxian zhij*i 中国地方志集成·湖北府县志辑 (Nanjing: Jiangsu Chinese Classics Publishing House, 2001), 180.

49 Yu, Que 余阙. "Cilizhou tianmen shuyuan bei" 慈利州天门书院碑. In S*iku quan shu* Vol. 1214 四库全书第1214册 (Shanghai: Shanghai Chinese Classics Publishing House, 1987), 400.

50 Zhao, Changweng 赵长翁. "Rulin shuyuan ji" 儒林书院记. In S*iku quan shu* Vol. 534 四库全书第534册 (Shanghai: Shanghai Chinese Classics Publishing House, 1987), 719.

51 Qian, Dehong 钱德洪. "Xiyin huiyu" 惜阴会语. In *Xu Ai, Qian Dehong, Dong Yun ji · Qian Dehong yulu shiwen jiyi*徐爱、钱德洪、董沄集·钱德洪语录诗文辑佚 (Nanjing: Phoenix Press, 2007), 177.

52 Wang, Yucheng 王禹偁 "Tanzhou yuelushan shuyuan ji" 潭州岳麓山书院记. In S*iku quan shu* Vol. 1086 四库全书第1086册 (Shanghai: Shanghai Chinese Classics Publishing House, 1987), 164.

53 See Xu, Bingyun 徐冰云. *Fengxin gudai shuyuan* 奉新古代书院 (Yichun: Fengxin County Chronicle Editorial Committee, Fengxin County Education Bureau, 1985), 73.

54 Xu, Xuan 徐铉. "Hongzhou huashan hushi shutang ji" 洪州华山胡氏书堂记. In *Siku quan shu* Vol. 1085 四库全书第1085册 (Shanghai: Shanghai Chinese Classics Publishing House, 1987), 251.

55 Xu, Xuan徐铉. "Hongzhou huashan hushi shutang ji" 洪州华山胡氏书堂记. In *Siku quan shu* Vol. 1085四库全书第1085册 (Shanghai: Shanghai Chinese Classics Publishing House, 1987), 251.

56 "Hualin shuyuan tiyong" 华林书院题咏. In *Fengxin gudai shuyuan* 奉新古代书院 (Yichun: Fengxin County Annal Editorial Committee, Fengxin County Education Bureau, 1985), 5–27.

57 "Hengyang xianzhi" Vol. 7 衡阳县志卷七. In *Liezhuan* Vol. 6 列传六. 79.

58 Wang, Shangning 汪尚宁. "Biyang shuyuan ji" 碧阳书院记. In *Yixian zhi* Vol. 14 黟县志卷十四. 58.

59 Wang, Yan 王俨. "Fengshan shuyuan ji" 凤山书院记. In *Zhongguo fangzhi congshu* 中国方志丛书 (Taibei: Chengwen Publishing House, 1985), 249–250.

60 Chen, Li陈澧. "Jupo jingshe ji" 菊坡精舍记. In *Xuxiu siku quan shu* Vol. 1537 续修四库全书第1537册 (Shanghai: Shanghai Chinese Classics Publishing House, 2002), 267.

166 *Regional Cultural Undertakings*

61 Hong, Mai 洪迈. "Zhoujun shuyuan" 州郡书院. In *Rongzhai suibi· Rongzhai sanbi* Vol. 5 容斋随笔·容斋三笔卷五 (Shanghai: Shanghai Chinese Classics Publishing House, 1978), 477.

62 Zhu, Xi朱熹. "Bailudong die" 白鹿洞牒. In *Zhuzi quan shu* (Shanghai: Shanghai Chinese Classics Publishing House; Hefei: Anhui Education Publishing House, 2002), 4585.

63 Zhu, Xi朱熹. "Qici bailudong chi'e" 乞赐白鹿洞敕额. In *Zhongguo lidai shuyuan zhi* Vol. 2 中国历代书院志第2册 (Nanjing: Jiangsu Education Press, 1995), 33.

64 Zou, Shouyi 邹守益. "Jiuhuashan yangming shuyuan ji" 九华山阳明书院记. In *Zou shouyi ji* Vol. 6 邹守益集卷六 (Nanjing: Phoenix Publishing House, 2007), 321–322.

65 Zou, Shouyi 邹守益. "Jiuhuashan yangming shuyuan ji" 九华山阳明书院记. In *Zou shouyi ji* Vol. 6 邹守益集卷六 (Nanjing: Phoenix Publishing House, 2007), 322.

66 Zhou, Bida 周必大. "Taihe xian longzhou shuyuan ji" 太和县龙洲书院记. In *Siku quan shu* Vol. 1147 四库全书第1147册 (Shanghai: Shanghai Chinese Classics Publishing House, 1987), 627.

67 Lü, Chongmi 吕崇谧. "Fengshan shuyuan beiji" 凤山书院碑记. In *Taiguxian zhi* Vol. 6 太谷县志卷六, 13–14.

68 Duan, Jian 段坚. "Chuangjian zhixue shuyuan beiji" 创建志学书院碑记. In *Nanyang fuzhi* Vol. 6 南阳府志卷六, 36.

69 Wang, Yuanzheng 王元正. "Heshan shuyuan ji" 鹤山书院记. In *Sichuan tongzhi* Vol. 80 四川通志卷八十 ((Chengdu: Bashu Publishing House, 1984), 2638.

70 Peng, Rushi 彭汝实. "Jiufeng shuyuan ji" 九峰书院记. In *Sichuan tongzhi* Vol. 80 四川通志卷八十 (Chengdu: Bashu Publishing House, 1984), 2630–2361.

71 Wu, Shengqin 吴省钦. "Tongchuan caotang shuyaun beiji" 潼川草堂书院碑记. In *Xuxiu siku quan shu* Vol. 1447续修四库全书 (Shanghai: Shanghai Chinese Classics Publishing House, 2002), 632.

72 Li, Changfu 李长馥. "Xiuziyun shuyuan qi" 修子云书院启. In *Sichuan tongzhi* Vol. 80四川通志卷八十 (Chengdu: Bashu Publishing House, 1984), 2633.

73 Li, Ba 李拔. "Benfu xuexiao" 本府学校. In *Funingfu zhi* Vol. 13福宁府志卷十三.

74 See Li, Ba 李拔. "Fu'an xuexiao" 福安学校. In *Funingfu zhi* Vol. 13福宁府志卷十三.

75 See "Hejing shuyuan." 和靖书院. In *Zhongguo fangzhi congshu*中国方志丛书 (Taibei: Chengwen Publishing House, 1985), 634.

76 Huang, Jin 黄溍. "Wenxue shuyuantian ji" 文学书院田记. In *Quan yuan wen* Vol. 953全元文 (Nanjing: Jiangsu Chinese Classics Publishing House, 1999), 328.

77 Huang, Jin 黄溍. "Mingzheng shuyuantian ji" 明正书院田记. In *Quan yuan wen* Vol. 95全元文 (Nanjing: Jiangsu Chinese Classics Publishing House, 1999), 246.

78 Li, Ba 李拔. "Ningde xuexiao" 宁德学校. In *Funingfu zhi* Vol. 13福宁府志卷十三.

79 Ding, Gang 丁钢, and Liu, Qi 刘琪. "Shuyuan yu zhongguo wenhua" 书院与中国文化. In *Shuyuan yu siguan guanxi yilanbiao*书院与寺观关系一览表 (Shanghai: Shanghai Education Publishing House, 1992), 207–226.

80 Yang, Tingyi 杨廷仪. "Heshan shuyuan beiji" 鹤山书院碑记. In *Qingzhou zhi* Vol. 43邛州志卷四十三.

81 Lan, Dingyuan 蓝鼎元. "Mianyang shuyuan beiji" 棉阳书院碑记. In *Congshu jicheng sanbian* 丛书集成三编 (Taibei: Taibei Xinwenfeng Publishing Company, 1997), 76.

82 Li, Zhanchun 李霑春. "Chuangjian chongzheng shuyuan beiji" 创建崇正书院碑记. In *Zhongguo fangzhi congshu*中国方志丛书 (Taibei: Chengwen Publishing House, 1985), 298.

83 Dai, Junheng 戴钧衡. "Shuyuan zayi sishou" 书院杂议四首. In *Zhongguo lidai shuyuan zhi* Vol. 9 中国历代书院志第9册 (Nanjing: Jiangsu Education Publishing House, 1995), 769.

84 Cui, Dao 崔焘. "Juanzhi yijin shuyuan shuji bingwen" 捐置益津书院书籍禀文. In *Baxian xinzhi* Vol. 8霸县新志卷八 (Taibei: Chinese Local Chronicles Series, 民国23), 911.

85 Fan, Zhongyan 范仲淹. "Doujian yilu" 窦谏议录. In *Siku quan shu* Vol. 1085 四库全书第1085册 (Shanghai: Shanghai Chinese Classics Publishing House, 1987), 791.

86 Xu, Xuan 徐铉. "Hongzhou huashan hushi shutang ji" 洪州华山胡氏书堂记. In *Siku quan shu* Vol. 1085 四库全书第1085册 (Shanghai: Shanghai Chinese Classics Publishing House, 1987), 215.

87 Shi, Jie 石介. "Taishan shuyuan ji" 泰山书院记. In *Culaishi xiansheng wenji* Vol. 19祖徕石先生文集卷十九 (Beijing: Zhonghua Book Company, 1984), 223.

88 Wang, Yucheng 王禹偁. "Tanzhou yuelushan shuyuan ji" 潭州岳麓山书院记. In *Siku quan shu* Vol. 1086四库全书第1086册 (Shanghai: Shanghai Chinese Classics Publishing House, 1987), 164.

89 Xu, Du 徐度. "Quesao pian" 却扫篇. In *Siku quan shu* Vol. 863四库全书第863册 (Shanghai: Shanghai Chinese Classics Publishing House, 1987), 753.

90 Dai, Junheng 戴钧衡. "Shuyuan zayi sishou cangshuji" 书院杂议四首·藏书籍. In *Zhongguo Lidai shuyuan zhi* Vol. 9 中国历代书院志第9册 (Nanjing: Jiangsu Education Publishing House, 1995), 769.

91 Liu, Yueshen 刘岳申. "Xishu shishi shuyuan ji" 西蜀石室书院记. In *Siku quan shu* Vol. 1204四库全书第1204册 (Shanghai: Shanghai Chinese Classics Publishing House, 1987), 261.

92 Song, Lian 宋濂. "Heshang zhuan" 和尚传. In *Yuanshi* Vol. 134 元史卷一百三十四 (Beijing: Zhonghua Book Company, 1976), 3259.

93 Zhu, Xi 朱熹. "Qici bailudong shuyuan chi'e" 乞赐白鹿洞书院敕额. In *Zhongguo Lidai shuyuan zhi* Vol. 2 中国历代书院志第2册 (Nanjing: Jiangsu Education Publishing House, 1995), 33.

94 Mao, Deqi 毛德琦. "Dongxue bang" 洞学榜. In *Zhongguo Lidai shuyuan zhi* Vol. 2 白鹿洞书院志卷二.

95 Zhu, Xi 朱熹. "Ba bailudong shuyuan suocang hanshu" 跋白鹿洞书院所藏汉书. In *Zhuzi quan shu*朱子全书 (Shanghai: Shanghai Chinese Classics Publishing House, 2002), 3851.

96 Wang, Mu 王霂. "Zundao shuyuan cangshu ji" 尊道书院藏书记. In *Zhongguo fangzhi congshu huabei* Vol. 191中国方志丛书华北第191号 (Taibei: Chengwen Publishing House, 1985), 277.

97 Xu, Kai 徐锴. "Chenshi shutang ji" 陈氏书堂记. In *Quantang wen* Vol. 888 全唐文卷八百八十八 (Beijing: Zhonghua Book Company, 1983), 9279.

98 Ma, Duanlin 马端临. "Xuexiao kao qi" 学校考七. In *Wenxian tongkao* Vol. 46 文献通考卷四十六 (Beijing: Zhonghua Book Company, 1986), 431.

99 Zeng, Liuyuan 曾留远. "Shilin shuyuan" 石林书院. In *Guixixian zhi* Vol. 4贵溪县志卷四.

100 Wei, Liaoweng 魏了翁. "Shu heshan shuyuan shimo" 书鹤山书院始末. In *Siku quan shu* Vol. 1172 四库全书第1172册 (Shanghai: Shanghai Chinese Classics Publishing House, 1987), 468–469.

101 See Chen, Gujia 陈谷嘉, and Deng, Hongbo邓洪波. *Zhongguo shuyuan zhidu yanjiu*中国书院制度研究 (Hangzhou: Zhejiang Education Press, 1997), 130.

102 Cheng, Jufu 程钜夫. "Dong'an shuyuan ji" 东庵书院记. In *Siku quan shu* Vol. 1202 四库全书第1202册 (Shanghai: Shanghai Chinese Classics Publishing House, 1987), 175.

103 Zheng, Yuanyou 郑元祐. "Yingchang shuyuan ji" 颖昌书院记, "Qiaowu ji" 侨吴集. In *Siku quan shu* Vol. 1216 (Shanghai: Shanghai Chinese Classics Publishing House, 1987), 535.

104 Ding, Shanqing 丁善庆. "Changshafu yuelu shuyuan xuzhi" 长沙府岳麓书院续志. In *Zhongguo lidai shuyuan zhi* Vol. 4 中国历代书院志第4册 (Nanjing: Jiangsu Education Publishing House, 1995), 508–515.

105 See Hu, Linyi 胡林翼. "Zhenyan shuyuan zhi·zhidian diqi" 箴言书院志·志典第七. In *Zhongguo lidai shuyuan zhi* Vol. 5 中国历代书院志第5册 (Nanjing: Jiangsu Education Publishing House, 1995), 197–237.

168   *Regional Cultural Undertakings*

106 Huang, Pengnian 黄彭年. "Wanjuanlou cangshu beiji" 万卷楼藏书碑记. In *Lizhenglue · xuexiao* 礼政略·学校.

107 See Hu, Zhaoxi 胡昭曦. *Sichuan shuyuan shi* 四川书院史 (Chengdu: Bashu Publishing House, 2000), 249.

108 Jiang, Xin 蒋信. "Longzhou shuyuan ji" 龙洲书院记. In *Yiyangxian zhi* Vol. 8益阳县志卷八.

109 See Li, Qi 李祁. "Caotang shuyuan cangshu ming" 草堂书院藏书铭. In *Siku quan shu* Vol. 1219 四库全书第1219册 (Shanghai: Shanghai Chinese Classics Publishing House, 1987), 753.

110 Zhang, Jiuzhang 张九章. "Moxiang shuyuan cangshu ji" 墨香书院藏书记. In *Qianjiangxian zhi* Vol. 3 黔江县志卷三, 43.

111 See Deng, Hongbo 邓洪波. *Mingqing shiqi jiangsu cangshu mulu jilue* 明清时期江苏藏书目录辑略 (Nanjing: Journal of Jiangsu Library, 1996 (1)).

112 See Li, Ying 李颖. *Jindai shuyuan cangshu kao* 近代书院藏书考 (Lanzhou: Library and Information, 1999 (1)).

113 See Huang, Jing 黄璟. "Xiandi shuyuan cangshu shuo" 仙堤书院藏书说. In *Chinese Local Chronicles Series* Vol. 347 中国方志丛书华北第347号 (Taibei: Chengwen Publishing House, 1985), 210–211.

114 Hou, Shaoying 侯绍瀛. "Zhaoyi shuyuan cangshulou ji" 昭义书院藏书楼记. In *Chinese Local Chronicles series* Vol. 134 中国方志丛书华北第134号 (Taibei: Chengwen Publishing House, 1985), 434.

115 Chen, Hongmou 陈宏谋. "Shenming shuyuan tiaogui yi li shixue shi" 申明书院条规以励实学示. In *Peiyuantang oucun gao · wenxi* Vol. 48 培元堂偶存稿 · 文檄卷四十八, 12.

116 See Cai, Yi 蔡仪, and Cai, Xiaochu 蔡晓初. *Shuyuan cangshu tan* Vol. 1 书院藏书谈 (Nanchang: Journal of Jiangxi Institute of Education, 2002).

117 Deng, Ju 邓炬. "Huayang shuyuan chushu guitiao" 华阳书院储书规条. In *Chinese Local Chronicles Series* Vol. 129 中国方志丛书华中第129号 (Taibei: Chengwen Publishing House, 1985), 306.

118 See Wang, He 王河. *Nansong shuyuan cangshu kaolue* Vol. 3南宋书院藏书考略 (Nanchang: Jiangxi Social Sciences, 1998).

119 See Xu, Youren 许有壬. "Fengshi shutang ji" 冯氏书堂记. In *Siku quan shu* Vol. 1211 四库全书第1211册 (Shanghai: Shanghai Chinese Classics Publishing House, 1987), 273–274.

120 Shao, Rui 邵锐. "Bailudong xue jinyue" 白鹿洞学禁约. In *Zhongguo lidai shuyuan zhi* Vol. 1 中国历代书院志第一册 (Nanjing: Jiangsu Education Publishing House, 1995), 747.

121 Zhao, Yingchen 赵映辰. "Guangze shuyuan chushu ji" 广泽书院储书记. In *Juluxian zhi* Vol. 12 巨鹿县志卷十二, 83.

122 Hu, Linyi 胡林翼. "Zhenyan shuyuan zhigui er" 箴言书院志·志规二. In *Zhongguo lidai shuyuan zhi* Vol. 5 中国历代书院志第5册 (Nanjing: Jiangsu Education Publishing House, 1995), 191.

123 "Xiyin shuyuan jieshu ju zhangcheng" 惜阴书院借书局章程. In *Zhongguo fangzhi congshu huazhong* Vol. 41 中国方志丛书华中第41号 (Taibei: Chengwen Publishing House, 1985), 212.

124 Deng, Hongbo 邓洪波. *Jianlun wanqing jiangsu shuyuan cangshu shiye de tese yu gongxian* Vol. 4 简论晚清江苏书院藏书事业的特色与贡献卷四 (Nanjing: Journal of Jiangsu Library, 1996).

125 Zhu, Xi 朱熹. "Luo canyi" 罗参议. In *Zhuzi quan shu* 朱子全书 (Shanghai: Shanghai Chinese Classics Publishing House; Hefei: Anhui Education Publishing House, 2002), 4749.

126 Zhu, Xi 朱熹. "Da caijitong" 答蔡季通. In *Zhuzi quan shu* 朱子全书 (Shanghai: Shanghai Chinese Classics Publishing House; Hefei: Anhui Education Publishing House, 2002), 4674.

127 See Guo, Qi 郭齐, and Yin, Bo 尹波. "Zhuxi ji" 朱熹集. In *Banben kao lue* Vol. 10 版本考略第10册 (Chengdu: Sichuan Education Publishing House, 1996), 5865.

128 See Chen, Gujia 陈谷嘉, and Deng, Hongbo 邓洪波. *Zhongguo shuyuan zhidu yanjiu* 中国书院制度研究 (Hangzhou: Zhejiang Education Publishing House, 1997), 236–245.

129 Gu, Yanwu 顾炎武. "Rizhi lu jishi" Vol. 18 日知录集释卷十八. In *Jianben ershiyi shi* 监本二十一史 (Changsha: Yuelu Publishing House, 1994), 664.

130 Liu, Guang 刘光. "Shangan wei jIng shuyuan zhi" 陕甘味经书院志. In *Zhonguo lidai shuyuan zhi* Vol. 6 中国历代书院志第6册 (Nanjing: Jiangsu Education Publishing House, 1995), 22.

131 See Chen, Gujia 陈谷嘉, and Deng, Hongbo 邓洪波. *Zhongguo shuyuan zhidu yanjiu* 中国书院制度研究 (Hangzhou: Zhejiang Education Publishing House, 1997), 245–326.

132 Wu, Zhujun 吴朱钧. "Xihu shuyuan chongzheng shumu ji" 西湖书院重整书目记. In *Congshu jicheng xu bian* Vol. 2 丛书集成续编第2册 (Taibei: Taibei Xinwenfeng Publishing Company, 1988), 522.

133 See Chen, Ji 陈基. "Xihu shuyuan shumu xu" 西湖书院书目序. In *Siku quan shu* Vol. 1222 四库全书第1222册 (Shanghai: Shanghai Chinese Classics Publishing House, 1987), 293.

134 See the specific situation of the book engraving in the Yuan dynasty. See Jin, Dasheng 金达胜, and Fang, Jianxin 方建新. "Yuandai hangzhou xihu shuyuan cangshu keshu shulue" 元代杭州西湖书院藏书刻书述略. In *Journal of Hangzhou University* Vol. 3 杭州大学学报第3期 ((1995).

135 See Zheng, Tinghu 郑廷鹄. "Bailudong zhi·Louban" Vol. 16 白鹿洞志·镂板卷十六. In *Zhonguo lidai shuyuan zhi* Vol. 1 中国历代书院志第1册 (Nanjing: Jiangsu Education Publishing House, 1995), 494.

136 See Zheng, Tinghu 郑廷鹄. "Bailudong zhi·Louban" Vol. 16 白鹿洞志·镂板卷十六. In *Zhonguo lidai shuyuan zhi* Vol. 1 中国历代书院志第1册 (Nanjing: Jiangsu Education Publishing House, 1995), 494.

137 Liu, Guang 刘光. "Shangan weijing shuyuan zhi" 陕甘味经书院志. In *Zhonguo lidai shuyuan zhi* Vol. 6 中国历代书院志第6册 (Nanjing: Jiangsu Education Publishing House, 1995), 22.

138 "Yinshu zhangcheng" 印书章程. In *Zhonguo lidai shuyuan zhi* Vol. 3 中国历代书院志第3册 (Nanjing: Jiangsu Education Publishing House, 1995), 366.

139 See Wang, Ruxing 王儒行. "Jingyuan ba" 经苑跋. In *Zhongguo shuyuan shi ziliao* 中国书院史资料 (Hangzhou: Zhejiang Education Publishing House, 1998), 1861–1862.

140 See Wang, Ruxing 王儒行. "Jingyuan ba" 经苑跋. In *Zhongguo shuyuan shi ziliao* 中国书院史资料 (Hangzhou: Zhejiang Education Publishing House, 1998), 1861–1862.

141 Liu, Guang 刘光. "Shangan weijing shuyuan zhi" 陕甘味经书院志. In *Zhonguo lidai shuyuan zhi* Vol. 6 中国历代书院志第6册 (Nanjing: Jiangsu Education Publishing House, 1995), 22–23.

142 Xie, Guozhen 谢国桢. "Jindai shuyuan xuexiao zhidu bianqian kao" 近代书院学校制度变迁考. In *Jindai zhongguo shiliao congkan xubian* Vol. 651 近代中国史料丛刊续编第651册 (Taibei: Taibei Wenhai Press, 1974), 8.

143 See Chen, Gujia 陈谷嘉, and Deng, Hongbo 邓洪波. *Zhongguo shuyuan zhidu yanjiu* 中国书院制度研究 (Hangzhou: Zhejiang Education Publishing House, 1997), 295–296.

144 See Li, Jingwen 李景文. "Qindai henan shuyuan keshu qianlun" 清代河南书院刻书浅论. In *Shixue yuekan* Vol. 5 史学月刊第5期 (1994).

145 See Li, Guojun 李国钧. *Zhongguo shuyuan shi* 中国书院史 (Changsha: Hunan Education Publishing House, 1994), 13.

146 Xu, Xuan 徐铉. "Hongzhou huashan hushi shutang ji" 洪州华山胡氏书堂记. In *Siku quan shu* Vol. 1085 四库全书第1085册 (Shanghai: Shanghai Chinese Classics Publishing House, 1987), 215.

147 Wang, Yuchen 王禹偁. "Zhu chao xian jiti hongzhou yimen hushi hualin shuzhai xu" 诸朝贤寄题洪州义门胡氏华林书斋序. In *Siku quan shu* Vol. 1086 四库全书第1086册 (Shanghai: Shanghai Chinese Classics Publishing House, 1987), 190.

148 Wang, Yuchen 王禹偁. "Tanzhou yuelushan shuyuan ji" 潭州岳麓山书院记. In *Siku quan shu* Vol. 1086 四库全书第1086册 (Shanghai: Shanghai Chinese Classics Publishing House, 1987), 164.

149 Ma, Duanlin 马端临. "Xuexiao kao qi" 学校考七. In *Wenxian tongkao* 文献通考 (Beijing: Zhonghua Book Company, 1986), 431.

150 Zhu, Xi 朱熹. "Hengzhou shigu shuyuan ji" 衡州石鼓书院记. In *Zhuzi quan shu* 朱子全书 (Shanghai: Shanghai Chinese Classics Publishing House; Hefei: Anhui Education Publishing House, 2002), 3783.

151 Hong, Mai 洪迈. "Zhoujun shuyuan" 州郡书院. In *Rongzhai suibi·Rongzhai sanbi* Vol. 5 容斋随笔·容斋三笔卷五 (Shanghai: Shanghai Chinese Classics Publishing House, 1987), 477.

152 Zhang, Shi 张栻. "Tanzhou chongxiu yuelu shuyuan ji" 潭州重修岳麓书院记. In *Siku quan shu* Vol. 1167 四库全书第1167册 (Shanghai: Shanghai Chinese Classics Publishing House, 1987), 506.

153 See Xu, Zi 徐梓. *Yuandai shuyuan yanjiu* 元代书院研究 (Beijing: Social Sciences Academic Press, 2000), 135–145.

154 See Bai, Xinliang 白新良. *Zhongguo gudai shuyuan fazhan shi* 中国古代书院发展史 (Tianjin: Tianjin University Press, 1995), 42–45.

155 Zhang, Fenghong 张凤孤. "Pingchuan shuyuan ji" 平川书院记. In *Sichuan tong zhi* Vol. 80. 四川通志卷八十 (Chengdu: Bashu Publishing House, 1984), 2632.

156 Li, Dongyang 李东阳. "Chongjian yuelu shuyuan ji" 重建岳麓书院记. In *Lidongyang ji* Vol. 5 李东阳集卷五 (Changsha: Yuelu Publishing House, 1985), 74.

157 Luo, Hongxian 罗洪先. "Shuixi shuyuan xiguan lou ji" 水西书院熙光楼记. In *Zhongguo fangzhi congshu* Vol. 231 中国方志丛书华中第231号 (Taibei: Chengwen Publishing House, 1985), 747.

158 Wang, Shouren 王守仁. "Wansong shuyuan ji" 万松书院记. In *Wang yangming quanji* Vol. 7 王阳明全集卷七 (Shanghai: Shanghai Chinese Classics Publishing House, 1992), 254.

159 *Qin shilu·gaozong shilu* Vol. 20 清实录·高宗实录卷二十 (Beijing: Zhonghua Book Company, 1985), 487.

160 "Donglou shuyuan ji" 东娄书院记. In *Zhongguo fangzhi congshu* Vol. 485 中国方志丛书华北第485号 (Taibei: Chengwen Publishing House, 1985), 747.

161 Yang, Jingkai 杨金铠. "Yuping shuyuan ji" 玉屏书院记. In *Heqingzhou zhi* Vol. 8 鹤庆州志卷八 2 (1894).

162 See Li, Guojun 李国钧. *Zhongguo shuyuan shi* 中国书院史 (Changsha: Hunan Education Publishing House, 1994), 887.

163 Zhang, Tingyu 张廷玉et al. "Xuanjv zhi yi" 选举志一. In *Mingshi* Vol. 69 明史卷六十九 (Beijing: Zhonghua Book Company, 1974), 1686.

164 Li, Guojun 李国钧et al. *Zhongguo shuyuan shi* 中国书院史 (Changsha: Hunan Education Publishing House, 1994), 541.

165 "Longhuang shuyuan" 龙光书院. In *Jiangxi tong zhi* Vol. 81 江西通志卷八十一 (1881), 9.

166 "Longhuang shuyuan" 龙光书院. In *Jiangxi tong zhi* Vol. 81 江西通志卷八十一 (1881), 9.

167 "Qian xinmei xiansheng nianpu·zhuting jushi nianpu xubian" 钱辛楣先生年谱·竹汀居士年谱续编. In *Beijing tushuguan cangzhenben nianpu congkan* Vol. 105 北京图书馆藏珍本年谱丛刊第105册 (Beijing: Beijing Library Press, 1999), 529.

Regional Cultural Undertakings 171

168 Tao, Shu 陶澍. "Suzhou ziyang, zhengyi liang shuyuan gaoshi" 苏州紫阳、正谊两书院告示. In _Xuxiu siku quan shu_ Vol. 1053 续修四库全书第1053册 (Shanghai: Shanghai Chinese Classics Publishing House, 2002), 601.

169 Liu, Boji 刘伯骥. _Guangdong shuyuan zhidu_ 广东书院制度 (Taibei: National Compilation and Translation Library, 1958), 278–283.

170 See Bai, Xinliang 白新良. _Zhongguo gudai shuyuan fazhan shi_ 中国古代书院发展史 (Tianjin: Tianjin University Press, 1995), 274.

171 See Huang, Zongxi 黄宗羲, and Quan, Zuwang 全祖望. "Yuelu zhuru xue'an" 岳麓诸儒学案. In _Song yuan xue'an_ Vol. 71 宋元学案卷七十一 (Beijing: Zhonghua Book Company, 1986), 2368.

172 See Bai, Xinliang 白新良. _Zhongguo gudai shuyuan fazhan shi_ 中国古代书院发展史 (Tianjin: Tianjin University Press, 1995), 274.

173 See "Wenxue chuan xu" 文学传序. In _Nanhai xian zhi_ Vol. 19 南海县志卷十九 (1911), 1.

174 See Li, Xupu 李绪朴. _Qindai guangdong puxue yanjiu_ 清代广东朴学研究 (Guangzhou: Guangdong Map Pulishing House, 2001), 199–219.

175 Wu, Yihan 武一韩. "Xinjian fengshan shuyuan ji" 新建凤山书院记. In _Taigu xian zhi_ Vol. 6 太谷县志卷六 (1741), 15.

176 Meng, Shenghui 孟生蕙. "Fengshan shuyuan beiji" 凤山书院碑记. In _Taigu xian zhi_ Vol. 6 太谷县志卷六 (1741), 24.

177 Ma, Shengwu 马绳武. "Jianli huiwen shuyuan beiji" 建立会文书院记. In _Chongxiu tianjin fu zhi_ Vol. 35 重修天津府志卷三十五 (1899), 9.

178 Xie, Yun 谢沄. "Muxiu yijiang shuyuan kuixingge sangshanta xu" 募修义江书院奎星阁桑山塔序. In _Yining xian zhi_ Vol. 6 义宁县志卷六 (1912–1949), 28.

179 See Cheng, Minsheng 程民生. _Songdai diyu wenhua_ 宋代地域文化 (Kaifeng: Henan University Press, 1997), 1–2.

180 See Yang, Qing 杨青. "Yanpin sixian xintan" 延平四贤新探. In _Zhuxi yu minxue yuanliu_ 朱熹与闽学源流 (Shanghai: Shanghai Sanlian Publishing House, 1990), 26–60.

181 Zhu, Xi 朱熹. "Da luocanyi" 答罗参议. In _Zhuzi quan shu_ 朱子全书 (Shanghai: Shanghai Chinese Classics Publishing House; Hefei: Anhui Education Publishing House, 2002), 4747.

182 Wang, Maohong 王懋竑. _Zhuxi nianpu·zhuzi nianpu_ Vol. 1 朱熹年谱·朱子年谱卷一 (Beijing: Zhonghua Book Company, 1998), 32.

183 Zhu, Xi 朱熹. "Er shi fengchou jingfu zengyan bingyi weibie" 二诗奉酬敬夫赠言并以为别. In _Zhuzi quan shu_ 朱子全书 (Shanghai: Shanghai Chinese Classics Publishing House; Hefei: Anhui Education Publishing House, 2002), 387.

184 Zhu, Xi 朱熹. "Da chengyunfu" 答程允夫. In _Zhuzi quan shu_ 朱子全书 (Shanghai: Shanghai Chinese Classics Publishing House; Hefei: Anhui Education Publishing House, 2002), 1871.

185 Discussion of academic exchange between Zhu Xi and Zhang Shi and their mutual influence. See Zhu, Hanmin 朱汉民, and Chen, Gujia 陈谷嘉. _Huxiang xuepai yuanliu_ 湖湘学派源流 (Changsha: Hunan Education Publishing House, 1992), 376–404.

186 Quan, Zuwang 全祖望. "Tonggu sanxiansheng shuyuan ji" 同谷三先生书院记. In _Xu xiu siku quan shu_ Vol. 1429 续修四库全书第1429册 (Shanghai: Shanghai Chinese Classics Publishing House, 2002), 609.

187 See Shu, Jingnan 束景南. _Zhuzi da zhuan_ 朱子大传 (Fuzhou: Fujian Education Press, 1992), 326–336.

188 See Li, Guojun 李国钧. _Zhongguo shuyuan shi_ 中国书院史 (Changsha: Hunan Education Publishing House, 1994), 650–658.

189 Huang, Zongxi 黄宗羲. "Zhe zhong wangmen xuean yi yuanwai qian xushan xiansheng dehong" 浙中王门学案一·员外钱绪山先生德洪. In _Mingru xuean_ Vol. 11 明儒学案卷十一 (BeijIng: Zhonghua Book Company, 1985), 225.

190 Huang, Zongxi 黄宗羲. "Zhe zhong wangmen xuean er langzhong wang longxi xian-sheng ji" 浙中王门学案二·郎中王龙溪先生畿. In *Mingru xuean* Vol. 12 明儒学案卷十二 (Beijing: Zhonghua Book Company, 1985), 238.

191 See Yang, Shenchu, Zhu, Hanmin, and Deng, Hongbo 杨慎初,朱汉民,邓洪波. *Yuelu shuyuan shi lue* 岳麓书院史略 (Changsha: Yuelu Publishing House, 1986), 92–103.

192 "Jiu yi" 九益. In *Zhongguo lidai shuyuan zhi* Vol. 7 中国历代书院志第7册 (Nanjing: Jiangsu Education Publishing House, 1995), 119.

193 Xu, Song 徐松. *Song huiyao jigao · chongru er* Vol. 4 宋会要辑稿·崇儒二之四 (Beijing: Zhonghua Book Company, 1957), 2189.

194 Zhu, Xi 朱熹. "Tanzhouwei jiaoshou cuo zhi yuelu shuyuan die" 潭州委教授措置岳麓书院牒. In *Zhuzi quan shu* 朱子全书 (Shanghai: Shanghai Chinese Classics Publishing House; Hefei: Anhui Education Publishing House, 2002), 2189.

195 Cheng, Yanji and Ling Rumian 程廷济, 凌汝绵. "Xuexiao zhi·shuyuan" 学校志·书院. In *Fuliang xian zhi* Vol. 3 浮梁县志卷三 (Nanchang: Jiangxi Provincial Library, 1960), 4–5.

196 Li, Yuanzhen 李元振. "Nanyang shuyuan ji" 南阳书院记. In *Nanyangfu zhi* Vol. 6 南阳府志卷六 (1684), 70.

197 Huang, Zongxi 黄宗羲 and Quan, Zuwang 全祖望. "Yuelu zhuru xue'an" 岳麓诸儒学案. In *Song yuan xue'an* Vol. 71 宋元学案卷七十一 (Beijing: Zhonghua Book Company, 1986), 2368.

198 See Zhu, Hanmin 朱汉民 and Chen, Gujia 陈谷嘉. *Huxiang xuepai yuanliu* 湖湘学派源流 (Changsha: Hunan Education Publishing House, 1992), 288–289.

199 Zhou, Yinghe 周应合. "Jian mingdao shuyuan" 建明道书院. In *Siku quan shu* Vol. 489 四库全书第489册 (Shanghai: Shanghai Chinese Classics Publishing House,

200 See Xu, Zi 徐梓. *Yuandai shuyuan yanjiu* 元代书院研究 (Beijing: Social Sciences Academic Press, 2000), 136–137.

201 Song, Lian 宋濂 et al. "Xuqian zhuan" 许谦传. In *Yuan shi* Vol. 189 元史卷一百八十九 (Beijing: Zhonghua Book Company, 1974), 4319.

202 Wang, Shouren 王守仁. "Nianpu san" 年谱三. In *Wang yangming quanji* Vol. 35 王阳明全集卷三十五 (Shanghai: Shanghai Chinese Classics Publishing House, 1992), 1290.

203 Mao, Deqi 毛德琦. "Xun fu cai shiying shiding donggui" 巡抚蔡士英示定洞规. In *Zhongguo lidai shuyuan zhi* Vol. 2 中国历代书院志第2册 (Nanjing: Jiangsu Education Publishing House, 1995), 141.

204 Gao, Huang 高璜. "Jing jiu guimo yi" 经久规模议. In *Zhongguo lidai shuyuan zhi* Vol. 2 中国历代书院志第2册 (Nanjing: Jiangsu Education Publishing House, 1995), 148.

205 Hu, Linyi 胡林翼. "Zhi xuan shi" Vol. 4 志选士第四. In *Zhongguo lidai shuyuan zhi* Vol. 5 中国历代书院志第5册 (Nanjing: Jiangsu Education Publishing House, 1995), 194.

206 See "Xihu shuyuan xiangding xujuan shuyuan shiyi" 西湖书院详定续捐书院事宜. In *Zhongguo fangzhi congshu* Vol. 349 中国方志丛书华中第349号 (Taibei: Chengwen Publishing House, 1985), 348–349.

207 "Guangnan shenshi gongyi shuyuan tiaogui" 广南绅士公议书院条规. In *Zhongguo fangzhi congshu* Vol. 27 中国方志丛书华中第27号 (Taibei: Chengwen Publishing House, 1985), 41.

208 See Li, Caidong 李才栋. *Jiangxi gudai shuyuan yanjiu* 江西古代书院研究 (Nanjing: Jiangsu Education Publishing House, 1993), 121–151.

209 *Qin shilu ·gaozong shilu* Vol. 20 清实录·高宗实录卷二十 (Beijing: Zhonghua Book Company, 1985), 488.

210 "Jing xiu shuyuan tiaogui" 敬修书院条规. In *Zhongguo difang zhi jicheng·hunan fu xian zhi ji* 中国地方志集成·湖南府县志辑 (Nanjing: Jiangsu Chinese Classics Publishing House, 2003), 99.

211 "Fenghu shuyuan zhangcheng" 丰湖书院章程. In *Zhongguo fangzhi congshu* Vol. 3 中国方志丛书华中第3号 (Taibei: Chengwen Publishing House, 1985), 158.

212 Hu, Linyi 胡林翼. "Zhi gui" Vol. 2 志规卷二. In *Zhongguo lidai shuyuan zhi* Vol. 5 中国历代书院志第5册 (Nanjing: Jiangsu Education Publishing House, 1995), 109.

213 See Bai, Xinliang 白新良. *Zhongguo gudai shuyuan fazhan shi* 中国古代书院发展 史 (Tianjin: Tianjin University Press, 1995), 195–196.

Appendix 1
Rites and Customs in Academies

The academy is a specific kind of education and cultural entity in ancient China. As a necessary part of the societal system, the academy performs a series of social functions, including but not confined to cultivating talents, updating knowledge, and civilizing society as a whole. Among these functions, social education and civilization are indispensable missions undertaken by academies set up by followers of Confucianism, who, when founding academies, always announced and proclaimed an ultimate goal of achieving civilization and edification of society. By civilizing and educating, what these Confucian supporters meant was to exert an imperceptible but long-lasting influence on the general public via promoting fundamental principles and values of Confucianism and setting examples of how individuals with high morals should behave and act. Therefore, just like when there is a breeze blowing over, light as it is, grasses still bend. And so it was how civilizing and educating process works. In other words, during the education and edification process, values and ethical principles of Confucianism would get promoted and permeate into different classes of society, with a specific focus on the lower class, the aim of which was to build and mold a unanimous value shared by everyone, thereby reforming the social customs and even the overall climate. Therefore, to conclude, one of the most vital goals in the process was to influence and consequently achieve reform and normalization of social customs by adopting elite Confucian ideas and values. As some scholars pointed out, "To educate the general public was in to equip them with high moralities exhibited by gentlemen and intellectuals with noble character, achieving an overall advancement as far as the social customs are concerned."[1] In order to achieve this goal, when setting up academies, Confucian followers particularly focused on the construction of a cultural atmosphere with the spirit of Confucianism and had this orientation practiced throughout the construction and decoration process, from the selection of lecture contents, the establishment of teaching principles, and the issuing of rules and regulations to the selection of appropriate contents on the horizontal inscribed board hung on the main hall, poetic couplets, and stone tablets, as well as the choice of names for pavilions, terraces, open halls, and dormitories, the selection of locations and design styles, and decisions as to who they should worship and how they should conduct subsequent ritual activities.

DOI: 10.4324/9781003332305-4

However, the values and ethical principles of Confucianism were not the only singular forces behind such educating and civilizing process. From the cultural atmosphere of academies, it could be seen that different levels of cultural forces were coexisting, integrating, and exchanging. Apart from the world views and value ideals promoted by Confucian elites, as well as the well-known noble mission of "cultivating one's morality, regulating one's family, governing the country, and making the world peaceful," there were also traces and existence of folk culture, together with even utilitarian values, which encouraged chasing gains and avoiding hazards. As a result, elite culture's and folk culture's two drastically different values were coexisting and integrating at the same time. An introduction and illustration of buildings and sacrifice activities held by academies will be set forth in an attempt to illustrate the rites and customs in academies as a whole.

Rites and Academy Buildings

Generally, the selection of locations, instructions, and designs of halls and buildings of academies spoke for specific value goals, ideologies, and aesthetic tastes. The cultural atmosphere of academies was thus exhibited via their buildings, designs, and spatial patterns, which, as has been mentioned previously, were influenced by Confucian values and some folk customs.

Confucian Values and Academy Buildings

As far as the selection of location was concerned, most of the famous academies in the Song dynasty were set up in tranquil mountain areas and forests endowed with graceful and scenic views. For example, Yuelu Academy was located in the valley of Mount Yue, alongside the western shore of River Xiang. According to historical documents, the view enjoyed by the academy was quite breathtaking, with "clear and crystal spring water running and winding in front of the main study hall, and the academy is widely acknowledged as boasting the most breathtaking views in Hu Nan areas."[2] In addition, "Mount Xiang is just located right in the back of the academy, with River Wen winding in the front. It is such a tranquil and quiet place, which was ideal for scholars to cultivate minds and study."[3] As for Shigu Academy, which was located in the valley of Stone Drum Mountain, "it is surrounded by several rivers and acclaimed as having the best views in the county."[4] Bailudong Academy "is enjoying breathtaking views of high mountains and crystal creeks, far away from the noisy world."[5] Songyang Academy and Taishan Academy were located in Mount Song and Mount Tai, respectively, all famous mountains listed as the Five Great Mountains. These locations of academies listed were what Zhu Xi talked about in *Records of Shigu Academy of Hengzhou* (衡州石鼓书院记), "when considering locations of academies, it is suggested that they should be founded in places with beautiful sights and views."[6]

The reason lying behind was to locate academies in places away from the mundane world, which would be benign for students and scholars to purify their polluted hearts and have their minds cultivated. It is widely known that since the

176 *Rites and Customs in Academies*

Song and Ming dynasties, what Confucian scholars pursued and aimed for was a spiritual realm in which "they were indifferent to and neutral about gains and benefits, just like how saints Confucius and Yan Hui behaved." Therefore, these scholars were more willing to be immersed in nature in which they could better mold minds and bodies and cultivate tastes, eventually achieving synchronization with the universe and a harmonious coexistence with the world. As a result, most academies were demanding or even particularly picky about the selection of locations. In the meantime, it is the view of many scholars that when digging out ways of obtaining Tao, meditation was an inevitable process individuals had to go through, which required a serene and peaceful place to conduct. Just as Zhu Xi pointed out,

> if set in noisy markets, how could an individual be able to actually read into what he was reading . . . The proper way should be to spend half a day reading and the other half meditating, and one could be delighted to witness his advancement in just a year or two.[7]

For scholars, academies located in tranquil and serene mountain areas were lands of idyllic beauty where they could concentrate their academic pursuits. That is to say, the selection of locations with breathtaking and excellent scenic views was an indication of the values and principles of Confucianism and was more out of a goal for scholars to better cultivate their minds and to be attentive to study, thus achieving synchronization in which they could act in the same rhythm of the universe rather than being a mere convenient access to a superficial enjoyment.

The overall design of buildings and sacrificing halls also conveyed the values and ethical principles of Confucianism. Take Yuelu Academy as an example,[8] which adopted a layout of zuomiao youxue (左庙右学; sacrifice and worship buildings were placed on the left and study halls on the right). To view the buildings as a whole, on the left side, there were buildings for conducting sacrificial ceremonies or activities, with Palace Da Cheng being the center, surrounded by three layers of yards. On the right side, there were buildings for study, with the study hall taking the central place surrounded by four layers of yards. There was an invisible but conspicuous axis dividing the right part of the academy and the left part. What was followed here was the principle of zuozu youshe (左祖右社; buildings for offering sacrifices to ancestors should be on the left, and buildings for honoring the Lord of Lands should be set on the right), stated in *Records on the Examination of Craftsmanship* (考工记)[9] . In addition, in the volume "The Meaning of Sacrifices" in *The Rites* (礼记·祭义), similar principles are stated: "buildings for honoring the Lord of Lands and Lord of Crops should be set on the right, and buildings for sacrificing ancestors should be put on the left." Just as one scholar had pointed out,

> the principles of *The Rites* had been conveyed and indicated via most of the ancestral buildings, from imperial palaces to great mansions. It could be said

Rites and Customs in Academies 177

that they were all put in arrangement and accordance with appropriateness and manners in the aspects of styles, decorations, and appearances. Additionally, as for designs and layouts, such spirit was also conveyed.[10]

The Confucian temple in Yuelu Academy was the place where activities to laud Confucius were conducted. With successive reconstructions, transformations, and expansions over the years, the temple had grown into a complete complex with three layers of yards. Alongside the axis, from the low to the top, there are zhaobi (a screen wall facing the gate of a house), shi paifang (large stone put in the archway), Da Cheng Gate, east and west yards, Da Cheng Palace, Ming Lun Hall, and Saints Temple, with Da Cheng Palace taking up the very central place and Saints Temple located on the highest point. The overall design was well-proportioned and well-arranged, reflecting the tradition of honoring teachers and esteeming the truth, as well as the fundamental principles of respecting seniors and teachers. Thus, to conclude, the buildings in Yuelu Academy embodied the spirit of Confucianism.

Besides, there were also groups of symbolic buildings which had conveyed the pursuit of values of Confucius, which is fully expressed by Zeng Dian[11] in the chapter "Forerunner Men" in *The Analects of Confucius* (论语·先进). As is recorded, "Zeng Dian would take a bath on the whim in River Yi and he was too happy that he can't help but dance, going home singing songs." It is the view of Zhu Xi and several other Neo-Confucians that

> if one reads works of Zeng Dian, he would be impressed and surprised to find that there was no desire for gains or benefits at all. In the meantime, it vividly indicated that the heavenly principle kept running through the whole universe, leaving no place uncovered.

It is acclaimed that the works of Zeng Dian vividly and fully conveyed his spirituality, which "was characterized by a broad mind and a synchronization where individuals could breathe at a rhythm that was the same of the universe."[12] As a result, many famous academies, such as Yuelu Academy, Bailudong Academy, Bailu Academy, and Shigu Academy, had special architectures to acknowledge and encourage the spirituality expressed by Zeng Dian, such as Fengyu Pavilion in Yuelu Academy, Bailudong Academy and Shigu Academy, Yonggui Bridge in Yuelu Academy, Yuyi Pavilion in Bailu Academy, and so on. Particularly, nowadays, in Bailudong Academy, there are still relics such as Feng Yu Stone, which was carved and engraved with characters "Feng Yu" and sentences such as "I agree with Zeng Dian," as well as other traces reflecting Zeng's spiritual realm.

Undoubtedly, these symbols or symbolic architectures conveyed and expressed respect for and acknowledgment of great minds in the past and a pursuit of their values, as is indicated in Zhu Xi's poetic work: "The water in Lake Ping had turned green and risen up. I stepped onto the bridge holding its red rails. The story of Zeng Dian had been passed on for thousands of years, but it is still vivid in

178 *Rites and Customs in Academies*

people's minds." In an inscription in Feng Yu Stone of Bailudong Academy, Hu Juren, a Neo-Confucian in the Ming dynasty, writes,

> Standing in the south of Five Seniors Peak and front of White Deer Cave (by which Bailudong Academy is located), the warm spring breeze blew through my arm sleeves. Truth and virtue should be studied and practiced every day, and thus, Zeng Dian was by no means alone as far as great minds are concerned.[13]

From the perspective of Confucian scholars, it is beneficial for scholars to study and explore the truth and virtue, surrounded by nature and symbolic architectures mentioned earlier, making the eventual accomplishment of synchronization with the universe a possibility. For example, some scholars stated that

> I enjoy hanging out with people with noble character and high morals. While having fun, we are also exchanging our views and understandings regarding the truth and virtues. We would sing and recite, believing that via this process, we are capable of a finding of Tao in our minds as well as an achievement of synchronization with the universe.[14]

Feng Shui Images and Academy Buildings

Apart from a reflection of elite culture, buildings in academies were also embodiments of folk customs and cultures. Take Yuelu Academy as one example. There were many buildings containing conceptual local customs and traditions. Hao Xi Stage, founded in the Qianlong period of the Qing dynasty, functioned as the main opera stage with both front door and rear door open wide, and the front door facing the gate of the academy and study hall was accompanied by two outstandingly large characters set on each side of the stage, which were "fu" (peace) and "shou" (longevity). On the outside walls of the stage, there were pictures of various Chinese legendary stories painted. The sunk panels of the stage are painted with tai chi and ba gua pictures, as well as pictures of bats (embodiments of peace) and the character "shou. On the huge white marble stones set on each side of the front gate, there were carved images like three lions playing balls (implying best wishes); plum trees, orchids, bamboos, and chrysanthemums (all symbols of noble persons); flowers and chickens (implying brilliance on accomplished splendor); and the egret and lotus (implying no corruption). These images were a combination of both elite culture and folk culture.

Feng shui originally appeared in *Burying Books* (葬书), written by Guo Pu, a scholar living in the Jin dynasty. In Guo's words, "by Feng Shui, an individual should first consider the presence and existence of water, then make sure that the place or location is free from strong winds."[15] The original purpose of feng shui was to find an ideal burial place for dead people, a place which hopefully would accumulate the vigor and the vitality in the universe and also protect people in the family still alive, thus eventually drawing on advantages and avoiding disadvantages. It is the belief of several scholars that feng shui should be emphasized because

> as long as the place of vitality was found, one's destiny could be changed subsequently. Thus, individuals could not only make their dreams into a reality, but they could also bring long-lasting glory and prosperity to their families. Additionally, good luck would always favor their descendants and offspring.[16]

Hence, it could be said that feng shui contained the traditional concept of universal vitality. Via great mountains and grand rivers in the universe, which were endowed with good luck or veiled with evil omens, people sought the goal of drawing on advantages and avoiding bad luck, thereby achieving the gains or benefits they were pursuing. As a matter of fact, this ideology fit right into the category of folk culture. If the values and principles conveyed by buildings in the academies were more of an awareness of Tao in the universe to offer scholars a correct direction leading to harmony and coexistence with the universe, then it could be said images related to feng shui were closely related to chasing gains and benefits in the real world.

As far as feng shui images were concerned, they could be illustrated from two aspects which were "veins of the dragon" (places where universal vigor and vitality were hidden) and fang wei (directions), respectively. Veins of the dragon generally referred to a magnificent range of mountains hidden with vigor and vitality. For example, Mount Heng was generally viewed as the vein of Yuelu Academy. It is recorded that "Mount Heng was located in the Li Gua of Ba Gua, standing for intelligence and knowledge. As the last peak of all 72 mountains in Heng Mount Range, Mount Heng was the mountain gathering knowledge and truth."[17] Here, again, Yuelu Academy was set as an example to set forth views of various scholars on veins of the dragon. Since the beginning of the Song dynasty, there were documents recording feng shui in Yuelu Academy. Nonetheless, none had touched on the concept of the veins of the dragon. In the letter to Zhu Xi, Zhang Shi mentioned the threat that feng shui of Yuelu Academy was a potential prey for other predators.

> The academy was on the position of An Shan, with excellent feng shui. It is not the first time that it was coveted by high officials and rich people as an ideal burial place. I went through the thistles and thorns yesterday and found out that the academy was actually in the valley surrounded by four different mountains, with a river running upfront. The view was so beautiful and amazing that I would go as far as to say it is like paradise. Now I just have one pavilion built and named it Feng Yu Pavilion. I hereby sincerely invite you to come over, and we could go climbing together.[18]

By talking about the perfect location the academy was enjoying, apparently Zhang Shi paid more attention to the experience of climbing the mountain, during

180 *Rites and Customs in Academies*

which climbers were offered a chance to comprehend Tao than mere possibility of avoiding evil omens and obtaining honor and fortune. Until the late Ming dynasty, in "Reconstruction of Yuelu Academy" (重修岳麓书院图志), the superintendent Wu Daoxing continued to express his criticism of the link that had been forcefully made between the location of the academy and luck. It is the belief of Wu Daoxing that borderlines were set to prevent coveters who kept harrying and bothering with no aim but to steal the location of the academy. Wu writes,

> Celebrities and men of power were indulged with the superstitious concept feng shui. They lent ready ears to nonsenses of so-called feng shui masters and deified Guo Pu. Consequently, it is commonly seen that they would go and dig out bodies of their family, moving and transferring bodies into other places, which is against the heavenly principle.[19]

Nonetheless, in the Qing dynasty, notions of wisdom and good luck implied in the veins of the dragon came to be accepted by scholars, which could be testified by descriptions about how the veins of the dragon got destroyed in works such as "A Sequel to Yuelu Academy in Chang Sha" (长沙岳麓书院续志), written by the superintendent Ding Shanqing, and "Supplements to Yuelu Academy" (岳麓续志补编), authored by Zhou Yulin. In the 19th year of the Jiaqing period, "there were groups of gentlemen and people of noble character going to local governments at different levels, all proposing that measures should be taken in order to protect the feng shui of Yuelu Academy." This was because, in Dragon King Pit, Back Blade Mountain, and Grand Land Valley, it is witnessed that people were chiseling and cutting through the mountain, which was against the rules. They asserted, "It would destroy the feng shui of Yuelu Academy." Afterward, governments issued official bans and set large stone billboards in the academy: chiseling of any kind was forbidden.[20] Later on, in the seventh year of the Tongzhi era, another ban was issued: no cutting or chiseling was allowed. In the tenth year of the Tongzhi era, a handwritten public statement was made stating that coal mining was completely banned in Yuelu Academy, and lands considered as the veins of the dragon were in the possession of the academy, which had the exclusive right of possession, control, and management.[21] Bans as such were issued for the purpose of protecting and maintaining feng shui of Mount Heng. On the one hand, bans acted as responses to appeal of scholars, and on the other hand, they illustrated the emphasis put on feng shui by these scholars. Furthermore, works like *Academies* (书院志) indicated that the concept of feng shui, a category of folk culture, had permeated into the daily life of scholars and intellectuals, who started to selectively buy notions that feng shui and veins of the dragon were beneficial to the advancement of one's academic achievement and performance on the imperial exams.

Apart from more and more focuses put on the veins of the dragon, concepts about good or ill luck related to orientations and facing directions of academies also came to be recognized by scholars of academies. For example, in the Ming dynasty, there was a change regarding the orientation and direction of Yuelu Academy in consideration of luck. According to "Reconstruction of Yuelu Academy,"

Rites and Customs in Academies 181

authored by Wu Daoxing, during the Zhengde period, there was one student from Chang Sha County who suggested a change of orientation of the academy because the feng shui of Yuelu Academy was bad and that's the reason the academy was rebuilt many times but still yet to achieve its desired effects. Now changes concerning orientations and facing directions must be made in order to get it done once and for all. The suggestion was echoed by Wu Shizhong, an adviser of the government: "The importance of reconstruction on academies should not be emphasized enough. Feng shui masters should be invited to view the geographical locations of the academy. If feng shui is bad, then changes must be made."[22] During the Qing dynasty, there were three changes made with regard to the location of Yuelu Academy, which were because of the considerations regarding luck and imperial exams. Wang Wenqing, the superintendent of Yuelu Academy at that time, once talked about a change that was made. Wang recalled,

> In accordance with the main direction set by Zhu Xi, near places where two mountains were annexed to each other and rivers running in the front, a path was opened up from the original memorial gate. After this change, there was a significant increase in the number of students passing the exam.[23]

In the second change, "officials in charge of academies, took in words of charlatans on luck of academies, and changed the facing direction of the very first gate to the right," which had caused "the rise of ill luck with continuous problems and illness in academies, almost leading to a shutdown." Later, the academy changed the orientation of the gate back, and "everything was brought back to normal."[24] From his repeated emphasis that "I had experienced these changes in person," by Wang Wenqing, who was a Confucian scholar qualified enough to represent the mainstream values in the Qing dynasty, it could be said that Wang had completely bought the notion of good and evil lucks caused by orientation and location of academy. Thus, if great minds such as Wang Wenqing had accepted essential notions of feng shui and its implications on relative images, then it is safe to say that feng shui concept found its way into academies.

No doubt, it was not an indiscriminate and wholesale acceptance. Rather, the acknowledgment was selective in nature. In "Views on Folk Customs" (风俗论), Wang Wenqing explicitly expressed his opposition to the link between places of burial and the possibility of fortune. Wang writes, "Graves were where those beloved people could rest in peace, not places where those alive schemed and planed for their own benefits. It is a pity that some people nowadays were befuddled and deceived by those self-acclaimed feng shui masters."[25] Hence, the attitude of Wang Wenqing toward feng shui testified to the existence of subtle and complex coordination between elite cultures and folk customs, which coexist but at the same time oppose each other.

There were also voluminous documents about other academies recording protection of the veins of the dragon and changes of orientation in order to advance academic accomplishments and increase the passing rate of imperial exams. For example, based on *Records of Shigu Academy*, thanks to changes in facing

182 *Rites and Customs in Academies*

directions of the gate, there was a remarkable increase in the passing rate of imperial exams in Shigu Academy. In the past, the grand gate of Shigu Academy faced toward North Qiao Building. In the late Jiaqing era, the gate was changed facing toward the southeast, which was upfront the River Xiang, expressing a wish for good luck. It is recorded, "As a result, the passing rate fell down tremendously, and problems arose incisively." This was because

> Rive Xiang flowed down directly toward the academy with unstopping force. Thanks to the high location of Shigu Academy and the fact that not many people lived there, the evil spirit was somehow reduced. Otherwise, there would be more disasters happening.

Therefore, the orientation of the gate was changed back in the Guangxu era. What's worth pointing out here was that after the change back, the number of students passing the exam was rising up again, and the names of candidates who successfully passed were taken down:

> Tan Ying from Anren County scored first place in the provincial exam conducted together in all southern provinces in the year of Yi Mou, which was for the first time for Anren County for 53 years. In the year of the Geng Chen metropolitan exam, there were four passers, who were Zhu Songyun from Hengyang and Tan Xinzhen, Yang Yidou, and Cheng Ding from Hengshan, with Tan Xinzhen scoring third place in the final round exam. Additionally, Chen Ding was selected as high officials' backup of the central government and was honored with the title of shujishi (high officials' backup) in the royal exam (additional exam on passers of highest imperial exams held by emperors).[26]

Consequently, it could be seen that in the opinion of scholars of academies at that time, there was a close link between feng shui and exam performances. Hence, builders of academies also preferred a location with good feng shui for good luck.

As far as the overall development and advancement of academies were concerned, the original purposes of having academies built were to illustrate ethics and morality, to improve the social climate and customs, and to promote fundamental value principles of Confucianism, which had been talked about and mentioned by many educationists in academies. Consequently, the founding fathers aimed that, via the education received in academies, their students would have a good moral and noble character, caring and loving the world, instead of purely chasing after fame. For example, while in charge of Yuelu Academy, Zhang Shi explicitly stated that the ultimate goal of education was not to help students prepare for imperial exams, not to teach them how to write essays in a polished rhetorical style, nor to guide them onto the way of glory and wealth. Rather, it is to "promote virtues and values of Confucian Saints to help people around the world."[27] Nonetheless, in the Qing dynasty, it is surprising to witness that wishes for good luck in exams

Rites and Customs in Academies 183

and promising political careers were openly expressed through feng shui images in academies, which even got acknowledged and accepted selectively by scholars. Hence, it could be said that folk culture indeed shaped academies tremendously in its own subconscious way.

Ritual Activities of Academy

Ritual activities refer to a series of activities held to pay tribute to God, ancestors, or other sacrificial targets as a way to show respect or request protection. Sacrificial activities, book collections, and lectures and seminars were generally regarded as the three most important cultural and education functions of academies.

The cultural motivations regarding sacrifices held in academies were rather complicated, with the most outstanding one being to reflect the continuance of traditional Confucian values and principles, as well as mainstream academic views. For example, under most circumstances, it is the Confucian saints and masters that got commemorated, as well as some other outstanding figures who perfectly represented and carried the academic mission and spirit. However, it should not be overlooked that there were also some activities being held for wishing good luck in imperial exams or having a smooth political career. As a matter of fact, some ceremonies were held merely for best wishes. Therefore, Wen Chang (a god in charge of academic performance in traditional Chinese legends), Kui (a god in charge of exams in traditional Chinese legends), Guan Yu (a god of martial arts), and the God of Lands were common figures for people to worship. Consequently, there was a continuous interaction and integration between rites and folk customs as far as sacrifices were concerned. Here, an attempted illustration will be set forth from the perspective of spreading Confucian values and praying for good luck in academic exam performance.

Confucian Orthodoxy and Sacrificial Ceremonies

One of the most vital aims of holding sacrificial activities in academies was to show respect and promote Confucian values and principles in an expressive and direct way, which hopefully and gradually would begin to take root in the general public. From the view of Zhu Xi and other masters, in sacrificing ceremonies, attendees expressed recognition and yearning for the inheritance of both ritual targets and their significance, which was a token of Confucian values and principles. As is stated by Zhu Xi,

> Ancient legends and stories were researched, rules about sacrifices and rituals were issued, and statues of saints and great minds were set in academies and schools. The ultimate goal was to convey a message that the academic views and values of these saints and masters should be respected and continued.[28]

In "Reconstruction of Lian Xi Study Hall in Jiangzhou" (江州重建濂溪先生书堂记), Zhu Xi clearly points out that the academic achievements of Zhou Dunyi

184 *Rites and Customs in Academies*

should be reevaluated from the perspective of promoting and continuing Zhou's academic thoughts, which should be studied and inherited.[29] In a sacrificing ceremony held in Bamboo Forest Study Hall, Zhu Xi set Zhou Dunyi, Cheng Yi, Cheng Hao, Zhang Zai, and Sima Guang as lauding targets. In "To Masters," Zhu put great emphasis on the inheritance of traditional Confucian values and principles, viewing sacrificial figures as receivers and expressers in different inheritance phases.[30] To sum up, it is traditional Confucian ethics and virtues that Zhu Xi wanted to promote and spread. And it is the academies that Zhu viewed as the main bases to carry out this function of passing on the inheritance. In conclusion, holding worshiping activities were nothing but means to accomplish the continuance of Confucian values and principles. Zhu Xi's conduct was largely accepted and acknowledged by most scholars in the late Song dynasty. In "Lecture Notes of Shangcai Academy" (上蔡书院讲义), Wang Bai, a Neo-Confucian in the late Song dynasty, mentions,

> The emperor adored and recommended the academic and thought system of Confucius, thus encouraging the advancement and development of education nationwide. Apart from building a mass of schools that were like bamboo shoots after a spring rain, many academies were also set up.[31]

Similarly, it is stated in "Tongwen Academy of Jianyang," authored by Xiong He, a Neo-Confucian scholar living in the transition period of the Song and Yuan dynasties, that "traditional Confucian principles and values should be recognized and promoted in order to train and cultivate people with talents."[32] In the second year (1235) of the Duanping era of the Song dynasty, an official whose last name was Cao from Pingjiang of Jiang Su, was said to

> have gifted temples and other houses to scholars. In addition, he bought acres of land and intended crops from lands to be sources of funding for scholars. Books of Hejing (Yin Zhun) and his friends and teachers were also put in the academy.

Thus, Huqiu Academy was subsequently set up, and a statue of Yin Zhun was set up and put in the temple for students to pay respects to. Liu Zai made his point that what Cao did was of great importance. Liu writes, "As a whole, it is to advocate those acclaiming virtues and ethics. In particular, it could be seen as a continuance of academic thoughts of Hejing."[33] In the fifth year (1257) of the Baoyou era of the Song dynasty, in the Temple of Chenglianxi Academy located in Baoqing of Hu Nan, a statue of Zhou Dunyi was set up for students to come to pay respect to.

> In the center of the academy, there was a temple specifically set up in memory of Zhou Dunyi, accompanied by two other great minds with noble character. The lecture hall was put in the back, with complete subsidiaries and facilities, such as fast rooms, janitor rooms, corridors, kitchen, and bathrooms.[34]

Gao Side wrote a memorial address in which he praised Zhou Dunyi for his "excellence and outstanding achievements, seen as the true inheritor of the academic system of Confucius and Mencius."[35] Thus, apparently, it is the view of post-Zhu scholars that ritual activities were closely related to the promotion of traditional Confucian values.

Similarly, ritual activities were unanimously accepted and imitated by people in later generations. In *Research on Academies of Yuan Dynasty*, Xu Zi points out that the reason Zhu Xi got expansive and wide worship across the country during the Yuan dynasty was due to a mutual recognition of Zhu's status in the Confucian system.[36] For example, in "Founding History of Academy in Raozhou Lu" (饶州路创建书院疏), by Wang Yun, it is stated that

> the academy was founded in a place with the best scenic views in Raozhoulu. The temple for honoring Zhu Xi was put in a very central place. Students were taught and cultivated in the academy, and they were encouraged to go to the temple. By doing so, generally, they were praying for the longevity life of the emperor. In addition, they could also pray for long-lasting prosperity and harmony in their own families. Last, this was a way to inherit and carry on the academic system of Zhu Xi.[37]

In the 31st year (1692) of the Kangxi era of the Qing dynasty, in "Memorial Address to Zhu Xi Written in Huangu Academy" (还古书院祀朱文公议), Wang Puzheng further explicitly points out,

It is of vital importance to pay homage to those great minds to inherit and continue the academic system. It follows that Zhu Xi should be respected in all places where academic lectures are held, and Zhu's academic thought system should be credited as orthodox.[38] Ziyang Academy of Hankou was founded in the 60th year (1721) during the reign of Emperor Kang Xi, with one of the purposes being to show respect to Zhu Xi, indicating a strong inclination to inherit those traditional Confucian values. In Vol. 2 of *Ziyang Academy* (紫阳书院志略), it is stated that

> Zhou Dunyi of the Song dynasty had succeeded the academic thought system of Mencius, which had been stalling for hundreds of years. Cheng Yi and Cheng Hao carried on what they learned from Zhou and passed it on to Yang Wanli, who passed it on to Li Tong, from whom Zhu Xi took over and continued.[39]

In "Spring Elegiac Address" (春祭文), "Birthday Elegiac Address" (生日祭文), "Autumn Elegiac Address" (秋正祭文), "Anniversary of Death Elegiac Address" (忌日祭文) and other elegiac addresses to Zhu Xi, it is stated that "the academic thought system of Zhu Xi could be traced back as far as to Confucius." Also, "Zhu Xi was so excellent and brilliant. He was like the sun and the moon in the sky, undertaking the responsibility of passing on Confucian values and principles." In addition, "Zhu Xi was quite knowledgeable and had a comprehensive understanding upon virtues and righteousness of Confucian system, thus becoming an

186   *Rites and Customs in Academies*

ideal successor." Furthermore, "Zhu Xi was born with a mission to inherit and pass on the Confucian academic and thought system and to practice it in person throughout his life."[40] In the early years of the Qianlong era, in Vol. 4 of *Huangu Academy* (还古书院志), titled "Sacrificial Rites" (祀典), it is explicitly pointed out that "temples must be set up in the academy to pay respect to Confucius and Zhu Xi as a way to indicate an inheritance of Confucianism."[41]

Such awareness of inheritance spoke itself in the selection of ceremony targets. As the founder and the most famous representative of the Confucian system, the status of Confucius was unanimously recognized and thus unmovable. Therefore, undoubtedly, Confucius was worshiped. As a matter of fact, there were Confucian temples in almost every academy. For example, there had been traditions of worshiping ceremonies held for the purpose of showing respect to Confucius in Yuelu Academy ever since its foundation in the ninth year (976) of the Kaibao era of the Northern Song dynasty.[42] Till the second year (999) of the Xianping era, when Li Yun undertook the bearing of having the Academy rebuilt, such tradition was kept, which could be proven by reserving a specific rice field, the crop of which was exclusively used for sacrificial activities. Zhun Shunmin, a scholar of the late Northern Song dynasty, while visiting Yuelu Academy, recorded what he had witnessed: "there was a grand Confucian temple in the academy. In addition, there was also an exquisite library equipped with intact corridors."[43] Similar ceremonies to mark Confucius were also held in Bailudong Academy. For example, in the fourth year (1001) of the Xianping era, Emperor Zhen Zong issued royal orders demanding classic books published by Directorate of Education be used as textbooks in academies and schools nationwide. In addition, Confucian temples must be set up in academies. In the fifth year of Xian Ping, when Bailudong Academy was under reconstruction, it is recorded that "ten more statues of Confucian masters were made and set up."[44] Since then, throwing ceremonies to show respect to Confucius had become an indispensable part of activities held in academies.

Apart from Confucius, several other Confucian masters were memorialized and respected. As mentioned earlier, in the third year (1192) of the Shaoxi era of the Southern Song dynasty, Zhu Xi had Bamboo Forest Study Hall built in Kaoting and requested that Zhou Dunyi, Cheng Yi, Cheng Hao, Zhang Zai, Shao Yong, Sima Guang, and Li Dong be worshiped and given sacrifices to together in the temple. Among these seven erudite Confucian masters, Zhou Dunyi, Cheng Yi, Cheng Hao, Zhang Zai, Shao Yong, and Sima Guang were acclaimed by Zhu Xi, who, in "Praises on Six Great Minds," speaks highly of their academic achievements in the development of Neo-Confucianism.[45] In the first year (1241) of the Chunyou period of the Song dynasty, military official Jiang Wanli had Bailu Academy set up and "built a Confucian temple accompanied with Ling Xing Gate." "A temple was also built for students to worship Cheng Yi, Cheng Hao, Zhou Dunyi, Zhang Zai, Shao Yong, and Zhu Xi, thus named Temple of Six Great Masters (六先生画像赞)."[46] In the first year (1314) of the Yanyou era of the Yuan dynasty, the statues of Zhu Xi and Zhang Shi were put in the Temple of Masters in the Yuelu Academy. In the Hongzhi era of the Ming dynasty, Chong Tao Temple was set up to pay respect to Zhu Xi and Zhang Shi.[47] In the hundreds of years afterward, the two masters continued to be given sacrifices in Yuelu Academy. Since the reign of the Kangxi era, Chongzheng Academy, located in Yun Nan, began to put statues of Zhou Dunyi, Cheng Yi, Cheng Hao, Zhang Zai, and Zhu Shi in the temple for students to show respect.[48] Among all masters adored in Bailudong Academy, Zhou Dunyi, Cheng Yi, Cheng Hao, Zhang Zai, Shao Yong, Zhu XI, Lu Jiuyuan, Huang Gan, Cai Shen, and Lin Zezhi were the most commonly seen ones being worshiped for their key status and remarkable achievement in the Confucian system. Therefore, it could be said that the selection of targets to worship was actually out of consideration for inheritance and continuance of Confucian thoughts. Huang Wenzhong, a scholar of the Yuan dynasty, remarked that the original purpose of having academies set up was to continue and pass on the thoughts and philosophies of saints. In this way, traditional Confucian values and principles got passed on and came to reach the general public. Thus, these scholars with great minds ought to be honored. In particular, Confucius should be of first priority because he was the founder of the overall Confucian academic system. Masters and intellectuals after Confucius were at most representatives of various branches of the original Confucian system and thus should be treated in different ways.[49] Academies, as symbols of Confucianism, were the main places where Confucian ethics was advanced and highlighted.

Omen Worship in the Academy

The god Wen Chang was generally viewed by the folk people and Taoists as the god in charge of political careers. It is pointed out by some scholars that "Wen Chang was actually a combination of reverence toward the God of Zi Tong by local people from Szechuan and a belief in successful academic and political accomplishments since Spring and Autumn Period and Warring States Period."[50] Kui (魁) was the deity in charge of academic writings in ancient China and was one of the 28 main stars in traditional Chinese astrology. Additionally, in the famous charm book *Xiaojing yuan shen qi* (孝经援神契) of the Eastern Han dynasty, there was the saying that Kui (奎) was in charge of how well a person could write. Consequently, people in later generations deified the Kui (奎) and started to worship it. As time passed by, the character 奎 was gradually changed into the character 魁, which was its homophone. Starting from the late Song dynasty, buildings such as the Kui Pavilion and the Wen Chang Hall started to be set up in several academies to pay respect to the gods Wen Chang and Kui.[51] As pointed out in some books, respect shown toward Wen Chang, Kui, and Guan was an indication of the integration of Confucianism and Taoism in academies. For instance, in the Chunyou period of the Song dynasty, Xijian Academy of Gaoan in Jiang Xi issued rules requiring Kui to be worshiped in hopes of "praying for more insights and brilliance on essay writings."

> The final result of the imperial exam at the metropolitan level came out. Just like the carp leaping over the dragon gate, the news was coming that those who had successfully passed the final exam were summoned by the emperor.

188   *Rites and Customs in Academies*

It is a relief to know that they are on the way leading to a bright political future, and the best is yet to come.[52]

Similarly, the Wen Chang Hall was built in the Yuzhang Academy of Nanchang in Jiang Xi for students and lecturers to pray for good luck in their academic achievements during the Southern Song dynasty.[53] Gradually, it is common for academies nationwide to hold various kinds of ceremonies to offer sacrifices to Wen Chang and Kui. For some influential academies, there were the Kui Pavilion and the Wen Chang Hall built inside. Even those less well-known academies developed and kept similar activities as well.

The purpose of ceremonies held in honor of Wen Chang and Kui was to pray for good luck in imperial exams and brilliant academic accomplishments. In "Reconstruction of the Wen Chang Hall in Fengshan Academy" (补修凤山书院文昌阁碑记), Tang Changkai of the Qing dynasty states,

> Generally speaking, the greatness of a man lends glory to a place and vice versa. That is to say, in places enjoying both views of mountains and waters, there shall be regular maintenance made. Additionally, Wen Chang is in charge of luck and wealth in the universe, as well as how well a candidate could perform in exams. Consequently, the halls where they lived must be the priority for maintenance and reconstruction compared with other tasks such as improving feng shui and advancing culture.

All these prayers for Wen Chang and Kui prove folk culture's permeation into and influence on academies.[54] But how different are academies in conducting their ceremonies in honor of Wen Chang and Kui? As stated earlier, people prayed to Wen Chang and Kui for good luck in performance in exams in the hope of successful political careers and accumulation of wealth. In comparison, while glorifying Confucian saints and masters, they were practicing a continuance and inheritance of traditional Confucian values and principles. So how did the two actually coexist and subsist together?

Again, we take Yuelu Academy in the Qing dynasty as an example. According to Vol. 1 of *Sequel to Yuelu Academy of Changsha* (长沙岳麓书院续志), authored by Ding Shanqing, in the seventh year of the Kangxi era, Wen Chang Hall was built and set behind the main lecture hall. In the 57th year (1792) of the Qianlong era, Bi Yuan, the governor in charge of Hu Guang areas, donated 100 golds in support of setting up the Kui Pavilion in the academy.[55] Some interesting facts could be cramped out if a comparison was made between honoring Confucian masters and sacrificing Wen Chang. During the Qianlong era, ceremonies and activities held in honor of both Confucian masters and Wen Chang must be in accordance with official regulations and rules and thus in charge of particular departments of the government. In "Increase on Public Funding for Sacrificial Activities" (新增丁祭公费记), Luo Dian recorded that 14 silvers were set aside by the department in support of worshiping activities. For activities held in honor of Confucian masters, the standard of Tai Lao should be

Rites and Customs in Academies 189

adopted (Tai Lao sacrifice generally consists of an ox, a sheep, and a pig). Shao Lao sacrifice (Shao Lao sacrifice generally consists of a sheep and a pig) should be followed when worshiping Wen Chang.[56] In the Jiaqing era, things changed. Ritual activities conducted in the Wen Chang Hall were hosted by the superintendent Yuan Mingyao, who, via his lobbying efforts, had raised approximately 1,055 silvers. Money was expended to buy farmlands, the earnings from which were particularly set aside for ritual activities. The ceremony date to worship Wen Chang was also changed to the third day of February every year, and the ceremonies adopted Tai Lao standard with budge being 20 silvers.[57] In contrast, in the first year of the Jiaqing era, the budget for holding activities in honor of Confucian masters was only 14 silvers. Even to add up earnings from 200 silvers funded by students, it is far away from 20 silvers, which was the budget for sacrificing Wen Chang.[58] These statistics indicate that at least in Yuelu Academy, Ritual activities for Wen Chang were superior to those of Confucian masters' sacrifices in both budget and adopted standards. Ritual activities to honor Confucian masters came to be dwarfed and squeezed out by a new trend, with priority being put on adoring Wen Chang and Kui for the sake of good luck in academic achievements.

What's worse, in some academies, the folk ritual culture had completely taken up worshiping activities in academies. Yingyuan Academy, founded in the eighth year (1869) of the Tongzhi period in Guang Dong Province, was one of the examples. The academy was the most famous one in Guang Dong, enjoying lots of funding and monetary support. Nonetheless, from the expenditure report on ritual expenses, targets for worshiping included only Wen Chang and Kui.[59]

In addition, in academies at county levels, there was a trend that more priority and focus were put on Wen Chang's and Kui's sacrifices. Jade Lake Academy of Ningxiang in Hu Nan, founded in the second year (1523) of the Jiajing period of the Ming dynasty, was originally built, among other purposes, to continue the academic thought systems of Hu Wufeng and Zhang Shi, two great Confucian masters. A historical record in the Qianlong era also illustrates that in ceremonies held, the sequence in which targets were sacrificed were Hu and Zhang, to begin with, then five worthies making great contributions to the advancement and development of the academy system, and in the end, Wen Chang and Kui.[60] But in the Jiaqing era, there was a change with regard to the order, with Wen Chang and Kui being worshiped first, then Hu and Zhang, and last, the five scholars.[61] Thus, to sum up, as far as the sequence of the figures worshiped in ceremonies held in Yutan Academy was concerned, there was a transition from prioritizing Confucian masters to prioritizing Wen Chang and Kui.

Besides, changes also occurred in how ceremonies were held, thus the aspect of standards. In the Qianlong era, there was no singular and separate ceremony specifically held in honor of Wen Chang. As for worship of Kui, it is not only put in the latter part of overall order, but the manners required were also pretty simple. As is recorded, "For candidates to sit in provincial exams, before they set off, they shall come to show respect to Kui by kneeling once and bowing three times." Till the Jiaqing era, Wen Chang was entitled to a singular and separate

190 *Rites and Customs in Academies*

ceremony, enjoying a standard of Tai Lao, the standard of which was even higher than those used in commemorating Hu Wufeng and Zhang Shi. In contrast, less and less attention seemed to be put on ceremonies held for Hu and Zhang, with the standard being Shao Lao, and only one memorial elegiac address was written in honor of the two, which was read together along with other addresses during the ceremony in the Jiaqing era. This was a sharp contrast compared with the past. It is claimed that the reason behind such change was because "it is inconvenient to conduct separate ceremonies when the statues of Hu and Zhang were seated in the same temple hall; thus, only one elegiac essay would suffice as an honor."[62] Apparently, the explanation was untenable and rather weak when the true reason was that less and less emphasis was put on the two masters. In the chapter "Rituals" in "Reconstruction of Yutan Academy" (重修玉潭书院辑略·礼文), Zhang Sijiong touches upon the reasons Wen Chang and Kui were getting more and more attention:

> Now academies all over the country begin to attach great importance to sacrifices for Wen Chang and Kui, who are generally viewed as in charge of performance in exams. Thus, it goes without saying that the two are worshiped for their capacities in this field.[63]

As a result, in Yutan Academy and other academies at county levels, the folk custom represented by a prayer for good luck in political and academic achievements started to permeate into academies, with more and more influences being exerted.

Some academies seemed to have witnessed continuous back-and-forth changes related to the fight between elite culture and folk culture. When initially founded in the Qianlong era, Fangting Academy "set up the statue of Confucius in the Central Hall and bought kits and utensils used for sacrifices." As time passed by, the academy began to put more emphasis on sacrifices made to Wen Chang and moved the Confucius statue first down to the first story of the Kui Pavilion and later again moved it to the back room of the Wen Chang Temple, which could be testified by historical documents recording such moving procedures: "Mayor Shi asked people to move and set the Confucius statue to the first story of the Kui Pavilion, and later on, at the request of Zhang Liqing, the statue was removed to the back room of the Wen Chang Hall."[64] This was strongly opposed by Ren Sizheng, who, out of the concern that "it is inappropriate to put the statue of a Confucian saint in the back room of the Wen Chang Hall," had a Confucian temple built in the rear of the academy for the exclusive use of worshiping Confucius. Subsequently, the overall layout of the academy is described as follows: "Standing in the Confucian temple and looking out, one could see there was the Kui Pavilion in the front and the Wen Chang Hall in the left, with the study hall being in the very center." Such location change of Confucius' statue was a strong indicator concerning both the waning and waxing of influential power of different cultural concepts in worshiping and sacrificing activities in academies.

Conclusion

The academy, as one of the most outstanding symbols of Confucian culture, was acclaimed to have fully expressed the traditional values and principles of Confucianism. In order to civilize the folk and cultivate the talented, Confucian scholars made continuous and unremitting efforts to promote Confucian traditional principles, with an aim to "coordinate different virtue values and systematize local customs of different places," eventually replacing folk culture with mainstream elite culture. However, in reality, the cultural atmosphere of academies exhibited an interaction and mutual influence in rites and customs, not in accordance with the goal of many Confucian scholars. Nonetheless, in the process of communication and promotion of particular thoughts and values, great ideals sometimes yield to reality. In this scenario, despite criticisms and attacks made by Confucian scholars, due to the fact that traditional folk cultures had taken deep roots in the daily life of the general public, it is very hard to accomplish changes. For instance, in "Worshiping Worthies of Town of Tongxiang Academy" (桐乡书院志·祀乡贤), Dai Junheng expresses his disagreement with the fad of worshiping Wen Chang:

> The trend nowadays is that folk culture has infiltrated our daily life. For example, the Wen Chang Hall and the Kui Pavilion were built for people to pray and worship regularly every year. It is believed that these two gods were in charge of performance in imperial exams and academic achievements. Some Confucian scholars have expressed their views and stances on this false and superstitious belief already, with which I agree.

Consequently, Dai asserts, "There should be one person with high morals and noble character selected in each place for locals to worship." He concludes, "Thus, in the worshiping practice, worshipers were offered a chance to practice and improve their manners and etiquette, daring not to act against the rites. What could they get from mere prayer to Wen Chang and Kui?" Nonetheless, Dai also recognized the difficulty faced:

> Sacrificial practices made toward Wen Chang and Kui should be called upon to stop and unroot the daydreams of some scholars who thought they could be endowed with a bright and brilliant future by simply paying respects to the two gods. Rather, Confucian values and principles should be recognized and restored. However, this is yet to come.[65]

Hence, Wen Chang and Kui were pretty influential at that time.

In contrast, some other scholars adopted another method in which they made several attempts to try to achieve a balance between the elite cultural concept and the folk cultural concept instead of completely denying and opposing the latter. For example, when Shenxiu Academy of Yueyang got rebuilt during the Guangxu period, Kui Guang Hall was built with a wish to bring brilliance to students' performance in imperial exams. Yue Hongying acclaims in "Reconstruction of

192 *Rites and Customs in Academies*

Yueyang Academy" (重修岳阳书院记), "It is beneficial to cultivate and nourish feng shui as encouraged by feng shui masters. Additionally, students were provided another place where they could come up and enjoy the views."[66] This sounded more like a defense for, on the one hand, he did not criticize the setting up of Kui Light Hall but, on the other hand, he gave it acclaim for it had offered students chances to visit and enjoy the view. Thus, it could be said that some concepts and views of the folk culture had already exerted a subconscious influence on the overall cultural climate of academies. Nonetheless, they were not yet fully accepted; thus, they were still in need of additional explanations to defend their rationality.

As a matter of fact, although for many scholars, elite culture and folk culture belonged to different categories, the two somehow achieved coexistence in their minds. Confucian scholars were encouraged to continue and inherit traditional values and principles of Confucianism and made continuous and endless cultivation of their minds and bodies. But it was known to these scholars that they were not living in a pure ideal world. Rather, they were influenced subconsciously but greatly by folk culture, going as far as to have begun to recognize and accept parts of folk culture. In a word, the interaction and integration of rites and customs in the cultural atmosphere of academies were expressions of the inner worlds of Confucian scholars.

Notes

1 Zhao, Changwong赵长翁. "Rulin shuyuan ji" 儒林书院记. In *Siku quan shu* Vol. 534 四库全书第534册 (Shanghai: Shanghai Chinese Classics Publishing House, 1987), 719.
2 Zhang, Shunmin 张舜民. "Shen xing lu" 郴行录. In *Siku quan shu* Vol. 1117四库全书第1117册 (Shanghai: Shanghai Chinese Classics Publishing House, 1987), 52.
3 Hu, Hong胡宏. "Yü qin hui zhi shu" 与秦会之书. In *Huhong ji*胡宏集 (Beijing: Zhonghua Book Company, 1987), 105.
4 Zhu, Xi朱熹. "Hengyang shigu shuyuan ji" 衡阳石鼓书院记. In *Zhuzi quanhsu* 朱子全书 (Shanghai: Shanghai Chinese Classics Publishing House & Hefei: Anhui Education Press, 2002), 3782.
5 Zhu, Xi 朱熹. "Bai lu dong die" 白鹿洞牒. In *Bailu dong zhi* Vol. 15白鹿洞志卷十五 (Beijing: Zhonghua Book Company, 1995), 236.
6 Zhu, Xi朱熹. "Hengzhou shigu shuyuan ji" 衡州石鼓书院记. In *Zhuzi quanshu* 朱子全书 (Shanghai: Shanghai Chinese Classics Publishing House &Hefei: Anhui Education Press, 2002), 3783.
7 Li, Jingde 黎靖德. *Zhuzi yu lei* Vol. 116朱子语类卷一百一十六 (Beijing: Zhonghua Book Company, 1986), 2806.
8 See Liu, Su柳肃. "Rujia jisi wenhua yu dongya shuyuan jianzhu de yishi kongjian" 儒家祭祀文化与东亚书院建筑的仪式空间. In *Journal of Hunan University* No. 6, 2007, 35–38.
9 *Records on the Examination of Craftsmanship* (考工记) is a book on a wide range of fields in artisanry. It dates from the late Spring and Autumn Period (770–5th cent. bc) and is transmitted as the last part of the Confucian Classic Zhouli. The task of the minister of works (司空) was the monitoring of official work for the royal palace, the capital and its surroundings, and the needs of the royal state of the Zhou dynasty (11th cent.–221 bc) in general.

10 Li, Yunhe 李允鉌. *Huaxia yijiang—zhongguo gudian jianzhu sheji yuanli fenxi*华夏意匠—中国古典建筑设计原理分析 (Tianjin: Tianjin University Press, 2005), 40.

11 Zeng Dian was a student of Confucius. He liked playing the piano and singing, believed in Confucianism, studied Confucianism, and put it into practice. He hated the current ethical code and was determined to change the status quo. Confucius regarded him as an enterprising man.

12 Zhu, Xi 朱熹. *Sishu zhangju jizhu*四书章句集注 (Beijing: Zhonghua Book Company, 1983), 130.

13 Hu, Juren 胡居仁. "Hjuren ti fengyushi" 文翰七·胡居仁题风雩石. In *Bai lu dong zhi* Vol. 15 白鹿洞志卷十五, ed. Zheng Tinggu郑廷鹄 (Beijing: Zhonghua Book Company, 1995), 416.

14 Wu, Daoheng 吴道行. "Shanshui" 山水. In *Chongxiu yuelu shuyuan tuzhi* Vol. 3 重修岳麓书院图志卷三 (Changsha: Yuelu Press, 2012), 41.

15 Gu, Pu 郭璞. "Zang shu" 葬书. In *Sikuquanshu* Vol. 808 四库全书 (Shanghai: Shanghai Chinese Classics Publishing House, 1987), 15.

16 Wang, Zilin 王子林. *Zi jin cheng fengshui* 紫禁城风水 (Beijing: Forbidden City Press, 2005), 26.

17 Zhou, Zhaonan 周召南. "Kangxi wu shen xiufu yuelu shuyuan shu yin" 康熙戊申修复岳麓书院疏引. In *Zhongguo lidai shuyuan zhi* Vol. 4 中国历代书院志 (Nanjing: Jiangsu Education Publishing House, 1995), 380.

18 Zhang, Shi 张栻. "Da zhuyuanhui mishu" 答朱元晦秘书. In *Zhangshi quanji* Vol. 21 张栻全集·南轩集卷二十一 (Changchun: Changchun Publishing House, 1999), 852.

19 Wu, Daoheng 吴道行. "Xu: jiangjie" 续·疆界. In *Chongxiu yuelu shuyuan tu zhi* Vol. 3 重修岳麓书院图志卷三 (Changsha: Yuelu Press, 2012), 47.

20 Ding, Shanqing 丁善庆. "Yuelu lai mai xian jin kai zao le shi" 岳麓来脉宪禁开凿勒石. In *Zhongguo lidai shuyuan zhi* Vol. 4 中国历代书院志 (Nanjing: Jiangsu Education Publishing House, 1995), 439.

21 Zhou, Yulin 周玉麒. "Jnzhi si kan si zang shi" 禁止私砍私葬示. In *Yuelu xu zhi bupian* 岳麓续志补编 (Changsha: Yuelu Press, 2012), 709.

22 Wu, Daoheng 吴道行. "Xing fu shuyuan zha fu" 兴复书院札付. In *Chongxiu yuelu shuyuan tuzhi* Vol. 6 重修岳麓书院图志卷六 (Changsha: Yuelu Press, 2012), 74.

23 Wang, Wenqing 王文清. "Yulu shuyuan si gongde zhengji lue" 岳麓书院四公德政纪略. In *Hunan wen zheng* 湖南文征·国朝, ed. Ruhuai Luo 罗汝怀 (Changsha: Yuelu Press, 2008), 2074.

24 Wang, Wenqing 王文清. "Yulu shuyuan si gongde zhengji lue" 岳麓书院四公德政纪略. In *Hunan wen zheng* 湖南文征·国朝, ed. Ruhuai Luo罗汝怀 (Changsha: Yuelu Press, 2008), 2074.

25 Wang, Wenqing 王文清. "Yulu shuyuan si gongde zhengji lue" 岳麓书院四公德政纪略. In *Hunan wen zheng* 湖南文征·国朝, ed. Ruhuai Luo 罗汝怀 (Changsha: Yuelu Press, 2008), 1674.

26 See Li, Yanghua李扬华. "Shiji" 事迹. In *Zhongguo lidai shuyuan zhi* Vol. 4 中国历代书院志 (Nanjing: Jiangsu Education Publishing House, 1995), 101–102.

27 Zhang, Shi张栻. "Tanzhou chongxiu yuelu shuyuan ji" 潭州重修岳麓书院记. In *Zhangshi quanji nanxuan ji* Vol. 10张栻全集·南轩集卷十 (Changchun: Changchun Publishing House, 1999), 693.

28 Zhu, Xi 朱熹. "Xinzhou zhou xue da cheng dian ji" 信州州学大成殿记. In *Zhuzi quanshu*朱子全书 (Shanghai: Shanghai Chinese Classics Publishing House, Hefei: Anhui Education Press, 2002), 3806.

29 Zhu, Xi朱熹. "Jiangzhou chongjian lianxi xiansheng shutang ji" 江州重建濂溪先生书堂记. In *Zhuzi quanshu*朱子全书 (Shanghai: Shanghai Chinese Classics Publishing House & Hefei: Anhui Education Press, 2002), 3740.

30 Zhu, Xi朱熹. "Cangzhou jingshe gao xian sheng wen" 沧州精舍告先圣文. In *Zhuzi quanshu*朱子全书 (Shanghai: Shanghai Chinese Classics Publishing House & Hefei: Anhui Education Press, 2002), 4050.

194   *Rites and Customs in Academies*

31 Wang, Bai王柏. "Shang cai shuyuan jiangyi" 上蔡书院讲义. In *Congshu jicheng* 丛书集成 (Beijing: The Commercial Press, 1936), 171.

32 Xiong, He熊禾. "Jianyang shu fang tong wen shuyuan shu" 建阳书坊同文书院疏. In *Siku quan shu* Vol. 1188四库全书第1188册 (Shanghai: Shanghai Chinese Classics Publishing House, 1987), 800.

33 Liu, Zai刘宰. "Pingjiang fu huqiu shan shuyuan ji" 平江府虎丘山书院记. In *Siku quan shu* Vol. 1170四库全书第1170册 (Shanghai: Shanghai Chinese Classics Publishing House, 1987), 612.

34 Gao, Side 高斯得. "Baoqingfu lianxi shutang ji" 宝庆府濂溪书堂记. In *Siku quan shu* Vol. 1182四库全书第1182册 (Shanghai: Shanghai Chinese Classics Publishing House, 1987), 53.

35 Gao, Side 高斯得. "Baoqingfu lianxi shutang ji" 宝庆府濂溪书堂记. In *Siku quan shu* Vol. 1182四库全书第1182册 (Shanghai: Shanghai Chinese Classics Publishing House, 1987), 54.

36 Xu, Zi徐梓. *Yuandai shuyuan yanjiu*元代书院研究 (Beijing: Social Sciences Academic Press, 2000), 158–159.

37 Wang, Yun王恽. "Raozhou lu chuangjian shuyuan shu" 饶州路创建书院疏. In *Siku quan shu* Vol. 1201四库全书第1201册 (Shanghai: Shanghai Chinese Classics Publishing House, 1987), 63.

38 Wang, Jinzheng汪晋征. "Huan gu shuyuan si zhu wengong yi" 还古书院祀朱文公议. In *Zhongguo fangzhi congshu*中国方志丛书 (Taibei: Cheng Wen Publishing 1985), 1299.

39 Dong, Guifu 董桂敷. "Dao tong" 道统. In *Zhongguo Lidai shuyuan zhi* Vol. 3中国历代书院志第 3 册 (Nanjing: Jiangsu Education Publishing House, 1995), 479–482.

40 Dong, Guifu 董桂敷. "Chuan jiwen" 春祭文. In *Zhongguo Lidai shuyuan zhi* Vol. 3中国历代书院志第 3 册 (Nanjing: Jiangsu Education Publishing House, 1995), 529–530.

41 Shi, Huang施璜. "Si dian" 祀典. In *Zhongguo Lidai shuyuan zhi* Vol. 8中国历代书院志第 8 册 (Nanjing: Jiangsu Education Publishing House, 1995), 559.

42 See Chen, Gujia陈谷嘉, and Deng, Hongbo邓洪波. "*Zhongguo shuyuan zhidu yanjiu*" 中国书院制度研究 (Hangzhou: Zhejiang Education Publishing House, 1997), 585–594.

43 Zhang, Shunmin张舜民. "Chen xing lu" 郴行录. In *Siku quan shu* Vol. 1117四库全书第1117册 (Shanghai: Shanghai Chinese Classics Publishing House, 1987), 52.

44 Wang, Yinglin王应麟. "Song chao sishu yuan" 宋朝四书院. In *Siku quan shu* Vol. 947四库全书第947册 (Shanghai: Shanghai Chinese Classics Publishing House, 1987), 353.

45 Zhu, Xi 朱熹. "Liu xiansheng huaxiang zan" 六先生画像赞. In *Zhuzi quanshu*朱子全书 (Shanghai: Shanghai Chinese Classics Publishing House, Hefei: Anhui Education Press, 2002), 4001–4003.

46 Liu, Yi刘绎. "Jian zhi" 建置. In *Zhongguo Lidai shuyuan zhi* Vol. 2中国历代书院志第 2 册 (Nanjing: Jiangsu Education Publishing House, 1995), 568.

47 Ding, Shanqing丁善庆. "Miao si" 庙祀. In *Zhongguo Lidai shuyuan zhi* Vol. 4中国历代书院志 (Nanjing: Jiangsu Education Publishing House, 1995), 414.

48 Zhang Tingyu 张廷玉et al. *Ming shi* Vol. 283明史卷二百八十三 (Beijing: Zhonghua Book Company, 1974), 7267.

49 Huang, Wenzhong黄文仲. "Shun chang shuang feng shuyuan Xin jian si xian tang ji" 顺昌双峰书院新建四贤堂记. In *Quan yuanwen* Vol. 46全元文第46册 (Nanjing: Jiangsu Chinese Classics Publishing House, 1999), 144.

50 Meng, Yan孟彦. *Shou jie Wenchang wenhua yan tao hui zong shu* 首届文昌文化研讨会综述 (Chengdu: Journal of Chinese Culture, 1996), 50–51.

51 Ding, Gang丁钢, and Liu, Qi刘琪. *Shuyuan yu Chinese culture*书院与中国文化 (Shanghai: Shanghai Education Publishing House, 1992), 41–42.

Rites and Customs in Academies 195

52 Yao, Mian 姚勉. "Xijian shuyuan ji kuixing zhu wen" 西涧书院祭魁星祝文. In *Siku quan shu* Vol. 1184四库全书第1184册 (Shanghai: Shanghai Chinese Classics Publishing House, 1987), 329.

53 Zhao, Yuhong 赵与鸿. "Yuzhang shuyuan wen chang ge ji" 豫章书院文昌阁记. In *Nanchang yi cheng wen zheng* Vol. 18南昌邑乘文征卷十八, 1935, 15.

54 Kang, Changkai 唐昌恺. "Bu xiu feng shan shuyuan wen chang ge bei ji" 补修凤山书院文昌阁碑记. In *zhongguo shuyuan shi ziliao* 中国书院史资料, eds. Chen Gujia 陈谷嘉 and Deng Hongbo 邓洪波 (Hangzhou: Zhejiang Education Publishing House, 1998), 1739–1740.

55 Ding, Shanqing 丁善庆. "Miao si" 庙祀. In *Zhongguo lidai shuyuan zhi* Vol. 4中国历代书院志四 (Nanjing: Jiangsu Education Publishing House, 1995), 414.

56 Ding, Shanqing 丁善庆. "Xin zeng ding si gong fei ji" 新增丁祭公费记. In *Zhongguo lidai shuyuan zhi* Vol. 4中国历代书院志四 (Jiangsu: Jiangsu Education Publishing House, 1995), 489.

57 Ding, Shanqing 丁善庆. "Wen chang tian qi" 文昌田契. In *Zhongguo lidai shuyuan zhi* Vol. 4中国历代书院志四 (Jiangsu: Jiangsu Education Publishing House, 1995), 426–427.

58 Ding, Shanqing 丁善庆. "Gong rang si dian cheng ci" 公襄祀典呈词. In *Zhongguo lidai shuyuan zhi* Vol. 4中国历代书院志四 (Jiangsu: Jiangsu Education Publishing House, 1995), 424.

59 Wang, Kaitai 王凯泰. "Ying yuan shuyuan zhi lue zhang cheng" 应元书院志略章程. In *Zhongguo lidai shuyuan zhi* Vol. 3中国历代书院志三 (Nanjing: Jiangsu Education Publishing House, 1995), 271.

60 Zhou, Zaizhi 周在炽. "Li wen" 礼文. In *Zhongguo lidai shuyuan zhi* Vol. 4中国历代书院志四 (Nanjing: Jiangsu Education Publishing House, 1995), 576–577.

61 Zhang, Sijiong 张思炯. "Li wen" 礼文. In *Zhongguo lidai shuyuan zhi* Vol. 4中国历代书院志四 (Nanjing: Jiangsu Education Publishing House, 1995), 637.

62 Zhang, Sijiong 张思炯. "Li wen" 礼文. In *Zhongguo lidai shuyuan zhi* Vol. 4中国历代书院志四 (Nanjing: Jiangsu Education Publishing House, 1995), 638.

63 Zhang, Sijiong 张思炯. "Li wen" 礼文. In *Zhongguo lidai shuyuan zhi* Vol. 4中国历代书院志四 (Nanjing: Jiangsu Education Publishing House, 1995), 637.

64 Ren, Sizheng 任思正. "Yi jian sheng xiang lou ji" 移建圣像楼记. In *zhongguo shuyuan shi ziliao* 中国书院史资料, eds. Chen Gujia 陈谷嘉 and Deng Hongbo邓洪波 (Hangzhou: Zhejiang Education Publishing House, 1998), 1743–1744.

65 Dai, Junheng 戴钧衡. "Si xiang xian" 祀乡贤. In *zhongguo shuyuan shi ziliao* 中国书院史资料, eds. Chen Gujia 陈谷嘉 and Deng Hongbo邓洪波 (Hangzhou: Zhejiang Education Publishing House, 1998), 1724–1726.

66 Zhong, Ying 钟英. "Chong xiu yueyang shuyuan ji" 重修岳阳书院记. In *Zhongguo lidai shuyuan zhi* Vol. 5中国历代书院志五 (Nanjing: Jiangsu Education Publishing House, 1995), 81.

Appendix 2
Rites and Conduct in Academies

Rites were significant in traditional Chinese culture. In both foreign affairs and people's daily life, there were rules regulating proper manners, which were indications of the spiritual pursuit of appropriate behaviors and conduct. Many Confucian classics written prior to the Qin dynasty talk about appropriate manners and specifications on rites, appearance, utensils, and behaviors. Nonetheless, research on the visual aspect of rites received comparatively less attention than the overall rites system and values on spirituality. As the most important media of traditional Chinese culture and thoughts, academies had attached great importance to the manner of appearances, which was regarded as a key part of improving a person's overall temperament and cultivation of the mind. Thus, academies subsequently issued and demanded students to continuously practice and behave in appropriate manners as a way to develop high morals and noble character. An attempt here is made to discuss traditional manners of appearances from the perspective of so-called chengren zhidao (cultivation and development of an individual's characters) in Confucian notions.

Origin of Ritual Conduct

According to *Doctrine of the Mean*, "there were 300 general manners and 3,000 specific manners."[1] As was mentioned by Qiu Xigui, "when it came to weiyi (expression of solemnness and nobleness), people were actually talking about how their appearances looked like."[2] *Commentary on Rites* (礼记正义)[3] explains why there were 3,000 specific items: "As for the number 3,000, what it is referred to were 3,000 different specific manners in five main fields, which were good luck, evil omen, military, guest, and wedding, as categorized in *The Offices of the Zhou* (周官)."[4] Therefore, the complexity of ancient manners could be thus seen, which included not only detailed regulations on appearances as a whole but also specific requirements on looks and expressions. Manners regarding appearances can be traced back to ages ago. In the chapter "History of Shang Dynasty" in *Records of the [Grand] Scribe* (史记·殷本纪), it is recorded that having achieved victories, the emperor would "ask officials in charge of instruments and music to play to manifest his achievements." The index of *Records of the [Grand] Scribe* (史记索引), in citing Zhang Xuan, comments, "Officials in charge of music knew how to behave appropriately, so the rites department became the department in

DOI: 10.4324/9781003332305-5

Rites and Conduct in Academies 197

charge of manners."[5] Based on these historical documents, Qiu Xigui proposed that "official positions in charge of rites exclusively had been set in the Shang dynasty."[6] As for specific contents of manners, it is detailed in the chapter "Terrestrial Offices" in *Rites of Zhou* (周礼·地官):[7]

> Particular methods must be adopted in order to cultivate offspring from families with high standings in society . . . so they were taught in total six different manners. The first one was concerned with how they should behave when worshiping or sacrificing. The second one was about how to hospitably receive guests. The third one was about when being called upon by the emperor. The fourth one was concerned about how to behave at a funeral. The fifth one was about army manners. And the last one was on how to behave when going out with friends to have fun.[8]

Because of such details regarding manners, there were officials appointed exclusively in charge of regulations on manners based on different occasions and circumstances. The chapter "Autumn Offices" in *Rites of Zhou* (周礼·秋官)[9] says, "Siyi (the officials in charge of regulating and standardizing how to behave when treating guests) were appointed and were in charge of rites on how to receive and treat national guests and how to behave, speak, and bow."[10]

Confucius was known to always have good manners ever since he was a child, and he was quite knowledgeable about manners. In the chapter "Confucius and His Families" in *Records of the [Grand] Scribe* (史记·孔子世家), it is recorded that when "Confucius was a little kid, occasionally he would set and play with utensils or objects used for sacrifice as a game, acting in accordance with appropriate manners."[11] *The Analects of Confucius* were written recordings of conversations between Confucius and his disciples, as well as how they acted while talking. Specifically, the chapter "In the Village" (乡党) details the manners of Confucius, including his appearance, behaviors, ways of speaking, outfits, and eating manners. From these, it could be seen that in order to have extrinsic appearance and intrinsic temperament coincide, Confucius always behaved differently in different scenarios and occasions. For example,

> Confucius seemed to be very obedient and not talkative. However, when he was in the temples and royal courts, he was well versed but still in a cautious way. When Confucius entered the door, he would bend over like a shrimp. If he stood, he never stood in the way. If he walked, he would keep away from stepping on the door sill. If he passed the emperor, he would wear a solemn and serious face, attentive on each step, and speak in a way that was so careful and slow as if he was sick and weak. If he was called upon to see the emperor, he would carefully gather up his robe before stepping on the steps and bend down, holding his breath. When he was permitted to retreat, on every step he backed off, his face was getting less solemn and less serious. He retreated so fast that he was like a bird. Even back settling in his seat, he was still submissive and obedient.

198 *Rites and Conduct in Academies*

In addition, it is also recorded, "When in fasting, specific bathrobe was exclusively used. As for eating and sleeping, during this period of time, Confucius would always turn down his normal diet and resting place."[12] Therefore, it could be seen that the manners of Confucius changed in accordance with different times, locations, and people, proving his emphasis and seriousness regarding appropriate manners.

Confucius' emphasis on manners also set the tone and explained why Confucian scholars put so much attention and focus on manners. Consequently, such a subject was mentioned and talked about in many Confucian classics. For example, in the chapter "Dresses and Caps Worn by Rulers" in *The Rites* (礼记·玉藻), it is written that "when offspring of aristocratic families grew up, they shall dress appropriately suitable for grand occasions such as royal courts. In addition, they must learn appropriate manners on how to behave before they were allowed to take up official positions. For example, the sound of jade pendants they wore as accessories must match their steps."[13] Thus, individuals' must always follow the rites' rules. Other rites' rules, such as how to walk, how to behave, and how to express oneself, are also detailed in "Dresses and Caps Worn by Rulers" in *The Rites*, which strongly shows the emphasis put by Confucianism on manners.

The Han dynasty witnessed constant advancements in manners, which evolved into a special knowledge. Some scholars were appointed official positions for their excellence and achievement in the study of manners. An exclusive system for such officials in charge of rites was set up from the central to local government. The chapter "Biographies of Confucian Scholars" in *The Book of Han* (汉书·儒林传) says that

> after the Han dynasty was founded, Xu Sheng from the state of Lu was the living example of these manners, and because of his good manners, Xu Sheng was appointed as an official exclusively in charge of rites during the reign of Emperor Xiao Wen. Xu Sheng then passed on his official position to his son Xu Yan and his grandson Xu Xiang. Xu Xiang was known for his talent in understanding and practicing the manners of worshiping and sacrificing. But Xu Xiang was not very knowledgeable in Confucian classics as his father, Xu Yan, who was quite well-versed in classics, though not a master yet. Xu Xiang was also awarded an official position in charge of rites and manners and was promoted to take charge of affairs of Guangling City. In addition, Xu Yan, Xu Manyi, Xu Hengsheng, and Xu Danci, who were from the family of Xu, were all awarded official positions in charge of rites and manners. The same went with Xiao Fen from Xiaqiu, who became the prefecture chief of Huaiyang due to his mastery of *The Rites*. Generally, when speaking of *song* (referring to rites and manners) at that time, people would think of the Xu family.[14]

Yan Shigo comments, "By *song*, generally it meant 'appearance manners' under this circumstance." In addition, Yan also cites, "It is mentioned in the *Ancient Rules of the (Former) Han* (汉旧仪)[15] as well, which records that two officials, last names being Xu and Zhang, were awarded official positions because of their good manners. They were not knowledgeable in classic books, but they behaved with such perfect manners that they were followed and imitated by people sent by states.[16] Thus, although Xu Sheng, Xu Xiang, and other family members of Xu were not masters of classics, they realized their political achievements thanks to their good manners. According to Su Lin, at that period of time, rongshi (容史; officials in charge of rites and manners) were sent by sovereigns of different vassal states to state Lu to study rites and manners, with a particular focus put on appropriate manners for worshiping and sacrificing. Hong Ye divided rites and manners in the early Han dynasty into three main categories:

> There were three sources of rites and manners. The first one was rules and regulations issued by the government since the foundation of the country, which was made by Shu Sun through the collection and systemization of ancient rites and rites of Qin. The second source came from manners of worshiping and sacrificing by the people of the state of Lu, which should be credited to the Xu family. It also included manners that were already lost when Confucius was still alive, which had become even reduced because of the book burnings of Qin. As for the very last source, it is the manners set in *Rites of the Lower Nobility* (士礼), mastered by Gao Tangsheng, that Xu Xiang and Xu Yan studied but not yet mastered.[17]

In other words, when it came to manners of the Han dynasty, it included "manners used in royal courts, which were pieced and integrated together by Shu Suntong, taking into consideration the ancient rites and manners of Qin," "manners used for ritual sacrifice by people of the Lu state," and manners talked about in *Rites of the Lower Nobility*, annotated and explained by Gao Taosheng. Thus, manners, with a particular focus on the overall appearance and outlook of an individual, became an indispensable part of rites. It is the opinion of Prof. Peng Lin that the reason people of Han gave such great importance to manners was *The Rites* lacked specific descriptions of appropriate manners used in worshiping and sacrificing occasions. If there was no example for people of later generations to imitate and study, and if ways of speaking and expressions were wanting, then such manners are not appropriate.[18] Manners got further refined in the Han dynasty. In "Appearance Manners" in *The New Book*, written by Jia Yi in the early Han, Jia divided manners into standing manners, sitting manners, walking manners, kneeling manners, bowing banners, kowtowing manners, manners for sitting in the carriages, manners for standing in the carriages, manners for military carriages, and so on—basically, every aspect of one's daily life.[19] In addition, a pursuit of the perfection of manners was carried on throughout the Han dynasty. Liu Xiang once made a formal request to Emperor Cheng in which he stated that "colleges and schools should be set up and ceremonies should be held. In this way, the music of courts and sacrifices could be promoted, and so could manners and ways of behavior."[20] Thus, it could be seen that manners were put together and treated the same as schools and music, strongly testifying great attention given by Confucian scholars in the Han dynasty.

200 *Rites and Conduct in Academies*

The pursuit of proper manners was inherited by the Confucian scholars after the Han dynasty, becoming their daily practice. In one poem collected in *Yonghua shi* (咏怀诗), Ruan Ji expresses his disagreement with such circumstances:

> those knowledgeable scholars were dressed properly in accordance with relative rules governing how they should wear. They strictly stick to regulations and ways of behavior. When they were in royal courts, they were in solemn faces, which I couldn't stand to see.[21]

As one of the Seven Intellectuals of Bamboo Forest (竹林七贤),[22] Ruan Ji aspired for personality (自然)[23] instead of education (教化).[24] Thus, it could be seen from this poem that Ruan opposed strict compliance with manners and rites in daily life at that time. According to *Principles of Yan Familial Instructions* (颜氏家训), in "Character and Conduct" (风操) of scholars, he states in the very beginning, "In *The Rites*, Confucius set forth examples on how to sweep the floor, how to use spoons and chopsticks, how to reply, and how to help seniors wash hands and faces."[25] Yan also agreed that there should be appropriate manners followed in daily life. Neo-Confucianist of the Song dynasty paid a higher degree of attention to manners, which were viewed as a vital means to cultivate the temperaments of Confucian scholars and to improve the social climate. Lü Xizhe set ways of talking, appearance, and behaviors as first priorities:

> The very first thing to study should be ways of behavior and manners as a whole. If an individual behaves in a proper way, it is an indication that he can handle things well. So what on earth are good manners? They are manifested through ways of talking, expression, appearance, and ways of dealing with different things.[26]

This comment was echoed by Zhu Xi, who stressed that graceful manners were "keys of cultivation to handle matters."[27] Consequently, the study of manners had been placed by many Song scholars in their teaching syllabus. To name just a few, there were *Study Handbook of Zhen Dexiu* (西山真先生教子斋规)[28] and *The Chronological Process of Learning* (程氏家塾读书分年日程),[29] which had all touched upon the study of manners.

Learning Rites in the Academy

Under the influence of Neo-Confucianism, academies in ancient China had attached great importance to the study of manners. When talking about the school mission of Yuelu Academy, Zhang Shi argues, "Academies are not places to gather students and teach them how to pass exams and achieve gains and honors. In addition, the mere study of essays and phraseologies is not enough."[30] Hence, the mission of academies, which should be to cultivate students and scholars, lay not only in the imparting of classics and knowledge but also in the nourishment of

Just like Zhang Sijiong said to students of Yutan Academy,

> what Confucian saints and intellectuals elaborated on was how to behave and act properly, not just mere obtainments of honors and benefits . . . in addition, academies were schools to cultivate students. In other words, if students could behave appropriately, not in a vulgar or rude way, then even if they were short of intellectual talents and fell behind in academic study, they were still outstanding among the ordinary and general public.[31]

Given this kind of notion, almost all academies set forth detailed rules on proper ways of talking, wearing clothes, and acting.

Proper Ways of Wording

Wording was an essential concept in Confucianism, which not only covered words themselves but also touched upon how to convey the words, such as expressions and overall appearance. Confucius put great emphasis on wording, which was juxtaposed together with fate and politeness. Confucius says,

> To become a person of good morals and noble character, one must understand the true meaning of fate; to handle things and matters skillfully, one must be of full politeness; to truly know a person, one must be able to pick up the undertones.

As was explained by Zhu Xi, "words speak of one's morals and virtues."[32] Confucius believed that wording was closely related to one's virtues and morals: "One who has a sweet tongue and always curries favors with others is likely not to be a noble person."[33] In addition, "A person with high morals is always careful about his words."[34] Thus, here it could be seen that Confucius drew a line between words and morals and highly valued a careful selection of words that would make a person noble. In addition, Confucius also fixed many specific requirements on wording: "One should stick to his promise made to friends." "It is better to act than to talk." "It is good qualities to listen more and to solicit opinions more. When in doubt, hold the tongue; whereas no doubt, one should also be mindful of his words. Thus, fewer and fewer mistakes would arise." "People with high morals prefer to act than to speak." "No talking while eating, and no talking prior to sleeping."

These suggestions on wording put forward by Confucius were carried on by academies and applied to daily education practice. For example, when teaching students how to talk appropriately, exercise on tone was given priority, which required a slow and steady pace. Cheng Duanli, in *The Chronological Process of Learning* (程氏家塾读书分年日程), points out that "when speaking, individuals should pay attention to the volume, which should not be too loud."[35] Cheng's suggestions were echoed and adopted by many academies and schools later on.

202 *Rites and Conduct in Academies*

While lecturing at Yingshan Academy, Fang Shimin advised students "to hold back the tongue when in anger."[36] Liang Tingnan requested students in Yuexiu Academy to "be careful when making a promise, which should be fulfilled once made, and be serious when talking, thus no flirting, deceiving, or being noisy and joking around."[37] Liang Dingfen demanded students in Duanxi Academy to speak in a soft and steady way,[38] which was beneficial in building up harmonious peer relationships. Li Laizhang valued friendship highly in that

> friendship was one of the five most important relationships in the world. Given its importance, when hanging out with friends, one should be honest and be respectful to each other. Only in this way could mutual inspection and mutual advancement be achieved.[39]

If when discussing and exchanging views on the study, students could not keep a calm mind, then questions would arise as to whether they could benefit from debating or not, which was echoed by Li Wenzhao, who believed that "arguments and quarrels only backfired mutual advancement among students."[40]

As for the content of words, it is the proposition of Confucius that individuals must understand that some can be said and some should be withheld. In *The Analects of Confucius*, it is recorded that "when reading the *Book of Songs* and the *Book of Documents*, as well as administering official affairs, Confucius would only speak Yayan (the official language of Zhou Dynasty)." Additionally, "Confucius avoided talking about benefits or gains but was willing to discuss virtue and destiny." Also, "Confucius never commented on the supernatural, mana, rebellion, or ghosts." Scholars of academies in the later generations inherited these thoughts and discouraged improper discussions. For example, Zheng Zhiqiao admonished students of Ehu Academy that "improper words would bring only more serious disasters than sword-sawing."[41] Zhu Yishen also told students of Ningxiu Academy, "People are more prone to rashly utter inappropriate words, such as insult and threats, which they would feel ashamed about throughout their lives. Hence, please remember that out of the mouth comes evil."[42] Bian Lianbao fiercely criticized that "there were even jokes and improper talking ways of butchers, small businessmen, and townsfolk uttered in the academy."[43] He pointed out that students should be mindful of their words and be cautious about their behaviors, with no judging and no speaking on untenable hearsays. For example, Cheng Duanli explicitly contended that "individuals should just speak as it is and shall not exaggerate or deceive."[44] In "Ten Commandments of the Cave" (洞学十戒), Gao Benheng of the Ming dynasty reminds students not to "exaggerate or make unfulfilled promises."[45] Li Yu, in "Rules and Regulations of Guanzhong Academy" (关中书院学程), emphasizes that there shall be "no talking on personal matters, no sharing on marital matters, no judging on officials or other people, and no commenting on state affairs or hearsays."[46] In "Rules and Regulations of Yuelu Academy" (岳麓书院学规), Wang Wenqing warns students not to "attack the shortcomings but ignore the advantages of others."[47] Peiying Academy proposed that students should not "utter the extreme, the obscene, or the absurd."[48]

As was emphasized by Yuexiu Academy, "don't judge people casually and don't utter vulgar and improper words."[49] In addition, in connecting words with the social climate,

> Individuals who are too arrogant to restrain their own behaviors or who are prone to judge people with mean words or who intend to comment on public and state affairs with no bounds shall not become pillars of support for the country. Rather, they only bring disgrace to the academy and exert a bad influence on social climates.[50]

Proper Ways of Dressing

The Analects of Confucius states,

> There are three things a person with high morals and noble character should pay particular attention on. They should wear solemn faces, thus restrained and formal, they should zhengyanse (have a serious expression) to make them look credible, and they should be mindful of their words and tones to avoid vulgar and falsity.

Here, by zhengyanse, what it meant was attention put on expressions and appearances. Just as Zhang Shi said that "a serious and proper expression on one's face speaks of honesty."[51] And Chen Xiangdao agrees, "when an individual wears a respectful face, he is not rude or bold; when he is honest, then his face not deceitful or flattering; when he is speaking in a soft way, then he is not vulgar or improper."[52] Hence, expression is closely related to one's intrinsic quality, which embodies virtues and emotional feelings. Thus, people cannot be more serious about appearances and expressions. It is suggested that if students want to become people of high morals and noble character, they should wear "soft" expressions. *The Analects of Confucius* states, "A person with high morals must take nine things seriously ... whether their faces are soft and mild, and whether their expressions are modest and respectful." Song Xingbing explains that "it is essential to wear a soft and mild expression on the face."[53] Most academies in later generations also requested students to "be solemn and serious" and "not to express anger, laziness, or neglectfulness."[54] For example, it is the rule of Yuexiu Academy that students "must be serious and solemn, restraining themselves from being vulgar or aggressive. In addition, they should learn how to control emotions, such as not venting out on a whim."[55] Gao Benheng, in "Ten Commandments of the Cave," points out that in daily life, students should be wary "not to fake their expressions and faces to obtain gains or benefits." Dou Keqin, from the perspective of interpersonal relationships, proposed that "a serious and solemn expression makes a firm and adamant person"; thus, "it is vital to learn how to speak and act in a solemn way." Lü Zuqian suggested that expressions and faces should change in accordance with different circumstances, as indicated in the rules he set for Lize Academy: "when lecturing in the seminars, lecturers should be speaking in a serious and solemn manner; while staying with students, they should be gentle and mild."[56]

The chapter "In the Village" in *The Analects of Confucius* set forth in detail how particular and even picky Confucius was on manners, such as matching the color and style of clothes and accessories with dates and occasions. Although most Confucian scholars did not devote particular care to luxury and style, they did stress appropriateness. *The Rites by Dai the Elder* (大戴礼记) states,[57]

> Confucius told Li that if he wanted to become a person with acclaiming morals, he must learn how to behave appropriately, which included a proper dressing style. Without proper attire, he would appear vulgar and crude. If he's viewed as vulgar and crude, he was disrespectful and rude, which would hinder him from making any progress in this world.[58]

Therefore, it is the belief of Confucius that when interacting and talking with people, one should be mindful of one's appearance, including how one should dress. Proper attire showed respect to others and to oneself. Consequently, there were many rules that could be found in academies about how students should dress. Generally, students were required to dress plainly and simply, not too flamboyantly or magnificently. Li Yu, when in Guanzhong Academy, emphasized, "One must act and take heed in dealing with any matter, living a hardworking and simple life." In addition, "There is no need to wear glamorous or flamboyant outfits."[59] Wang Wenqing also required students of Yuelu Academy to "live a simple and plain life."[60] In addition, they must be attentive to cleanness and tidiness and not wear weird or inappropriate outfits. Yuexiu Academy had a rule in the entry "Tidy and Clean Dressing":

> Students shall not wear weird or improper outfits. Nor shall they live a luxurious life. In addition, they must be attentive to cleanliness and tidiness. Even if they are alone at home, they must dress themselves appropriately, which means they shall always have socks on even in the hottest summer.[61]

In drafting "Rules and Regulations of Duanxi Academy" (端溪书院生徒住院章程), Liang Dingfen emphasized something similarly: "students shall not dress in improper outfits, nor shall they be allowed to have their feet bare when getting together."[62] Chen Shouqi, in "General Affairs of Aofeng Academy" (拟定鳌峰书院事宜), states that "students must regularly tidy their dresses." In addition,

> they shall not huddle together before class begins. Rather, they should tidy their dresses and wait to sign in in order . . . when signing in, they must wear properly with their hats on and wait in line instead of pushing ahead against each other.[63]

Huang Shubing asked students of Mingdao Academy to "regularly check attires, hats, belts, and shoes to make sure they are dressed in a proper way."[64]

Rites and Conduct in Academies 205

Li Liangzhang held the belief that if an individual dressed untidily or inappropriately, then he was no different from uneducated townsfolk. What's worse, improper clothing would be detrimental to his cultivation of mind and virtues. He admonishes in "Lianshan Academy" (连山书院榜文) that

> nowadays, there are some students who are rather loose. When idling away, they don't dress properly. Rather, their heads and feet are completely bare. They joke around with each other, thinking they are funny or humorous. I view these behaviors as no different from those of townsfolk, such as small businessmen and matchmakers. Hence, not only do they appear improperly extrinsically, they are uninhibited and unrestrained inside.[65]

Proper Ways of Behaving

Apart from having rules regarding words and clothing, discussed earlier, ancient academies also made rules governing the daily activities of students, such as when to get up and rest and how to sit, stand, walk, see, and listen. As a whole, students in academies must strictly follow daily schedules and behave in a way as required.

Generally speaking, there was usually a mica plate in each academy that would be beaten and stricken to remind students to get up, study, or rest. For example, as was ruled by Yuexiu Academy,

> there was a mica plate placed in front of the study hall. When the sun came out in the early morning of the first and fifteenth days of each lunar month, servants would beat and strike the plate. The first strike reminded students to get up and get dressed. The second strike was the time students should have themselves seated, ready to study and read. When it is time to study the explanations on classics or essay-writing techniques, students would go to the platform of the hall, bowing three times before putting forward their questions. At night, students would be dismissed and allowed to rest until another strike on the mica plate, which was also a reminder for students who wanted to keep studying at night.[66]

As a matter of fact, apart from the first and fifteenth days, the other days of the month went just the same as this. Duanxi Academy required students "to get up at the dim light of dawn and to rest at the second strike at night drum, thus fixing and sticking to a regular timetable which gave students plenty of time to study."[67]

In addition, there were detailed and particular rules governing how to worship, pay respect to superintendents, salute teachers, and communicate with their peers. For example,

> in the first and fifteenth days of each lunar month, when students were living in academies, they would get up at the first rays of the morning sun, dress, and wait in line following the teacher to pay their respect to Zhu Xi. Normally, they burned incenses, kneeled thrice, and kowtowed six times.

Then the teacher would face southwest and students northeast, bowing to each other respectfully. After the sacrificial ceremony, everyone was allowed to enter the study hall, with students sitting on the east and west sides, facing each other, bowing. Then, students were allowed to get dismissed and went back to their dorms. On important days, such as Chinese New Year and Chinese New Year's Eve, students would dress up and pay their respect to teachers, with teachers bowing them back. Then students bowed to each other. When students on leave came back, they should go to see teachers and let them be notified about their whereabouts as a way of paying respect. Afterward, students went to greet their peers, with everyone bowing to each other. When the tutoring day came, students lined up in front of teachers, bowing before putting forward their questions. They should not sit down until the teacher was seated. When the discussion was over, they again bowed and retreated. Whenever students in academies came across their teachers, they must stop walking, waiting for the teachers to pass by first. And when they met their peers, they bowed at each other. If a student joined a group, all group members must stand up to welcome and greet the newcomer. The same went with when someone was leaving, and everyone would be seeing him off. When sitting together, students should sit in the order of age.[68]

The Learning Principles of Cheng Duanmeng 程端蒙 *and Dong Zhu* 董铢 (程董二先生学则) was acclaimed by Zhu Xi as "having kept a light-hearted and free spirit"[69] and was widely adopted by most of academies in later generations. For example, Yuexiu Academy borrowed some of these rules when making its own rules in regulating students' manners of walking, sitting, and standing. It was ruled that

students shall have fixed dormitories assigned. While sitting, they must sit by age, with their backs straight and legs retracted. They shall not cross their legs and shake their feet. They shall not be permitted to rest until seniors go to bed, and shall not talk before resting. Neither shall they be permitted to nap during the day. While walking, they must walk slowly, standing behind seniors, and should never stand with their backs against people with higher positions. They shall not step on the sills of the doors nor lean on the doors while standing, and shall not look around nor pry into private matters of others.[70]

In *The Chronological Process of Learning* (程氏家塾读书分年日程), which was issued officially by Directorate of Education of the Yuan dynasty, Cheng Duanli details how to sit, walk, stand, and talk, which exerted great influence on both private schools and academies. For example, some rules had been borrowed by academies such as Jiangdong Academy when formalizing their own rules. The rule stated, "While sitting, students should sit straight with no shaking feet and hands. They shall not lie down or lean around." Also, "While walking, students should walk at a slow and steady pace with hands hidden in their sleeves. They shall not leap forward." Furthermore, "As for standing, students must stand very straight with their hands crossed submissively, and they shall not lean or tilt." Last, "While bowing, students must lower their heads and bend down and shall

Rites and Conduct in Academies   207

never retract their hands until they were finished greeting or saluting. They must take bowing seriously."[71] While drafting "Rules of Guanzhong Academy" (关中书院学程), Li Yu demanded students to "walk at a slow and steady pace and bow in a graceful and appropriate manner. While sitting and standing, students must sit and stand up very straight."[72] The same went with Yuelu Academy, which also required students "to correct inappropriate manners and to behave in a solemn and serious way."[73] When setting up rules for Suanxue Academy, Sun Yi underlined the need that

> students must listen attentively and not cut in rudely. They shall ask questions cautiously and stand and sit up very straight. While walking, they must walk steadily and peacefully, even when striding. Overall, they must calm down and concentrate on studying, avoiding distractions of any kind.[74]

Mingdao Academy required students to

> sit straight and stand still with hands retracted submissively as if they were statutes. While sleeping, students shall not make any noises. They must clear up their minds and build up defensive walls inside their hearts against any distractions. It is okay if they are as mute as fish, as long as they are not gossiping or joking around. In this way, they could gradually achieve self-cultivation.[75]

All these rules and regulations in governing manners of students in academies could be rather trivial and detailed, but there is little doubt that they were acclaimed as embodiments of Confucian values and principles.

Cultural Significance of Ritual Conduct

There were quite a few historical documents recording manners, such as tones, expressions, and behaviors in Confucian classics such as *The Rites of the Zhou*, *The Analects of Confucius*, and *The Etiquette and Rites*. Manners were manifested in self-cultivation, family management, and administration of state affairs, which became the guidance leading to the ultimate accomplishment of Tao. In the Han dynasty, manners were getting more and more attention and focus, adopted by academies when writing rules and regulations. Ancient Chinese academies took the responsibility and mission of cultivating talents and, apart from the transmission of Confucian classics, values, and principles, were also devoted to the refinement of the temperaments and virtues of students. Hence, a demanding requirement on manners of students was as beneficial to students in improving their moralities and characters as to advancing their academic progress. Thus, academies gave great importance to the manners of students and integrated education of manners into daily activities.

One of the main outstanding principles of Confucianism was the unity of mind and body, which focused on the pursuit of coordination between intrinsic virtues

208 *Rites and Conduct in Academies*

and extrinsic behaviors. The principle itself was reasonable in that individual's conscious virtues and value principles were under the unremitting influence of the social environment while the two were interacting with each other. On the one hand, it is proposed that one's face was the index of one's heart. On the other hand, by constantly refining and correcting manners, an individual could make himself conform to the recognized social protocols, thus improving his overall cultivation. *The Rites by Dai the Elder* (大戴礼记) states,

> Generally speaking, people could get to know an individual by simply observing his manners, such as appearance, expressions, and ways of talking. If people speak highly of his manners, then he must be a respectable one. If his manners are criticized, then he is not a good person.[76]

Thus, as the saying went, one's face was the index of one's heart, and manners were manifestations of one's nature. If an individual was kind-hearted, then, in reality, he must be a nice person with an amiable appearance and manners. In addition, besides the influence of the intrinsic mind on extrinsic appearance, Some Confucian scholars also noticed that appropriate manners and behaviors worked in encouraging the advancement of self-cultivation. The chapter "Music" in *The Rites* (礼记·乐记) notes, "Negligence or carelessness of manners, slight as they could be, were indications of a disdain attitude deep inside one's heart."[77] Since inner virtue was decisive of one's outer appearance and manners, and at the same time, one's manners could bring a great influence on self-cultivation, then it could be said an individual achieved the state of perfection only when there was a harmonious relationship found between inner virtues and outer manners. The chapter "The record on example" in *The Rites* (礼记·表记) states that

> a person with high morals and noble character should learn how to dress up and study appropriate manners before pursuing self-cultivation. It follows that if a person doesn't take such things as how to dress up seriously, there shall be no appropriate manners. If a person is ashamed of appropriate manners, he shall never master talking skills. If a person considers talking skills as trivial, he shall never become a person with high morals.[78]

Therefore, it could be said that the intrinsic virtues of a person with high morals and noble character must be compatible with how he appeared, such as his attires, expressions, ways of talking, and behaviors, and the two supplemented each other. The emphasis put on the unity of mind and body by Confucian scholars also indicated the importance of appropriate manners, for only when a person acted properly could he become a respectable person with acclaiming virtues. In the meantime, it testified to a possibility that inner cultivation could be realized through extrinsic polishing of one's behaviors. For example, Kong Yingda said,

> When it comes to virtues, it is more of a spiritual aspect of an individual that finds its manifestation through the extrinsic behaviors of such a person.

Rites and Conduct in Academies 209

That is to say, an individual with high morals and noble virtues shall act and behave appropriately in daily life.[79]

There were quite a few Confucian classics talking about the mutual influence of inner virtues and outer behaviors. For example, the chapter "Exercising government" in *The Analects of Confucius* (论语·为政) says, "Zi Xia consulted Confucius about the notion of filial piety, and Confucius told him, 'to know whether a person truly has filial piety or not, just observe his facial expressions when serving his parents.'" Zhu Xi agreed and said that

> when serving parents, it is difficult for an individual to keep appropriate facial expressions all the time. Hence, to see whether a person has filial piety, the facial expressions of the individual should be taken into consideration apart from running errands or supporting parents with alimony.[80]

Also, the chapter "The meaning of sacrifices" in *The Rites* (礼记·祭义) states that "if an individual truly loves and respects his parents, he must treat his parents' heart and soul with gentleness and mildness, which are manifested by delight and happiness on his face."[81] Therefore, the notion of filial piety is intertwined closely with facial expressions and other manners, which are natural revelations of how an individual thinks of his parents deep inside his heart. In other words, since appearance and manners are outward manifestations of inner temperament, then the study of appropriate manners also helps in cultivating and refining the virtues and morals of an individual. In a word, one's expressions, tones, and behaviors are compatible with inner feelings, thus the expression "an accordance between facial expressions and virtues."[82] Additionally, this mutual influence between the inner and the outer was also emphasized in the ritual study of the Confucian thought system. The chapter "The great suburban sacrifice" in *The Rites* (礼记·郊特牲) states that

> rites focus on a deeper understanding and respect. Mere knowledge of how to worship, such as how to place utensils, is not enough, and such knowledge shall rest in the exclusive charge of worshiping officials. Hence, the rites look simple at first sight but get more difficult when trying to explore the fundamentals.[83]

Therefore, the essentials of the ritual study lie in its invisible justifications, and a mere ability to handle worshiping utensils is far away from true mastery of the rites, the essence of which should be consistency and unification between behaviors and cognition. The chapter "Questions of Zeng Zi" in *The Rites* (礼记·曾子问) states, "For a person with high morals and noble character, he shall behave consistently with how he thinks deep in his mind."[84] Kong Yingda explains that

> when attending wedding or funeral ceremonies, it is very important to coordinate inner feelings with outward behaviors, which, in other words, is to have

210 *Rites and Conduct in Academies*

feelings expressed via appropriate conduct and acts. Thus, one should wear tidy and neat funeral apparel, qicui (齐缞), to indicate he had lost female family members, wear hats with checks to show respect, and wear cucui (粗缞) to express sorrow and grief.[85]

As a consequence, if an individual wants to truly express what he feels deep in his heart, he would need to rely on things in the outer world such as apparel, expressions, and behaviors. In a word, the manifestation of rites in an individual is based on manners and appearance, which in turn rely on how the individual feels in his heart, thus a complete process of rite practice from the external to the internal.

Such integration of inside with outside has found its further advancement in Confucianism of the Song dynasty, particularly on the cultivation of obedience. Mencius asserts that "when studying, there was no other goal other than retrieval of a lost heart." Hence, it is Mencius' view that the fundamental aim of studying was to call back a wandering heart. This view was highly acclaimed by Zhu Xi, who viewed "obtainment of a lost heart" as "the top priority of study."[86] In the meantime, Zhu Xi also recognized the importance of obedience, viewing it as "the first priority of Confucian classics." Zhu states that "obedience is the first priority in Confucian classics, which should be an unstopping and incessant process throughout the time."[87] Of all kinds of cultivation proposed by Zhu Xi, the cultivation of obedience was listed as one of the most important ones. In essence, the cultivation of obedience was the same as the retrieval of a lost heart, as proposed by Mencius. The two views were closely related to each other. Therefore, Zhu Xi, when elaborating and lecturing, always mentioned the two together: "by obedience, it means that an individual shall have a say in places of mind where he dominates." In addition, "obedience indicates a dominance power of an individual, which shall be the beginning of everything." Zhu also added, "to control one's heart, an individual must be obedient in the first place." "If only one could not control his heart and follow the rules, he is disobedient." As for the practice of cultivation of obedience proposed by Zhu Xi, it all came down to the cultivation of the mind, which, in other words, was to learn how to settle and calm down. The cultivation of obedience cannot be accomplished without daily practice. Therefore, Zhu Xi proposed that

> in order to truly master the cultivation of obedience, one must not talk too much. He shall be serious and manifest in a solemn manner, being attentive to his behaviors and facial expressions, and having his thoughts organized at the same time. Meanwhile, he must dress up and tidy his apparel and hats so as to win people's respect.[88]

Thus, it could be seen that what Zhu Xi emphasized was also a process of practice through the extrinsic to the intrinsic so as to accomplish mastery of good manners, cultivation of obedience, and advancement of virtues and morals.

As a consequence, views of manners and appearance prescribed by Confucian scholars, especially those scholars of the Song and Ming dynasties, exerted a deep influence on education in ancient academies. Lots of academies also agreed and acknowledged the good influence of appearance and manners on the retrieval of a lost heart and the cultivation of obedience. During the Qianlong era, Li Lianzhang, who was the county mayor of Lianshan of Guang Dong Province, founded Lianshan Academy as one of his attempts to improve the local cultural climate. Quite often, he would go to the academy and give lectures himself, with the focus being on the cultivation of mind and body. In "Rules of Lianshan Academy" (连山书院榜文), Li admonishes that

> students must dress up and be attentive to their outer appearance. When bowing and saluting, they should follow appropriate manners. By doing so, they are not only pursuing proper manners that are pleasing to people, but they are also cultivating their minds and bodies and restraining evil thoughts, if any. Additionally, they could easily win respect and recognition from people around, who shall observe and go back to imitate and learn, which helps improve an overall social climate.[89]

Furthermore, Li Liangzhang points out,

> For people whose appearance is tidy and pleasing, they must be masters at controlling their minds. They never unleash those evil thoughts, which is very important to scholars . . . if people could be serious, calm and, quietly solemn all the time, be attentive to their manners, and make timely adjustments and corrections, then in the long term, good habits are formed, and all behaviors and daily practices are nothing but their natural manifestations. This is true even for the highest level of morals.[90]

Hence, from the point of view of Li Lianzhang, when pursuing good manners, people are not doing so to present a pleasing and delightful appearance; they are also aiming for the cultivation of their minds and bodies. It is the process of restraint on bodies by correcting the wild nature of human beings, which eventually promotes the development of human nature. As a matter of fact, the idea of the unity of mind and body and the cultivation of the mind through refinement and regulation of daily behaviors was adopted and recognized by many academy educationists. For example, Dou Keqin of Douyang Academy proposed that "if an individual is in good manners, then accordingly, he is strengthening his morals and virtues. Hence, a dual practice of both cultivation of mind and behaviors."[91] His views were also shared by Zheng Zhiqiao, who believed that "apparel and hats could restrain one's straying and wandering minds. If an individual is not attentive to his appearances such as outfits and hats, then he must be lazy and careless."[92]

212 *Rites and Conduct in Academies*

Some academies went steps further, equaling serious and solemn manners with obedience. For example, Zheng Zhiqiao writes in "Rules and Regulations of Ehu Academy" (鹅湖书院学规) that

> the so-called obedience refers to tidy and graceful appearance manners and the finding of a lost heart. In daily life, a person shall be obedient and restrain his heart all the time, and regardless if he is working or resting, socializing or meditating, he shall keep such manners.[93]

Here, by restraining one's heart, one is also cultivating his obedience. Some other academies divided obedience into two parts: the outer one and the inner one. "The former is identical to serious and solemn behaviors. The latter involves clammed and concentrated hearts."[94] Thus, it could be seen that inner obedience is more of a notion in spirituality, while extrinsic obedience focuses more on appearance and manners, which is an indispensable part of the cultivation of obedience.

The reason behind such emphasis on training of appropriate behaviors lies in a deficiency of good manners at that time. "Despite of their hard work in studying classics, many scholars' and students' overall behaviors were contrary to what's stated in classics and were so intolerable to the eyes that they were just like vulgar townsfolk."[95] Li Lianzhang agreed: "I'm very concerned for students and scholars nowadays. Some of them want talent and intelligence. And for those who are indeed blessed with wits beyond measure, they are frivolous, luxurious, sly, and conceited."[96] Li's worries were not untenable, for self-conceit and self-satisfaction certainly exerted a bad influence on academic achievements. The very first rule of "Rules and Regulations of Longhu Academy" (龙湖书院学规) states,

> Flighty people shall never be trusted and are doomed to be nobody. If they think their talents are qualified enough for them to be conceited and take pride jauntily, they are wrong. And they shall witness no progress in their academic study. Even if they are capable of accomplishing remarkable academic achievements, the chance of which I believe is quite remote, deep inside my heart, I look down upon them.[97]

Hence, academies paid great attention to students' manners, alert to any signs of flirting and flight, which were under fierce attack by superintendents. In "Rules and Regulations of Guiyan Academy" (桂岩书院学规), Bian Lianbao stresses that "despite problems of various kinds, I think flirtatious behaviors are the worst."[98] As a result, many academies relied on daily training in manners to discourage flirtation in academies.

Zhu Xi viewed the cultivation of extrinsic manners, intrinsic minds, and ultimate accomplishment of Tao as a whole and complete process. It is the belief of Zhu Xi that "flirtation is extremely evil. An individual who is cocky and overbearing shall never grasp the essentialities of what he studies."[99] Zhu Xi's view was adopted and reiterated by superintendents of most academies. For example, Bian Lianbao, in admonishing students of Guiyan Academy, stated that

Rites and Conduct in Academies 213

flightiness leads to restlessness, which in turn results in low efficiency. This is true even for the most intelligent person in the world because if he is not focusing his mind, his observation, and his five senses on the study. How could he be able to contemplate the ultimate truth hidden deep inside? No wonder people like such are still outsiders despite years of studying, which is nothing but futile.[100]

Zhu Tingfang seconds this in "Regulations of Xingxian Academy" (兴贤书院条约):

Scholars ought to take pride in righteousness, solemnness, honesty, and simplicity. They should also stay away from flippant and flighty ones who like to boast and brag about themselves, judge people, and joke around. Even if they are as talented as or even more talented than Cao Zhi,[101] they bring nothing but shame to scholars' groups.[102]

Consequently, the key to correcting and improving such a climate lay in the daily practice of good manners. Huang Shisan stated, "Scholars should be on guard against any signs of cavalier attitudes and be attentive to their ways of talking, behaviors, outfits and hats, and overall appearances."[103] Since manners play such a vital role in the cultivation of virtues and academic achievements, academies, burdened with tasks of polishing the morals of students and imparting knowledge, ought to set training in good manners as a priority.

Conclusion

As stated earlier, there are plenty of pre-Qin literature documents about manners, which became an integral part of Confucianism. Hereafter, despite different degrees of treatment received in different periods of time, manners successfully guarded their place in the Confucian system throughout the process of mind cultivation, family management, and state affairs administration. Furthermore, manners integrated themselves into daily life, practiced and followed by people subconsciously, generating a profound effect in cultivating minds and improving the social climate.

As was pointed out by Yang Rubin, "the ideal education in the Confucian system is a harmonious state between intrinsic cultivation and extrinsic behaviors."[104] Such a state shall become a reality on the premise of the unity of mind and body highlighted by Confucian scholars. It relies on the constant practice of cultivation, such as the practice of manners, which advance inner virtue and morals via standardization of manners. In the process, an individual's body is transformed from uncivilized flesh into a moralized and spiritualized body, gradually squashing the inherent evil, so civil nature characterized by high morals comes to prevail.

Ancient academies put emphasis on the unification of the pursuit of Tao and the pursuit of knowledge, aiming to raise students with perfect personalities. Manners were recognized and adopted by academies in their rules and regulations for their

214 *Rites and Conduct in Academies*

profound influence in cultivating students with such personalities. Hence, manners were no longer a mere option but a must for academies in educating students. Nowadays, contemporary education tends to value knowledge delivery more than virtue cultivation, and consequently, many schools have yet to include manners cultivation in their current education system. As a result, the social climate keeps deteriorating and is in high need of improvement. Here, the manners of ancient academies could offer some lessons and insights for schools today.

Notes

1 Zhu, Xi 朱熹. *Sishu zhangju jizhu*四书章句集注 (Beijing: Zhonghua Book Company, 1983), 35.
2 Qiu, Xigui 裘锡圭. "Shi qiang pan ming jie shi" 史墙盘铭解释. In *Gu wenzi lunji*古文字论集 (Beijing: Zhonghua Book Company, 1992), 377.
3 Sun Yirang 孙诒让 (1848–1908), was a late Qing period (1644–1911) Confucian scholar. He hailed from Rui'an, Zhejiang, and was from 1867 on secretary (主事) in the Ministry of Justice (刑部), yet he soon retired because of illness. From then on, he dedicated himself to the study of the Confucian classics, the masters and philosophers, Chinese history, and Chinese characters and language. In his later years, he supported the academy in Wenzhou and was head of the Zhejiang Study and Teaching Group. During his lifetime he was known for his study of the classic *Rites of the Zhou*. In the preface to this study, he explained that it was important to investigate all steps of the transmission of such a texts, from the Tang period stone slab versions and the Song and Ming period prints.
4 Zheng, Xuanzhu 郑玄 and Kong, Yingda 孔颖达. *Liji zhengyi* Vol. 1礼记正义卷1 (Shanghai: Shanghai Chinese Classics Publishing House, 2008), 3.
5 Si, Maqian司马迁. "Yin ben ji" 殷本纪. In *Shiji* Vol. 3史记卷3 (Beijing: Zhonghua Book Company, 1963), 109.
6 Qiu, Xigui 裘锡圭. "Shi qiang pan ming jie shi" 史墙盘铭解释. In *Guwenzi lunji* 古文字论集 (Beijing: Zhonghua Book Company, 1992), 377.
7 Terrestrial Offices refers to Overseer of Public Affairs (Minister of Education) with 78 officials looked after the local administration, especially the royal domain around the capital, and its inhabitants.
8 Sun, Yirang 孙诒让. *Zhouli zhengyi* Vol. 26 周礼正义卷26 (Beijing: Zhonghua Book Company, 2013), 1010.
9 Autumn Offices refers to Overseer of Penal Affairs (Minister of Justice) with 66 officials were responsible for jurisdiction.
10 Sun, Yirang 孙诒让. *Zhouli zhengyi* Vol. 71 周礼正义卷71 (Beijing: Zhonghua Book Company, 2013), 3009.
11 Si, Maqian 司马迁. "Kong zi shi jia" 孔子世家. In *Shiji* Vol. 47 史记卷47 (Beijing: Zhonghua Book Company, 1963), 1906.
12 See Zhu, Xi 朱熹. *Sishu zhangju jizhu* 四书章句集注 (Beijing: Zhonghua Book Company, 1983), 117–122.
13 Zheng, Xuan 郑玄 and Kong, Yingda 孔颖达. *Liji zhengyi* Vol. 39礼记正义卷39 (Shanghai: Shanghai Chinese Classics Publishing House, 2008), 1191.
14 Ban, Gu 班固. "Ru lin zhuan" 儒林传. In *Hanshu* Vol. 88 汉书卷88 (Beijing: Zhonghua Book Company, 1964), 3614.
15 A fragmentary collection of administrative rules and prescriptions of the Former Han period. The book was compiled by Wei Hong (伟宏), during the Later Han period, but it was lost at an early point of time. Wei Hong hailed from the commandery of Donghai (modern Yancheng, Shandong) and was a disciple of Xie Manqing (谢曼卿), a

teacher of the Confucian classics. During the reign of Emperor Guangwu, the founder of the Later Han dynasty, he was appointed court gentleman for consultation (议郎). The text includes documents like the imperial diary, designations of court officials, and the number and hierarchies of officials in the Central Palace and the household of the heir apparent.

16 Ban, Gu 班固. "Ru lin zhuan" 儒林传. In *Hanshu* Vol. 88 汉书卷88 (Beijing: Zhonghua Book Company, 1964), 3615.

17 Hong, Ye 洪业. "Yi li yin de xu" 仪礼引得序. In *Yin de di liu hao* Vol. 6 引得第六号 (Beijing: Yenching University Library Compilation Department, 1932), i–ii.

18 Peng, Lin彭林. *Zhongguo gudai liyi wenming*中国古代礼仪文明 (Beijing: Zhonghua Book Company, 2013), 50.

19 Jia, Yi贾谊. *Xin shu jiao zhu*新书校注 (Beijing: Zhonghua Book Company, 2000), 227–229.

20 Ban, Gu 班固. "Li yue zhi" 礼乐志. In *Hanshu* Vol. 22 汉书卷22 (Beijing: Zhonghua Book Company, 1964), 1033.

21 Ruan, Ji 阮籍. "Yong huai shi." In *Xian qin han wei jin nan bei chao shi*先秦汉魏晋南北朝诗 (上) (Beijing: Zhonghua Book Company, 1983), 508.

22 "Seven Intellectuals of Bamboo Forest" refer to Ji Kang, Ruan Ji, Shan Tao, Xiang Xiu, Liu Ling, Wang Rong, and Ruan Xian, the seven of whom enjoyed drinking, singing and having fun in Bamboo Forest of Hui County of He Nan.

23 A proposition of Laozi which was to act in accordance with one's nature.

24 Rules and regulations in Feudalism.

25 Wang, Liqi王利器. *Yan shi jia xun ji jie* Vol. 2颜氏家训集解卷2 (Beijing: Zhonghua Book Company, 2007), 59.

26 Huang, Zongxi黄宗羲. *Song yuan xue an* Vol. 23宋元学案卷23 (Beijing: Zhonghua Book Company, 2011), 904.

27 Zhu, Xi朱熹. *Sishu zhangju jizhu*四书章句集注 (Beijing: Zhonghua Book Company, 1983), 104.

28 Zhen Dexiu (真德秀; 1178–1235), style Xishan Xiansheng (西山先生), was a scholar and philosopher of the Southern Song period. He hailed from Jianzhou (modern Andao, Fujian) and earned the jinshi degree in 1199. He was appointed imperial diarist and vice minister in the Court of Imperial Sacrifices and took over the offices of prefect of Quanzhou and then of Fuzhou before he became drafter in the Imperial Secretariat, vice minister of rites, and then minister of revenue. Later on, he was a Hanlin academician and finally vice counselor. Zhen Dexiu is often mentioned side by side with Wei Liaoweng (魏了翁; 1178–1237), both together called Master Xishan and Master Heshan.

29 *The Chronological Process of Learning* is a school curriculum or learning portfolio compiled by the Yuan scholar Cheng Duanli (程端礼; 1271–1345). He hailed from Yinxian (鄞县; near modern Ningbo, Zhejiangg) and was educational instructor (教諭) of Jianping and Jiande, later director (山長) of the academies in Jiaxuan (稼轩书院) and Jiangdong (江东书院), then again prefectural instructor in Qianshan, and finally teacher in Taizhou. Cheng Duanli was a disciple of Shi Mengqing (史蒙卿; 1247–1306) and was instructed in the teachings of the Neo-Confucian master Zhu Xi. The three-juan-long book was compiled in a chronological manner and describes the method of how Zhu Xi studied the ancient writings. It serves as a model for the Confucian scholar to read and learn from the ancient classical texts and is therefore a very important source for the history of education in ancient China.

30 Zhang, Shi 张栻. "Zhang zhou chongxiu yuelu shuyuan ji" 潭州重修岳麓书院记. In *Zhangshi ji* Vol. 3 张栻集册3 (Beijing: Zhonghua Book Company, 2015), 900.

31 Zhang, Sijiong 张思炯. "Yutan shuyuan qie yao si tiao" 玉潭书院切要四条. In *Zhongguo lidai shuyuan zhi* Vol. 4 中国历代书院志册4 (Nanjing: Jiangsu Education Press, 1995), 632.

Rites and Conduct in Academies

32 Zhu, Xi 朱熹. *Sishu zhangju jizhu* 四书章句集注 (Beijing: Zhonghua Book Company, 1983), 195.

33 Zhu, Xi 朱熹. *Sishu zhangju jizhu* 四书章句集注 (Beijing: Zhonghua Book Company, 1983), 48.

34 Zhu, Xi 朱熹. *Sishu zhangju jizhu* 四书章句集注 (Beijing: Zhonghua Book Company, 1983), 133.

35 Cheng, Duanli 程端礼. *Cheng shi jia shu dushu fen nian ri cheng* 程氏家塾读书分年日程 (Hefei: Huangshan Publishing House, 1992), 9.

36 Fang, Shimin 方世敏. "Ying shan shuyuan xue gui" 瀛山书院学规. In *Zhongguo lidai shuyuan zhi* Vol. 8 中国历代书院志册8 (Nanjing: Jiangsu Education Press, 1995), 401.

37 Liang, Tingnan 梁廷柟. "Yuexiu shuyuan xue gui" 粤秀书院学规. In *Zhongguo lidai shuyuan zhi* Vol. 3 中国历代书院志册3 (Nanjing: Jiangsu Education Press, 1995), 17.

38 Liang, Dingfen 梁鼎芬. "Duan xi shuyuan sheng tu zhu yuan zhang cheng" 端溪书院生徒住院章程. In *Zhongguo lidai shuyuan zhi* Vol. 3 中国历代书院志册3 (Nanjing: Jiangsu Education Press, 1995), 385.

39 Li, Laizhang 李来章. "Lian shan shuyuan xue gui" 连山书院学规. In *Zhangguo lidai shuyuan zhi* Vol. 3 中国历代书院志册3 (Nanjing: Jiangsu Education Publishing House, 1995), 320.

40 Li, Wenzhao 李文炤. "Yuelu shuyuan xue gui" 岳麓书院学规. In *Zhongguo shuyuan xuegui ji cheng* Vol. 2 中国书院学规集成册2, ed. Deng Hongbo 邓洪波 (Shanghai: Zhongxi Book Company, 2011), 1035.

41 Zheng, Zhiqiao 郑之侨. "Xin you quan zhu sheng ba ze" 辛酉劝诸生八则. In *Zhongguo lidai shuyuan zhi* Vol. 11 中国历代书院志册11 (Nanjing: Jiangsu Education Publishing House, 1995), 178.

42 Zhu, Yishen 朱一深. "Ning xiu shuyuan tiao yue" 凝秀书院条约. In *Zhongguo lidai shuyuan zhi* Vol. 2 中国历代书院志册2 (Nanjing: Jiangsu Education Publishing House, 1995), 322.

43 Bian, Lianbao 边连宝. "Gui yan shuyuan xue yue ba ze" 桂岩书院学约八则. In *Renqiuxian zhi* Vol. 11 任邱县志卷11 (Taibei: Chengwen Publishing House Co., Ltd, 1976), 1541.

44 Cheng, Duanli 程端礼. *Chengshi jia shu du shu fen nian ri cheng* 程氏家塾读书分年日程 (Hefei: Huangshan Publishing House, 1992), 9.

45 Gao, Benheng 高贲亨. "Dong xue shi jie" 洞学十戒. In *Zhongguo shuyuan xue gui ji cheng* Vol. 2. 中国书院学规集成册2, ed. Deng Hongbo 邓洪波 (Shanghai: Zhongxi Book Company, 2011), 649.

46 Li, Yong 李颙. "Guan zhong shuyuan xue cheng" 关中书院学程. In *Er qu ji* Vol. 13 二曲集卷13 (Beijing: Zhonghua Book Company, 1983), 118.

47 Wang, Wenqing 王文清. "Yuelu shuyuan xue gui" 岳麓书院学规. In *Zhongguo lidai shuyuan zhi* Vol. 4 中国历代书院志册4 (Nanjing: Jiangsu Education Publishing House, 1995), 436.

48 Yan, Yaoxi 阎尧熙. "Pei ying shuyuan quan xue shi ze" 培英书院劝学十则. In *Zhongguo xueyuan xuegui jicheng* Vol. 1 中国书院学规集成册1, ed. Deng Hongbo 邓洪波 (Shanghai: Zhongxi Book Company, 2011), 16.

49 Lang, Tingnan 梁廷柟. "Yuexiu shuyuan xue gui" 粤秀书院学规. In *Zhongguo lidai shuyuan zhi* Vol. 3 中国历代书院志册3 (Nanjing: Jiangsu Education Publishing House, 1995), 17.

50 Lang, Tingnan 梁廷柟. "yue xiu shuyuan xue gui" 粤秀书院学规. In *Zhongguo lidai shuyuan zhi* Vol. 3 中国历代书院志册3 (Nanjing: Jiangsu Education Publishing House, 1995), 17.

51 Zhang, Shi 张栻. "Nan xuan xiansheng lunyu jie" 南轩先生论语解. In *Zhang shi ji* Vol. 1 张栻集册1 (Beijing: Zhonghua Book Company, 2015), 173.

52 Chen, Xiangdao 陈祥道. "Lunyu quanjie" 论语全解. In *Ru cang* 儒藏 (Beijing: Peking University Press, 2008), 87.

Rites and Conduct in Academies   217

53 He, Yan 何晏 and Xing, Bing 邢昺. "Lunyu zhu shu" 论语注疏. In *Shisanjing zhu shu* 十三经注疏, ed. Li Xueqin 李学勤 (Beijing: Peking University Press, 1999), 229.

54 Fang, Shimin 方世敏. "Yingshan shuyuan xuegui" 瀛山书院学规. In *Zhongguo lidai shuyuan zhi* Vol. 8 中国历代书院志册8 (Nanjing: Jiangsu Education Publishing House, 1995), 401.

55 Lang, Tingnan 梁廷枏. "Yuexiu shuyuan xuegui" 粤秀书院学规. In *Zhongguo lidai shuyuan zhi* Vol. 3 中国历代书院志册3 (Nanjing: Jiangsu Education Publishing House, 1995), 17.

56 Lü, Zuqian 吕祖谦. "Lize shuyuan qian dao simian gui yue" 丽泽书院乾道四年规约. In *Lu Donglai wenji* Part 4 Vol. 10 吕东莱文集册4) 卷10 (Shanghai: The Commercial Press, 1937), 247.

57 During the Former Han period, books on ritual matters with a length of 131 chapters were gathered, one by the Confucian scholar Dai De (戴德; Dai the Elder [大戴]), who compiled a collection of 85 chapters (called *The Rites by Dai the Elder*), and one by his nephew Dai Sheng (戴圣), with a length of 49 chapters, which was accordingly called *The Rites by Dai the Younger*. At the end of the Later Han, the book of Dai De ceased to be taught at the Imperial College and was overshadowed by the compilation of Dai Sheng, which then became the orthodox classic on rituals, together with *The Etiquette and Rites* and *Rites of the Zhou*.

58 Fang, Xiangdong 方向东. *Dadai liji hui xiao jijie* 大戴礼记汇校集解 (Beijing: Zhonghua Book Company, 2008), 949.

59 Li, Yong 李颙. "Guanzhong shuyuan xue cheng" 关中书院学程. In *Er qu ji* Vol. 13 二曲集卷13 (Beijing: Zhonghua Book Company, 1996), 117.

60 Wang, Wenqing 王文清. "Yuelu shuyuan xuegui" 岳麓书院学规. In *Zhongguo lidai shuyuan zhi* Vol. 4 中国历代书院志册4 (Nanjing: Jiangsu Education Publishing House, 1995), 436.

61 Liang, Tingnan 梁廷枏. "Yuexiu shuyuan xuegui" 粤秀书院学规. In *Zhongguo lidai shuyuan zhi* Vol. 3 中国历代书院志册3 (Nanjing: Jiangsu Education Publishing House, 1995), 17.

62 Liang, Dingfen 梁鼎芬. "Duanxi shuyuan sheng tu zhuyuan zhangcheng" 端溪书院生徒住院章程. In *Zhongguo lidai shuyuan zhi* Vol. 3 中国历代书院志册3 (Nanjing: Jiangsu Education Publishing House, 1995), 385.

63 Chen, Shouqi 陈寿祺. "Niding aofeng shuyuan shiyi" 拟定鳌峰书院事宜. In Deng Hongbo 邓洪波, *Zhongguo shuyuan xuegui jicheng* Vol. 1 中国书院学规集成册1 (Shanghai: Zhongxi Book Company, 2011), 543.

64 Huang, Shubing 黄舒昺. "Mingdao shuyuan xuegui" 明道书院学规. In *Zhongguo lidai shuyuan zhi* Vol. 6 中国历代书院志册6 (Nanjing: Jiangsu Education Publishing House, 1995), 356.

65 Li, Laizhang 李来章. "Lianshan shuyuan bang wen" 连山书院榜文. In *Zhongguo lidai shuyuan zhi* Vol. 3 中国历代书院志册3 (Nanjing: Jiangsu Education Publishing House, 1995), 317.

66 Liang, Tingnan 梁廷枏. "Yuexiu shuyuan xuegui" 粤秀书院学规. In *Zhongguo lidai shuyuan zhi* Vol. 3 中国历代书院志册3 (Nanjing: Jiangsu Education Publishing House, 1995), 16.

67 Liang, Dingfen 梁鼎芬. "Duanxi shuyuan sheng tu zhuyuan zhangcheng" 端溪书院生徒住院章程. In *Zhongguo lidai shuyuan zhi* Vol. 3 中国历代书院志册3 (Nanjing: Jiangsu Education Publishing House, 1995), 385.

68 Liu, Xizai 刘熙载. "Longmen shuyuan kecheng liu ze" 龙门书院课程六则. In *Zhongguo shuyuan xuegui ji cheng* Vol. 1 中国书院学规集成册1, ed. Deng Hongbo 邓洪波 (Shanghai: Zhongxi Book Company, 2011), 119.

69 Zhu, Xi 朱熹. "Ba cheng dong er xiansheng xue ze" 跋程董二先生学则. In *Zhuzi quan shu* Vol. 24 朱子全书册24 (Hefei: Anhui Education Press, 2010), 3879.

70 Zhou, Ruli 程瑞礼. *Chengshi jiashu dushu fen nian ri cheng* 程氏家塾读书分年日程 (Hefei: Huangshan Publishing House, 1992), 3.

218 *Rites and Conduct in Academies*

71 Zhou, Ruli 程瑞礼. *Chengshi jiashu dushu fen nian ri cheng* 程氏家塾读书分年日程 (Hefei: Huangshan Publishing House, 1992), 9.

72 Li, Yong 李颙. "Guanzhong shuyuan xuecheng" 关中书院学程. In *Er qu ji* Vol. 13 二曲集卷13 (Beijing: Zhonghua Book Company, 1996), 117.

73 Wang, Wenqing 王文清. "Yuelu shuyuan xuegui" 岳麓书院学规. In *Zhongguo lidai shuyuan zhi* Vol. 4 中国历代书院志册4 (Nanjing: Jiangsu Education Publishing House, 1995), 436.

74 Sun, Yirang 孙诒让. "Suan xue shuyuan xuegui" 算学书院学规. In *Zhongguo shuyuan xuegui ji cheng* Vol. 1 中国书院学规集成册1 (Nanjing: Jiangsu Education Publishing House, 1995), 440.

75 Huang, Shubing 黄舒昺. "Ming dao shuyuan xue gui" 明道书院学规. In *Zhongguo lidai shuyuan zhi* Vol. 6 中国历代书院志册6 (Nanjing: Jiangsu Education Publishing House, 1995), 356.

76 Fang, Xiangdong 方向东. *Dadai liji huijiao jijie* 大戴礼记汇校集解 (Beijing: Zhonghua Book Company, 2008), 949.

77 Kong, Yingda 孔颖达. *Liji zhengyi* Vol. 49礼记正义卷四十九 (Shanghai: Shanghai Chinese Classics Publishing House, 2008), 1553.

78 Kong, Yingda 孔颖达. *Liji zhengyi* Vol. 61礼记正义卷六十一 (Shanghai: Shanghai Chinese Classics Publishing House, 2008), 2065.

79 Kong, Yingda 孔颖达. *Liji zhengyi* Vol. 61礼记正义卷六十一 (Shanghai: Shanghai Chinese Classics Publishing House, 2008), 2068.

80 Zhu, Xi 朱熹. *Sishu zhangju jizhu* 四书章句集注 (Beijing: Zhonghua Book Company, 1983), 56.

81 Kong, Yingda 孔颖达. *Liji zhengyi* Vol. 55礼记正义卷五十五 (Shanghai: Shanghai Chinese Classics Publishing House, 2008), 1818.

82 Kong, Yingda 孔颖达. *Liji zhengyi* Vol. 51礼记正义卷五十一 (Shanghai: Shanghai Chinese Classics Publishing House, 2008), 638.

83 Kong, Yingda 孔颖达. *Liji zhengyi* Vol. 36礼记正义卷三十六 (Shanghai: Shanghai Chinese Classics Publishing House, 2008), 1087.

84 Kong, Yingda 孔颖达. *Liji zhengyi* Vol. 27礼记正义卷二十七 (Shanghai: Shanghai Chinese Classics Publishing House, 2008), 791.

85 Kong, Yingda 孔颖达. *Liji zhengyi* Vol. 27礼记正义卷二十七 (Shanghai: Shanghai Chinese Classics Publishing House, 2008), 791.

86 Li, Jingde 黎靖德. *Zhuzi yülei* Vol. 59朱子语类卷五十九 (Beijing: Zhonghua Book Company, 2011), 1412.

87 Li, Jingde 黎靖德. *Zhuzi yülei* Vol. 12朱子语类卷一十二 (Beijing: Zhonghua Book Company, 2011), 210.

88 Li, Jingde 黎靖德. *Zhuzi yülei* Vol. 12朱子语类卷一十二 (Beijing: Zhonghua Book Company, 2011), 211.

89 Li, Laizhang 李来章. "Lianshan shuyuan bangwen" 连山书院榜文. In *Zhongguo Lidai shuyuan zhi* Vol. 3 中国历代书院志第3册 (Nanjing: Jiangsu Education Publishing House, 1995), 317.

90 Li, Laizhang 李来章. "Lianshan shuyuan bangwen" 连山书院榜文. In *Zhongguo Lidai shuyuan zhi* Vol. 3 中国历代书院志第3册 (Nanjing: Jiangsu Education Publishing House, 1995), 317.

91 Dou, Keqin 窦克勤. "Zhuyang shuyuan xuegui" 朱阳书院学规. In *Zhongguo Lidai shuyuan zhi* Vol. 6 中国历代书院志第6册 (Nanjing: Jiangsu Education Publishing House, 1995), 439.

92 Zheng, Zhiqiao 郑之侨. "Renxu shi zhusheng shiyao" 壬戌示诸生十要. In *Zhongguo Lidai shuyuan zhi* Vol. 11 中国历代书院志第11册 (Nanjing: Jiangsu Education Publishing House, 1995), 181.

Rites and Conduct in Academies 219

93 Zheng, Zhiqiao 郑之侨. "Ehu shuyuan xuegui" 鹅湖书院学规. In *Zhongguo Lidai shuyuan zhi* Vol. 11 中国历代书院志第11册 (Nanjing: Jiangsu Education Publishing House, 1995), 172.

94 Shao, Songyuan 邵松元. "Mingdao shuyuan richeng" 明道书院日程. In *Zhongguo Lidai shuyuan zhi* Vol. 6 中国历代书院志第6册 (Nanjing: Jiangsu Education Publishing House, 1995), 369.

95 Shen, Qiyuan 沈起元. "Loudong shuyuan guitiao" 娄东书院规条. In *Zhongguo xueyuan xuegui jicheng* Vol. 1 中国书院学规集成第1册, ed. Deng Hongbo邓洪波 (Shanghai: Zhongxi Book Company, 2011), 257.

96 Li, Laizhang 李来章. "Lianshan shuyuan xuegui" 连山书院学规. In *Zhongguo Lidai shuyuan zhi* Vol. 3 中国历代书院志第3册 (Nanjing: Jiangsu Education Publishing House, 1995), 321.

97 Yu, Liyuan 余丽元. "Longhu shuyuan zhi" 龙湖书院志. In *Zhongguo Lidai shuyuan zhi* Vol. 10 中国历代书院志第10册 (Nanjing: Jiangsu Education Publishing House, 1995), 41.

98 Bian, Lianbao 边连宝. "Guiyan shuyuan xueyue baze" 桂岩书院学约八则. In *Ren qiuxian zhi* Vol. 11任邱县志卷十一 (Taibei: Cheng Wen Publishing Co., Ltd, 1976), 1531.

99 Li, Jingde 黎靖德. Zhuzi *yule* Vol. 12朱子语类卷一十二 (Beijing: Zhonghua Book Company, 2011), 503.

100 Bian, Lianbao 边连宝. "Guiyan shuyuan xueyue baze" 桂岩书院学约八则. In *Ren qiuxian zhi* Vol. 11任邱县志卷十一 (Taibei: Cheng Wen Publishing CO., LTD, 1976), 1531.

101 Cao Zhi (192–232) was a famous scholar and poet of Three Kingdoms period who is mostly known for his ability to write a poem in just seven steps. Here, Cao Zhi is cited as a measurement to determine whether a student is intelligent or not.

102 Shen, Tingfang 祝廷芳. "Xingxian shuyuan tiaoyue baze" 兴贤书院条约八则. In *Zhongguo shuyuan xuegui jicheng* 中国书院学规集成, ed. Deng Hongbo 邓洪波 (Shanghai: Zhongxi Book Company, 2011), 705.

103 Huang, Shisan 黄式三. *Lunyü hou an*论语后案 (Nanjing: Phoenix Publishing House, 2010), 12.

104 Yang, Rubin 杨儒宾. "Rujia shenti guan" 儒家身体观. In *Gu wenzi lunji*古文字论集 (Taibei: In Journal of Institute of Chinese Literature and Philosophy, Academia Sinica 1996), 21.

Bibliography

Ancient Literature

Badong xian zhi 巴东县志, 1880 A.D.

Bai Juyi 白居易. *Bai ju yi ji* 白居易集. Shanghai: Shanghai Chinese Classics Publishing House, 1999.

Ban Gu班固. *Hanshu* 汉书. Beijing: Zhonghua Book Company, 1962.

Baoding fu zhi 保定府志, 1881 A.D.

Bao Hui 包恢. "Bizhou gaolue" 敝帚稿. In *Siku quanshu* 四库全书. Shanghai: Shanghai Chinese Classics Publishing House, 1987.

Ba xian xinzhi 霸县新志, 1934 A.D.

Beijing Library北京图书馆ed. *Beijing tushuguan cangzhenben nianpu cong kan* 北京图书馆藏珍本年谱丛刊. Beijing: Beijing Library Press, 1984.

Bi Yuan 毕沅. *Xu zizhi tongjian* 续资治通鉴. Beijing: Zhonghua Book Company, 1957.

Cao Weijing 曹惟精. *Chenhou shuyuan zhi* 郴侯书院志, 1863 A.D.

Cao Yanyue 曹彦约. "Canggu ji" 昌谷集. In *Siku quanshu* 四库全书. Shanghai: Shanghai Chinese Classics Publishing House, 1987.

Cha Duo 查铎. "Shuixi huitiao" 水西会条. In *Congshu jicheng* 丛书集成. Shanghai: Shanghai Commercial Press, 1936.

Changzhi xian zhi 长治县志, 1894 A.D.

Chen Bangzhan 陈邦瞻. *Songshi jishi benmo* 宋史纪事本末. Beijing: Zhonghua Book Company, 1977.

Chen Duanli 程端礼. "Weizahi ji" 畏斋集. In *Siku quanshu* 四库全书. Shanghai: Shanghai Chinese Classics Publishing House, 1987.

Chen Duanxue 程端学. "Jizhai ji" 积斋集. In *Siku quanshu* 四库全书. Shanghai: Shanghai Chinese Classics Publishing House, 1987.

Chen Ji 陈基. "Yibai zhaigao" 夷白斋稿. In *Siku quanshu* 四库全书. Shanghai: Shanghai Chinese Classics Publishing House, 1987.

Chen Li 陈澧. "Dongshu ji" 东塾集. In *Xuxiu siku quanshu* 续修四库全书. Shanghai: Shanghai Chinese Classics Publishing House, 2002.

Chen Wenwei陈文蔚. "Kezhai ji" 克斋集. In *Siku quanshu* 四库全书. Shanghai: Shanghai Chinese Classics Publishing House, 1987.

Chen Xianzhang 陈献章. *Chen xianzhang ji* 陈献章集. Beijing: Zhonghua Book Company, 1987.

Chen Zhensun陈振孙. "Zhizhai shulu jieti" 直斋书录解题. In *Siku quanshu* 四库全书. Shanghai: Shanghai Chinese Classics Publishing House, 1987.

Chen Zhu陈著. "Bentang ji" 本堂集. In *Siku quanshu* 四库全书. Shanghai: Shanghai Chinese Classics Publishing House, 1987.

Bibliography   221

Cheng Bi程珌. "Luoshui ji" 洛水集. In *Siku quanshu* 四库全书. Shanghai: Shanghai Chinese Classics Publishing House, 1987.

Cheng Hao 程颢, "Cheng Yi" 程颐. In *Ercheng ji* 二程集. Beijing: Zhonghua Book Company, 1960.

Cheng Jufu程钜夫. "Xuelou ji" 雪楼集. In *Siku quanshu* 四库全书. Shanghai: Shanghai Chinese Classics Publishing House, 1987.

Cheng Tingzuo程廷祚. "Qingxi ji" 清溪集. In *Congshu jicheng xubian* 丛书集成续编. Taipei: Taipei Xinwenfeng Publishing Company, 1988.

*Chong xiu shifang xina zhi*重修什邡县志, 1929 A.D.

Chong xiu tianjin fu zhi 重修天津府志, 1875–1908 A.D.

Dai Fengyi 戴凤仪. *Shishan shuyuan zhi* 诗山书院志. Xiamen: Xiamen University Press, 1995.

Dai Zhen戴震. *Daizhen wenji* 戴震文集. Beijing: Zhonghua Book Company, 1980.

Dali xian zhigao 大理县志稿, 1917 A.D.

"Dayuan shengzheng guo chao dianzhang"大元圣政国朝典章. In *Xuxiu Siku quanshu* 续修四库全书. Shanghai: Shanghai Chinese Classics Publishing House, 2002.

*Dean xian zhi*德安县志, 1862–1875 A.D.

Deng Mu邓牧. "Boya qin" 伯牙琴. In *Siku quanshu* 四库全书. Shanghai: Shanghai Chinese Classics Publishing House, 1987.

Ding Shanqing 丁善庆. *Changsha yuelu shuyuan xuzhi* 长沙岳麓书院续志, 1862 A.D.

Dong Guifu 董桂敷. *Ziyang shuyuan zhilue* 紫阳书院志略, 1806 A.D.

Dong Hao 董诰. *Quan tang wen* 全唐文. Beijing: Zhonghua Book Company, 1983.

Du You 杜佑. *Tong dian* 通典. Hangzhou: Zhe jiang Chinese Classics Publishing House, 1988.

Duan Yucai段玉裁."Jingyunlou ji" 经韵楼集. In *Xuxiu siku quanshu* 续修四库全书. Shanghai: Shanghai Chinese Classics Publishing House, 2002.

Fan Ye范晔. *Houhan shu* 后汉书. Beijing: Zhonghua Book Company, 1965.

Fan Zhongyan 范仲淹. "Fanwenzheng bieji" 范文正别集. In *Siku quanshu* 四库全书. Shanghai: Shanghai Chinese Classics Publishing House, 1987.

Fang Hongshou 方宏绶. *Yingshan shuyuan zhi* 瀛山书院志, 1794 A.D.

Fang Xuanling房玄龄 et al. *Jin shu* 晋书. Beijing: Zhonghua Book Company, 1974.

Fang Zude 方祖德. *Yingshan shuyuan zhi* 瀛山书院志, 1774 A.D.

*Fenghuang ting zhi*凤凰厅志, 1823 A.D.

*Fuliang xian zhi*浮梁县志, 1783 A.D.

*Funing fu zhi*福宁府志, 1912–1949.

Fu Weisen 傅维森. *Duanxi shuyuan zhi* 端溪书院志, 1900 A.D.

Gao Long高隆et al. *Donglin shuyuan zhi* 东林书院志, 1881 A.D.

Gao Side高斯得. "Chitang cungao" 耻堂存稿. In *Siku quanshu* 四库全书. Shanghai: Shanghai Chinese Classics Publishing House, 1987.

Gao Panlong高攀龙. "Gaozi yishu" 高子遗书. In *Siku quanshu* 四库全书. Shanghai: Shanghai Chinese Classics Publishing House, 1987.

*Guangnan fu zhi*广南府志, 1905 A.D.

*Guixi xian zhi*贵溪县志, 1862–1875 A.D.

Gu Xiancheng顾宪成. "Gu wenduangong yishu" 顾文端公遗书. In *Xuxiu siku quanshu* 续修四库全书. Shanghai: Shanghai Chinese Classics Publishing House, 2002.

Gu Yanwu顾炎武. *Gu tinglin shiwenji* 顾亭林诗文集. Beijing: Zhonghua Book Company, 1959.

Gu Yanwu 顾炎武. *Ri zhi lu jishi* 日知录集释. Annot. Huang Rucheng 黄汝成. Changsha: Yuelu Press, 1994.

Gui Zihua 桂滋华. *Changlin hecheng guishi zongpu* 长林河城桂氏宗谱, 1895 A.D.

222 *Bibliography*

Guo Qi 郭齐, "Yin Bodian" 尹波点. In *Zul xi ji* 朱熹集. Chengdu: Sichuan Education Publishing House, 1996.

*Haiyang xian zhi*海阳县志, 1900 A.D.

*Hangzhou fu zhi*杭州府志, reprinted 1875–1908 A.D.

*Hangzhou fu zhi*杭州府志, 1922.

Han Yu 韩愈. *Han yu quanji* 韩愈全集. Shanghai: Shanghai Chinese Classics Publishing House, 1997.

Hao Jing郝经. "Linchuan ji" 凌川集. In *Siku quanshu* 四库全书. Shanghai: Shanghai Chinese Classics Publishing House, 1987.

He Changling贺长龄. "Naian wencun" 耐庵文存. In *Xu xiu siku quanshu* 续修四库全书. Shanghai: Shanghai Chinese Classics Publishing House, 2002.

*Heqing zhou zhi*鹤庆州志, 1894 A.D.

Hong Liangji 洪亮吉. *Hong liang ji ji* 洪亮吉集. Beijing: Zhonghua Book Company, 2001.

Hong Mai洪迈. *Rongzhai suibi* 容斋随笔. Beijing: Zhonghua Book Company, 1978.

*Huanggang xian zhi*黄冈县志, 1882 A.D.

Hu Hong 胡宏. *Hu hong ji* 胡宏集. Beijing: Zhonghua Book Company, 1987.

Hu Peihui胡培翚. "Yanliushi wenchao" 研六室文钞. In *Xuxiu siku quanshu* 续修四库全书. Shanghai: Shanghai Chinese Classics Publishing House, 2002.

Hu Shian胡师安 et al. "Yuan xihu shuyuan chongzheng shumu" 元西湖书院重整书目. In *Congshu jicheng xubian* 丛书集成续编. Taipei: Taipei Xinwenfeng Publishing Company, 1988.

Huang Gan黄榦. "Mianzhai ji" 勉斋集. In *Siku quanshu* 四库全书. Shanghai: Shanghai Chinese Classics Publishing House, 1987.

Huang Linggeng 黄灵庚, ed. *Lǚ zu qian quanji* 吕祖谦全集. Hangzhou: Zhe jiang Chinese Classics Publishing House, 2008.

Huang Pengnian黄彭年. "Taolou wenchao" 陶楼文钞. In *Xuxiu siku quanshu* 续修四库全书. Shanghai: Shanghai Chinese Classics Publishing House, 2002.

*Huangzhou fu zhi*黄州府志, 1884 A.D.

Huang Zongxi 黄宗羲. *Mingru xue an* 明儒学案. Beijing: Zhonghua Book Company, 1985.

Huang Zongxi 黄宗羲. "Quan Zuwang" 全祖望. In *Songyuan xue an* 宋元学案. Beijing: Zhonghua Book Company, 1986.

Huizhou fu zhi 惠州府志, 1881 A.D.

Hu Linyi 胡林翼. *Zhenyan shuyuan zhi* 箴言书院志, 1866 A.D.

*Hunan tongzhi*湖南通志, *Xuxiu siku quanshu*续修四库全书. 1875–1908.

Ji Jun纪昀. "Siku quanshu zongmu" 四库全书总目. In *Siku quanshu* 四库全书. Shanghai: Shanghai Chinese Classics Publishing House, 1987.

Jiang Yanxi 蒋廷锡. *Gujin tushu jicheng* 古今图书集成. Beijing: Zhonghua Book Company, 1986.

*Jianyang xian zhi*建阳县志, 1821–1850.

*Jiaohe xian zhi*交河县志, 1917 A.D.

Jiao Xun焦循. "Diaogu ji" 雕菰集. In *Xuxiu siku quanshu* 续修四库全书. Shanghai: Shanghai Chinese Classics Publishing House, 2002.

*Jiaqing shanyin xian zhi*嘉庆山阴县志, 1936.

*Jiaying zhou zhi*嘉应州志, 1898 A.D.

Jie Xisi揭傒斯. "Wenan ji" 文安集. In *Siku quanshu* 四库全书. Shanghai: Shanghai Chinese Classics Publishing House, 1987.

*Jingding jiandang zhi*景定建康志, 1736–1976 A.D.

*Jing xian zhi*泾县志, 1806 A.D.

*Jülu xian zhi*巨鹿县志, 1886 A.D.

Ke Shaomin 柯绍忞. *Xin yuan shi* 新元史. Beijing: Zhonghua Book Company, 1988.

Lan Dingyuan 蓝鼎元. "Luzhou chuji" 鹿洲初集. In *Congshu jicheng sanbian* 丛书集成三编. Taibei: Taipei Xinwenfeng Publishing Company, 1997.

Li Anren李安仁. *Shigu shuyuan zhi* 石鼓书院志, 589 A.D.

Li Dongyang 李东阳. *Li dongyangji* 李东阳集. Changsha: Yuelu Book Club, 1985.

Li Fu李绂. "Mutang chugao" 穆堂初稿. In *Xuxiu siku quanshu* 续修四库全书. Shanghai: Shanghai Chinese Classics Publishing House, 2002.

Li Jingdei 黎靖德, ed. *Zhu zi yu lei* 朱子语类. Beijing: Zhonghua Book Company, 1986.

Li Qi李祁. "Yunyang ji" 云阳集. In *Siku quanshu* 四库全书. Shanghai: Shanghai Chinese Classics Publishing House, 1987.

Li Tao李焘. *Xu zizhi tongjian changbian* 续资治通鉴长编. Beijing: Zhonghua Book Company, 1979.

Li Xinchuan李心传. "Jianyan yilai xinian yaolu" 建炎以来系年要录. In *Siku quanshu* 四库全书. Shanghai: Shanghai Chinese Classics Publishing House, 1987.

Li Xiusheng 李修生, ed. *Quan yuan wen* 全元文. Nanjing: Jiangsu Ancient Books Publishing House, 1999.

Li Yong 李颙. *Er qu ji* 二曲集. Beijing: Zhonghua Book Company, 1996.

Li Yanghua 李扬华. *Guochao shigu zhi* 国朝石鼓志, 1880 A.D.

Li Yingsheng 李应升. *Bailudong shuyuan zhi* 白鹿洞书院志, 1622 A.D.

Liao Xingzhi 廖行之. "Xingzhai ji" 省斋集. In *Siku quanshu* 四库全书. Shanghai: Shanghai Chinese Classics Publishing House, 1987.

Lingui xian zhi 临桂县志, 1802 A.D.

Lin Wenju林文俊. "Fangzhai cungao" 方斋存稿. In *Siku quanshu* 四库全书. Shanghai: Shanghai Chinese Classics Publishing House, 1987.

Lin Xiyi林希逸. "Zhuxiyan zhai shiyigao xu ji" 竹溪鬳斋十一稿续集. In *Siku quanshu* 四库全书. Shanghai: Shanghai Chinese Classics Publishing House, 1987.

Liu Guangfen 刘光蕡. *Shangan weijing shuyuan zhi* 陕甘味经书院志, 1936.

Liu Xu 刘昫 et al. *Jiu tang shu* 旧唐书. Beijing: Zhonghua Book Company, 1976.

Liu Yi 刘绎. *Bailuzhou shuyuan zhi* 白鹭洲书院志, 1871 A.D.

Liu Yueshen 刘岳申. "Shenzahi ji" 申斋集. In *Siku quanshu* 四库全书. Shanghai: Shanghai Chinese Classics Publishing House, 1987.

Liu Zai刘宰. "Mantang ji" 漫塘集. In *Siku quanshu* 四库全书. Shanghai: Shanghai Chinese Classics Publishing House, 1987.

Liu Zongzhou 刘宗周. "Zhengren shehuiyi" 证人社会仪. In *Congshu jicheng* 丛书集成. Shanghai: Shanghai Commercial Press, 1936.

*Luancheng xian zhi*栾城县志, 1872 A.D.

*Lueyang xian zhi*略阳县志, 1904 A.D.

Lu Jiuyuan 陆九渊. *Lu jiuyuan ji* 陆九渊集. Beijing: Zhonghua Book Company, 1980.

Lu Shiyi 陆世仪. "Futing xiansheng yishu" 桴亭先生遗书. In *Siku quanshu* 四库全书. Shanghai: Shanghai Chinese Classics Publishing House, 1987.

Lu You 陆游. "Weinan wenji" 渭南文集. In *Siku quanshu* 四库全书. Shanghai: Shanghai Chinese Classics Publishing House, 1987.

Ma Duanlin 马端临. *Wenxian tongkao* 文献通考. Beijing: Zhonghua Book Company, 1986.

Mao Deqi 毛德琦. *Bailu shuyuan zhi* 白鹿书院志, 1910 A.D.

*Ming Shilu*明实录. History Institute of Taipei Academia Sinica, 1967.

Miu Quansun 缪荃孙. "Xu beizhuan ji." In *Jindai zhongguo shiliao congkan* 近代中国史料丛刊. Taipei: Taipei Wenhai Publishing House, 1983.

224   *Bibliography*

Nanling xian zhi 南陵县志, 1912–1949.

Nanyang fu zhi 南阳府志, 1694 A.D.

Ouyang Shoudao 欧阳守道. "Xunzhai ji" 巽斋集. In *Siku quanshu* 四库全书. Shanghai: Shanghai Chinese Classics Publishing House, 1987.

Ouyang Xiu 欧阳修. *Ouyangxiu quan ji* 欧阳修全集. Beijing: Zhonghua Book Company, 1986.

Ouyang Xiu 欧阳修et al. *Xin wudai shi* 新五代史. Beijing: Zhonghua Book Company, 1974.

Ouyang Xiu 欧阳修et al. *Xin tang shu* 新唐书. Beijing: Zhonghua Book Company, 1975.

Ouyang Xuan 欧阳玄. "Guizhai wenji" 圭斋文集. In *Siku quanshu* 四库全书. Shanghai: Shanghai Chinese Classics Publishing House, 1987.

Puqi xian zhi 蒲圻县志, 1836 A.D.

Qianjiang xian zhi 黔江县志, 1894 A.D.

Qian Long 乾隆. *Xu wenxian tong kao* 续文献通考. Hangzhou: Zhe jiang Chinese Classics Publishing House, 1988.

Qian Yiji 钱仪吉. "Beizhuan ji" 碑传集. In *Jindai zhongguo shiliao congkan* 近代中国史料丛刊. Taipei: Taipei Wenhai Publishing House, 1983.

Qimen xian zhi 祁门县志, 1873 A.D.

"Qinding daqing huidian shili" 钦定大清会典事例. In *Jindai zhongguo shiliao congkan sanbian* 近代中国史料丛刊三编. Taipei: Taipei Wenhai Publishing House, 1983.

Qing shi lu 清实录. Beijing: Zhonghua Book Company, 1985.

Qingyuan xian zhi 清苑县志, 1934 A.D.

Qi xian zhi 杞县志, 1788 A.D.

Quan Zuwang 全祖望. "Jieqiting ji waibian" 鲒埼亭集外编. In *Xuxiu siku quanshu* 续修四库全书. Shanghai: Shanghai Chinese Classics Publishing House, 2002.

Ruan Yuan 阮元. "Gujing jingshe wenji" 诂经精舍文集. In *Congshu jicheng* 丛书集成. Shanghai: Shanghai Commercial Press, 1936.

Sanyuan xian xinzhi 三原县新志, 1880 A.D.

Shandan xian zhi 山丹县志, 1835 A.D.

Shanhua xian zhi 善化县志, 1877 A.D.

Shaoguan fu zhi 韶关府志, 1873 A.D.

Shaozhou fu zhi 韶州府志, 1874 A.D.–1876 A.D.

Shehong xian zhi 射洪县志, 1875–1908 A.D.

Shen Defu 沈德符. *Wanli yehuo bian* 万历野获编. Beijing: Zhonghua Book Company, 1959.

Shi Huang 施璜. *Huangu shuyuan zhi* 还古书院志, 1843 A.D.

Shi Jie 石介. *Zulaishi xiansheng wenji* 徂徕石先生文集. Beijing: Zhonghua Book Company, 1984.

Shisan jing zhusu 十三经注疏. Beijing: Zhonghua Book Company, 1980.

Shunchang xian zhi 顺昌县志, 1912–1949.

Sichuan tongzhi 四川通志, 1797 A.D.

Si Maguang 司马光. *Zizhi tongjian* 资治通鉴. Beijing: Zhonghua Book Company, 1956.

Sima Guang 司马光. "Chuanjia ji" 传家集. In *Siku quanshu* 四库全书. Shanghai: Shanghai Chinese Classics Publishing House, 1987.

Song Lian 宋濂. "Song xueshi quanji" 宋学士全集. In *Siku quanshu* 四库全书. Shanghai: Shanghai Chinese Classics Publishing House, 1987.

Song Lian 宋濂 et al. *Yuanshi* 元史. Beijing: Zhonghua Book Company, 1976.

Songyuan fangzhi congkan 宋元方志丛刊. Beijing: Chinese Publishing House, 1990.

Suian xian zhi 遂安县志, 1930.

Suining xian zhi 睢宁县志, 1886 A.D.

Su Shi 苏轼. *Su dongpo quanji* 苏东坡全集. Beijing: Zhonghua Book Company, 1986.

Su Tianjue 苏天爵. "Cixi wengao" 滋溪文稿. In *Siku quanshu* 四库全书. Shanghai: Shanghai Chinese Classics Publishing House, 1987.

Sun Fu 孙复. "Sunmingfu xiaoji" 孙明复小集. In *Siku quanshu* 四库全书. Shanghai: Shanghai Chinese Classics Publishing House, 1987.

Sun Guangxian 孙光宪. *Beimeng suo yan* 北梦琐言. Beijing: Zhonghua Book Company, 2002.

Sun Xidan 孙希旦. *Li ji ji jie* 礼记集解. Beijing: Zhonghua Book Company, 1989.

Suzhou fu zhi 苏州府志, 1883 A.D.

Taigu xian zhi 太谷县志, 1796 A.D.

Tang Su 唐肃. "Danya ji" 丹崖集. In *Xuxiu siku quanshu* 续修四库全书. Shanghai: Shanghai Chinese Classics Publishing House, 2002.

Tao Shu 陶澍. "Tao wenyi gong quanji" 陶文毅公全集. In *Xuxiu siku quanshu* 续修四库全书. Shanghai: Shanghai Chinese Classics Publishing House, 2002.

Tuo Tuo 脱脱 et al. *Song shi* 宋史. Beijing: Zhonghua Book Company, 1985.

Wang Bai 王柏. "Luzhai ji" 鲁斋集. In *Congshu jicheng* 丛书集成. Shanghai: Shanghai Commercial Press, 1936.

Wang Dang 王谠. *Tang yu lin* 唐语林. Beijing: Zhonghua Book Company, 1987.

Wang Daokun 汪道昆. "Taihan ji" 太函集. In *Xuxiu siku quanshu* 续修四库全书. Shanghai: Shanghai Chinese Classics Publishing House, 2002.

Wang Fuzhi 王夫之. *Songlun* 宋论. Beijing: Zhonghua Book Company, 1964.

Wang Guowei 王国维. *Wang guowei yishu* 王国维遗书. Shanghai: Shanghai Chinese Classics Publishing House, 1983.

Wang Hui 王恽. "Qiujian ji" 秋涧集. In *Siku quanshu* 四库全书. Shanghai: Shanghai Chinese Classics Publishing House, 1987.

Wang Kaitai 王凯泰. *Yingyuan shuyuan zhilue* 应元书院志略, 1870 A.D.

Wang Maohong 王懋竑. *Zhu xi nian pu* 朱熹年谱. Beijing: Zhonghua Book Company, 1984.

Wang Shouren 王守仁. *Wang yangming quanji* 王阳明全集. Shanghai: Shanghai Chinese Classics Publishing House, 1992.

Wang Tingdian 王颋点. *Zhou xue dian li* 庙学典礼. Hangzhou: Zhe jiang Chinese Classics Publishing House, 1992.

Wang Xu 王旭. "Lanxuan ji" 兰轩集. In *Siku quanshu* 四库全书. Shanghai: Shanghai Chinese Classics Publishing House, 1987.

Wang Yingchen 汪应辰. "Wending ji" 文定集. In *Siku quanshu* 四库全书. Shanghai: Shanghai Chinese Classics Publishing House, 1987.

Wang Yinglin 王应麟. "Yu hai" 玉海. In *Siku quanshu* 四库全书. Shanghai: Shanghai Chinese Classics Publishing House, 1987.

Wang Yinglin 王应麟. "Siming wenxian ji" 四明文献集. In *Congshu jicheng xubian* 丛书集成续编. Taipei: Taipei Xinwenfeng Publishing Company, 1988.

Wang Yong 王栐. *Yanji yimou lu* 燕翼诒谋录. Beijing: Zhonghua Book Company, 1981.

Wang Yucheng 王禹偁. "Xiaoxu ji" 小畜集. In *Siku quanshu* 四库全书. Shanghai: Shanghai Chinese Classics Publishing House, 1987.

Wei Liaoweng 魏了翁. "Heshan ji" 鹤山集. In *Siku quanshu* 四库全书. Shanghai: Shanghai Chinese Classics Publishing House, 1987.

Wei Songtang 魏颂唐. *Fuwen shuyuan zhilue* 敷文书院志略, 1936.

Wen Tianxiang 文天祥. *Wen tianxiang quan ji* 文天祥全集. Beijing: China Bookstore Publishing House, 1985.

226 Bibliography

Wen Ying 文莹. *Xiangshan ye lu* 湘山野录. Beijing: Zhonghua Book Company, 1984.

Wu Shengqin 吴省钦. "Baihua qiangao" 白华前稿. In *Xuxiu siku quanshu* 续修四库全书. Shanghai: Shanghai Chinese Classics Publishing House, 2002.

Wu Yong 吴泳. "Helin ji" 鹤林集. In *Siku quanshu* 四库全书. Shanghai: Shanghai Chinese Classics Publishing House, 1987.

Xiangyang fu zhi 襄阳府志, 1885 A.D.

Xia Xie 夏燮. *Ming tong jian* 明通鉴. Changsha: Yuelu Press, 1999.

Xiaogan xian zhi 孝感县志, 1882 A.D.

Xiao Lianggan 萧良榦. "Jishan huiyue" 稽山会约. In *Congshu jicheng* 丛书集成. Shanghai: Shanghai Commercial Press, 1936.

Xie Jin 解缙 et al. *Yongle dadian* 永乐大典. Beijing: Zhonghua Book Company, 1960.

Xiong He 熊禾. "Wuxuan ji" 勿轩集. In *Siku quanshu* 四库全书. Shanghai: Shanghai Chinese Classics Publishing House, 1987.

Xiuning xian zhi 休宁县志, 1694 A.D.

Xu bian liang chao gang mu bei yao 续编两朝纲目备要. Beijing: Zhonghua Book Company, 1995.

Xu Chengrao 许承尧. *Xishi xian tan* 歙事闲谈. Huangshan: Huangshan City Book Club, 2001.

Xu Du 徐度. "Quesao pian" 却扫篇. In *Siku quanshu* 四库全书. Shanghai: Shanghai Chinese Classics Publishing House, 1987.

Xu Jingxi 徐景熹. *Fuzhou fu zhi* 福州府志. Fuzhou: Haifeng Publishing House, 2001.

Xu Song 徐松. *Songhuiyao jigao* 宋会要辑稿. Beijing: Zhonghua Book Company, 1957.

Xu xiu jianshui zhou zhi 续修建水州志, 1731 A.D.

Xu xiu xingye xian zhi 续修兴业县志, 1778 A.D.

Xu Xuan 徐铉. "Qisheng ji" 骑省集. In *Siku quanshu* 四库全书. Shanghai: Shanghai Chinese Classics Publishing House, 1987.

Xuyi xian zhigao 盱眙县志稿, 1891 A.D.

Xu Youren 许有壬. "Zhizheng ji" 至正集. In *Siku quanshu* 四库全书. Shanghai: Shanghai Chinese Classics Publishing House, 1987.

Xu Yuanjie 徐元杰. "Meiye ji" 梅野集. In *Siku quanshu* 四库全书. Shanghai: Shanghai Chinese Classics Publishing House, 1987.

Xue Jüzheng 薛居正. *Jiu wudai shi* 旧五代史. Beijing: Zhonghua Book Company, 1976.

Xue Xi 薛熙. *Ming wen zai* 明文在. Changchun: Jilin People's Publishing House, 1998.

Xue Xuan 薛瑄. "Dushu lu" 读书录. In *Siku quanshu* 四库全书. Shanghai: Shanghai Chinese Classics Publishing House, 1987.

Xuzuan jvrong xian zhi 续纂句容县志, 1904 A.D.

Yan Jue 严毅. *Donglin shuyuan zhi* 东林书院志, 1662–1722 A.D.

Yanping fu zhi 延平府志, 1796–1820.

Yaojiang shuyuan zhilue 姚江书院志略, 1794 A.D.

Yao Mian 姚勉. "Xuepo ji" 雪坡集. In *Siku quanshu* 四库全书. Shanghai: Shanghai Chinese Classics Publishing House, 1987.

Yang Shiqi 杨士奇. "Dongli wenji" 东里文集. In *Sikuan quanshu* 四库全书. Shanghai: Shanghai Chinese Classics Publishing House, 1987.

Yang Wanli 杨万里. "Chengzahi ji" 诚斋集. In *Siku quanshu* 四库全书. Shanghai: Shanghai Chinese Classics Publishing House, 1987.

Ye Mengdei 叶梦得. *Shi lin yan yu* 石林燕语. Beijing: Zhonghua Book Company, 1984.

Ye Shi 叶适. *Yeshi ji* 叶适集. Beijing: Zhonghua Book Company, 1961.

Yinign xian zhi 义宁县志, 1821 A.D.

Yu Minzhong 于敏中, ed. *Ri xia jiu wenkao* 日下旧闻考. Beijing: Beijing Chinese Classics Publishing House, 1983.

Yu Que 余闕. "Qing yang ji" 青阳集. In *Siku quanshu* 四库全书. Shanghai: Shanghai Chinese Classics Publishing House, 1987.

Yuan Fu 袁甫. "Mengzhai ji" 蒙斋集. In *Siku quanshu* 四库全书. Shanghai: Shanghai Chinese Classics Publishing House, 1987.

Yuan Shuyi 苑书义, ed. *Zhang zhi dong quanji* 张之洞全集. Shijiazhuang: Hebei People's Publishing House, 1984.

Yuan Xie 袁燮. "Qiezhai ji" 絜斋集. In *Siku quanshu* 四库全书. Shanghai: Shanghai Chinese Classics Publishing House, 1987.

Yuan Zhen 元稹. *Yuan zhen ji* 元稹集. Beijing: Zhonghua Book Company, 1982.

Yunnan fu zhi 云南府志, 1696 A.D.

Yun xian zhi 郧县志, 1866 A.D.

Zan Ning 赞宁. *Song gao seng zhuan* 宋高僧传. Beijing: Zhonghua Book Company, 1987.

Zengxiu ganquan xian zhi 增修甘泉县志, 1837 A.D.

Zhang Boxing 张伯行. *Zheng yi tang wenji* 正谊堂文集. Beijing: Zhonghua Book Company, 1985.

Zhanghua xian zhi 漳化县志, 1836 A.D.

Zhang Nai 张鼐 et al. *Yushan shuyuan zhi* 虞山书院志, 1573–1620 A.D.

Zhang Shi 张栻. "Guisi mengzi shuo" 癸巳孟子说. In *Siku quanshu* 四库全书. Shanghai: Shanghai Chinese Classics Publishing House, 1987.

Zhang Shi 张栻. "Nanxuan ji" 南轩集. In *Siku quanshu* 四库全书. Shanghai: Shanghai Chinese Classics Publishing House, 1987.

Zhang Shunmin 张舜民. "Huaman ji" 画墁集. In *Siku quanshu* 四库全书. Shanghai: Shanghai Chinese Classics Publishing House, 1987.

Zhang Tingyu 张廷玉 et al. *Mingshi* 明史. Beijing: Zhonghua Book Company, 1974.

Zhang Yanyu 张廷玉 et al. *Qingchao wenxian tongkao* 清朝文献通考. Hangzhou: Zhejiang Chinese Classics Publishing House, 1988.

Zhang Zhuo 张篇. *Chaoye qianzai* 朝野佥载. Beijing: Zhonghua Book Company, 1979.

Zhaoqing fu zhi 肇庆府志, 1876 A.D.

Zhao Suosheng 赵所生, & Xue Zheng Xing 薛正兴. *Zhongguo lidai shuyuan zhi* 中国历代书院志. Nanjing: Jiangsu Education Press, 1985.

Zhejiang tong zhi 浙江通志, 1899 A.D.

Zhenan fu zhi 镇安府志, 1892 A.D.

Zhen Dexiu 真德秀. "Xishan wenji" 西山文集. In *Siku quanshu* 四库全书. Shanghai: Shanghai Chinese Classics Publishing House, 1987.

Zheng Tinghu 郑廷鹄. *Bailudong zhi* 白鹿洞志, 1566 A.D.

Zheng Yuanyou 郑元祐. "Qiaowu ji" 侨吴集. In *Siku quanshu* 四库全书. Shanghai: Shanghai Chinese Classics Publishing House, 1987.

Zhong Shizhen 钟世桢. *Xinjiang shuyuan zhi* 信江书院志, 1867 A.D.

Zhou Bida 周必大. "Wenzhong ji" 文忠集. In *Siku quanshu* 四库全书. Shanghai: Shanghai Chinese Classics Publishing House, 1987.

Zhou Dunyi 周敦颐. *Zhou dunyi quan shu* 周敦颐全书. Nanchang: Jiangxi Education Press, 1985.

Zhou Mi 周密. "Guixin zazhi" 癸辛杂志. In *Siku quanshu* 四库全书. Shanghai: Shanghai Chinese Classics Publishing House, 1987.

Zhou Wei 周伟 et al. *Bailudong shuyuan zhi* 白鹿洞书院志, 1584 A.D.

Zhu Jieren 朱杰人, Yan Zuozhi 严佐之, & Liu Yongxiang 刘永翔, eds. *Zhuzi quanshu* 朱子全书. Shanghai: Shanghai Chinese Classics Publishing House; Hefei: Anhui Education Press, 2002.

Zhu Ruixi 朱瑞熙. *Bailu dong shuyuan guzhi wuzhong* 白鹿洞书院古志五种. Beijing: Zhonghua Book Company, 1984.

228 *Bibliography*

Zhu Xi 朱熹. *Sishu zhangju jizhu* 四书章句集注. Beijing: Zhonghua Book Company, 1983.

Zhu Yizun 朱彝尊. *Jing yi kao* 经义考. Beijing: Zhonghua Book Company, 1998.

Zhuzi jicheng 诸子集成. Shanghai: Shanghai Bookstore, 1986.

Zou Yuanbiao 邹元标. "Yuanxue ji" 愿学集. In *Siku quanshu* 四库全书. Shanghai: Shanghai Chinese Classics Publishing House, 1987.

Monographs

Bai Xinliang 白新良. *Zhongguo shuyuan fazhan shi* 中国书院发展史. Tianjin: Tianjin University Press, 1995.

Benjamin A. Elman 艾尔曼. *Cong lixue dao puxue—zhonghua diguo wanqi sixiang yu shehui bianhua mianmian guan* 从理学到朴学—中华帝国晚期思想与社会变化面面观. Trans. Zhao Gang赵刚. Nanjing: Jiangsu People's Publishing House, 1997.

Cai Shangxiang 蔡上翔. *Wangjing gongnian pukao lue* 王荆公年谱考略. Shanghai: Shanghai People's Publishing House, 1973.

Cai Yuanpei 蔡元培. *Cai yuanpei quanji* 蔡元培全集. Beijing: Zhonghua Book Company, 1984.

Chen Gujia 陈谷嘉. Deng Hongbo 邓洪波. *Zhongguo shuyuan zhidu yanjiu* 中国书院制度研究. Hangzhou: Zhejiang Education Press, 1997.

Chen Gujia 陈谷嘉. Deng Hongbo 邓洪波. *Zhongguo shuyuan shi ziliao* 中国书院史资料. Hangzhou: Zhejiang Education Press, 1998.

Chen Lai 陈来. *Zhuzi zhexue yanjiu* 朱子哲学研究. Shanghai: East China Normal University Press, 2000.

Chen Rongjie 陈荣捷. *Zhuxue lunji* 朱学论集. Taiwan: Taiwan Student Book Compan, 1982.

Chen Wenyi 陈雯怡. *You guanxue dao shuyuan—cong zhidu yu linian de hudong kan songdai jiaoyu de yanbian* 由官学到书院—从制度与理念的互动看宋代教育的演变. Taibei: Taibei Lianjing Publishing Company, 2004.

Chen Yuanhui 陈元晖, Yin Dexin 尹德新, & Wang Bingzhao 王炳照. *Zhongguo gudai de shuyuan zhidu* 中国古代的书院制度. Shanghai: Shanghai Education Press, 1981.

Cheng Minsheng 程民生. *Songdai diyu wenhua* 宋代地域文化. Kaifeng: Henan University Press, 1997.

Deng Hongbo 邓洪波. *Zhongguo shuyuan shi* 中国书院史. Shanghai: Oriental Publishing Center, 2004.

Dennis H. Long 丹尼斯·H.朗. *Quanli lun* 权力论. Beijing: China Social Sciences Press, 2000.

Ding Gang丁钢, & Liu Qi刘琪. *Shuyuan yu zhongguo wenhua* 书院与中国文化. Shanghai: Shanghai Education Press, 1992.

Edgar Bodenheimer E. 博登海默. *Falixue—fazhexue jiqi fangfa* 法理学—法哲学及其方法. Beijing: Huaxia Publishing House, 1987.

Fan Kezheng 樊克政et al. *Zhongguo shuyuan shi* 中国书院史. Taiwan: Wenjin Publishing House, 1995.

Fang Yanshou 方彦寿. *Zhuxi shuyuan yu menren kao* 朱熹书院与门人考. Shanghai: East China Normal University Press, 2000.

Feng Youlan 冯友兰. *Zhongguo zhexueshi xinbian* 中国哲学史新编. Beijing: People's Publishing House, 1988.

Gu Shusen 顾树森. *Zhongguo lidai jiaoyu zhidu* 中国历代教育制度. Jiangsu: Jiangsu Education Press, 1981.

Bibliography 229

Han Guoqing 韩国磐. *Suitang wudaishi lunji* 隋唐五代史论集. Hong Kong: Joint Publishing, 1979.

He Huaihong 何怀宏. *Xuanju shehui ji qi zhongjie* 选举社会及其终结. Beijing: Beijing Sanlian Bookstore, 1998.

Hou Shaowen侯绍文. *Tangsong kaoshi zhidu shi* 唐宋考试制度史. Yaiwan: Commercial Press, 1973.

Hou Wailu 侯外庐. *Zhongguo sixiang tongshi* 中国思想通史. Beijing: People's Publishing House, 1995.

Hou Wailu 侯外庐, Qiu Hansheng 邱汉生, & Zhang Qizhi 张岂之. *Song ming lixue shi* 宋明理学史. Beijing: People's Publishing House, 1997.

Hu Qing 胡青. *Shuyuan de shehui gongneng ji qi wenhua tese* 书院的社会功能及其文化特色. Wuhan: Hubei Education Press, 1996.

Hu Zhaoxi 胡昭曦. *Sichuan shuyuan shi* 四川书院史. Chengdu: Bashu Publishing House, 2000.

Huang Jinxing 黄进兴. *You ru shengyu—quanli, xinyang yu zhengdang xing* 优入圣域—权力、信仰与正当性. Xi'an: Shanxi Normal University Press, 1998.

Huang Liuzhu黄留珠. *Zhongguo gudai xuanguan zhidu shulue* 中国古代选官制度述略. Shanxi: People's Publishing House, 1989.

Huang Meiyin 黄玫茵. *Tangdai jiangxi diqu kaifa yanjiu* 唐代江西地区开发研究. Taibei: College of Arts, Taiwan University, 1995.

Ji Xiaofeng 季啸风. *Zhongguo shuyuan cidain* 中国书院辞典. Hangzhou: Zhejiang Education Press, 1996.

John Meshill. *Academy in Ming China: A History Essay*. Tucson：The University of Arizona Press, 1982.

Joseph Needham 李约瑟. *Zhongguo kexue jishu shi* 中国科学技术史. Beijing: Science Press, 1990.

Lai Xinxai 来新夏. *Zhongguo gudai tushu shiye shi* 中国古代图书事业史. Shanghai: Shanghai People's Publishing House, 1990.

Li Bing 李兵. *Shuyuan yu keju guanxi yanjiu* 书院与科举关系研究. Wuhan: Central China Normal University Press, 2005.

Li Caidong李才栋. *Bailudong shuyuan shilue* 白鹿洞书院史略. Beijing: Science Press, 1989.

Li Caidong 李才栋. *Jiangxi gudai shuyuan yanjiu* 江西古代书院研究. Nanchang: Jiangxi Education Press, 1993.

Li Guojun 李国钧et al. *Zhongguo shuyuan shi* 中国书院史. Changsha: Hunan Education Press, 1994.

Linda Walton. *Academies and Society in Southern Sung China*. Hawaii: University of Hawaii Press, 1999.

Li Shen 李申. *Zhongguo rujiao shi* 中国儒教史. Shanghai: Shanghai People's Publishing House, 1999.

Li Shuhua 李书华. *Zhongguo yinshuashu qiyuan* 中国印刷术起源. Hong Kong: New Asia Institute, 1962.

Li Wenzhi 李文治 & Jiang Taixin 江太新. *Zhongguo zongfa zongzu zhi he zutian yizhuang* 中国宗法宗族制和族田义庄. Beijing: China Social Sciences Press, 2000.

Li Xubai 李绪柏. *Qingdai guangdong puxue yanjiu* 清代广东朴学研究. Guangzhou: Guangdong Map Publishing House, 2001.

Liu Boji 刘伯骥. *Guangdong shuyuan zhidu yange* 广东书院制度沿革. Taiwan: National Institute of Compilation and Translation, 1958.

Liu Feng 刘丰. *Xianqin lixue sixiang yu sh hui de zhenghe* 先秦礼学思想与社会的整合. Beijing: China Renmin University Press, 2003.

Bibliography

Liu Guojun 刘国钧. *Zhongguo de yinshua* 中国的印刷. Shanghai: Shanghai People's Publishing House, 1960.

Liu Hong 刘虹. *Zhongguo xuanshi zhidu shi* 中国选士制度史. Changsha: Hunan Education Press, 1992.

Liu Qihua 刘起釪. *Shangshu xueshi* 尚书学史. Beijing: Zhonghua Book Company, 1989.

Liu Xingyan 刘行炎et al. *Chuanbo xue* 传播学. Wuhan: University Press, 1994.

Liu Zehua 刘泽华. *Xianqin shiren yu shehui* 先秦士人与社会. Tianjin: Tianjin People's Publishing House, 2004.

Lü Simian 吕思勉. *Suitang wudai shi* 隋唐五代史. Shanghai: Shanghai Chinese Classics Publishing House, 1984.

Mou Zongsan 牟宗三. *Xinti yu xingti* 心体与性体. Shanghai: Shanghai Chinese Classics Publishing House, 1999.

Qian Jibo 钱基博. *Hunan jin bainian xuefeng* 湖南近百年学风. Beijing: China Renmin University Press, 2004.

Sheng Langxi 盛朗西. *Zhongguo shuyuan zhidu* 中国书院制度. Beijing: Zhonghua Book Company, 1934.

Shu Jingnan 束景南. *Zhuzi dazhuan* 朱子大传. Fuzhou: Fujian Education Press, 1992.

Sima Yunjie 司马云杰. *Wenhua shehui xue* 文化社会学. Beijing: China Social Sciences Press, 2001.

Sun Benwen 孙本文. "Shehuixue yuanli" 社会学原理. In *Minguo congshu* 民国丛书. Shanghai: Shanghai Bookstore, 1992.

Wang Bingzhao 王炳照. *Zhongguo gudai sixue yu jindai sili xuexiao yanjiu* 中国古代私学与近代私立学校研究. Jinan: Shandong Education Press, 1997.

William T. Rowe. *Save the World—Chen Hongmou and Elite Consciousness in Eighteenth Century China*. Stanford, CA: Stanford University Press, 2001.

Wu Han 吴晗, Fei Xiao Tong 费孝通et al. *Huangquan yu shenquan* 皇权与绅权. Shanghai: Shanghai Observatory, 1949.

Wu Renan 吴仁安. *Ming qing shiqi shanghai de zhuxing wangzu* 明清时期上海的著姓望族. Shanghai: Shanghai People's Publishing House, 1997.

Wu Wanju吴万居. *Songdai shuyuan yu songdai xueshu zhi guanxi* 宋代书院与宋代学术之关系. Taiwan: Taiwan Literature, History and Philosophy Publishing House, 1991.

Wuyishan zhu xi yanjiu zhongxin 武夷山朱熹研究中心, ed. *Zhu xi yu min xue yuanliu* 朱熹与闽学源流. Shanghai: Shanghai SDX Joint Publishing Company, 1990.

Xiao Yongming 肖永明. *Beisong xinxue yu lixue* 宋新学与理学. Xi'an: Shaanxi People's Publishing House, 2000.

Xie Guozhen谢国桢. "Jindai shuyuan xuexiao zhidu bianqian kao" 近代书院学校制度变迁考. In *Jindai zhongguo shiliao congkan xubian* 近代中国史料丛刊续编. Taibei: Wenhai Publishing House, 1983.

Xiong Chengdi 熊承涤, ed. *Zhongguo gudai jiaoyushi xinian* 中国古代教育史系年. Beijing: People's Education Press, 1985.

Xu Bingyun 徐冰云. *Fengxin gudai shuyaun* 奉新古代书院. Yichun: Fengxin County Annal Editorial Committee and Fengxin County Education Bureau, 1985.

Xu Yanping 徐雁平. *Qingdai dongnan shuyuan yu xueshu ji wenxue* 清代东南书院与学术及文学. Hefei: Anhui Education Press, 2007.

Xu Zi 徐梓. *Yuandai shuyuan yanjiu* 元代书院研究. Beijing: Social Sciences Academic Press, 2000.

Yang Busheng 杨布生. "Peng Dingguo" 彭定国. In *Zhongguo shuyuan wenhua* 中国书院文化. Taibei: Taiwan Huanglong Press, 1997.

Yang Nianqun 杨念群. *Ruxue diyuhua de jindai xingtai--sanda zhishi qunti hudong de bijiao janjiu* 儒学地域化的近代形态—三大知识群体互动的比较研究. Beijing: Beijing SDX Joint Publishing Company, 1997.

Yang Shenchu 杨慎初, Zhu Hanmin 朱汉民, & Deng Hongbo 邓洪波. *Yuelu shuyuan shilue* 岳麓书院史略. Changsha: Yuelu Book Press, 1986.

Yu Yingshi 余英时. *Zhuxi de lishi shijie* 朱熹的历史世界. Beijing: Beijing SDX Joint Publishing Company, 2004.

Zhang Chuting 张楚廷. "Zhang Chuan sui" 张传遂. In *Hunan jiaoyu shi* 湖南教育史. Changsha: Yuelu Press, 1994.

Zhang Liuquan 章柳泉. *Zhongguo shuyuan shihua--songyuan mingqing shuyuan de yanbian jiqi neirong* 中国书院史话—宋元明清书院的演变及其内容. Beijing: Science Press, 1981.

Zhang Liwen 张立文. *Songming lixue yanjiu* 宋明理学研究. Beijing: University Press, 1985.

Zhang Xiumin 张秀民. *Zhongguo yinshua shi* 中国印刷史. Shanghai: Shanghai People's Publishing House, 1989.

Zhang Zhongli 张仲礼. *Zhongguo shenshi--guanyu qi zai shijiu shiji zhongguo shehui zhong zuoyong de yanjiu* 中国绅士—关于其在十九世纪中国社会中作用的研究. Trans. Li Rongchang 李荣昌. Shanghai: Press of Shanghai Academy of Social Sciences, 1991.

Zhao Tongxi 赵同喜. *Tangdai kaoxuan zhidu* 唐代考选制度. Taiwan: The Compilation Committee of Series of Books on Examination and Selection System, 1983.

Zhou Qingshan 周庆山. *Chuanbo xue gailun* 传播学概论. Beijing: Beijing University Press, 2004.

Zhu Hanmin 朱汉民. *Huxiang xuepai yu yuelu shuyuan* 湖湘学派与岳麓书院. Beijing: Science Press, 1991.

Zhu Hanmin 朱汉民. *Song ming lixue tonglun--yizhong wenhua xue de quanshi* 宋明理学通论—一种文化学的诠释. Changsha: Hunan People's Publishing House, 2000.

Zhu Hanmin 朱汉民, & Chen Gujia 陈谷嘉. *Huxiang xuepai yuanliu* 湖湘学派源流. Changsha: Hunan Education Press, 1992.

Zhu Hanmin 朱汉民, Deng Hongbo 邓洪波, & Gao Fengyu 高峰煜. *Changjiang liuyu de shuyuan* 长江流域的书院. Wuhan: Hubei Education Press, 2004.

Articles

Bai Xinliang 白新良. "Shi lun qing chu shuyuan de huifu yu fazhan" 试论清初书院的恢复和发展. In *Zhongguo shuyuan* Vol. 5 中国书院第5辑. Changsha: Hunan Education Press, 2003.

Cai Yi 蔡仪, & Cai Xiaochu 蔡晓初. "Shuyuan cangshu tan" 书院藏书谈. In *Jiangxi jiaoyu xueyuan xuebao* 江西教育学院学报, No. 1, 2002.

Cao Songye 曹松叶. "Song yuan ming qing shuyuan gaikuang" 宋元明清书院概况. In *Zhongshan daxue yuyan lishi yanjiusuo zhoukan* Vol. 10, 中山大学语言历史研究所周刊, No. 111–115, 1929–1930.

Chen Dongyuan 陈东原. "Shuyuan shi lue" 书院史略. In *Xuefeng* Vol. 1 学风, No. 9, 1931.

Chen Keng 陈铿. "Cong (xingshi hunyin) kan mingqing zhiji de difang shenshi" 从〈醒世姻缘〉看明清之际的地方士绅. In *Xiamen daxue xuebao* 厦门大学学报, No. 4, 1984.

Chen Yuanping 陈平原. "Jie du bei zuo wei shenhua de qinghua guoxue yuan" 解读被作为神话的清华国学院. In *Science Times* 科学时报, 1995.

Cheng Shunying 程舜英. "Fojiao dui zhongguo jiaoyu he shuyuan zhidu de yingxiang" 佛教对中国教育和书院制度的影响. In *Yuelu shuyuan yi qian ling shi yi zhounian jinian*

232 Bibliography

wenji Vol. 1, 岳麓书院一千零一十周年纪念文集第1辑, Changsha: Hunan People's Publishing House, 1986.

Deng Guangming 邓广铭. "Wang Anshi zai beisong rujia xuepai zhong de diwei" 王安石在北宋儒家学派中的地位—附说理学家的开山祖问题. In *Jiaoyu yu rensheng* 北京大学学报, No. 2, 1991.

Deng Hongbo 邓洪波. "Ming qing shiqi jiangsu cangshu mulu jilue" 明清时期江苏藏书目录辑略. In *Jiangshu tushuguan xuebao* 江苏图书馆学报, No. 1, 1996.

Deng Hongbo 邓洪波. "Jian lun wanqing jiangsu shuyuan cangshu shiye de tese yu gongxian" 简论晚清江苏书院藏书事业的特色与贡献. In *Jiangsu tushuguan xuebao* 江苏图书馆学报, No. 4, 1999.

Deng Hongbo 邓洪波. "Tang dai minjian shuyuan yanjiu" 唐代民间书院研究. In *Zhongguo shuyuan* Vol. 3 中国书院第3辑. Changsha: Hunan Education Press, 2000.

Deng Hongbo 邓洪波. "Nansong shuyuan yu lixue de yitihua" 南宋书院与理学的一体化. In *Hunan daxue xuebao* 湖南大学学报, No. 3, 2004.

Deng Hongbo 邓洪波. "Ru xue quanshi de pingmin hua mingdai shuyuan jiangxue de xin tedian" 儒学诠释的平民化：明代书院讲学的新特点. In *Hunan daxue xuebao* 湖南大学学报, No. 3, 2005.

Gao Jichun 高纪春. "Songgaozong chunian de wanganshi pipan yu luoxue zhi xing" 宋高宗初年的王安石批判与洛学之兴. In *Zhongzhou xue kan* 中州学刊, No. 1, 1996.

Gao Mingshi 高明士. "Shuyuan jisi kongjian de jiaoyu zuoyong" 书院祭祀空间的教育作用. In *Zhongguo shuyuan* Vol. 1 中国书院第1辑. Changsha: Hunan Education Press, 1997.

Gong Pengcheng 龚鹏程. "Lun tangdai de wenxue chongbai yu wenxue shehui" 论唐代的文学崇拜与文学社会. In *Wantang de shehui yu wenhua* 晚唐的社会与文化. Taibei: Taipei Student Bookstore, 1990.

Gu Hongyi 顾宏义. "Shilun songdai shuyuan de guanxue hua" 试论宋代书院的官学化. In *Zhongguo shuyuan* Vol. 2 中国书院第2辑. Changsha: Hunan Education Press, 1998.

Gu Weiying 古伟瀛. "Ming qing bianju xia de shuyuan" 明清变局下的书院. In *Zhongguo shuyuan* Vol. 5 中国书院第5辑. Changsha: Hunan Education Press, 2003.

Hu Shi 胡适. "Shuyuan de lishi yu jingshen" 书院的历史与精神. In *Jiaoyu yu rensheng* 教育与人生, No. 9, 1923.

Hu Shi 胡适. "Shuyuanzhishi lue" 书院制史略. In *Dong fang zazhi* Vol. 21东方杂志, No. 3, 1924.

Huang Kuanzhong 黄宽重. "Nansong liangzhelu shehui liudong kaocha" 南宋两浙路社会流动考察. In *Songshilun cong* 宋史论丛. Taibei: Taibei New Wenfeng Publishing Company, 1993.

Huang Xinxian 黄新宪. "Qing dai fujian shuyuan de ruogan tese jiqi dangdai jiazhi" 清代福建书院的若干特色及当代价值. In *Zhongguo shuyuan* Vol. 5 中国书院第5辑. Changsha: Hunan Education Press, 2003.

Jin Dasheng 金达胜, & Fang Jianxin方建新. "Yuandai hangzhouxihushuyuan cangshu" 元代杭州西湖书院藏书. In *Journal of Hangzhou University* 杭州大学学报, No. 3, 1995.

Jin Xudong 金旭东. "Shi lun songdai de enyin zhidu" 试论宋代的恩荫制度. In *Yunnan shehui xueke* 云南社会科学, No. 2, 1985.

Li Caidong 李才栋. "Jianlun woguo shuyuan de qiyuan" 简论我国书院的起源. In *Yuelu shuyuan yi qian ling shiyi zhounian jinian wenji* 岳麓书院一千零一十周年纪念文集. Changsha: Hunan People's Publishing House, 1986.

Li Caidong 李才栋. "Guanyu zhongguo shuyuan zhidu yanjiu de tongxun" 关于中国书院制度研究的通讯. In *Zhongguo shuyuan* Vol. 2 中国书院第2辑. Changsha: Hunan Education Press, 1998.

Li Caidong 李才栋. "Guanyu shuyuan jianghui de jige wenti" 关于书院讲会的几个问题. In *Zhongguo shu yuan* Vol. 4 中国书院第4辑. Changsha: Hunan Education Press, 2002.

Li Jingwen 李景文. "Qingdai henan shuyuan keshu qianlun" 清代河南书院刻书浅论. In *Shixue yuekan* 史学月刊, No. 5, 1994.

Li Junxiu 李峻岫. "Shi lun hanyu de daotongshuo jiqi mengxue sixiang" 试论韩愈的道统说及其孟学思想. In *Kongzi yuanjiu* 孔子研究, No. 6, 2004.

Li Ying 李颖. "Jindai shuyuan cangshu kao" 近代书院藏书考, In *Tushu yu qingbao* 图书与情报, No. 1, 1999.

Linda Walton 琳达·沃尔顿. "Nansong shuyuan de dilifenbu" 南宋书院的地理分布. Trans. Deng Hongbo邓洪波. In *Hunandaxue xuebao*湖南大学学报, No. 1, 1991.

Liu Qi 刘琪, & Zhu Hanmin 朱汉民. "Xiangshui jiaojing tang shuping" 湘水校经堂述评. In *Yuelu shuyuan yi qian ling shiyi zhounian jinian wenji* Vol. 1, 岳麓书院一千零一十周年纪念文集第1辑. Changsha: Hunan People's Publishing House, 1986.

Liu Yihui 柳诒徵. "Jiangsu shuyuanzhi chugao" 江苏书院志初稿. In *Jiangsu guoxue tushuguan niankan* 江苏国学图书馆年刊, No. 4, 1931.

Liu Zijian 刘子健. "Luelun songdai difang guanxue yu sixue de xiaozhang" 略论宋代地方官学与私学的消长. In *Songshi yanjiu ji* Vol. 4宋史研究集. Taibei: Editorial Board of Taibei Zhonghua Series, 1969.

Liu Zijian 高明士. "Tangdai sixue de fazhan" 唐代私学的发展. In *Taida wenshi zhexue bao* Vol. 20, 台大文史哲学报 1971.

Peng Yongjie 彭永捷. "Lun rujia dao tong ji songdai lixue de chuantong zhi zheng" 论儒家道统及宋代理学的道统之争. In *Wen shi zhe* 文史哲, No. 2, 2001.

Robert Hymes. "Lu Jiuyuan: shuyuan yu xiangcun shehui wenti" 陆九渊: 乡村与社会问题. In *Songdai sixiang shi lun* 宋代思想史论, ed. Hoyt Cleveland Till Man and Trans. Yang Lihua. Beijing: Social Science Academic Press, 2003.

Song Xi宋晞. "Songdai shi dafu dui shangren de taidu" 宋代士大夫对商人的态度. In *Songshi yanjiulun cong* Vol. 1. 宋史研究论丛, 1962.

Su Yunfeng 苏云峰. "Guangya shuyuan1888–1903" 广雅书院 (1888–1902). In Tai Wan 台湾, *"Zhongyang yanjiu yuan" jindai shi yanjiu suo jikan* "中央研究院"近代史研究所集刊, No. 13, 1984.

Wang Ermin 王尔敏 et al. "Ruxue shisuhua jiqi duiyu minjian" 儒学世俗化及其对于民间风教之浸濡. In *Ming qing shehui wenhua shengtai* 明清社会文化生态. Taibei: Taipei Commercial Press, 1997.

Wang He 王河. "Nansong shuyuan cangshu kaolue" 宋书院藏书考略. In *Jiangxi shehui kexue* 江西社会科学, 1998.

Wang Jianliang 王建梁. "Qingdai shuyuan yu hanxued hudong yanjiu" 清代书院与汉学的互动研究. Ph. D diss., Beijing: Peking Normal University, 2002.

Wang Lanyin 王兰荫. "Hebei sheng shuyuan zhi" 河北省书院志. In *Shida yuekan* Vol. 25师大月刊, No. 29, 1936.

Weng Tongwen 翁同文. "Tangdai sixue de fazhan" 印刷术对于书籍成本的影响. In *Taida wenshi zhexue bao* Vol. 8 宋史研究集. Taibei: Editorial Board of Taiwan Zhonghua Series, 1976.

Wu Jingxian 吴景贤. "Anhui shuyuan zhi" 安徽书院志. In *Xuefeng* Vol. 2学风, No. 4–8, 1932.

Wu Zongguo吴宗国. "Tangdai shizu jiqi shuailuo" 唐代士族及其衰落. In *Tangshi xuehui lunwen ji* 唐史学会论文集. Xi'an: Shaanxi People's Publishing House, 1986.

Xiao Yongming肖永明, & Tang Yayang 唐亚阳. "Shuyuan yu shehui jiaohua" 书院与社会教化. In *Zhongguo shuyuan* Vol. 5 中国书院第5辑. Changsha: Hunan Education Press, 2003.

234 *Bibliography*

Xu Maoming 徐茂明. "Shishen de jianshou yu quanbian qingdai suzhou panshi jiazu de jiafeng yu xintai yanjiu" 士绅的坚守与权变：清代苏州潘氏家族的家风与心态研究. In *Shixue yue kan* 史学月刊, No. 10, 2003.

Xu Zi 徐梓. "Lun yuandai shuyuan de xuexiao hua" 论元代书院的学校化. In *Zhongguo shuyuan* Vol. 2 中国书院第2辑. Changsha: Hunan Education Press, 1998.

"Yanjiu yuan zhangcheng" 研究院章程. In *Qinghua zhoukan* 清华周刊, No. 360, 1925.

Yu Yingshi 余英时. "Zhonguo jin shi zonhjiao lunli yu shangren jingshen" 中国近世宗教伦理与商人精神. In *Yu yingshi wenji* 余英时文集Vol. 3余英时文集第3卷. Guilin: Guangxi Normal University Press, 2004.

Zhang Yin 张崟. "Gujing jingshe zhi chugao" 诂经精舍志初稿. In *Wenlan xuebao* Vol. 2, 文澜学报, 1936, No. 1.

Zhu Hanmin 朱汉民. "Nansong lixue yu shuyuan jiaoyu" 南宋理学与书院教育. In *Zhongguo zhexue* Vol. 16,中国哲学. Changsha: Yuelu Book Press, 1993.

Zou Chonghua 邹重华. "Songdai sichuan shuyuan kao jian lun songdai shuyuan yanjiu de ruogan wenti" 宋代四川书院考—兼论宋代书院研究的若干问题. In *Zhonguo shuyuan* Vol. 3 中国书院第3辑. Changsha: Hunan Education Press, 2000.

Index

Academy annals 147, 150; *see also Annals of...*

Academy of imperial China (the Academy): authoritarian power, subservience to 41; book collecting in the academies 135–142; book engraving in the academies 135, 142–147; cultivation of regional talents and 147–154; diffusion of Confucianism from Academy to Society 13–18; interlocking of Confucianism and 11–13; manners and etiquette in 177, 189, 191, 196–214; obedience in 210–212; omen worship in 187–190; politics and state policy to 18–41; public lectures offered by 31, 128, 149, 152–156; *see also* Bailudong Academy; sacrificial ritual; Yuelu Academy

Ai *see* Duke Ai

Analects of Chen Hao（尊道录）144

Analects of Confucius 116, 202–204, 207; *Annotations on the Analects of Confucius* (Zhu Xi) 25; *Commentary on Analects*（论语精义）(Zhu Xi) 3; "Exercising Government" 209; "Forerunner Men" 177; "In the Village" 197, 204; Zhu Xi's request for copies of 137

Analects of Zhu Xi（朱子语类）69, 117

Anding Academy 119, 162

"Annal of Confucian Scholars of Shi-Liu School"（士刘诸儒学案）, in *Scholarly Annals of Song and Yuan Periods*（宋元学案）114

"Annal of the Confucian Scholar Hu Hong"（五峰学案）, in *Scholarly Annals of Song and Yuan Periods*（宋元学案）121

"Annal of the Scholars of Nanxuan School"（南轩学案）, in *Scholarly*

Annals of Song and Yuan Periods（宋元学案）115

Annals of Academies（书院志）143

Annals of Bailudong Academy（白鹿书院志）(Li Mengyang) 58

Annals of Bailudong Academy（白鹿书院志）(Mao Deqi) 52, 58

Annals of Bailudong Academy（白鹿洞志，又名：白鹿洞书院志）(Zheng Tinghu) 53, 54, 56, 144

Annals of Classics in Zhenyan Academy（箴言书院典籍志）(Hu Linyi) 138

annals of counties, prefectures, and provinces *see* county annals

"Annals of Donglou Academy"（东娄书院记）150

Annals of Huangu Academy（还古书院志）81

Annals of Mingdao Academy（明道书院志）147

Annals of Shenye Academy（莘野书院四斋说）147

Annals of Songyang Academy（嵩阳书院志）147

"Annals of Wansong Academy"（万松书院记）(Wang Shouren) 150

Annals of Xinjiang Academy（信江书院志）(Zhong Shizhen) 56

"Annals of Yuping Academy"（玉屏书院记）(Yang Jinkai) 150

Annals of Ziyang Academy（紫阳书院志略）(Dong Guifu) 60

Annals of Ziyun Academy（敕赐紫云书院志）(Li Zhuoran) 147

"Annals, The"（年谱）in Appendix 1 to *The Complete Works of Wang Yangming*（王阳明全集卷·年谱附录一）88

Aofeng Academy 162, 204

Back Blade Mountain 180

Bailu Academy（白鹭书院）37, 177

236 *Index*

Bailudong Academy, Jiangxi 20, 124, 129; ancestral buildings 52, 69, 81; *Annals of Bailudong Academy* (白鹿书 院志) (Li Mengyang) 58; *Annals of Bailudong Academy* (白鹿书院志) (Mao Deqi) 52, 58; *Annals of Bailudong Academy* (白鹿洞志,又名:白鹿洞书院志) (Zheng Tinghu) 53, 54, 56, 144; books loaned by 141; destruction and abandonment of 21–23; disrepair and mismanagement of 30; "Four Great Academies" of Song dynasty 129; figures of worship at 57–60, 62, 63, 64, 66, 69, 84, 85, 92, 95; God of Lands 60; "Homage to Sages on Completion of Bailudong Academy" (白鹿洞成告 先圣文) (Zhu Xi) 56; "Longterm Plan of Bailudong Academy" (经久规模议) (Gao Huang) 160; Loyalty Temple 59, 62; "Notes on Shrine of Confucian Ancestors of Bailudong Academy" (白鹿洞书院宗儒祠记) (Yang Lian) 13; literati lectures at 153; *Petition to Rebuild Bailudong Academy* (申修白鹿书院状) (Zhu Xi) 23; *Reconstruction of Book Pavilion in Bailudong Academy* (白鹿书院重建书阁记) (Cao Yanyue) 18; "Records of Shrine of Confucian Ancestors" (宗儒祠记) of Bailudong Academy (Yang Lian) 63; renovation of 92, 96; restoration of 24–25, 77, 136–137; *Restoration of Bailudong Acaemy* (重修白鹿洞书院记) 11; sacrificial rituals at 51; Sages Temple (Sanxian Temple) 58, 81; Saints' Hall 65; Shicai ceremony at 65; *Statutes of Bailudong Academy* (白鹿洞书院揭示) (Zhu Xi) 12, 14–15, 25, 36, 149; teachers at 130, 161; Two-Sage Shrine 64; Yuan Fu efforts at 96; Zhu Xi's lectures at 130; Zhu Xi's repairs to/reconstruction/restoration of 130, 136–137, 161

Bailuzhou Academy of Ji'an County, Jiangxi Province 37: creation of 56; Gong Temple 58; neglect and abandonment of 30; *Rules and Regulations of Bailuzhou Academy* (白鹭洲书院学规) (Wang Mingcong) 15

Baisha Xin Xue 57

Bai Xinlian 28, 37, 38, 152, 162

Baiyan Peak 133

Bamboo Forest: Seven Intellectuals of 200

Bamboo Forest Study Hall 184, 186

Bangyan 70

Banzuo 69, 70

Baoding County: Lianchi Academy 138

Baoqing (Bao Qing) era 122

Baoqing, Hunan: Chenglianxi Academy 184

Baoxin County, Jiangzhou Prefecture 22

Bao You period 80, 184

behaving and behavior, Confucian advice regarding 205–207

"Biographies of Confucian Scholars" in *The Book of Han* (汉书·儒林传) 198

"Biographies of Confucian Scholars" of *The Ming Dynasty* (明史·儒林传) 31

"Biographies of Three Masters" (三先生祠 行状) (Zhan Li) 66

"Biography of Zhu Xi" (行状) (Huang Gan) 82

Biquan Academy 115–116, 152, 155

Blackmar, F. W. 1

Bodenheimer, Edgar E. 2

book collecting in the academies 135–142

book engraving in the academies 135, 142–147

Book of Changes (易经): engraving plates for 144; *Notes of Yu on the Book of Changes* (周易虞氏义笺) 123

Book of Documents: Confucius' reading of 202; *Commentary on Book of Documents* (书集传) (Zhu Xi) 117

Book of Filial Piety see filial piety

Book of Governors and Magistrates (牧令书) 7

Book of Han (汉书·儒林传) 198

Book of Rites (礼记) 2, 5, 49, 60, 65; *Annotations to the Book of Rites* (Sun Xidan) 54; engraving plates for 144

Book of Songs (诗经): Confucius' reading of 202; *Similarities and Differences of Mao Xiang's and Zheng Xuan's Annotations to the Book of Songs* (诗毛郑异同辨) (Zeng Zhao) 123

book pavilion *see Reconstruction of Book Pavilion in Bailudong Academy* (白鹿书院重建书阁记) (Cao Yanyue)

Bo Yi 55

Buddha, worship of 132

Buddhism 64, 133; academy used to diminish influence of 129; Confucian resistance of 75; flourishing of 93; Han Yu's refutation of 72, 76; Zhou Bida's opinion of 131; Zhu Yi's rejection of 97, 129–131

"cai" (vegetables for cooking) 53

Cai Jing 59

Index 237

Cai Jitong 142
Cai Qing 58
Cai Shen 57, 85, 116, 187
Cao Cheng (commoner in Ying-tianfu) 22, 51
Cao Cheng (wealthy man in Songcheng) 136
Cao from Pingjiang 80, 184
Caotang Academy, Mount Yu of Jiang Xi 132, 139
Caotang Temple 132
Cano Yanyue 18
Cao Zhi 213, 219n101
Changchun Immortal House 129
Changsa City 50, 116, 124
Changsa County 50, 57; Yuelu Academy 58–60, 180, 188
Changas County School 55
Chang Sha County 181
Changsu County 31, 99
Chaoyang 134
Chaozhou 52, 143
Chen Baisha 57
Chen Chun 116
Chen Dalun 88
Chen family, Jiangzhou 141; *see also* Dongjia Academy
Cheng brothers 26, 55, 56, 117, 156; *see also* Cheng Hao; Cheng Yi; Neoconfucianism
Chengdu 139
Cheng Duanli 201–202, 206, 215
Cheng Duanmeng 15, 206
Chengdu City 139
Cheng (Emperor) 199
Cheng family: Feilin Academy 125
Cheng Hao: death of 73; *see also* Cheng Yi and Cheng Hao
Cheng Hao Memorial Hall, Jiankang Prefectural School 55
Chenghua, reign of 31
Cheng Nan (Chengnan) Academy 116, 152, 156
chengren zhidao (cultivation and development of character) 196
Cheng Shaokai 95
Chen Guija 146
Cheng Tingzuo 9
Cheng Yi and Cheng Hao 24, 26, 28, 57, 66, 93, 99–100, 184–187; disciples of 155; as representative scholars of Confucian Daotong School 73–74, 77–90; theories of essential principles of the world 121; worship of 56, 93, 99; *see also* Cheng Hao; Cheng Zhu

Chengzhou 134
Chengzi (Emperor) 32
Chen Hao 55, 56, 144
Chen Hongmou 140
Chenhou Academy 36
Chen Jiding 162
Chen Jixin 67
Chen Kang 128
Chen Kengzhi 6
Chen Li 102, 128, 153
Chen Mi 161
Chen Qi 159
Chen Rongjie 76
Chen Xiangdao 203
Chen Yi 55, 56
Chen Yuegu 151
Chen Xianzhang 100
Chenzhou: Huxi Academy 88
Chenzhou County 124
Chen Zhu 94
Chongdao Temple 56
Chongning Reform 21
Chongning reign 59
Chongwen Academy, Hangzhou City 119
Chongzhen (Chong Zhen) reign 89
Chongzheng Academy 13, 56, 134, 187; "Tablet Inscription of Creation of Chongzheng Academy" 153
Chunyou (Chun You) reign 25, 52, 56, 58, 82, 95, 137, 161, 186, 187
Chunxi (Chun Xi) reign 21, 23, 24, 25, 53, 77, 78, 86, 92, 94, 117, 129, 130, 136, 137, 156, 157
Cihu Academy 58, 94; *Records of Cihu Academy* 87, 95
clothes *see* dress and dressing, Confucian advice regarding
Commentary of Zuo (左传 · 成公十三年) 2, 48, 69
Confucian doctrine 13, 71–76, 79, 81, 83, 90, 91, 135
Confucianism: Confucius and 186, 187; diffusion of 13–18; etiquette and 4; political ideal of 38; pre-Qin 3; Qingli Educational Reform's impact on 21; rites and 2–3; role of the Academy in social interlock of scholars and 9–18; societal control exerted by 2, 5; as soul of the Academy 11; successor lineage of 71–74; *see also* Daotong; Neo-Confucianism
Confucian revival movement 73
Confucian scholars: Confucianism and 6, 75; early Qing 39; sense of moral

238 *Index*

mission and social responsibility of 66–68; *see also* Mencius; Wang Yingming

Confucian Way 38, 89; *see also* Daotong

Confucius: death of 81; dressing, thoughts on 203–205; emphasis on wording by 201–203; good manners of 197–200; hometown of 4, 19; psalm to 66; respect for 5; statues of 27, 50, 64, 77, 190; temples dedicated to 52; worship of 30, 51, 54, 55, 78, 92, 93, 99, 186; Xiansheng 61; as Xianshi (Sage of Sages) 56, 79; Yayan spoken by 202; *see also Analects of Confucius*; Daotong

county annals, various 146–147

County Annals of Laoting(乐亭县志) 123

County Annals of Nanhai(南海县志) 122

cultivation: of Confucian scholars 13; of family 17; of mind 95, 196, 205; moral 12, 66, 67, 90, 121; of obedience 210–212; personal spiritual 5; of psychological and behavioral laws 10; of regional talents 147–154; talent 14, 30, 68, 135, 141, 145, 147; self- 15, 17, 20, 207, 208; of virtues 213

Dai De 217n57
Dai Junheng 51, 55, 60, 66, 68, 135, 136
daily inspections 17
daily life: Confucian rites in 9, 12; Confucian values in 65; feng shui in 180; folk culture and 191; obedience in 212; rules and manners in 196, 199, 200, 207, 213; *Rules for Learning by Cheng Duanmeng and Dong Zhu*(程董学则) and 15; student 203, 205; "Ten Commandments of the Cave" (Gao Beheng) and 203
daily teaching 33
Dai Ming 146
Dai Sheng 217n57
Dai the Elder: *Rites* 204, 208, 217n57
Dai the Younger *see* Dai Sheng
Dai Zhen 118, 162
Da Ke 136
Daliang Academy of Henan 59
Daoguang reign 16, 102, 119, 120, 123, 140, 146, 151, 152, 154
Daonan Sacrificial Hall 64
Daonan Temple 92
Daotong (Confucian orthodoxy) 38; academy sacrifice and 71–92; Mencius and 71–74, 77, 79, 82, 86, 87, 89, 93;

Wang Yangming and 89–90; Zhu Xi and 79, 81, 82, 84, 85, 93
Daotong of Shi Jie 73
Daotong of Sun Fu 73
Daozhou 51
Daozhou Lianxi Academy 27
Dazhong Xiangfu period 21, 22, 51, 137
Dazhu County 138
Dengdong Academy 125
Deng Hongbo 19, 138, 146
Diaotai Academy 133
Ding Shanqing 58, 188
Doctrine of Mean(中庸) (*Doctrine of the Mean*) 94, 117, 122, 196
doctrine: Chen Baisha 57; Confucian 13, 71–76, 79, 81, 83, 90, 91, 135; Daotong 87; Xin Xue 87; Yangming (Wang Yangming) 89, 98; Yang Wenyuan Gong 95; Zhou 28, 32; Zhu Xi 88, 93, 97
Donghu Academy 94, 117
Dongjia Academy 125, 137, 141
Donglai 160
Donglai School of Thought 121
Donglin (Dong Lin) Academy 34, 39–40, 91–92, 157
Donglou Academy 150
Donglu 19
Dongshan Academy 17, 33, 153
Dongting Lake 126
Dongyang 138, 159
Dong Zhu 15
Dou Kequin 211
Doushan Academy 157
Douyang Academy 211
Dou Yujun 136
Dragon Gate 187
dragon, veins of 179–181
dress and dressing, Confucian advice regarding 198, 203–205
Duan Jian 131
Du Fu 132
Duke Ai 2, 5
Duke Cheng 48
Duke of Huiguo 83
Duke of Lishan 87
Duke of Zhou 55, 73, 74, 75, 80, 87
Duke Yan 77, 78
Duke Yin 2
Duke Zou 78
Duzhou Academy 100
Duzong 25

Eastern Han dynasty 56, 187
Eastern Jin dynasty 50, 76, 129

Index 239

Eastern Lu 128
Ehu Academy 37, 153, 202, 212
elegiac addresses (Zhu Xi) 185
Elman, Benjamin A. 39, 118
eunuch director 136
eunuchs 34
Explanation of the Diagram of the Utmost Extreme (太极图说), annotations to 116
"Explanations of the Classics" in *The Book of Rites* (礼记·经解) 2
Explaining Simple and Analyzing Compound Characters (说文解字) 123

family: cultivation of 16, 17; filial piety and 18
family interests: state power and 1, 10
Family Rituals That Ever Existed (古今家祭礼) 117
Fan Feng 146
Fang Shimin 202
Fangting Academy 190
Fang Xinru 146
Fang Xuejian 64, 92
Fang Yanshou 83, 116
Fanyang 136
Fan Yinnian 88
Fan Zhongyan 62
Feilin Academy 125
Fei Xiaotong 8
Fei Yuanlong 132
Fengcheng 151
Fenghu Academy 161–162
Fenghuang 161
Feng Mengzhou 138, 141
Fengming Academy 138
Fengshan Academy 128, 131, 153, 188
feng shui 179–183, 192
Fengxin, Jiangxi 127
Fengyi, Guangxi 134
Feng Yu Stone of Bailudong 177–178
Fengzhou 134
filial piety 14, 15, 17, 60; *Amendment to the Classic of Filial Piety* (孝经刊误) (Zhu Xi) 117; Confucius on 209; family and 18
Five Classics, The 32, 83
five constant virtues" (三纲五常) (five rules) 13, 43n42, 97
Five Dynasties period 19, 125, 137, 152
Five Great Mountains of China 175
five most important relationships 202
Five Rites 77, 144
five sages 99
Five Seniors Peak of Mount Lu 178

five senses 213
five worthies 189
folk culture 28, 175, 178, 179, 180; academies/academic culture and 183, 188, 192; feng shui and 178–183
folk customs 16, 17, 19; prayer for good luck 190; "Views on Folk Customs" (Wang Wenqing) 181; *see also* gods
folk ritual culture 189
Four Books, The (四书) 13, 32, 91, 94, 128; annotations (Zhu Xi) 82, 83; *Interlinear Analysis of and Collected Commentaries on the Four Books* (四书章句集注) (Zhu Xi) 83
Four Gentlemen Memorial Hall 95
Four Masters of Mingzhou: *Continued Tablet Inscriptions of Four Masters of Mingzhou* (四明教授厅续壁记) 20
four natural human consciences (四端) 13, 43n43
Four Worthies Hall, Shuangfeng Academy 64
Fujian Province 19, 36, 161; academies in 57, 158; Aofeng Academy 162; Hanquan Academy 156; Huanxi Academy 143; Liangshan Academy 138; Li Ba as governor of 132, 133; Min School 155
Fuwen Academy, Hangzhou 119
Fuxi (Emperor) 73
Fuxi (sage) 99
Fugu Academy, Anfu 88

Ganquan School, Zengcheng, Guangdong Province 157
Gao'an 59: Xijian Academy 187
Gao'an City: Guiyan Academy 125, 148
Gao Benheng 202, 203
Gaobiao Mountain 132
Gao Deng 55
Gao Erxiu 58
Gao Huang 160
Gao Mingshi 49, 51
Gao Panlong 34
Gao Shitai 157
Gao Side 80, 185
Gao Tangsheng 199
Gaoxin 73
Gao Yao 71, 74
general public: academies open to 141; academies' printing of books for 135; attempts to make Daotong understandable to 82; education of 16, 123, 127; folk culture and 191; influence

240   *Index*

of ritual on 70; promotion of Confucian values in 9, 128, 129, 134, 174, 183, 187
Geng Chen metropolitan exam 182
Geng Ju 99
Geng Wenkai 146
God of Lands 60
God of Zi Tong 187
gods 5, 48, 65, 183, 191; *see also* Guan Yu; Kui; Wen Chang
Gong County 126
Gong Dao 133
gongsheng (tribute students) 8
Gong Shitai 57
Gongyi Academy 161
Goose Lake, meeting of 94
Guangde Academy 126
Guangdong Province 122, 134, 145, 153, 157, 159
Guangfu Academy 133
Guangling City 198
Guangnan Prefecture, Yunnan 161
Guangxi Provinces 119, 134, 154
Guangxu era 36, 59, 60, 123, 125, 134, 138, 139, 144, 146, 147, 150, 160, 182
Guangya Bookstore 144
Guangze Academy 142
Guanzhong Academy 202, 204
Guangzhou 144
Guan School 114, 116
Guan Yu 183, 187
Guixi, Jiangxi 137
Guiyan Academy 125, 148, 212
Guiyang 88
Guiyue 14
Guizhou 132
Gujing Academy 56, 101, 102, 119, 120
Guo Pu 180
Guo Songdao 152
Gu Wen Shang Shu 76
Gu Xiancheng 34, 92, 99
Gu Yanwu 6, 7

Han Changli 84
Han dynasty 101–103, 199–200
Han learning 101–103, 118–119
Han Shijun 162
Han Yu 37, 71–73, 76; *Critical Investigations of Han Yu's Essays* 117
Hao Xi Stage 178
Hao Yulin 16
Hengzhou: *Records of Shigu Academy of Hengzhou* (衡州石鼓书院记) 20, 175
Heshan Academy 91, 131, 133, 137–138
He Xun 84

History of Chinese Academies (Li Guojun) 67
"History of Shang Dynasty" in *Records of the [Grand] Scribe* (史记·殷本纪) 196
History of Song (宋史) (Tuotuo) 82
History of the Ming Dynasty (明史・选举志) 30
Hong Mai 22, 23, 148
Hongwu 29
Hong Ye 199
Hongzhi reign 31, 56, 58, 63, 81, 84, 99, 130, 186
Hou Kui 55
Huacheng Temple 130
Huaihua City 124
Huaitang Academy 87, 94
Huaiyang 198
Huang Donfa 100
Huang Gan 23, 57, 63, 82, 85, 116, 130, 161, 187
Huanggang County, Hubei Province 52, 162
Huang Honggang 159
Huanghua Academy 146
Huang Ji 87
Huangliao Academy 125
Huang Mengxing 159
Huangu Academy 186
Hu Anguo 115
Huangqing (Huang Qing) period, Yuan dynasty 126
Huang Shubing 146
Huangu Academy 40, 84, 185, 186
Hu Anguo 140, 149
Huang Wan 89
Huang Wenzhong 55, 64, 187
Huang Yuanzhi 11
Huang Zhen 100
Huang Zongxi 34, 115, 162
Hu Aqiu 134
Hubei Province 52, 53, 115, 126, 128, 159, 160, 162
Hubei Wuchang Bookstore 139
Hu Dashi 152, 158
Hunan Province 36, 57, 65, 80, 115, 116, 120, 124, 125, 126, 127, 138, 140, 143, 148, 152, 155, 156, 157, 158, 161
Hundred Poems About Lingnan (南海百咏) (Fang Xinru) 146
Hu Peihui 102
Huxiang School 11, 23, 115, 116, 120, 121, 127, 152, 155, 156, 158
Hu Zhaoxi 138, 163
Hu Zhongyao 136
Hymes, Robert 10

innate moral goodness *see* moral goodness, innate

Institutional History of the Song Dynasty (宋会要辑稿) 157

Jade Book (玉篇) 123
Jade Lake Academy 189
jade pendants 198
Jiajing reign: Biyang Academy 128; Confucian ethics and morality 13; Fugu Academy 88, 127; Hejing Academy 133; Heshan Academy 131; Jade Lake Academy 189; Jishan Academy 159; Jiufeng Academy 132; large-scale bannings and closures of academies during 31–33; Mount Jiuhua Academy 130; Wansong Academy 150; worship of Yangming (Wang Yangming) during 89, 97–99; Yuelu Academy 57, 84
Jianchang Prefecture 125
Jiangdong Academy 206
Jiangdong Province 86, 96, 158
Jiangnan (Jiang Nan) Province 35, 54, 86
Jiangning Province 142, 160, 162
Jiangsu (Jiang Su) Province 19, 80, 91, 101, 162
Jiang Wanli 56, 58, 186
Jiang Wenzhong Gong Temple 58
Jiangxi Province: academies in 37, 125; Chens in 141; Dongjia Academy 137, 141; Education Department 58; Fuli Academy 97; Hualin Mountain and Taoism in 127; Lushan as Buddhist religious center 129; Provincial Surveillance Commission 144; Tang dynasty and 19; Xiangshan Academy 31; Xijian Academy 59; Yuzhang Academy 59; *see also* Bailudong Academy
Jiang Yi 61, 63, 80
Jiangzhou Prefecture 77, 78, 92, 125
Jiankang 143
Jianning county 84
jiansheng 8, 70
Jianyang County 158, 184
Jiatai period, Song dynasty 130
Jiaxi period 52, 142
Jiaxuan 215
Jinhua Academy 114, 162
jinshi examination 8, 153, 160–161
Jishan Academy 159, 162
Jiujiang 162
Jiujiang City 125
Jixian Academy 19

Kaibao reign 50, 136, 186
Kaifeng 139; Daliang Academy 162; *Prefectural Annals of Kaifeng* 146
Kaixi reign 84, 137
Kangxi Emperor 4, 35; attitude to academies of 37–38; edict regarding workship of Zhu Xi 83, 84–85
Kangxi era 11; Bailudong Academy during 15, 85, 160; Chongzheng Academy during 56; Daliang Academy during 52, 59; Dongling Academy during 39; Guanzhong Academy during 40; Seven-Sage Academy during 59; Yaojiang Academy during 100; Yuelu Academy during 60, 162, 188; Ziyang Academy during 81; Ziyun Academy during 147
Kaoting 56, 79, 80
Kaoting Academy 17, 84
King Wen of Zhou *see* Wen (King)
King Wu of Zhou *see* Wu (King)
Kong clan 77
Kong Ji 74, 85, 86, 93
Kong Yingda 208–210
Kui (奎) (god of exams) 60, 183, 187–192
Kui Light Hall 192
Kui Pavilion, Yijiang Academy 52, 59, 70, 154, 187–191

Lan Dingyuan 134
Lianchi Academy, Baoding 138
Liang Dingfen 202, 204
Liangshan Academy 138
Liang Tingnan 153, 202
liang (unit of weight for precious metals) 52, 60
Liao City 36
Li Ba 132, 133
Li Caidong 19, 25, 37, 125
Li Dong 155
Li Faga 58
Li Fu 17 Li Liangzhang 205, 211
Lin Miaogui 134
Li Qi 62
Li Tong 78
Liu Bangcai 159
Liu Banzhong 120
Liu Boji 151
Liu Feng 5
Liu Gong 57, 67, 84, 142
Liu Guangye 143, 145
Liu Junguan 153
Liu Junsheng 153
Liu Qihui 86
Liu Qingzhi 130

242 *Index*

Liu Renji 137
Liu Wenmin 159
Liu Xiang 199
Liuyang County 124
Liu Yuanqing 97
Liu Yue 25
Liu Zai 80, 184
Liu Zehua 6
Liu Zihe 137
Li Xue works of Zhi Xi 116, 117
Li Xupu 153
Li Yong 40
Li Yunze 50, 51, 57, 92, 127
Li Zhongcheng Temple 58
Li Zhongsu 162
Longcheng Academy 119
Longgang Academy 16, 88
Longguang Academy 151
Longhu Academy 212
Longmen Acadeny 120, 139
Longqing reign 97
Longshan Academy 143
Longxi Academy 143
Longxing, Municipal School of 55
Longxing Prefecture 125
Longzhou Academy 131, 138
Loudong Academy 102
Lou Liang 30
Lu Jiuling 86, 87, 88, 95
Lu Jiuyuan 57, 158; as figure of worship
    81, 87, 94, 97; Hu Hong's thought
    distinct from 121; Xin Xue School and
    85–87, 94–97, 100, 117, 130; Zhu Xi
    and 156; *see also* Lu Xue (Lu School)
Luo 61, 82
Luo Congyan 78, 155
Luo Dian 102, 188
Luo Rufant 89
Luo School 61, 73, 82
Luo Tao 19
Luoyuan Academy 162
Lü Sheng 77
Lu Xue (Lu School) 94, 95
Lü Zuqian 95, 149; articles on conduct in
    Guiyue（规约）14; *Close Thoughts* 117;
    Daotong and 91; on expressions and faces
    203; Master's Temple built on site of
    lecture by 52; opinion of Huxiang School
    121; Wu School and 156; Xuancheng
    Academy and 90; Zhu Xi and 156

manners and etiquette 177, 189, 191,
    196–214
Mao Deqi 52, 58

Maoshan Academy, Jiangning 20
Mao Xiang 123
Maoyuan, Municipal School of 55
Meihua Academy 160
Mencius（孟子）(book) 137; *Annotations
    to Mencius* 25; Daotong affirmed in 72;
    "Devotion" (final chapter of) 71; Zhu
    Xi's explanatory notes to 122
Mencius 61; Daotong in the wake of
    79, 81–90, 93, 95; *Essential Ideas of
    Mencius*（孟子要略）(Zhu Xi) 117;
    ethical self-discipline theory of 121;
    four outstanding Confucian scholars
    after 73–74; hometown of 4, 19, 127;
    On Mencius（孟子说）(Zhang Shi) 116;
    Zhou Dunyi as inheritor of system of
    185
Meng clan 77
Meng Ke 56
Meng Shenghui 153
Meng Yuan 159
Mianyang Academy 145
Mianzhu 161
Mingdao (Chen Hao) 55
Mingdao Hall, Municipal School of
    Jiankang 55
Mingdao (Ming Dao) Academy 143, 147,
    159, 204, 207
Mingdao reign 22
Ming dynasty 6–7; Bailudong Academy
    during 56–60, 62–64, 81, 141; banning
    and destruction of academies during
    33–37, 39; book engraving business
    during 143; Chenghua reign 131, 132;
    Confucian schools of thought during
    121; development of academies during
    28–31, 33; emergence of Yangmingism/
    worship of Wang Yangming during
    88–90, 92, 97–100; Fengshan Academy
    founded during 128, 153; Hongzhi
    reign 58, 63, 81, 130; Hunan Province
    academies during 124, 125; Jian
    Guoxiang 69; Jiajing reign 97, 98, 144;
    Min School's importance during 121;
    Neo-Confucianism during 115, 117;
    public lectures offered during 155–156;
    Wang Ji 16; Wanli period 64; Yunshan
    Academy 126; Zhang Yi 13; Zhan Li
    66; Zhan Ruoshi 57; Zhengde reign 128;
    Zheng Tinghu 53, 54, 56; Zhengtong
    reign 84; Zhu Xi's enshrinement during
    83–84; Zhu Xi's school of thought
    during 121, 122
Mingjing Academy 88, 159

Mingzheng Academy 133
Mingzhou, Four Masters of 20
Mingzong (Ming Zong) (Emperor) 19
Min School 155
moral being: man as 75
moral character 182, 191, 196; cultivation of 67; faith and 65–66
moral customs 2
moral evaluation 8
moral goodness, innate: Xin Xue's advocation of 98, 117
morality 3, 5; Confucian 11–18, 64, 65, 175, 201; improving 207; Neo-Confucian 93; rites associated with 6
moral mission 66–68
moral order 86
moral principles 10, 28; Buddhists' failure to observe 131; secular 129
moral role models 9
morals and virtues: words in relationship to 201–203
moral sensibilities 23
moral standards 4; feudal Chinese society 43
moral studies 4
moral values 84
Mount Bahua 159
Mount Gu 101
Mount Heng 179, 180
Mount Jiuhua 130
Mount Kuang 19
Mount Lu 97
Mount Ment 126
Mount Mingzhao 117
Mount Song 171
Mount Tai 29, 81, 175
Mount Yuelu 50
Mount Yuexiu 119
Mou Zongsan 121

Nanfeng Prefecture 125
Nangan 159
Nangu Academy 39
Nanguang Academy 126
Nanjian Prefecture 155
Nanjing 32
Nanjing Academy 101
Nankang Prefecture 23, 54, 64, 77, 136
Nankang Military Region 125, 129
Nanxuan School 115
Neo-Confucianism: academies' ties with 148; Cheng Hao 93; Cheng Yi 93; *Close Thoughts* as introductory book of 156; Emperor Chengzi's promulgation of

32; Emperor Lizong's promotion of 25; establishment of academies and 24, 118; Hu Dashi 158; Hu Hong 23, 121; Hu Juren 178; Huxiang School 115, 127, 152; Li Dong 93; Li Xue studies 117; Lu Zuqian 14, 52; Mencius and 72; merging of Zhu and Lu 96–97; Min School 116; Shao Yong 93; Sima Guang 93; Wang Yingming 12; Wei Liaoweng 91; worship of scholars of 77–78; Wu Cheng 96; Xiong He 80; Xu Qian 159; Yin Tun 133; Yuan Xie 20; Zhang Shi 11; Zhou Dunyi 51, 92, 93; Zhu Xi 4, 24, 32, 56, 61, 73–75, 83, 122, 155, 177; Zhu Xue of 94
Neo-Confucian Scholars (道学传) (Tuotuo) 82
Nine Classics, The (九经) 137
Nine-Sage Academy 59

obedience in the academy 210–212
omen worship in the academy 187–190
ontology theory 94
Ouyang De 59
Ouyang Shoudao 161
Ouyang Xiu 73

Pan Ciming 77
public cultural resources 142, 145
public lectures offered by academies 31, 128, 149, 152–156
public library 141, 142
public opinion 32, 34
public property 22
public, the *see* general public
public welfare 27, 58
Prefectural Annals of Funing (福 宁府 志) 133
Prefectural Annals of Kaifeng (开封府 志) 146
private academies 26, 36, 38, 122
private schools 19

Qiandao (Qian Dao) reign 14; Hanquan Academy during 116; Lu Jiuyuan 86; Yuelu Academy during 57, 67, 127, 152; Zhu Xi 127, 152, 155, 157
Qian Daxin 102–103
Qian Dehong 157
Qianlong (Emperor): academy superintendents, decree regarding 161; support of academies by 35, 38–41, 150–151
Qianlong (Qian Long) reign: Bailuzhou Academy during 15; ceremony of Dingji

244 *Index*

70; Daongshan Academy during 17; farmland converted into academies during 132–133; Fengshan Academy restored during 131; Han learning during 100, 102; Hao Xi Stage 178; Huangu Academy during 81, 186; Kui Pavilion 60; Nanguang Academy during 126; Shinan Academy during 18; support of academies during 35, 38–41; Wenfeng Academy created during 132; Wenjin Academy during 52; Ziyang Academy 151; *see also* Qian Daxin

Qiantang County 101

Qian Zhuting 103

Qiaonan Academy 152

Qimen County 33

Qing dynasty 1, 4; academies and social mores during 16; Bailudong Academy during 15, 52; Chen Tingzuo 9; Dai Junheng 55, 60, 66, 68; Daliang Academy 59; development of academies during 35, 39; Gu Yanwu 6; Han learning during 100; Huangu Academy 40, 81; Huang Yuanzhi 11; Huang Zongxi 34; Li Fu 17; Lumen Academy during 53; Sun Xidan 55; Wang Xuntai 18; Wenjin Academy during 52; Wu Rui 16; Xinjiang Academy 56; worship of Zhu Xi during 83, 84; Zhenyan Academy 54; Yaojiang Academy 100; Yingshan Academy 58; Zhu Yizun 29; Yan Ruoqu 76; Yuelu Academy 69, 70; Ziyang Academy 60

Qingli Education Reform 21

Qing rulers: suspicions of academies 37

Qingyuan Party ban 24

Qin Hui 23

Qin (imperial): *Integration of Pre-Qin Dynasty Rites in Society* (先秦礼学思想与社会的整合) (Liu Feng) 5; pre-Qin Confucians 3, 5, 92, 213

Qingtian County 88

Qingyuan reign 86, 117

Qingyuan Party Ban 24

Quanshan 57

Quanzhou 215n28; Supervision Bureau 27

Quan Zuwang 87, 98, 100, 121, 122, 156, 162

Qi Tongwen 22

Qu Zuwang 87, 98, 100, 121, 122, 156, 162

Raozhoulu Academy 185

Raozhou Prefecture 125

Raozhou Road 80

"Records of Biquan Academy"（碧泉书院上梁文）(Hu Hong) 115

"Records of Cheng Hao Memorial Hall in Jiankang Prefectural School" (建康府学明道先生祠记) 55

"Records of Cihu Academy" (慈湖书院记) (Wen Jiweng) 87, 95

"Records of Construction of Four Worthies Hall in Shuangfeng Academy" (顺昌双峰书院新建 四贤堂记) 64

"Records of Donghu Academy" (东湖书院记) (Yuan Xie) 68

"Records of Farmlands of Mingzheng Academy"（明正书院田记）(Huang Jin) 133

"Records of Fengshan Academy"（新建凤山书院记）(Wu Yihan) 153

Records of Gujing Academy (西湖诂经精舍记) (Ruan Yuan) 101

Records of Heshan Academy (鹤山书院记) 91

"Records of Jiufeng Academy"（九峰书院记）(Peng Rushi) 132

"Records of Jupo Academy"（菊坡精舍记）(Chen Li) 128

"Records of Library in Zhaoyi Academy" (昭义书院藏书楼记) (Hou Shaoying) 140

"Records of Nanyang Academy"（南阳书院记）(Li Yuanzhen) 158

Records of Qian Zhuting Being Worshiped in Zhongshan Academy (钱竹汀先生入祀钟山书院记) 103

"Records of Reconstruction of Daonan Sacrificial Hall" (重建道南祠记) (Huang Wenzhong) 64

Records of Rixin Academy (日新书院记) 99

Records of Shigu Academy of Hengzhou (衡州石鼓书院记) (Zhu Xi) 20

Records of Shinan Academy (石南书院记）18

Records of Shishan Academy (诗山书院志· 颁胙说) 69

"Records of Shrine of Confucian Ancestors" (宗儒祠记) of Bailudong Academy 63

Records of Six Great Masters Academy (杜洲六先生书院记) (Quan Zuwang) 100

"Records of Studies" in *The Book of Rites* (礼记·学记) 49, 53

Records of Tianzhang Academy（天章书院记）(Hao Yulin) 16

Records of Words and Deeds of Eminent Persons of the Song Period (八朝名臣言行录) 117

Records of Xiangshan Academy (象山书院记) (Yuan Fu) 11

"Records of Yangming Academy in Jiuhuashan" (九华山阳明书院记) (Zou Shouyi) 130

"Records of Yan Yan Memorial Hall in Changshu County School" (平江府常熟县学吴公祠记) 55

Records of Yaojiang Academy (姚江书院记) (Shao Yancai) 100

Records of Yuelu Academy in Tanzhou (潭州岳麓山书院记) (Li Yunze) 50

"Records of Zhou Dunyi Memorial Hall in Shaozhou State School" (韶州州学濂溪先生祠记) 55

Renzong era 82

"Restoration of Cihu Academy" (重修慈湖书院本末记) (Huang Xianglong) 58

"Restoration of Diaotai Academy" (重修钓台书院记) (Huang Jin) 133

Restoration of Gujing Academy (重修诂经精舍记) (Yu Yue) 102

Restoration of Yuelu Academy in Tanzhou (潭州重修岳麓 书院记) 11

Restoration of Bailudong Academy (重修白鹿洞书院记) (Yuan Fu) 11

Restoration of Donglin Academy (重修东林书院记) (Xiong Cilyu) 39

"Restoration of Xuancheng Academy" (重修宣成书院 记) (Guangzu) 90

Restoration of Xuancheng Academy (复修宣成书院 记) (Li Fu) 17

Revolt of the Three Feudatories 38

Ruan Ji 200

Ruan Yuan 56, 100–102, 119, 122–123, 153

Ruixi Academy 145, 162

Rulin Academy 126

sacrifice: appropriate manners for 199; Shao Lao 189; Tai Lao 189; tools and utensils for 190, 197; Wen Chang and Kui 188–191

"Sacrificial Rites" in *Huangu Academy* (还古书院志) 186

sacrificial ritual, academic 2, 4, 48–103, 189–191; academy sacrifice and Daotong (Confucian orthodoxy) 38, 71–92; academy sacrifice and shift of learning mindset 92–103; functionality of 60–70; overview of 48–60

San Yisheng 71

Scholarly Annals of Song and Yuan Periods (宋元学案) 114, 115, 152, 158

seminars and conferences 17, 148, 183

Shandong Province 29, 162, 214

Shao Bao 31, 58

Shaoding reign 35, 86–87, 96

Shaohao 73, 73

Shao Lao sacrifice 189–190

Shao Rui 141

Shaosheng, period of 21

Shaoxi period 53, 56, 69, 77, 93, 117, 186

Shaoxing: Jishan Academy 162

Shaoxing period 23, 151

Shao Yancai 100

Shao Yong 57, 66, 77, 78, 79, 80, 99, 186, 187

Shaozhou 55; Mingjing Academy 88

Shecai, ritual of 52

shengyuan 6–7

Shengyuan reign 129

Shennong 73

Shen Tingfang 162

Shicai, ritual of 49, 52–54, 65, 69, 77

Shidian, ritual of 49, 52–54, 56, 65, 89

Shigu Academy 22, 37, 59, 84, 124, 128, 143, 148, 157, 175, 177, 188; *Records of Shigu Academy* (Zhu Xi) 20, 175, 181–182

Shi Jie 73, 76

Shi Tanglong 58

Shuixi Academy 89

Shuiyue Temple 132

Shunzhi reign 35, 36, 37, 58, 159

Sima Guang 77, 78, 79, 93, 184, 186

Sima Qian 101

Six Classics 61–62, 66, 91

Six Gentlemen Hall, Yuelu Academy 57, 58, 67, 69

Six Great Masters 186

Six Great Masters Academy 100

Six Great Minds 186

Sixian Academy 159

Sixue 49

Song dynasty 3, 6–8; academies during 20–23, 25–28, 30, 52–53, 55–59, 61, 152–153, 155; book engraving 142–143; Cao Yanyue 18; Cheng Duanmeng 15; Chen Zhu 94; Chunxi period 53; Confucian Way during 38; Dong Zhu 15; "Four Great Academies" of 124, 129; *History of Song* (Tuotuo) 82; *Institutional History of the Song Dynasty* (宋会要辑稿) 157; Jiatai

246   *Index*

reign 130; Jin dynasty, conflict with 23; Jingding reign 90, 133; jinshi qualification 8; Kaixi reign 84, 137; Li Daochuan 122; Lu Jiuyuan 85, 86; Luo School 73; Lu Zuqian 121; Neo-Confucianism and 118; Northern 21, 51, 55, 57, 73, 92; prosperity of academies during 13; *Records of Words and Deeds of Eminent Persons of the Song Period* (八朝名臣言行录) 117; regional schools and academies during 121–127, 129–138; sacrificial rituals of the academy perfected during 48; *Scholarly Annals of Song and Yuan Periods* (宋元学案) 114, 115, 152, 158; Shaoxi period 53, 56, 69, 77, 93, 117, 186; Shaoxing era 151; Southern 3, 10, 11, 14, 20, 52, 53, 74, 77, 91, 93; three sages of 81; Wei Liaoweng 91; Wu Feng 96; Xianchun reign 95; Xiong He 80; Yuan Fu 96; Yuan Xie 20; *see also* Zhu Xi
Song Xiangxing 58
Songyang Academy 20, 22, 147, 175
Stone Classics 137
Stone Drum Mountain 175
Sun Fengji 50
Sun Fu 73, 136
Sun Guangzu 33
Sun Qifeng 146
Sun Xidan 54, 55, 61
Sun Xingyan 101, 119
Sun Yi 207
Sun Yirang 214n3
Sun Zhou 22
Su Shi 73
Su Tianjue 143

Tai Chi 156
Taihe County 19, 131, 159
Taiji Academy 26
Tai Ping Xing Guo (Taiping Xingguo) 22
Taishan Academy 136, 175
Taizong reign, Yuan dynasty 26, 50
Tai Zu (Taizu) (Emperor) 29, 31
talent cultivation *see* cultivation
Tang dynasty: academies during 123–125; Confucian doctrine passed from 71–76; Gaozong reign 55; Han Yu 37, 52; imperial examinations during 8; Ouyang De 59; private academies during 19; social changes during 6; talent cultivation by 148; Yan Zhenqing 59; Yuanhe reign 128; Zhenguan period 50
Tang period literature 144

Tang Jin 96
Tang Laihe 15
Tang Su 51
Tan Xinzhen 182
Tanzhou 57
Taoism 72, 75, 76, 93, 97; academy/academic scholars and 178–180, 187; Buddhism and 127–134; Hualin Mountain and practice of 127–129; manners and 207; Mount Jiuhua and 130–131; Yuexiu Mountain temple 129; Zhu Xi's concerns regarding 130
Taoqiu 127
Tao Shu 120, 152
Tao Yuanming 59, 62, 66
theory of Han learning 56
theory of learning through heart or mind 100
Theory of Mind 4, 87; *see also* Lu Jiuyuan; Xin-Xue; Wang Yangmin
theory of two hearts 75, 76
three aspects of Daotong 75
Three Essays of Hong Mai 22, 23
Three Feudatories, Revolt of 38
three major undertakings of the academy 48, 50
Three Masters, biographies of 66
Three Offerings ritual 54
Three Rituals Classics 24, 42n48
three points, the 12
three principles, the 13, 43n42, 97
Three Sages Temple 81, 84
three sages, the 72
Three-School System of Tanzhou 22
Tianbao (Tian Bao) era 50
Tianbao period 50
Tianjin 153
Tianmen Academy 126
Tianqi era 31, 34
Tianquan Academy 157
Tianyang 134
Tianzhang Academy 16
Tian Zhen Mountain 88
Tong Juyi 100
Tongwen Academy of Jianyang 80, 184
Tongxiang Academy 68, 191
Tongzhi era: Chenhou Academy 36; Gujing Academy 120; Yingyuan Academy 60; Yuelu Academy 135; Xiyin Academy 142; Xuehai Academy 123
Tuotuo 82

Walton, Linda 126
Wang Bai 184

Index 247

Wang Chang 119
Wang Cui 26
Wang Ji 16
Wang Jinzheng 81, 84
Wang Mingcong 15
Wang Mingsheng 118, 119
Wang Shouren 150
Wang Tong 73
Wang Wenqing 102, 181
Wang Xuntai 18
Wang Yangming 85, 87–90, 96–100, 127, 130; academies developed by 32; *Complete Works* 88; Jishan Academy founded by 159; Rixin Academy and 99; worship of 90, 97, 99; Yaojiang Academy and 100; *see also* Xin Xue; Yangmingism; Yuelu Academy
Wang Yucheng 50, 127, 148
Wang Yun 80, 185
Wang Zeng 22
Wanli reign 31, 33, 64, 84, 92, 97
Wansong Academy 150
Warring States period 3, 6, 25, 187
Wei Gao 132
Weijing Academy 144, 145
Wei Liangqi 159
Wei Liangzheng 159
Wei Liaoweng 91, 131, 137, 215
Wei Qi 91
weiyi 196
Wei Yuan 152
Wei Zhongxian 34
Wen'an 86
Wen Chang 59–60, 183, 187–191
Wen Chang Hall 59–60, 187–188
Wencheng (Want Yangming) 90
Wenching (Marquis) 89
Wenfeng Academy 132
Wengong Academy 142
Wenguo 77
Wenhu 88
Wenjin Academy 52
Wen Jiweng 87, 95
Wen (King of Zhou) 53, 59, 61, 71, 72, 74, 75, 87, 99
Wenxuan (Emperor) 50; King Wenxuan Temple 56
Wenzong Academy 95
Wrong, Dennis H. 1
Wucheng County 101
Wu Daoxing 180, 181
Wu from Hefei 161
Wugang City 126
Wuhua Academy 146

Wu Jinhua 39
Wu (King of Zhou) 55, 58, 61, 72, 74, 75, 87
Wuma River 131
Wu Rongguang 120, 153
Wu Rui 16
Wu School 117, 156
Wu Xiang 133
Wuxing District 119
Wu Xunchao 146
Wuyi Academy 117, 142, 158
Wuyi Mountain 57
Wuyishan 130
Wu Yihan 142
Wu Yong 24
Wuyuan 157, 159
Wu Yubi 30
Wu Zetian (Empress) 8
Wuzhou 143

Xia Jie 97
Xiangshan Academy 31, 94, 117; Lu Jiuyan 86–87; rebuilding of 31; *Records of Xiangshan Academy* (Yuan Fu) 11; Yuan Fu and 96; Xin Xue School and 117
Xiangshan School of Thought 156
"Xiangshan shuyuan ji" (象山书院记) (Yuan Fu) 87
Xiangshui Jiaojingtang Academy 120
Xianping reign 51
Xiansheng 49, 53, 54, 55, 56, 61, 63, 65
Xianshi 49, 53, 54, 55, 56, 61, 63, 65
Xianxian 49, 55
Xiao Fen 198
Xiaogan 160
Xiaojing yuan shen qi (孝经援神契) 187
Xiaopi Academy 30
Xiao Qiu 159
Xiaozong (Emperor, Song dynasty) 23, 24, 25
Xiao Wen (Emperor) 198
Xiaowu Emperor 50
Xiaqiu 198
Xie Guozhen 145
Xie Jieheng 138
Xie Manqing 214n15
Xie Tingjie 128
xieyuan degree 153
Xie Yun 154
Xihu Academy 143, 144, 160
Xijian Academy 59, 187
xin (mind) 94, 95

248 *Index*

Xingjiang Academy 56
Xingye County 18
"Xing zhuang" (Huang Gan) 82
Xinquan Academy 157
Xin Xue, School of 4, 94–100; Baisha
  Xin Xue 57; Jiangmen Xin Xue 100;
  Li Fu 17; Lu Jiuyuan 85, 86, 87, 94,
  117; Lu school's promotion of 86; Lu
  Xue and 94; Lu-Wang Xin Xue 88;
  Shuixi Academy 150; Wang Ji 16; Wang
  Yingming and 88–89; Yang Jian and 88;
  Ye Mengde 137; Yuan Fu 96; *see also*
  Donghu Academy; Xiangshan Academy
  117
Xiong Can 146
Xiong Cilyu 39
Xiong He 80, 82, 94, 184
Xiong Juechang 132
xiucai (秀才) exam 6, 70
Xiuning County 157
Xizong (Emperor) 34
Xuancheng: Zhixue Academy 89
Xuancheng Academy 17, 90
Xuan De era 210
Xuanxiu Peak 136
Xuan Yuan 79
Xuanzong (Emperor) 8
Xuchang, Henan 128
Xu Danci 198
Xuegu Academy 151
xuegui (学规) 14
Xuehai Academy 119m 123, 144, 153
Xue Kan 88
Xue Xuan 100
xueyue (学约) 14
Xue Zongkai 159
Xu family 198–199
Xu Manyi 198
Xun Kuang 76
Xunzhen Temple 128
Xunzi 3, 76
Xupu County 124
Xu Qian 159
Xu Shen 101, 102
Xu Sheng 199
Xu Xiang 199
Xu Xuan 127, 148
Xu Yan 198
Xuyang County 125
Xu Zaishu 152
Xu Zi 29, 159

Yang Lian 13
Yangmingism 32, 57, 88

Yangming School of Mind 4, 88–90,
  96, 98–100, 121, 157; *see also* Wang
  Yangming
Yang Rubin 213
Yang Ruli 95
Yang Tingyi 133
Yangtze River 27, 28, 118, 137, 157
Yang Weizhong 26
Yang Xiong 73
Yang Yungong 51
Yangzhou: Anding Academy 119, 162;
  Meihua Academy 160
Yan Jie 101
Yan Shigo 198
Ya Yan Memorial Hall, Changshu County
  School 55
Yanyou period 56, 126, 136, 138, 186
Yan Zhenqing 66
Yao (Emperor) 71
Yao (sage) 55, 72, 73, 74, 75, 80, 85, 87,
  97, 99; Way of 89
Yaojiang Academy 90, 98, 100, 115
Yao Nai 162
Yayan language 202
Ye Mengde 137
Yi-Luo School: *Origins of the Yi-Luo
  School* (伊洛渊源录) (Zhu Xi) 117, 144
Yingchang 138
Yingchang Academy 141
Ying Dian 88
Yingshan Academy 58, 66, 202
Yingtianfu 22
Yingtianfu Academy 20, 51, 124, 137, 148
Yingtian (Ying Tian) Mountain 86
Yingyuan Palace 129
Yining Prefecture 125, 154
Yin Tun 133
Yi Yin 71, 74
Yongkang County 88
Yongle reign 83
Yongze Academy, Guixi 143
Yongzheng reign 4, 9, 35, 38, 40, 60, 134,
  150, 152
Yongzhou Supervision Bureau 27
Yongzhou City 124
You Jiugong 158
You Jiuyan 152, 158
Yuan Dynasty 26–30, 55–64, 80–84;
  academies established during 124–126,
  149; ancestral temples during 51;
  Gong Shitai on 57; sacrificial rituals
  of 83; *Scholarly Annals of Song and
  Yuan Periods* 114, 115, 121, 122,
  152; worship of Zhu Xi during 80,

84; Tuotuo 82; Xuancheng Academy destroyed during 90; Yuelu Academy during 56

Yuan Fu 11, 87, 96

Yuanhe reign 128

Yuan Kuoyu 37

Yuan Xie 20, 68

Yuanyou period 52

Yuelu Academy 20; book collections and libraries of 136, 138, 140; ceremony of Dingji 70; Chongdao Ancestral Hall 84; Confucian temple 177, 186; decline and disrepair of 21, 30; feng shui of 178–182; Han-learning scholars worshiped at 102; Hu Hong's request to revitalize 23; Huxiang and 116; influence of 124, 152; Liu Gong's restoration of 67; Li Yunze's rebuilding of 92; Li Zhongcheng Temple 58; number of people memorialized at 52; Ouyang Shoudao 161; reconstruction of 50; *Restoration of Yuelu Academy in Tanzhou* (潭州重修岳麓 书院记) 11; Sanlu Temple 59; school mission of 200; *Sequel to Yuelu Academy Annals in Changsha* (长沙岳麓书院续志) 35, 58–60, 180, 188; Sima Qian worshiped at 101; Six Gentleman Hall 67, 69; spirit of Confucianism embodied by the buildings of 177; superintendents of 161, 162; Wen Chang Hall 60; Zhang Sunmin's visit to 51; Zhang Shi and Zhu Xi worshiped at 56; Zhang Shi as teacher at 155; Zhu Dong's founding of 57; Zhu Xi's lectures at 127, 157, 158; Zou Hao 66; zuomiao youxue layout of 176

Yun County 126

Yunge Academy 30

Yunan Academy 147

Yun Nan 187

Yunnan poems 146

Yunshan Academy 126

Yu Yingshi 7

Yu Yue 102

Yuzhang Academy, Nanchang 59, 188

Zeng Bian 159

Zengcheng 157

Zeng clan 77

Zeng Dian 177, 178

Zeng Gao 19

Zeng Guofan 152

Zeng Shen 74, 79, 84, 93

Zeng Zhao 123, 153

Zeng Zi 87, 128

Zhang Jiuzong Academy 148

Zhang Juzheng 33

Zhang Liuquan 50

Zhang Mu 146

Zhang Nanxuan 84

Zhangpu: Liangshan Academy 138

Zhang Qia 96

Zhang Shi 11, 56, 90, 91, 115, 116; as Hu Hong's disciple 155; Huxian School of Thought of 120, 121, 156, 158; lectures and teaching at Yuelu Academy 127, 152, 158, 161; on the mission of academies 149; Zhu and Zhang Conference 156

Zhang Shiba 67

Zhang Shu 146

Zhang Sunmin 51

Zhang Xun 158

Zhang Yuanbian 157

Zhang Zai 24, 57, 66, 78, 79, 80, 82, 83, 93, 100

Zhang Zhenyi 17

Zhang Zhidong 16

Zhang Zhongli 6, 7

Zhangzhou: Municipal School 55; Zhuxi Academy 143

Zhang Zi 77

Zhang Yi 13

Zhan Ruoshi 31, 32, 57, 98, 157

Zhao, Duke of 74

Zhao Fu 26

Zhao Jin 88

Zhaoqing: Duanxi Academy 60, 151; Ruixi Academy 162

Zhao Rumo 131

Zhao Yanxian 86

Zhaoyi Academy 140

Zhao Yingchen 141

Zhejiang Province 23, 101; Han learning in 119; Jinhua Academy 162; Nanyuan Academy 138; Yangming academies in 88; Yingshan Academy 58

Zhen Dexiu 91, 200

Zhengde Academy 126

Zhengde era 31, 32, 58, 89, 98, 99, 128, 130, 133

Zhenghe Confucianism 91

Zhenghe reign 77

Zheng Liangchen 52

Zheng Tinghu 53, 56, 144

Zhengtong (Zheng Tong) (Emperor) 82

Zheng Xuan 54, 101, 102; *Annotations to the Book of Songs* 123

250 *Index*

zhengyanse 203
Zhengyi Academy 151
Zheng Yu 96
Zheng Zhiqiao 202, 211, 212
Zhenzong (Emperor, Song Dynasty) 21, 22, 51, 136
Zhili Prefecture 159
Zhishengxianshi (sage of sages) 56
Zhishun period, Yuan dynasty 52, 91
Zhi Xue Academy in Xuancheng 89
Zhiyuan reign, Yuan dynasty 26, 27, 29, 126
Zhizheng reign 90, 143
Zhongding day 54, 65
Zhongshan Academy 9, 102, 119, 160
Zhong Shizen 56
Zhongzi 52
Zhou Bida 131
Zhou Jihua 146
Zhou Dunyi: academic/ancestral halls dedicated to 55, 81, 84; Bailudong Academy and 57, 69, 83, 84; Confucianism/Neo-Confucianism and 66, 93; Daotong and 80–82; Daozhou Lianxi Academy resolution 27–28; Lianxi Academy and 51–52, 78; Seven Sage Academy and 59; Wang Yangming's advocacy of 89; worship of 26, 52, 61, 64, 77, 78, 82, 83; Zhulin Academy and 56, 77; Zhu Xi's worship and advocacy of 79, 85
Zhou dynasty 82, 202
Zhou Muyan 31
Zhou, Rites of the 197, 207
Zhou Shi 84
Zhou Tong 88
Zhou Zhongfu 101
Zhuangyuan 70
Zhuanxu 73

Zhu Dong 50
Zhuge Liang 37, 59, 62
Zhuge Temple 59
Zhulin Academy 53, 56, 77, 78, 79, 93
Zhu Songyun 182
Zhu Xi: academic works by 116–117; *Complete Collection of Zhu Xi* (朱子全书) 4; Daotong and 79, 81, 82, 84, 85, 93; Li Dong as teacher of 56; Liu Yue as disciple of 25; Li Xue 116–117; Neo-Confucianism of 4, 24, 32, 56, 61, 73–75, 83, 122, 155, 177; *Records of Shigu Academy in Hengzhou* (衡州石鼓书院记) 20; repairs to/reconstruction/restoration of Bailudong Academy 21, 23, 53; school of thought 32; *Statutes of Bailudong Academy* (白鹿洞书院揭示) 12, 14; worship of 57, 59; Zhulin Academy and 56
Zhuxi Academy 143
Zhu Xue 94
Zi Si 56, 87
Ziyang Academy 60, 81, 102, 119, 143, 162; number of students enrolled at 151; temple farmlands granted to 132
Ziyang Temple 52, 85
Ziyun Academy 132, 147
Ziyun Mount 115
Zou: Duke of 77, 78
Zou Boqi 153
Zou Chonghua 25
Zou Hao 59, 66
Zou Shouyi 88, 97, 127, 130
Zou Yuanbiao 157
Zuo: *Commentary of Zuo* (左传 · 成公十三年) 2, 48, 69
zuomiao youxue 176
Zuo Zongtang 152

Ingram Content Group UK Ltd.
Milton Keynes UK
UKHW022211120323
418470UK00005B/10